CONNECTIONIST MODELS OF NEUROCOGNITION AND EMERGENT BEHAVIOR

From Theory to Applications

Progress in Neural Processing • 20

Proceedings of the 12th Neural Computation and Psychology Workshop

CONNECTIONIST MODELS OF NEUROCOGNITION AND EMERGENT BEHAVIOR

From Theory to Applications

Birkbeck, University of London   8 – 10 April 2010

Editor

Eddy J Davelaar

University of London, UK

W World Scientific

NEW JERSEY • LONDON • SINGAPORE • BEIJING • SHANGHAI • HONG KONG • TAIPEI • CHENNAI

Published by

World Scientific Publishing Co. Pte. Ltd.

5 Toh Tuck Link, Singapore 596224

USA office: 27 Warren Street, Suite 401-402, Hackensack, NJ 07601

UK office: 57 Shelton Street, Covent Garden, London WC2H 9HE

British Library Cataloguing-in-Publication Data
A catalogue record for this book is available from the British Library.

Progress in Neural Processing — Vol. 20
CONNECTIONIST MODELS OF NEUROCOGNITION AND EMERGENT BEHAVIOR
From Theory to Applications
Proceedings of the 12th Neural Computation and Psychology Workshop

ISBN-13 978-981-4340-34-2
ISBN-10 981-4340-34-0

Printed in Singapore.

PREFACE

This volume collects together most of the papers presented at the Twelfth Neural Computation and Psychology Workshop (NCPW12) held in 2010 at Birkbeck College (England). The conference invited submissions on neurocomputational models of all cognitive and psychological processes. The special theme of this conference was "From Theory to Applications", which allowed submissions of pure theoretical work and of pure applied work. This topic highlighted the extent to which computational models of cognition and models in general are integrated in the cognitive sciences.

As before, NCPW12 was characterized by the largely informal atmosphere and the presence of a single-track schedule. NCPW12 included keynote talk by James L. McClelland, Peter J. B. Hancock and Jochen J. Steil. Together they covered a wide-ranging set of cognitive topics and research methodologies.

The chapters in this book cover a wide range of research topics in neural computation and psychology, including cognitive development, language processing, higher-level cognition, but also ecology-based modeling of cognition, philosophy of science, and real-world applications.

Apart from presenting contributions to the 2010 workshop, this book also includes commentaries highlighting some important aspects of modeling. Readers may welcome these additions that help the more reflective process of what computational modelers can do and how to go about doing it.

I would like to thank John Bullinaria, Angelo Cangelosi, Bob French, and Julien Mayor for advice and support on organizing the workshop, Stéphane Argon for let me use the templates for the conference website and Rachel Wu with whom a London-specific NCPW logo was created. The workshop was supported most generously by the *Society for the Study of Artificial Intelligence and Simulation of Behaviour* (AISB) and the *2nd European Network for the Advancement of Artificial Cognitive Systems, Interaction and Robotics* (EUCogII).

NCPW12 continued the tradition of a small, friendly meeting and we look forward to future installments of the Neural Computation and Psychology Workshop.

Eddy J. Davelaar

CONTENTS

INTRODUCTION

EDDY J. DAVELAAR

Birkbeck, University of London, Department of Psychological Sciences,
Malet Street, London, WC1E 7HX, United Kingdom

This chapter introduces the topics presented in this book. The first part highlights trends and questions that form a common thread across chapters. In the second part, an overview will be given of the topics addressed in the different sections.

1. Trends in Cognitive Modeling

The chapters in this book are diverse in the topics that they address, reflecting the diversity of the researchers involved in neural computation and psychology. Nevertheless, a set of common questions appear from these contributions that warrant some pause for reflection.

1.1. *Agent-World Interaction*

Several chapters touch on the importance of understanding cognition as the product of interacting systems. At first blush, these systems may simply be different brain areas, but a recurrent theme is that understanding cognition requires placing models of cognitive development within the environment. This places a strong emphasis on the need for a suitable model of the environment itself. Clearly, the complexity (or simplicity) of the environmental model will affect the interaction-dependent components of the cognitive model. This type of dynamic modeling is known in research fields that physically place cognitive models within real-world scenarios, such as in cognitive robotics.

Creating models of the environment is done explicitly in chapters dealing with visual illusions (Byrne, Corney & Lotto), sentence comprehension (Frank), and developmental disorders (Thomas, Knowland & Karmiloff-Smith). Given the requirement to be explicit about the environment-agent interaction in these different areas, it is not unlikely that the similar techniques that allow cognitive models to be compared will eventually be applied to modeling the environment. This would further extend the boundaries of the field of cognitive modeling.

1.2. *What are Models for?*

This book presents chapters in which models are used in a wide-ranging number of ways. Not only does the community of modelers use a large number of different model architectures, they also employ them in different ways (see Stafford). For example, a self-organizing map (SOM) can be used as a statistical tool for cluster analysis (Lopez, Bonin, Vermeulen, Meot & Mermillod), but also to look at how interacting developing representations lead to better performance (Althaus & Mareschal).

The choice and use of representations are worth pointing out. Apart from the well-known distinction between distributed and localist representations, this choice is orthogonal to the question what the representation itself is used for. In several chapters, the representation is emergent and its structure is the focus of investigation (e.g., Hannagan & Grainger). In other chapters, the representation is simply to facilitate the simulations and what is being represented (e.g., units of language) is the focus of investigation. The wide-spread use of both types of representations and research focus may lead to a resurrection of the representation debate in cognitive science with detailed analytical knowledge about the utilities of both types.

2. Overview of the Book

2.1. *Visual perception and attention*

If cognition is the result of evolutionary adaptation, then which parameters in the environment were the crucial ones that sculpted our cognitive system? Byrne, Corney and Lotto outline an ecology-based approach to cognitive modeling by which we can understand why certain cognitive behaviors have emerged in the first place. Plebe takes the developmental view and focuses on environmental-driven learning in early visual cortical areas. The modeling work reveals how certain visual selectivity emerges through exposure to the environment. Attentional processing is addressed by Harrison and De Kamps who develop a brain-based model of the ventral and dorsal streams of visual processing. Although the authors start with a classical artificial neural network, they show how to bridge levels of description and build a realistic spiking neuron model of feature-based attention.

Attention and learning are closely related. Children's learning is sensitive to the social context in which events happen. Yurovsky, Wu, Yu, Kirkham and Smith look at individual differences in the distribution of attention in young children while they learn to associate auditory and visual stimuli. Their modeling work focus on a complex data set of eye-movements. The brain can be seen as a large statistical device that extracts the relevant statistics of the environment and map them onto behavioral actions. Lopez, Bonin, Vermeulen, Meot and Mermillod use neural networks to ascertain whether the spatial frequency of faces contains diagnostic information for categorizing emotional expressions.

2.2. *Speech and language*

A complex problem in machine learning and neural computation is how relevant features are abstracted from the input. The brain has the computational power to learn these features in an unsupervised way. What are these features and how are they used in ongoing cognitive development? Klein, Osindero, ten Bosch and Boves model speech perception using restricted Boltzmann machines. They focus on the ability of these neural networks to learn to categorize speech input without the need of fine-tuning connection weights. Althaus and Mareschal address the impact of verbal labeling on object categorization in early infancy. In the process of developing a model that can account for this effect, they develop a new unsupervised learning algorithm that allows two developing networks to interact with each other during learning. Further in language development, children transit from one-word utterance stage to a two-word utterance stage. Nyamapfene models this transitional phase and addresses the importance of multimodal temporal processing.

The more complex the models become, the harder it becomes to understand why a model is able to perform the computations that it does. Hannagan and Grainger address why a model of visual word recognition is able to learn words invariant of their spatial location. Their analyses provide an elegant understanding of how invariance and flexibility are closely linked. A related question in visual word recognition concerns the functional units with which people read words. Smith and Monaghan focus on digraphs and their effect in reading words and nonwords. They make predictions using a computational model of reading which are tested in an experiment. Loth and Davis compare two computational models of word recognition in their ability to account for response congruency effects. This analysis highlights the importance of understanding the inner working of cognitive models and the surprising conclusions that can be drawn from this enterprise. Finally, Frank takes an information-theoretic approach to sentence comprehension by explicating the ecology in which the comprehender lives. This world knowledge is shown to have a major influence in the ability of understanding sentences and situations that unfolds over a sequence of words.

2.3. *High-level cognition*

Whereas the current contributions largely focus on development of cognitive abilities, cognitive processes interact in complex ways to give rise to higher-level cognitive behavior. Elhalal and Usher build on previous models of memory and develop a neurocomputational model of free recall memory which combines activation-based processes with a distributed context. They reveal how this new model is able to better capture a wide range of memory phenomena. Wichert addresses the question of how higher-level reasoning is instantiated in associative neural networks. His contribution shows how an associative memory model based on neuronal cell-assemblies is able to make inferences about the environment. In psychology it is widely known that cognitive performance varies among individuals. Statistical procedures are used to capitalize on co-variation to learn about latent cognitive functions. Cooper and Davelaar show how computational models can play an important role in understanding why and how performance on several tasks covaries.

2.4. *Applications and methodologies*

Apart from the chapters that feature computational models, several chapters abstract away from task-dependent cognitive models and address their use in more practical environments.

Adaptive control systems have a natural place within the study of neurodynamics and cognition. Boza and Guerra present an ongoing project on a control system with several interacting modules that exhibits self-optimizing behavior. Garletti provides an overview of her research on developing a method of creating a cognitive profile of students who follow on-line courses in written French. This profile is then used in formative feedback, facilitating the learning of students.

Brain imaging data from studies on semantics can be hard to interpret and analyze. Levy and Bullinaria tackle this problem using their framework of lexical semantics. They show how the semantic representations in their models can be used to investigate brain activation profiles from neuroimaging studies.

Thomas, Knowland and Karmiloff-Smith use neural networks as a tool to investigate which parameters account for developmental regression in autism. They simulate a large population of neural networks with variability in their parameter settings to highlight the critical parameters. These parameters can be seen as proxies for risk and protective factors.

2.5. *Philosophy of computational science*

Cognitive modeling is an integrative enterprise and is arguably the only method that allows full experimental control over the environment and the inner workings of the cognitive system. However, as seen in the preceding chapters, there exists great variability is the type of models used and the topics addressed. What a particular model is developed to do may not always be clear from articles. Stafford surveys how computational modelers present their computational work and relate this to the impact that the work has on the research communities within and outside the domain of the article.

An often repeated sentiment in the computational modeling community is that cognitive models should be as simple as possible. The appeal of Occam's razor may lead to oversimplifying computational models. Shillcock and colleagues take up the gauntlet and cautiously provide an argument against simplicity as the dominant principle constraining model development. This particular contribution has sparked some debate at the meeting and several commentaries were included. Pitt and Myung point out several caveats to the simplicity view.

In the final chapter, Steil reviews current trends in cognitive robotics and addresses both the question of what models are for and the question of simplicity/complexity within the domain of cognitive robotics.

Finally, I would like to thank the various researchers that reviewed the contributions. They are in alphabetical order: John Bullinaria, Emma Byrne, Rick Cooper, Colin Davis, Stefan Frank, Thomas Hannagan, David Harrison, Michael Klein, Joe Levy, Martial Mermillod, Padraic Monaghan, Abel Nyamapfene, Alessio Plebe, Richard Shillcock, Marie Smith, Tom Stafford, Marius Usher, and Andrzej Wichert.

AN ECOLOGY-BASED APPROACH TO PERCEPTUAL MODELLING

E. L. Byrne

Division of Community Health Sciences, The University of Edinburgh Medical School, Teviot Place, Edinburgh, EH8 9AG, United Kingdom
E-mail: emma.byrne@ucl.ac.uk

D. P. A Corney

Department of Computing, University of Surrey Guildford, Surrey, GU2 7XH, United Kingdom
E-mail: d.corney@surrey.ac.uk

R. B. Lotto

UCL Institute of Ophthalmology, University College London 11-43 Bath Street, London, EC1V 9EL, United Kingdom
E-mail: lotto@ucl.ac.uk

The emergence of any organism's brain and behaviour cannot be explained solely by examining the organism itself. We must look beyond the organism and model the ecology as well. This is the philosophical difference between the approach that we propose and the traditional approaches that seek to model behaviour and/or neural networks. We propose treating features of the ecology as independent variables and determining which parameter values are sufficient for particular types of behaviour to arise.

Biologically-inspired perceptual modelling has so far largely proceeded by mimicking known neural features or observed behaviours. However, these approaches do not explicitly model the source of the perception: the ecology. The approach described here is novel in that it focuses on the ecology of visual agents and their adaptation to their ecology, rather than being limited to imitating aspects of a particular animal's physiology or behaviour. This approach allows us to build counterfactual ecologies in which we can identify parameter values that are sufficient for the emergence of particular features of perception. Furthermore it allows us to extract the common strategies adopted by all agents in a given class of ecologies. We demonstrate the value of this approach by describing an ecology-based model of the perception of several optical illusions.

1. Introduction

Perception is the process of turning sense data into meaningful signals that influence behaviour. That sense data is almost always ambiguous. Sense organs conflate several features of the environment. Eyes, for instance, receive a signal that is dependent on illumination, transmittance and reflectance of light from the world. Ambiguity must be minimised by taking context into account. In order to model perceptual systems, whether to understand their natural counterparts, or to build autonomous artificial intelligence, we require a more complete understanding of how ambiguity is resolved. In this chapter we will focus on the modelling of visual perception, but similar arguments hold for other sensory modalities.

Biologically-inspired perceptual modelling has so far focused on existing animal visual systems. Typical models mimic either known neural architecture or observed behaviour, as we discuss in Section 3. However, these existing architectures and behaviours are end-products of a process of evolution and development within a given ecology: they are consequences of the need to resolve ambiguity and survive within a given ecology.

Here we propose an alternative approach: ecology-based modelling. This approach has a fundamentally different emphasis to existing, bio-inspired methods. Rather than imitating aspects of a particular animal's physiology, behaviour or development, this approach focuses on the ecology of an agent, be it machine, human or other animal. For the purposes of these models, an ecology consists of two components: the external environment in which an agent must operate, and its behaviours therein that enable the agent's survival (see Table 1 for terminology). Crucially, the ecological parameters are the *independent* variables in the model, and the features of perception that emerge are the dependent variables. This leads to sufficiency proofs for the range of feature values that are adequate for the emergence of perceptual phenomena such as colour constancy, brightness constancy, size constancy etc.

There are two strengths to this approach for addressing general questions of ambiguity resolution. Firstly, we can define "counterfactual ecologies" — ones with features deliberately chosen to be different from those found in nature — and analyse the resulting perceptual systems. This allows us to define and test falsifiable hypotheses regarding the effect of ecological parameters on the evolution of perceptual systems.

Ecology-based modelling provides sufficiency proofs for features of ecologies that lead to the emergence of perceptual phenomena. By modelling both extant and counterfactual ecologies we can explore where perceptual

Table 1. Terminology used in this chapter to refer to parts of the ecology-based model.

Environment	A set of parameter values defining the distribution of features such as spatial frequency, illumination etc.
Scene	An individual set of surfaces and illuminants derived from the distributions that make up the environment.
Stimulus	The presentation of a scene at the network's eye
Behaviour	Actions that are the result of the effect of prior experience and of stimuli, but that are rewarded on the basis of the underlying scene.
Counterfactual ecology	Simulated ecology with features different from those found in nature

phenomena emerge and where they do not. We provide a motivating example in this chapter: the emergence of the general class of lightness illusions, and of the specific case of White's illusion, based on a recent demonstration.[1]

Secondly, once a naturalistic ecology has been defined, multiple agents can adapt to it, and their common features can be extracted and differences measured. Whereas the modelling of any one extant system restricts our findings to a single point in the space of all possible solutions, generating multiple systems allows us to search for more general answers.

In this chapter we discuss this ecology-based approach in more detail, develop a formal framework for the approach, and give examples of its use in building models of the perceptual spaces of human neural processing.

2. Empirical Vision: Perception as Ambiguity Resolution

All sensory modalities that conflate multiple features of the environment inevitably experience ambiguity. To take the example of vision: the intensity of the stimulus (s) that falls onto the eye from an object in the world depends on both the illumination (i) and the object's reflectance (r, the fraction of incident light that is reflected). Because $s = i \times r$, any given stimulus intensity can represent more than one possible combination of r and i. It is typically the properties of an object's surface (r) that are of most interest to the observer, and yet the visual system only ever has direct access to s. By extending this simple example to spectral power distributions, where the same relationships hold at each wavelength in the visible spectrum, equivalent ambiguity can be found in colour perception.

Resolving the ambiguity of visual images is the central challenge facing any visual system.[2-6] Animals as different as humans and bumble bees can consistently judge the colour of surfaces under differently coloured illumination.[7] When vision is 'fooled' however, as when viewing an optical illusion, it is clear that the goal of vision is not to accurately represent the physical qualities of information falling on the eye, but rather to represent what that information historically meant for survival.[1] Brains do this by making assumptions about what information is likely to mean, given what it meant previously, both in the history of the individual organism and of the species. Recent psychophysical experiments on humans suggest a general framework for resolving image uncertainty. Central to this hypothesis is that the brain encodes statistical relationships between images and scenes in past visual experience.[6]

One compelling example consistent with the "empirical vision" hypothesis is the Cornsweet illusion. Figure 1a demonstrates the standard Cornsweet illusion. The left hand side of the stimulus appears to be a darker grey than the right hand side of the stimulus, when in fact they are physically identical. Repeated experiments have demonstrated that the lightness gradient in the centre of the stimulus induces this effect. We might consider the effect in terms of the characteristics of the human visual system, and describe the effect in terms of neurophysiology, for example. However, we can provide a more general explanation for this effect, and perhaps begin to determine why it emerged, if we instead consider what the gradient has "meant" in the past.

Figure 1b shows a more ecologically detailed Cornsweet illusion: as well as the gradient in the stimulus, there are clues to the nature of the objects in the surrounding scene that give rise to the gradient.[8] The centres of the "top" and "bottom" surfaces are identical shades of grey in the stimulus (i.e. they reflect an equal fraction of incident light), but the top surface appears to have a much lower reflectance than the bottom surface. This version demonstrates the ecological meaning of lightness gradients in stimuli: the same amount of light would reach the eye from a dark surface under a strong illuminant as from a lighter surface under a weaker illuminant.

Each half of the gradient in the standard Cornsweet illusion is consistent with the highlights and shadows induced by a single source of illumination at a curved boundary. Both the lightness gradient and (in the more ecologically detailed version) the orientation of the surfaces are consistent with two surfaces of different reflectance under different illuminants. We might hypothesize that this is why the Cornsweet illusion arises, but we need a

(a) Standard Cornsweet illusion.   (b) Enhanced Cornsweet illusion (Reproduced with permission from ref 8.)

Fig. 1.   The Cornsweet illusion. Two identical patches of grey appear to be different if placed either side of a suitable lightness gradient. A colour version of (b) may be found at www.lottolab.org, with several variants.

new form of modelling to pursue this hypothesis. In short, we need a type of model that allows us to determine which ecological characteristics (such as curvature, illumination variance and so on) are required for a perceptual effect to arise, as well as considering how they are encoded by the observer.

3. Current Approaches to Perceptual Modelling

The aim of this section is not to provide a comprehensive survey of the wide range of perceptual models that have been developed, but rather to briefly discuss some of the key approaches and how they differ from our proposal.

The goal of many modelling approaches can be summarized thus: 1) measure the human (or other animal) responses to a particular set of stimuli; 2) measure the predictions of a model in response to equivalent stimuli; 3) adjust the model to minimize any discrepancies. Rarely is any counterfactual modelling attempted, which would allow the hypotheses to be tested through falsification.[9] Even an accurate model cannot by itself explain *why* certain features emerged, not under what conditions they would *not* emerge. For example, it may be observed that bees harvest nectar from flowers of particular colours under varied illumination, and based on this, a model may be built which correlates with bee behaviour very closely, and shows color constancy. Suppose that a (presumably simulated) counterfactual world were then created where flower colour was unrelated to its nectar production, and bees were allowed to adapt to this world. If such bees still exhibited colour constant behaviour, then it would suggest that such behaviour is *not* best explained in terms of the need to see flower colours consistently under varying illumination.

The very long tradition of psychophysics is restricted to the first of the three steps listed above, including very precise measurements of responses to a wide range of stimuli. In practice, however, the stimuli used are often very simple compared to natural stimuli. For example, the careful generation and control of visual stimuli, and careful use of instructions to subjects, allows systematic measurements of differences between brightness and lightness.[10] These approaches may tell us what we see, but not how or *why*.

Many models are effective on simple stimuli, such as with just two or three luminance regions (e.g. surfaces), but are untested on more complex, natural images. For example, the well-known anchoring model of human lightness perception uses a combination of "local frameworks" and simple rules such as "bright is white" and "large is white".[11] Such methods do not reliably scale up to complex scenes with multiple luminance regions, which are frequently encountered in natural scenes.

Fine tuning of models is sometimes needed to produce a closer fit to observed psychophysical results. Examples include various weighting or tuning parameters,[11,12] which typically offer no explanation as to how such parameters are represented or optimized in biological systems.

A number of mathematical models of neurons have been proposed, one of the more successful being the Hodgkin-Huxley model.[13] This is arguably too greatly simplified to be a faithful model of a biological neuron (for example, it ignores different types of neurotransmitter), while also being too complex for large scale network models. A more scalable model using simpler neurons has been demonstrated as a powerful tool for machine vision,[14] but makes no claim to explain *why* such networks of neurons should come into being in the first place. With growing computing power, the more recent model of Izhikevich and Edelman[15] has been developed, consisting of a million neurons with nearly 500 million synapses. This type of model can be used to investigate brain disorders such as the effect of strokes, Alzheimer's disease and Parkinson's disease. The exciting possibility of real-time simulations of cortical systems could be realized within a few years[a].

---

[a]http://www.izhikevich.org/human_brain_simulation/why.htm

Some models of perception are very faithful to observations, but only in limited circumstances, such as requiring a constant, uniform illumination, or only modelling brightness and not lightness perception[b]. One family of models that corresponds closely to psychophysical results on a wide range of stimuli is the filter models of Blakeslee and McCourt.[12,16] The model consists of a tunable set of filters that share broad features with the responses of cells found in the visual cortex. When presented with a greyscale image, the filter's output is closely correlated with the brightness perceived when a human subject is presented with a similar stimulus. However, such models do not attempt to predict the reflectance of surfaces, but only the perceived brightness of a stimulus, and are therefore unable to explain lightness constancy in more natural scenes under spatially heterogeneous illumination.

A very different kind of perceptual model is the attempt to identify regions of the brain associated with different aspects of (mostly visual) perception. While fMRI modelling provides us with ever more detail about the activities of different brain regions in response to different stimuli,[17] the flow of information between brain areas is sometimes overlooked. Recent work has used simulated fMRI scans on a virtual collection of neurons, representing a simplified model of the visual cortex.[18] This is *not* an attempt to provide a realistic model of how the brain actually works, but rather to develop a Bayesian analytical method which discovers coupling between cortical areas, with some success. This approach, along with brain lesion studies, neuron recordings, and so on, tells us what happens in the brain and where, but not *why*.

"Sparse coding" models[19] can be seen as an attempt to explain the characteristics of cells in the visual cortex in terms of the visual ecology. Such models are very powerful and may lead to great insights into the nature of visual neurophysiology. However, the work typically lacks counterfactual testing that, we argue, would provide stronger support for the models. Also, these models are limited to describing possible forms of visual coding, rather than tackling wider problems in vision, such as resolving ambiguity.

Most models of perception are based on human subjects, and so provide little insight into the physiological and/or computational principles of vision found across all visual animals. Given that humans are but one product of evolution, much can be gained by comparing human perception to that of other animals if we are to understand the evolutionary and adaptive rea-

---

[b]Here, lightness is the apparent reflectance of a surface, and brightness is the apparent intensity of light coming from a surface.

sons being our own physiology and behaviour. Any animal is the end result of a long process of evolution, and historical accident cannot be separated from more general tendencies by observation alone. Also, we have very limited access to past experiences of individuals and species. Simulation can give us total control over the life and evolutionary histories of simulated individuals. One interesting attempt to model natural visual behaviour involved simulating a variety of fish in a physically-realistic virtual ocean.[20] Although the emphasis was on generating a realistic computer animation, the model did include a simple visual system capable of colour perception, foveation and visual navigation.[21]

In summary, a wide range of models of perception have been developed, and continue to be developed. These provide great insight into perception, but rarely address the question of its origins.

4. What is Ecology-Based Modelling?

In order to provide explanatory models of the underlying regularities of visual behaviour, it is not enough to describe specific, extant networks. Whilst single organism models give us an insight into *what* the features of perception are, it will not enlighten us as to *why* they have arisen. Furthermore, single organism models resist generalization, being only single points in the space of "solutions" to the problem of ambiguity.

In order to develop explanatory models that indicate the general emergent causes of visual behaviour, it is necessary to model the visual ecologies from which they emerge. The parameters defining such a model, such as the distribution of surface sizes or reflectances, can then be varied. In effect, the features of the ecology are independent variables in the model, whilst the emergence (or not) of certain types of perception is the dependent variable. The aim is to discover a set of critical parameter values of scenes (i.e., conditions in the world) that are sufficient for visual behaviours to emerge. Figure 2 summarizes the proposed framework.

One assumption that lies behind the notion of ecology-based modelling is that the computational principles that enable robust behaviour in ambiguous environments are preserved across different neural architectures. This premise is intuitive, given that for many tasks, such as colour constancy, the visual performance of species as divergent as humans and bees is similar despite the dissimilarity of their eyes and brains.[7] It is also supported by studies that show that artificial networks of vastly different components generate behaviours that are indistinguishable from natural systems.[1,22] This assumption leads us to treat artificial neural networks (and

- Materials
  - a model of the ecology,
  - a population of agents that are free to adapt.
- Methods
  - treat the ecology as the independent variable, and explore the parameter values of this ecology,
  - let agents adapt to these ecologies.
- Observations
  - measure the change in behaviour with respect to the different ecologies.
  - measure the variety of distinct model variants produced.
- Outcome
  - sufficiency proofs of which ecological features are consistent with which types of perception.

Fig. 2. A framework for an ecology-based approach to perceptual modelling

other such computational tools), not as models of brains, but as an adequate representation of the processes that relate environment to behaviour.

It is this environment-behaviour link that ecology-based modelling can be used to uncover. Extant living organisms demonstrate that the parameter values of the ecology *as it is* are sufficient for the behaviours we observe to have emerged. However, ecological modelling allows us to examine ecologies *as they might be*. We can create counterfactual ecologies where the values of, for example, the variance of illumination, or the ratios between the variance of illumination and the variance of reflection are different to those observed in the natural world. One could then ask, for example, does colour constancy emerge in a world with constant illumination? If not, then how much must illumination vary before colour constant behaviour emerges? By varying these and other scene distributions (such as spatial frequencies) we expect to uncover the critical values of scenes that are engender colour constancy. These counterfactual worlds allow us to determine the ranges of the values that are sufficient for such behaviours to emerge.

The ranges of parameter values in the different environments that we model can then be related to the behaviours that emerge. In the illustrative example in Figure 3 we can see how we might quantitatively analyse the relationship between environmental parameter values and behaviour.

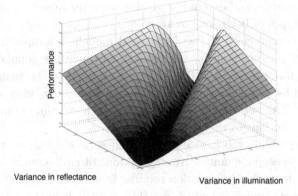

Fig. 3. Example of an ecology space. (Note: this is not based on model outputs and is for illustration only.) Areas of the parameter space that are sufficient for some behaviour (e.g. lightness constancy) to emerge are indicated by high values on the (vertical) performance axis. However, there are areas of the parameter space (i.e. ecologies) where lightness constancy fails to emerge, such as where the variance in illumination and in reflectance is the same. This results in the trough in the performance surface.

For a real example of a qualitative analysis of the relationship between environmental parameter values and behaviour, see Section 5.

In Figure 3, we consider two features of a simulated, simplified visual environment: the variance of the reflectance of different surfaces; and the variance of the intensity of illumination across space. The dependent variable is some measure of the behaviour of an agent (such as a simulated animal), after it has adapted to its environment. In this example, the behaviour of interest is lightness constancy, i.e. the ability to perceive a surface as unchanging, even when the illumination changes.

An organism's ecology is the interplay between the environment, and the behaviours necessary for survival within that environment. The brain is a manifestation of its historical interaction with its ecology: this much is, we hope, axiomatic. A general framework for resolving image uncertainty based on the hypothesis that the brain encodes statistical relationships between images and scenes in past visual experience is supported by recent psychophysical experiments (see Ref. 6 and references therein). However, this work does not allow us to furnish explanations of the origins of specific behaviours in terms of these ecological drivers. In order to determine the effect of ecology on the emergence of brain and behaviour, it is necessary but not sufficient to examine organisms themselves. We must look beyond the organism and model the ecology and treat features of the ecology as independent variables and determine which parameter values are sufficient for particular types of behaviour to arise.

A further advantage of the ecology-based modelling approach is that it allows us to generate multiple individuals, and multiple populations of individuals, in order to measure the variety of solutions to the visual problems presented by a single ecology. This is analogous to the work done by Marder *et al.*[22] This set of individuals is, in effect, a sampling from the set of all possible solutions to the problem of vision.

A major stumbling block to developing these models arises from the fact that the necessary quantitative descriptions of environmental, physiological and behavioural information relating to each variable are lacking, even after it has been decided which variables to include in the model. Yet, if the principles of vision are to be discovered, quantitative descriptions of the relations between real-world environments, sensory images and vision must form the basis of explanatory models that identify the necessary and sufficient features of ecologies that lead to robust vision.

A further issue is that of computational complexity. As the number of features defining a simulated ecology is increased, the simulation becomes more useful as a (presumably) truer reflection of reality; but it also requires more computational resources. This trade-off is of course true of any computational modelling and simulation approach.

5. Motivating Example: White's Illusion

A number of explanations have been advanced for simultaneous lightness contrast effects, the most commonly advanced one being centre-surround physiology.[23] This explanation of the effect shown in Figure 4 is that the lightness of a grey patch is "boosted" early in visual physiology when that patch is in a darker context, and that its lightness is attenuated when surrounded by a lighter context.

This explanation is unsatisfactory on two levels: firstly, it is unsatisfactory as an explanation *qua* explanation. Although it tells us *how* the lightness contrast effect may emerge in physiology it doesn't advance an explanation as to *why* that might be the case (i.e. why such a physiology would exist). Secondly, as an explanation it fails on a counterexample: White's illusion.

In the case of White's illusion[24] (Figure 5), the effect experienced is the inverse of the simultaneous lightness contrast illusion: the grey patch that appears lighter actually has (on average) a lighter surround than the grey patch that looks darker.

Fig. 4. Simultaneous lightness contrast. The left and right central squares are identical intensities of grey, but the left hand square (on a dark background) usually appears lighter than the right hand square (on a lighter background).

We can posit an informal explanation for this effect – the patches that look lighter appear to "belong" to a dark background, obscured by lighter bars and vice versa. In each case, if the obscuring bars are removed from consideration, on the assumption that they are under a different illumination, then the stimulus is reduced to the simultaneous lightness contrast stimulus, and the effects of White's illusion are now consistent with the effects of the simultaneous lightness contrast effect. This still does not explain how this heuristic came about, if indeed it is used at all. However, we can test the contribution of figure/background separation on the emergence of White's illusion directly, by using ecological modelling.

5.1. *An Ecology-Based Model of White's Illusion*

Ecology-based modelling allows us to address the two shortcomings of the physiological model of the perception of lightness contrast illusions. Firstly, it allows us to create a common framework that explains both the "standard" lightness contrast effect and White's illusion, as well as modelling the more general perception of complex scenes under heterogeneous illumination. Secondly, it allows us to build an explanatory model based on distal causes of perception, i.e. the ecology in which visual agents must survive, and the possible evolutionary origins of observed perceptions.

An ecology-based model was recently introduced to explore the perception of various lightness illusions, including White's illusion.[1] We discuss this work here and relate it back to the framework of ecology-based modelling presented in Figure 2. In this work, the ecology (Figure 2: materials) was defined as a set of achromatic reflective surfaces under spatially-

Fig. 5. White's illusion. The shorter grey bars near the centre of the figure are identical in reflectance, but the left hand bar (on a black strip) usually appears lighter than the right hand bar (on a white strip).

heterogeneous illumination. The surfaces were arranged in a naturalistic fashion, consistent with distributions observed in nature. Specifically, each scene tended to consist of a few large surfaces and many small surfaces, generated by the "dead leaves" algorithm.[25] The illumination varied smoothly across the surfaces, typically including shadows as well as brightly-lit regions.

In one set of experiments, all the surfaces were in the same plane, perpendicular to the line of sight. The goal in all the experiments was to predict the reflectance (i.e. the fraction of light reflected) of the surface at the centre of the stimulus, irrespective of the illumination. This is non-trivial given the ambiguity caused by the varied light sources as discussed in Section 2. A set of artificial neural networks (Figure 2: materials) was trained to make this prediction, before being tested with previously unseen stimuli. The networks used were very simple multi-layer perceptrons, trained by the standard backpropagation algorithm (Figure 2: methods). Preliminary results showed that other general-purpose machine learning algorithms, such as support vector machines, produced equivalent results, showing that the results are *not* due to specific properties of artificial neural networks.

When presented with typical naturalistic stimuli, the networks were capable of correctly predicting the reflectance of the target to a high degree of accuracy (Figure 2: observations). When presented with "optical illusion" stimuli, including the Vasarelly illusion, Mach band stimuli, the Chevreul illusion and the Hermann grid, the networks gave predictions that were more faithful to prior experience of scenes than to the physical properties of the stimulus being shown, much as human subjects do. In other words, the networks "saw" the same illusions as humans do. Note that these illusions are all variations of the simple simultaneous lightness contrast illusion (Figure 4).

In a second set of experiments, some of the surfaces were in a second plane, which was nearer to the observer and had many gaps in it, allowing parts of the more distant plane to remain visible (Figure 2: methods). Where two planes were used, each had independent spatially-heterogeneous lighting. This is similar to the effect of looking at a scene through the branches of a tree, for example, where the near and far portions of the visual field have effectively independent light sources. A new set of artificial neural networks was trained in this environment, using the same training regime as before, and again learning to predict the reflectance of the surface in the middle of the field of view. In some cases, this would be the "foreground" mask, in others, the "background" layer. These networks exhibited similar behaviour as the first set, namely they correctly predicted the reflectance in naturalistic scenes, and gave responses equivalent to the human perception of various illusory stimuli (Figure 2: observations).

Both sets of networks were also presented with the White's illusion stimulus, the "opposite" of the simultaneous lightness contrast effect (Figure 5. When the networks had been trained in a 3D environment, then they gave human-like responses, i.e. they "saw" the illusion. However, the networks that had only ever experienced a 2D environment did not (Figure 2: observations).

This suggests that White's illusion can best be explained in terms of the visual ecology. When presented with surfaces on implicitly different planes under independent sources of illumination, the networks learned to ignore information arising from surfaces that were *not* co-planar with the target. Since illumination of each plane is independent, only co-planar information provides statistical information about the probable source of the illumination, and hence the target. Thus, changing the ecology (by introducing multiple layers) leads directly to a change in adaptive behaviour (the networks response to White's stimulus), showing a causal link between the two, and demonstrating that lightness constancy without depth perception is sufficient to explain some types of perception but not all (Figure 2: outcome).

6. Discussion

Ecology-based modelling, as described in this chapter, is a novel approach to the computational modelling of perception. Rather than focusing on particular networks or behaviours in order to determine *how* we see the world, ecology-based modelling models the parameters of the ecology in order to determine *why* we see the way we do.

But first let us stress that we are *not* suggesting that research into *how* we see the world is unnecessary or unimportant. We believe that describing perception in terms of neuroscience, and more generally addressing the mind-body problem, is of utmost importance, and is a very exciting area of ongoing research across a range of disciplines. However, there is a risk that in becoming too focused on specific low-level explanations, and particular tools for generating them (such as fMRI analysis or single-neuron recording), we may lose sight of a broader question: if neuroscience teaches us how the brain produces perception, we still need to ask why the human brain evolved the way it did. Why does it produce the perceptions that it does? We believe that an ecology-based approach to perceptual modelling allows us to better address such questions, by allowing us to explore "counterfactual" ecologies, where observed aspects of perception no longer emerge, as well as simulating ecologies consistent with our understanding of our own world.

One possibility for future work is to combine the ecology-based modelling described here with existing perceptual models. For example, one could start with a relatively sophisticated model of perception, such as a neuro-physiological model of the visual cortex, and then place this in a simulated environment and allow it to adapt. The inclusion of prior knowledge in this way has the benefit of allowing experiments to be performed on more realistic models, but at the cost of including strong assumptions about the systems under investigation.

Ecology-based models consist of a model of the ecology and a population of agents that are free to adapt within that ecology. The ecology is the relationship between an environment and the behaviours necessary to survive therein. The ecology-based model allows us to treat the parameters of the ecology as independent variables, that is, we can systematically investigate the different environments and different behaviours. As a result we can state which combinations of parameters are sufficient for the emergence of perception.

The proofs provided by the ecology-based modelling technique are of the nature of sufficiency proofs. That is to say, whilst the models don't demonstrate how perception necessarily emerged, they do at least allow us to limit our investigation to the space of parameters that are consistent with the emergence of certain types of behaviour.

In short, this chapter has argued that ecology-based modelling is an approach that complements existing methods of understanding perception, and that it fills an important gap in the repertoire of explanations provided by other methods.

References

1. D. Corney and R. B. Lotto, *PLoS Computational Biology* **3**, e180 EP (September 2007).
2. R. B. Lotto and D. Purves, *Nature Neuroscience* **2**, 1010(November 1999), PMID: 10526341.
3. R. B. Lotto and D. Purves, *Proceedings of the National Academy of Sciences of the United States of America* **97**, 12834(November 2000), PMID: 11058148.
4. R. Clarke and R. B. Lotto, *Vision Research* **49**, 1455(May 2009), PMID: 19286002.
5. R. B. Lotto and D. Purves, *Journal of Cognitive Neuroscience* **13**, 547(July 2001), PMID: 11506656.
6. D. Purves and R. Lotto, *Why We See What We Do: An Empirical Theory of Vision* (Sinauer Associates, February 2003).
7. A. Werner, R. Menzel and C. Wehrhahn, *Journal of Neuroscience* **8**, 156(January 1988).
8. D. Purves, A. Shimpi and R. B. Lotto, *J. Neurosci.* **19**, 8542(October 1999).
9. K. Popper, *The Logic of Scientific Discovery* (Basic Books, New York, NY, 1959).
10. L. Arend and B. Spehar, *Perception and Psychophysics* **54**, 446 (1993).
11. A. Gilchrist, C. Kossyfidis, F. Bonato, T. Agostini, J. Cataliotti, X. Li, B. Spehar, V. Annan and E. Economou, *Psychol Rev* **106**, 795(October 1999).
12. B. Blakeslee and M. E. McCourt, *Vision Research* **44**, 2483 (2004).
13. L. Abbott and T. Kepler, Model neurons: From Hodgkin-Huxley to Hopfield, in *Statistical Mechanics of Neural Networks*, 1990.
14. W. Maass, R. Legenstein and H. Markram, A new approach towards vision suggested by biologically realistic neural microcircuit models, in *Biologically Motivated Computer Vision*, 2002.
15. E. M. Izhikevich and G. M. Edelman, *Proceedings of the National Academy of Sciences* **105**, 3593(March 2008).
16. B. Blakeslee and M. E. McCourt, *Vision Research* **39**, 4361 (1999).
17. N. Hadjikhani, A. Liu, A. Dale, P. Cavanagh and R. Tootell, *Nature Neuroscience* **1**, 235 (1998).
18. L. Lee, K. Friston and B. Horwitz, *NeuroImage* **30**, 1243 (2006).
19. B. Olshausen *et al.*, *Nature* **381**, 607 (1996).
20. X. Tu and D. Terzopoulos, Artificial fishes: Physics, locomotion, perception, behavior, in *Proceedings of the 21st annual conference on Computer graphics and interactive techniques*, 1994.
21. D. Terzopoulos and T. Rabie, Animat vision: active vision in artificial animals, in *Proc. Fifth Inter. Conf. Computer Vision (ICCV95)*, June 1995.
22. A. A. Prinz, D. Bucher and E. Marder, *Nature Neuroscience* **7**, 1345 (2004).

23. S. Palmer, *Vision science: Photons to phenomenology* (MIT press Cambridge, MA., 1999).
24. M. White, *Perception* **8**, 413 (1979).
25. A. B. Lee, D. Mumford and J. Huang, *International Journal of Computer Vision* **41**, 35 (2001).

EARLY DEVELOPMENT OF VISUAL ABILITIES

Alessio Plebe

Dept. of Cognitive Science, Messina
Messina, Italy
* E-mail: alessio.plebe@unime.it

In this paper I argue for a developmental view of some of the basic visual processes in humans. The support provided for this position comes from a variety of sources. There are results from psychological, anthropological, and neurophysiological studies here reviewed, that show how even certain low-level visual processes depend on environmental-driven learning. In addition, a neurocomputational model of the lower visual pathway in the cortex is provided that replicates features of two main visual processing functions: orientation selectivity in V1 (primary visual cortex) and corner selectivity in V2 (secondary visual cortex). These functions emerge in the model purely by exposure to stimuli.

1. Introduction

The visual modality is the primary means by which humans obtain information about the surrounding world. Concrete thinking is formed to a considerable degree on the basis of visual notions with language and abstract thinking developing later. Vision in newborns is far from the powerful visual perception of older infants or adults. This paper deals with some of the key processes underpinning visual perception: the ability to detect the basic features of shape, like line orientation, and the subsequent use of this fundamental element to construct more complex percepts of shape, such as corners. The claim made here is that these processing skills become possible because of learning in the visual system, and especially in the visual cortex, in the early period after birth. This learning process, in fact, begins even before birth. While higher visual abilities, like object recognition, are widely acknowledged to unfold during development, it is often claimed that lower level visual processing is instead innate.[1,2]

The arguments used in support of the developmental nature of some of the main early visual abilities come from the review of a series of studies that converge on this thesis, from very different points of view: anthropological, psychological and neurophysiological; and from a neurocomputational model. In the review I cover several visual mechanisms that seem to strongly depend on learning. In the modeling work discussed the focus is necessarily a narrow one, which concentrates on two key types of processing, the one taking place in V1, the primary visual cortex, and in V2, the secondary visual cortex. In V1 the model reproduces specific aspects of the ability to detect oriented lines, known from early results in neuroscience to be one of the fundamental types of low-level processing in the vision of mammals.[3–5] For V2 instead, only very recent research endeavors have begun to shed light on its role.[6–8] The model discussed here addresses one piece of evidence supplied by recent studies on V2, that is, that this area contributes to visual perception in detecting slightly more complex features than those processed in V1, such as corners.[9,10]

The purpose of including a neurocomputational model in support of the main argument is in line with the use of computing as a way of modeling cognitive functions, contrasted with explanatory computations.[11] There is also a more specific grounding of this model, in that it adheres to the theoretical framework of neuroconstructivism,[12,13] that implies not only a focus on cognitive development and how it is linked to the development of the underlying neural structures in the brain, but also requires, according to the neuroconstructivist perspective, a certain design criteria for modeling, that can be summarized as follows:

(1) avoiding any predefined design of the mature computational system of recognition, at least at the cortical level;
(2) reproducing, at the cortical level, the basic plasticity mechanisms and the epigenetic conditions of development;
(3) constraining the architecture of the model as much as possible so as to set the hierarchy of functional stages according to current knowledge on the corresponding hierarchy in the biological visual system.

Neural computation of vision has already contributed to explain several facts of human vision under the neuroconstructivist perspective.[14] The two most orignal results provided by this model are the following:

- reproduction of environmental-dependent anysotropy of orientation selectivity in area V1;
- reproduction of corner selectivity emergence in V2, by exposure to stimuli.

2. Psychological and neurophysiological evidence of visual development

There is evidence found in a wide range of disciplines that undermines the idea that humans possess a large set of innate visual processing abilities, or, at least, drastically reduce the number of abilities that are effectively predefined. Before discussing the neurocomputational model, the core of my argument, I will briefly review some of this evidence.

2.1. *Cases in visual anthropology*

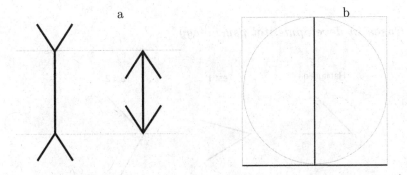

Fig. 1. Two optical illusions: a) the Müller-Lyer, where people typically perceive that the left line segment is longer than the right line segment, when in fact they are the same length; b) the "horizontal-vertical" illusion, where the vertical line is perceived as being longer than the horizontal one.

Some visual illusions are thought to derive from lower-level processing, and to be strong support for the supposed universal and innate nature of those processes. The Müller-Lyer illusion (see Fig. 1) has been cited by Fodor,[1,2] for the rigid persistence of the illusion, even in cases where we know it to be mistaken. Fodor and Pylyshyn claim that this rigidity of the visual modules in their stereotypical deliverance to the higher cognitive systems about how the world appears, demonstrate that these visual modules come equipped to manage stimuli in their proper predefined ways.

Following the steps pioneered first by Rivers[15] in his historical attempt to combine ethnographic method with psychophysical tests during the Torres Strait expedition, Segall and his group[16] performed an extensive investigation of visual illusions, on 17 small-scale societies. In the case of the Müller-Lyer illusion, by varying the lengths of the two segments and asking

26

subjects which of the two is longer, researchers can estimate the magnitude of the visual illusion for each by estimating the length difference at which a subject perceives the line segments as equal. They show that individuals who grow up in visual environments sharply different from that of western countries, such as the San people, African foragers from the Kalahari Desert, are virtually immune to the illusion.

Another similar illusion, the "horizontal-vertical", has also been found to be strongly culturally dependent: people living in flat, open environments like those of the Fenlands, in eastern England, are more susceptible to it than those living in heavily urbanized environments characterized by tall constructions such as those found in Glasgow, Scotland.[17]

2.2. *Cases in developmental psychology*

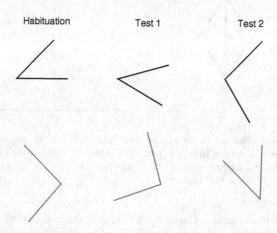

Fig. 2. Stimuli used in experiments of angle perception by Ref. 18, habituation stimuli were acute (upper) in half cases, and obtuse (lower) in the other half.

One of the first types of evidence suggesting that learning from the environment was necessary in order to develop vision in the early period just after birth, was given by the so-called *kitten carousel experiment*.[19] In this experiment, a kitten was connected to one end of a pivotal arm by a harness and neck yoke, and left relatively free to walk about. At the other end of the arm, a second kitten was forced to passively follow the locomotion induced in the arm by the first kitten. As result of this visual-motor deprivation the second animal was almost blind, recovering only after a week of free movement. It is obviously not possible to test human infants with procedures of induced temporary deprivation, but several clever and reliable methodologies have been designed to study the early development of visual abilities[20,21] . I mention here only results concerning the two processes addressed in my model: orientation and angle selectivity.

It is known from early studies using visual evoked potentials that orientation selective mechanisms are almost absent at birth and can only be detected after the second postnatal month,[22] with infants at about 3 months of age discriminating stimuli oriented at 5° versus 15°.[23] More recently it has been observed[24] that even at 5 years the orientation discrimination thresholds of children is 4–5 times less than that of adults.

Difficulties in identifying angles has been analyzed in a study[18] where, following habituation, children were tested either with a change in orientation of the same angle, as in Test 1 of Fig. 2, or with a change in the angle alone, leaving one segment unchanged, Test 2 of the same figure. 6-week-old infants succeeded in Test 1 and failed Test 2, while the 14-week-olds did the opposite. Interpretation of this and further studies on angles is not straightforward,[25] but the key point here is that this feature also seems to require months of learning for the visual system to process it adequately.

2.3. *Cases in neurophysiology*

The unfolding of visual processing skills during development is a direct consequence of the maturation of neurophysiological structures, such as the visual cortex in particular. There is an extensive amount of literature on the necessity of sensorial experience for the development of V1 in mammals, and on the shaping effect of the environment[26–28] . When kittens are reared in visual environments that are made up of stripes at one orientation, they demonstrate a deficit in visual acuity for orientations which were not present in the early visual environment, confirmed by the lack of cells responding to other orientations in V1[29] .

As for cases in developmental psychology, for obvious reasons no equivalent data is available for humans, however, important details on the development of circuits in the human visual cortex have been revealed by a study[30] on brains without neurological disease obtained at autopsy, ranging from 24 weeks gestation up to 5 years. In V1, while intracolumnar vertical connections, which link neurons representing the same point in the visual field, develop prenatally at 28-29 weeks of gestation, lateral intercolumnar connections, fundamental for orientation selectivity, develop later and slowly. They first emerge prenatally at about 37 weeks of gestation, but the more adult-like patchiness of the projection can be found only after 8 weeks postnatal.

Less data is available today on V2, a few studies on monkeys[31,32] suggest that the functional organization mature considerably later in V2 than in the primary visual cortex. The large V2 receptive fields, responsible for angle selectivity, are mostly absent until 4 weeks of age, and still immature as late as 8 weeks of age.

3. Modeling lower visual areas

This section will introduce the model, the rationale for its design, its mathematical background and the details of each component.

3.1. *Mathematics for developing artificial cortical maps*

A fruitful mathematical framework for simulating cortical maps in a developmental perspective is the concept of *self-organization*, that has been the object of several proposals for artificial neural network schemes. The first implementation was proposed by[33,34] in models of the development of aspects of the visual system, based exclusively on the local interaction of neurons. The difficulties related to the system of differential equations in this early formulation made it unsuitable for building cognitive models. Kohonen's SOM (*Self-Organizing Maps*) made the mechanism of self-organization maps popular, thanks to its efficiency and simplicity.[35,36] However, the winner-takes-all mechanism at the basis of the SOM, is a significant departure from the behavior of biological cortical circuits. It works as a mathematical substitution for the effect of lateral connections, but only assuming fixed connections and uniform neighborhoods. Today, several models are available that still offer the necessary simplicity for being used in the simulation of higher level cognitive function, but without the SOM winner-takes-all simplified mechanism.[37]

In our model, we use the LISSOM architecture (*Laterally Interconnected Synergetically Self-Organizing Map*),[38] which implements flexible and modifiable lateral connections of both excitatory and inhibitory types.

In a LISSOM sheet of neurons, the activation of each neuron is due to the combination of afferents, excitatory, and inhibitory connections. Since the excitatory and inhibitory contributions depends on the activation of neighbor neurons on the same sheet, the computation is recursive in time, in general 10 steps are sufficient for convergence.

3.2. *Overall structure of the model*

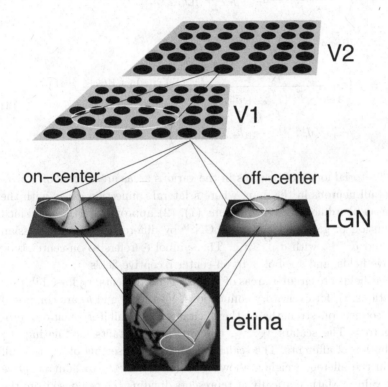

Fig. 3.   Overall scheme of the model.

An outline of the modules that make up the model is shown in Fig. 3. By calling x a neuron in the LGN (*Lateral Geniculate Nucleus*), y a neuron in V1, and z in V2, and being r and c bidimensional coordinates in the maps, and v the retinal input, the model is based on the following equations:

$$x_{r,c}^{(\odot)} = f\left(\left(\vec{g}_{r_A}^{(\sigma_N)} - \vec{g}_{r_A}^{(\sigma_W)}\right) \cdot \vec{v}_{r,c}\right) \tag{1}$$

$$x_{r,c}^{(\circledcirc)} = f\left(\left(\vec{g}_{r_A}^{(\sigma_W)} - \vec{g}_{r_A}^{(\sigma_N)}\right) \cdot \vec{v}_{r,c}\right) \tag{2}$$

$$z_{r,c}^{(k)} = f\left(\frac{\gamma_X}{1 + \gamma_N \vec{I} \cdot \vec{a}_{r,c}} \vec{a}_{r,c} \cdot \vec{y}_{r,c} + \gamma_E \vec{e}_{r,c} \cdot \vec{z}_{r,c}^{(k-1)} - \right.$$
$$\left. \gamma_H \vec{h}_{r,c} \cdot \vec{z}_{r,c}^{(k-1)}\right) \tag{3}$$

$$y_{r,c}^{(k)} = f\left(\frac{\gamma_X}{1 + \gamma_N \vec{I} \cdot \left(\vec{a}_{r,c}^{(\odot)} + \vec{a}_{r,c}^{(\circledcirc)}\right)}\left(\vec{a}_{r,c}^{(\odot)} + \vec{a}_{r,c}^{(\circledcirc)}\right)\left(\vec{x}_{r,c}^{(\odot)} + \vec{x}_{r,c}^{(\circledcirc)}\right) + \right.$$
$$\left. \gamma_E \vec{e}_{r,c} \cdot \vec{y}_{r,c}^{(k-1)} - \gamma_H \vec{h}_{r,c} \cdot \vec{y}_{r,c}^{(k-1)}\right) \tag{4}$$

where vectorial forms of neurons in the various areas are vectors of activations of all neurons in the map, where a lateral connection exists with the neuron at coordinates r, c. Equations (1), (2) approximate the combined contribution of gangliar cells and LGN[39] by differences of two Gaussian $\vec{g}^{(\sigma_N)}$ and $\vec{g}^{(\sigma_W)}$, with $\sigma_N < \sigma_W$. The symbol $\odot$ refers to on-center type receptive fields, and symbol $\circledcirc$ to off-center receptive fields.

Their fields are circular areas of radius r_A for afferents, r_E for inhibitory connections, r_H for excitatory connections. Vectors $\vec{e}_i$ and $\vec{h}_i$ are composed by all connection strengths of the excitatory or inhibitory neurons projecting to i. The scalars γ_X, γ_E, and γ_H, are constants modulating the contribution of afferents. The scalar γ_N controls the setting of a push-pull effect in the afferent weights, allowing inhibitory effects without negative weight values. Mathematically, it represents dividing the response from the excitatory weights by the response from a uniform disc of inhibitory weights over the receptive field of neuron i. Vector $\vec{I}$ is just a vector of 1's of the same dimension of $\vec{x}_i$. Maps V1 and V2 have their own different sets of field radius and gamma parameters. The function f is a piecewise linear approximation of the sigmoid function. k is the time step in the recursive procedure.

All connection strengths adapt according to the general Hebbian principle, and include a normalization mechanism that counterbalances the overall increase of connections of the pure Hebbian rule. The following, for example, is the equation in the case of the afferent synaptic strengths in

V2:

$$\Delta \vec{a}_{r,c} = \frac{\vec{a}_{r,c} + \eta_A x_{r,c} \vec{v}_{r,c}}{\|\vec{a}_{r,c} + \eta_A x_{r,c} \vec{v}_{r,c}\|} - \vec{a}_{r,c}, \tag{5}$$

where η_A is the afferent learning rate. Similar equations hold for the excitatory and inhibitory connection strengths in V2, as well as in V1. The size of V1 is of 96×96 neurons, V2 of 36×36 neurons.

3.3. *Stimuli simulation*

The mature visual functions are not implicit in the model definition, they will be learned during the development, therefore a component of the model are the sets of stimuli, that replicate in essence natural conditions. It is known that important development in V1 occurs during the pre-natal phase, under the "learning" of the responses to spontaneous waves of activity traveling along the retina.[40] These waves are simulated by synthetic random blobs. A second set of synthetic blobs, arranged in a corner, have been used as an experimental condition for angle development in V2, as will be discussed in §4.2. The third set is made up by a collection of 100 real objects, the COIL-100,[41] where for each of the objects, 72 different views are available.

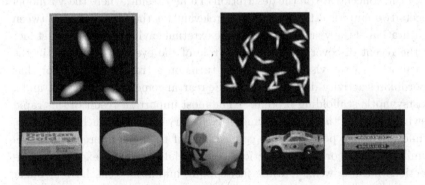

Fig. 4. Stimuli used during the development: in the top row synthetic blobs as spontaneous retinal waves, and angular blobs used for V2, in the bottom row real objects of the COIL-100 collection.

4. Visual abilities learnt by the model

At the end of the simulated period of development, the resulting organization in the V1 and V2 maps was analyzed, the first with respect to the selectivity to line orientations, the second for the ability to identify angles.

4.1. *Orientation selectivity in model V1*

In model V1, most neurons respond selectively to a specific orientation, and the organization of the arrangement of orientation preferences over the map is similar to natural V1, with repeated patterns of gradually changing orientations, broken by a few types of discontinuity. The most common are fractures, lines where the orientation changes abruptly, and pinwheel centers, spots surrounded by cells sensitive in turn to all orientations. Since similar results have been already achieved in several computational models of V1 – a survey in[42] – including models based on LISSOM,[43,44] details on these aspects will not be described here.

Table 1. Changes in the main parameters of equation (4) after eye opening.

	γ_X	γ_E	γ_H
pre-natal	1.0	0.9	0.9
after eye opening	0.7	0.5	1.2

I will concentrate on the description of a new result, where the V1 model meets two empirical facts, especially relevant for the relationship between maturation of the visual cortex and the external environment. The first fact is the recent discovery of the crucial role of the eye opening event in the maturation of the visual cortex, that turns on a transcription factor that coordinates activity-dependent synaptic rearrangement in the cortex, and a postsynaptic scaffolding protein.[45] The most important result of this rapid rewiring is that the star pyramidal excitatory cells are much less active, while inhibitory post-synaptic connections of thalamic afferents increase. Similar to intracortical connections, pyramidal-pyramidal excitatory connections become weaker, while fast-spiking inhibitory cells have stronger activity.[46] In the model this reconfiguration can be replicated by changing the main parameters balancing in equation (4) the relative weight of afferent, excitatory, and inhibitory connections in the V1 map, values are in Tab. 1.

The second fact is the peculiar feature of the orientation selectivity in V1, known as *oblique effect*. It is a higher sensitivity to cardinal vs. oblique contours,[47] observed in V1 of several mammals, humans included,[48] which may encode a bias in environmental information content in that horizontal and vertical contours occur more frequently than others.

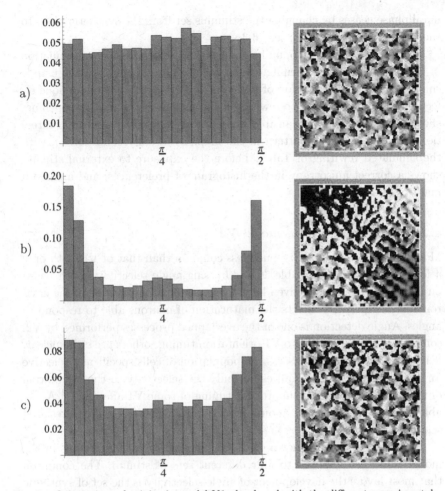

Fig. 5. Orientation selectivity in model V1, developed with the different experimental conditions: a) pre-natal development only, b) no simulated reconfiguration after eye-opening, c) simulated reconfiguration according to Tab.1. For each condition, on the left the histogram of preferences in orientation of all cells, on the right the map of preferences, with orientation coded as gray level, from black, horizontal, to white, vertical.

Within the model these two facts seem to be in strong correlation, in that anisotropy in orientation preference occurs only after the eye opening period, while spontaneous activity gives rise to an initial isotropic map. Moreover, if no rewiring is applied at the eye opening transition, the environmental driven experience distorts the map too much towards cardinal preferences, disrupting the smooth organization of V1. In the model the pre-natal phase ceases by changing the stimulus set from the synthetic blobs to the COIL-100 real objects, see §3.3.

With reference to Fig. 5, under condition a), which lacks any stimulation in the period after eye opening, the arrangement of patterns in the map is smooth, and the distribution of preferences is flat, without any oblique effect. Condition b), where no rewiring has been simulated after eye opening, shows a very strong, implausible excess of preferences for cardinal directions, and an irregular pattern in the map. Eventually condition c), with the simulated rewiring of Tab. 1 before the exposure to external stimuli, shows a correct anisotropy in the histogram of preferences, and a smooth map.

4.2. Angle selectivity in model V2

Modeling responses of V2 is much less common than that of V1, with only a few recent studies available[49,50] addressing angle selectivity, both based on LISSOM. The results given herein concern how, in the model, the environmental experience affects the maturation of neurons able to respond to angles. Angle detection is one of the overlapped processes performed by V2, some of which are similar to V1 orientation tuning, others are still unclear, it is therefore difficult to assess the population of cells specifically selective for angles. This feature requires not only the selectivity to the orientation of the half lines, but also suppressive tuning of some V1 afference.[51] Available data[9,10] suggests that about one third of V2 neurons come to respond selectively to angles.

In Fig. 6 results are shown of the angular selectivity of neurons in the model V2, when exposed to four different sets of stimuli. The condition that most favors the development of angle selectivity is the set of synthetic corner patterns, as a couple of elongated Gaussian blobs, with a coincident end point. However, the exposure to natural objects of the COIL collection leads to a consistent angular selectivity in the map. It is interesting how the resulting map reflects the nature of the set of objects experienced, with a limited number of neurons responding to angles when the objects seen during the development are roundish. Table 2 gives the percentage of units significantly responding to angles in the different developmental conditions. It can be seen that the exposure to all possible combinations of objects give the percentage that is the closest to the amount of angle selective neurons found in biological V2.

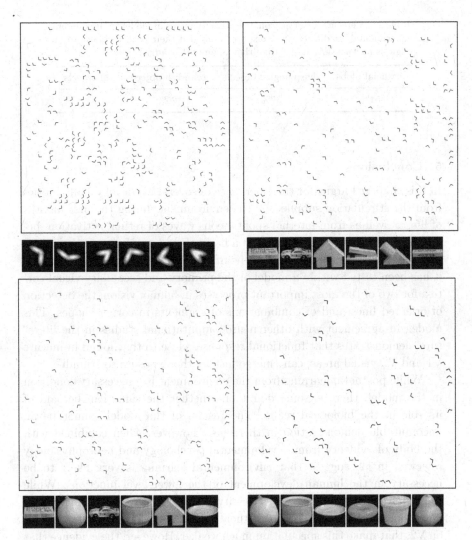

Fig. 6. Angular selectivity in model V2, developed with different sets of stimuli: synthetic random angular blobs on the top left, objects with sharp angles on top right, all objects on bottom left, roundish objects on bottom right.

Table 2. Percentages of neurons selective to angles in model V2 in different experimental conditions. Neurons are counted if their peak response to an angle is at least 30% larger than that of any other angle.

artificial blobs	sharp angled objects	roundish objects	all objects
51%	37%	25%	35%

5. Conclusions

In this chapter I argue for the emergence of several low-level visual abilities from the stimulation supplied by the environment during the first months of life, as well as from internal spontaneous waves of retinal activation, before birth. This argument hinges on a body of evidence from psychological, anthropological, physiological and neurocomputational studies. Moreover, it has been tested within a model of the primary and secondary visual cortex, for two of the most important processes in human vision: the detection of oriented lines, and of combinations of segments in corner shapes. This model, in agreement with other neurocomputational studies in the literature, demonstrates that functional responses close to that found in mature V1 and V2 visual areas, can emerge just by the exposure to stimuli.

While postnatal learning from the environment is a necessary condition in the model, there is some doubt on whether the same can be said of its role in the biological realm. The results of the model cannot be an unconfutable demonstration in this sense, however, when combined with the body of evidence from developmental psychology and neurophysiology reviewed in §2, suggest that environmental learning is very likely to be necessary in the human development of the lower-level functions. While the empirical support for the necessity of environmental learning in the development of area V1 is broad, there is a lack of developmental studies on V2, that make this speculation much weaker. However, the evidence that in primates functional organization matures considerably later in V2 than in V1,[32] strongly suggests that the role of environmental learning should be even more important for V2 than for V1.

If low-level visual abilities in humans are mostly learned, it is necessary to understand how this thesis fares with regard to the question on why natural selection did not equip us with a ready-to-go visual system, at least in its very basic abilities. For the higher cognitive functions, like those supported by the prefrontal cortex, a reasonable explanation of the protracted maturation is to allow humans the powerful flexibility in coping with environmental variance and the challenges such instability presents.[52] Some scholars speculate that the extreme plasticity of the human brain is in fact the key solution of natural evolution, in the so-called variability selection hypothesis.[53] However, it is unlikely that the advantage in entrusting early visual processes, like line and corner detection, to instructivist somatic interactions, may lay in the necessity of coping with different environments. With the exception of experimental settings, the environments of mammals are rich enough and varied enough with respect to line or corner orientation, therefore, specializing vision for layouts of the environment significantly different with respect to these features is not useful.

I believe, that in fact, the differences in seeing among people of various cultures is mostly due to the higher visual areas, and to the interaction with language, like in the case of colors.[54,55] I would guess that the reason for the sensorial driven developmental stage in lower vision is to avoid the genetic coding of complex functional patterns, that engages hundred of millions of neurons in the visual pathway. It is an externalization strategy, that relies upon strong regularities of the environment, in building functions that capture these regularities. What make objects visible as entities distinct from their background is very often the gradient in light or hue, along contour lines, with corners being the most prominent cues of many three dimensional objects. The general-purpose learning of frequent coincidences of patterns in retinal space is sufficient for reliably developing large scale organization of connections in the major visual areas of the cortex.

References

1. J. Fodor, *Philosophy of Science* **51**, 23 (1984).
2. Z. Pylyshyn, *Behavioral and Brain Science* **22**, 341 (1999).
3. D. Hubel and T. Wiesel, *Journal of Physiology* **148**, 574 (1959).
4. D. Hubel and T. Wiesel, *Journal of Physiology* **195**, 215 (1968).
5. W. Vanduffel, R. B. Tootell, A. A. Schoups and G. A. Orban, *Cerebral Cortex* **12**, 647 (2002).
6. J. Hegdé and D. C. Van Essen, *Journal of Neuroscience* **20**, 4117 (2000).
7. A. Plebe, The ventral visual path: Moving beyond V1 with computational models, in *Visual Cortex: New Research*, eds. T. A. Portocello and R. B. Velloti (Nova Science Publishers, New York, 2008) pp. 97–160.
8. J. Hegdé and D. C. Van Essen, *Cerebral Cortex* **17**, 1100 (2007).
9. M. Ito and H. Komatsu, *Journal of Neuroscience* **24**, 3313 (2004).
10. A. Anzai, X. Peng and D. C. V. Essen, *Nature Neuroscience* **10**, 1313 (2007).
11. G. Piccinini, *Synthese* **in press** (2007).
12. S. R. Quartz and T. J. Sejnowski, *Behavioral and Brain Science* **20**, 537 (1997).

13. G. Westermann, D. Mareschal, M. H. Johnson, S. Sirois, M. S. Spratling and M. S. C. Thomas, *Developmental Science* **10**, 75 (2007).

14. R. Miikkulainen, J. Bednar, Y. Choe and J. Sirosh, *Computational maps in the visual cortex* (Springer-Science, New York, 2005).

15. W. H. R. Rivers, Vision, in *Physiology and Psychology, Part I: Reports of the Cambridge Anthropological Expedition to Torres Strait*, ed. A. C. Haddon (Cambridge University Press, Cambridge (UK), 1901)

16. M. Segall, D. T. Campbell and M. J. Herskovits, *The influence of culture on visual perception* (Bobbs Merill, New York, 1966).

17. H. Ross, Environmental influences on geometrical ilusions, in *Proceedings of the Sixth Annual Meeting of the International Society of Psychophysicists*, ed. F. Müller (Würzburg, Germany, 1990).

18. L. B. Cohen and B. A. Younger, *Infant Behavior and Development* **7**, 37 (1983).

19. R. Held and A. Hein, *Journal of Comparative and Physiological Psychology* **56**, 872 (1962).

20. A. Slater, Visual perception, in *Blackwell Handbook of Infant Development*, eds. G. Bremner and A. Fogel (Nova Science Publishers, New York, 2002)

21. P. Gerhardstein, G. Shroff and K. Dickerson, The development of object recognition through infancy, in *New Directions in Developmental Psychobiology*, eds. B. C. Glenyn and R. P. Zini (Nova Science Publishers, New York, 2009)

22. J. Atkinson, O. Braddick, J. Wattam-Bell, B. Hood and F. Weeks, *Perception* **18**, p. 492 (1989).

23. M. H. Bornstein, S. J. Krinsky and A. A. Benasich, *Journal of Experimental Child Psychology* **41**, 49 (1986).

24. T. L. Lewis, A. Kingdon, D. Ellemberg and D. Maurer, *Journal of Vision* **7**, 1 (2007).

25. L. B. Cohen and C. H. Cashon, Infant perception and cognition, in *Handbook of Psychology: Developmental psychology*, eds. R. M. Lerner, D. K. Freedheim, I. B. Weiner, M. A. Easterbrooks and J. Mistry (John Wiley, New York, 2003) pp. 65–90.

26. D. Hubel and T. Wiesel, *Journal of Neurophysiology* **26**, 1003 (1963).

27. T. Wiesel and D. Hubel, *Journal of Neurophysiology* **28**, 1041 (1965).

28. M. P. Stryker, H. Sherk, A. G. Leventhal and H. V. Hirsch, *Journal of Neurophysiology* **41**, 896 (1978).

29. G. G. Blasdel, D. Mitchell, D. Muir and J. Pettigrew, *Journal of Physiology* **265**, 615 (1977).

30. A. Burkhalter, K. L. Bernardo and V. Charles, *Journal of Neuroscience* **13**, 1916 (1993).

31. T. A. Coogan and D. C. Van Essen, *The Journal of Comparative Neurology* **372**, 327 (1996).

32. B. Zhang, J. Zheng, I. Watanabe, I. Maruko, H. Bi, E. L. S. III and Y. Chino, *Proceedings of the Natural Academy of Science USA* **101**, 5862 (2005).

33. C. von der Malsburg, *Kibernetic* **14**, 85 (1973).

34. D. J. Willshaw and C. von der Malsburg, *Proceedings of the Royal Society of London* **B194**, 431 (1976).

35. T. Kohonen, *Biological Cybernetics* **43**, 59 (1982).

36. T. Kohonen, *Self-Organizing Maps* (Springer-Verlag, Berlin, 1995).

37. G. Wallis and E. Rolls, *Progress in Neurobiology* **51**, 167 (1997).

38. J. Sirosh and R. Miikkulainen, *Neural Computation* **9**, 577 (1997).

39. J. E. Dowling, *The Retina: An Approachable Part of the Brain* (Cambridge University Press, Cambridge (UK), 1987).

40. F. Sengpiel and P. C. Kind, *Current Biology* **12**, 818 (2002).

41. S. Nayar and H. Murase, *International Journal of Computer Vision* **14**, 5 (1995).

42. L. Schwabe and K. Obermayer, *Neural Networks* **16**, 1353 (2003).

43. J. A. Bednar and R. Miikkulainen, *Neurocomputing* **69**, 1272 (2006).

44. A. Plebe and R. G. Domenella, *Neural Networks* **20**, 763 (2007).

45. S. P. Gandhi, J. Cang and M. P. Stryker, *Nature Neuroscience* **8**, 9 (2005).

46. A. Maffei, S. B. Nelson and G. G. Turrigiano, *Neural Networks* **7**, 1353 (2004).

47. B. Li, M. R. Peterson and R. D. Freeman, *Journal of Neurophysiology* **90**, 204 (2003).

48. C. S. Furmanski and S. A. Engel, *Nature Neuroscience* **3**, 535 (2000).

49. A. Plebe, *Neurocomputing* **70**, 2060 (2007).

50. Y. F. Sit and R. Miikkulainen, *Neural Computation* **21**, 762 (2009).

51. B. D. B. Willmore, R. J. Prenger and J. L. Gallant, *Journal of Neuroscience* **30**, 2102 (2010).

52. S. R. Quartz, Toward a developmental evolutionary psychology: Genes, development, and the evolution of the human cognitive architecture, in *Evolutionary Psychology – Alternative Approaches*, eds. S. Scher and F. Rauscher (Kluwer, Dordrecht (NL), 2003) pp. 185–210.

53. R. Potts, *American Journal of Physical Anthropology* **107**, 93 (1999).

54. D. Roberson, J. Davidoff, I. R. Davies and L. R. Shapiro, *Cognitive Psychology* **50**, 378 (2005).

55. A. Plebe, M. Mazzone and V. De la Cruz, Colors and color adjectives in the cortex, in *New Directions in Colour Studies*, eds. C. Biggam, C. Hough, D. Simmons and C. J. Kay (John Benjamins, Amsterdam, 2010) p. in press.

A DYNAMICAL NEURAL SIMULATION OF FEATURE-BASED ATTENTION AND BINDING IN A RECURRENT MODEL OF THE VENTRAL STREAM

D. G. Harrison* and M. De Kamps

School of Computing, University of Leeds,
Leeds, West Yorkshire, LS2 9JT, UK
* E-mail: pab2dgh@leeds.ac.uk

Visual attention can be deployed to locations within the visual array (spatial attention), to individual features such as colour (feature-based attention), or to entire objects (object-based attention). Objects are composed of features to form a perceived 'whole'. This compositional object representation reduces the storage demands by avoiding the need to store every type of object experienced. However, this approach exposes a problem of binding these constituent features (e.g. form and colour) into objects. The problem is made explicit in the higher areas of the ventral stream as information about a feature's location is absent. For feature-based attention and search, activations flow from the inferotemporal cortex to primary visual cortex without spatial cues from the dorsal stream, therefore the neural effect is applied to all locations across the visual field.[1-4]

We present a model of the ventral stream (based on the Closed Loop Attention Model (CLAM) of visual search[5]) which explains this behaviour. The model also demonstrates a mechanism of binding together colour and form features from AIT through a coincidence mechanism within primary visual cortex. The visual search simulations also demonstrate how neural activations propagate from the inferotemporal cortex to enhance activity across the primary visual cortex. As CLAM is built on top of MIIND,[6] dynamical simulations can be generated from the model using Wilson-Cowan dynamics[7] to simulate neural populations and add a temporal aspect to the model. The simulations are realised as 2 and 3 dimensional graphical displays which allows the flow of activations for a simulation to be visualised.

1. Introduction

The ability to see our environment is something most of us take for granted. However, the world we see around us is just an illusion created by our visual system from the small proportion of received stimuli that make our attention.[8] The mind stitches together these snapshots of the world, using our expectations of what the environment should contain, to create a sufficiently accurate model that allows us to interact with the real external world as if perceiving it whole. The brain has a limited processing bandwidth,[9] so the area of the visual field that is being attended to must be carefully chosen for effective reconstruction of the mental image.

William James' contention in 1890 that "Everyone knows what attention is" [10, pp403] comes no doubt from the everyday experience of using attention to examine a part of a scene, such as an object, with greater detail than other less 'salient' parts of the scene, such as background. However, James' statement of a common knowledge of this innate ability belies an equally common ignorance of the neural processes by which attention is deployed.

1.1. *Spatial Attention*

Visual attention can be deployed to locations in the visual field to increase neural sensitivity for neurons whose receptive fields are enclosed within the attended to location. The neural mechanism for spatial attention is to increase the effective contrast of stimuli within the locus of attention[11,12] and to reduce the response of neurons sensitive to unattended locations.[13] This is described as the contrast gain model.[13]

1.2. *Feature-Based Attention*

Treisman and Gelade[14] detail a set of basic features (such as orientation, colour and direction of motion) to which neurons are sensitive. When attention is directed to one of these fundamental features neurons sensitive to that feature are modulated such that the response to stimuli that match the coded for feature is increased, and others are depressed. The selectivity of the feature-sensitive neurons is a continuum: a neuron sensitive to horizontal lines will see a response gain to the presence of a horizontal line within its receptive field, a depressed response for the presence of a vertical line and a diminished response to intermediate orientations. The level of modulation depends on the similarity between the coded for feature and the stimulus.[15,16] Sàenz et al[2] present results consistent with the feature similarity gain model[13] while showing that the attentional effects are dependent on the presence of competing stimuli.

1.3. *Object-Based Attention*

Objects are composed of features to form a perceived 'whole'. These features are bound to each other through spatial relationships, such that attending to any component feature of an object causes selection of all other object features.[17] This compositional object representation reduces the storage demands by avoiding the need to store every type of object experienced. The effect of object-based attention has been described as a shrinking of the receptive fields of neurons around the attended object.[18]

A number of studies have found that feature-based attentional effects occur across the visual field.[1–4,19,20] The Sàenz *et al* studies[2,19] used fMRI to test if feature-based attention produces global modulation of cortical populations. The studies presented overlapping fields of upwards or downwards moving dots in one visual hemifield to which the subject's attention was directed, and a single field of moving dots in the contralateral hemifield. Every twenty seconds subjects changed their attention between the upwards or downwards moving dots in the attended to hemifield. This effectively alternated the trial conditions between attended and ignored stimuli moving in the same direction, or in opposite directions. Their results show that attention to a feature modulates responses of neurons sensitive to that feature across the visual array, including the ignored stimuli in the contralateral hemifield.

We introduce a neural model of attention that postdicts this effect as neural activations generated by AIT neurons in a feedback network are applied throughout the visual field as a consequence of the interareal connection structure. The neurons in the reverse network coding for features are modulated by task-relevant information originating in higher areas, such as prefrontal cortex, through object and feature representations in AIT to the lower visual areas. The model features widening neural receptive fields in subsequently higher visual areas, such that the receptive fields of neurons in AIT are the entire visual field. Furthermore, a recent study by Zhang and Luck,[20] using a similar experimental paradigm to Sàenz *et al* but recording cortical activity via EEG, demonstrates this attentional modulation occurs only in cases where the attended to feature is in competition with distractors. We interpret this result as a consequence of binding: without neural activations from distractor features the representation in AIT is unambiguous, so the attentional neural cascade is not required.

2. The Model

The Closed Loop Attention Model (CLAM) of Visual Search proposed by van der Velde and de Kamps[5] includes the generation of saliency maps that are used to select a location to which attention is directed. CLAM consists of layers of neural networks that mimic the layered organisation of the human visual cortex, including the two primary cortico-visual pathways identified by Mishkin *et al*:[21] the ventral pathway from area V1 (striate cortex) to the anterior inferotemporal cortex (AIT) responsible for object recognition; and the dorsal pathway from area V1 to the posterior parietal (PP) region for spatial vision.

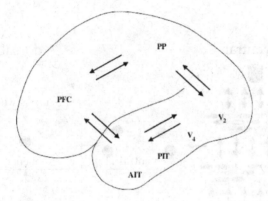

Fig. 1. The overall connection structure of the CLAM. PFC = prefontal cortex; AIT = anterior infero-temporal cortex; PIT = posterior infero-temporal cortex; PP = posterior parietal cortex.

Visual search comprises a bidirectional flow of activation between the lower and higher visual areas, in terms of bottom-up (stimulus-driven) and top-down (attentional/user-driven) processes. In the bottom-up flow, homogeneity in cells' receptive fields is penalised through layer local inhibition (e.g. the biased competition model of Desimone and Duncan[8]). A similar mechanism models the effect of attention via the top-down flow, except the top down maps generated by either the dorsal or ventral stream are primed for a cued location (or object/feature set) by the prefrontal cortex.

Unlike Feature Integration Theory and Guided Search, CLAM models these flows by two neural networks for each of the dorsal and ventral streams, with activations flowing from V1 to higher visual areas in one network, and an identical network propagating activations from higher areas to V1. Each pair of networks interact through local microcircuits via a disinhibition mechanism to enhance or suppress activations of features and positions[22] through a gating mechanism acting on similar activations in the two networks.

The time required to traverse these layers and interact are in line with experimental timing observations: Constantinidis and Steinmetz measured the activity of neurons which responded to the location of a singleton (target), finding that activity for both singleton and distractors were initially similar, but after a period of 180ms after stimulus presentation activity in the target selective neuron exceeded those of the distractors,[23] providing strong evidence that global saliency is not due to feedforward processes only.

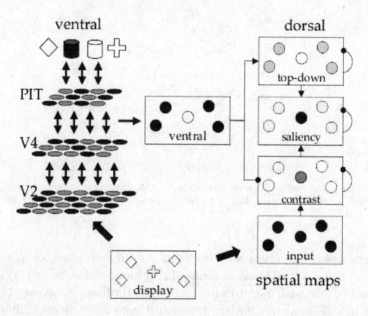

Fig. 2. Outline of CLAM showing interaction between the ventral and dorsal stream. This paper is concerned with modelling the ventral stream only.

The process of global saliency in CLAM is shown in figure 2. When presented with the input as shown in 'display', processing occurs in parallel in both the ventral and dorsal streams, initially in a feedforward manner. In the dorsal stream the display is processed into an input map of activated spatial locations. At this stage the identity of the objects at each location are unknown. In the ventral stream a winning object is selected through either biased competition or via endocortical activation of a target representation (i.e. cueing the selection of a particular object) and a ventral map is produced retinotopically. The input map and ventral maps are then combined into the contrast map by inhibition, such that activations in the ventral map mask out similar locations in the input map so only locations in the input map not selected in the ventral map remain. The ventral map also retinotopically activates a 'top-down' map in the dorsal stream. This copy of the ventral map performs inhibitory competition such that activations are reduced in the top-down map when multiple locations are active in the ventral map. The top-down map and contrast maps then combine through inhibitory competition in a retinotopic manner to create a saliency map.

2.1. *The Implementation*

The model of the ventral stream consists of a five-layer artificial neural network, with layers corresponding to V1, V2, V4, posterior inferotemporal (PIT) and anterior inferotemporal (AIT) cortical areas. Each layer receives input from overlapping neighbourhoods of neurons in its preceding area and outputs to the next higher area such that the effective receptive field size increases towards higher visual areas. Evidence for the increasing receptive field structure from V1 to V2 is provided by Sincich and Horton.[24] This forward network is trained using backpropagation: input/output pattern pairs are iteratively applied to the network, output errors are propagated back to the input layer, and network weights are adjusted to reduce the error until a threshold is reached. In addition to the forward network a reverse network, structurally identical to the forward but with activations propagating from higher to lower areas, is trained from the forward network via Hebbian learning.

The application of a pattern to the input layer of the trained network causes activations to be propagated through the intermediate layers where form features are combined into successively more complex units, terminating in AIT where the presence of complex objects is signalled by the activation of neurons coding for each learned object. The forward pass loses spatial information with each ascent to a higher visual area, where the neurons are spatially unaware but activate strongly for the existence of the features to which they are tuned occurring anywhere within their receptive fields. Conversely, activation of the AIT neurons in the reverse network generates a cascade from the feature domain to the spatial domain as each area passes activations to lower visual areas. A corollary to the AIT nodes being spatially agnostic is that the reverse network causes a spreading of neural activity throughout the lower visual areas.

The model is implemented using MIIND,[6] an open source library of tools for creating neural network simulations. MIIND includes advanced features that can be used to convert a biologically unrealistic artificial neural network (ANN) to more biologically plausible dynamical networks, with neural outputs being more accurately modelled with population firing rates[25,26] using Wilson-Cowan population dynamics.[7] This conversion is necessary as the networks can only be trained as ANN's, but these networks do not correlate well with the properties of real cortical neurons.[27] Conversion of the ANN to a dynamical simulation allows the time course of the system to be visualised and explored.

A simple example serves best to introduce the basic features of ClamLib. In Fig. 6 a small ANN is shown. It is a feedforward network and the activity of the nodes is given by

$$o = f(\sum_i w_i x_i), \tag{1}$$

where o is the activity of a node, w_i is the weight of its i-th input and x_i is the activity of another node which is connected to the i-th input of this node. The sigmoid function $f(x)$ is smooth and often given by:

$$f(x) = \frac{1}{1 + e^{-x}}. \tag{2}$$

In this particular case, it means that for $x \to -\infty, f(x) = 0$ and $x \to \infty, f(x) = 1$. A natural way to interpret this in neural terms is to say that for high negative input a node is inhibited, whereas for high positive input it is stimulated or excited.

Wilson-Cowan dynamics is a simplified model of the behaviour of a group of spiking neurons. The population firing rate of a group of neurons is the fraction of neurons that fires in a short time window, Δt, divided by Δt. Wilson-Cowan dynamics is given by:

$$\tau \frac{dE}{dt} = -E + f(\sum_i w_i E_i) \tag{3}$$

Here, E is the population firing rate of the group, E_i are the firing rates of other populations, which are connected to the group via weighted connection i (with weight w_i). Although the original motivation for this dynamics has been criticised, the dynamics can also be inferred from sophisticated methods for modelling population dynamics and has recently been shown to reproduce neuronal dynamics very reliably in some cases.[28]

Equation 3 gives a very direct interpretation for the activation in ANNs as given by equation 1: if $\frac{dE}{dt} = 0$, equation 3 reads:

$$E = f(\sum_i w_i E_i),$$ (4)

i.e. if the sigmoids are identical in both equations, the equations are identical as well. The sigmoid in equation 3 arises from neuroscience considerations and will not be of the form of equation 2, but this is a minor issue.

This gives a direct interpretation for the activation of ANNs: they represent steady state activation of neural populations described by Wilson-Cowan dynamics. While equation 3 looks suspiciously like equations describing leaky-integrate-and-fire neurons, these describe discontinuous behaviour of individual neurons: the membrane potential is reset after a spike. It is therefore incorrect to associate these dynamics with population dynamics.

This suggests a direct possibility for converting ANNs into networks of dynamical simulations. DynamicNetworks are objects that can be instantiated using MIIND's DynamicLib library. DynamicNetworks can be used to simulate networks of populations described by Wilson-Cowan dynamics. The most direct way of associating ANNs with neural dynamics is to generate Wilson-Cowan dynamics simulation from a trained ANN such that there is a one-to-one mapping between nodes of the ANN and the DynamicNetwork. The weights in the DynamicNetwork are the same as the weights between corresponding nodes in the ANN. The main complication is that the network needs input to something interesting. Input in a DynamicNetwork is provided by an extra node which runs an algorithm that provides constant input.

When converting the ANN to a population-based model a complication arises in the representation of negative ANN weights as the firing rate of a collection of neurons. This impedance was overcome by replacing each ANN node in the forward and reverse networks with a micro-circuit of six neural populations with four input nodes and two output nodes: one coding for positive ANN weights and the other coding for negative weights (see figure 3a). Both of these nodes output positive spike rates, but the negative nodes' outputs are implicitly considered as negative values. The four input nodes ensure that the output nodes of a circuit fire exclusively.

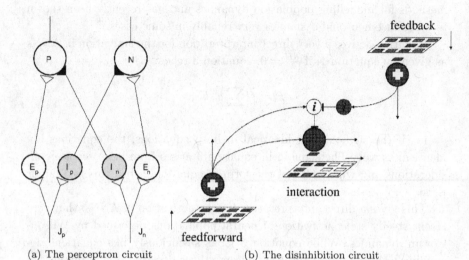

(a) The perceptron circuit (b) The disinhibition circuit

Fig. 3. Cortical micro-circuits. a) The perceptron circuit: Ep - Excitatory positive input; Ip - Inhibitory positive input; En - Excitatory negative; In - Inhibitory input; P - Positive output; N - Negative output. Image from[25] b) The disinhibition circuit: the feedforward network activates an excitatory and inhibitory neuron in the interaction layer. Matching activation in the feedback and feedforward networks causes a disinhibition of the interaction network via inhibition of the inhibitory neuron activated by the feedforward network.

During the conversion to a dynamical network the forward and reverse networks are coupled through another cortical circuit joining the positive and negative populations of the forward and reverse networks (see figure 3b). The circuit acts to gate activations between the two networks through a disinhibition mechanism driven by matching activations in the joined forward and reverse networks. For a positive activation in the forward network the output and gating nodes of the disinhibition circuit receive activations from the forward network, such that the output node is excited and inhibited equally after a settling period in which the output of the gating node catches up with the innervation of the output node. This steady state is maintained by activations in the forward network. If a positive activation occurs in the feedback network, the disinhibition node is activated in the disinhibition circuit causing the gating node to be inhibited, allowing the output node of the disinhibition circuit to output spikes. A similar mechanism occurs for matching negative activations in the forward and reverse networks. Note that in cases of mismatched activations, the output node of the disinhibition circuit will not emit spikes.

3. A Binding Problem

The distributed representation of a scene in terms of the 'what' and the 'where' poses a problem of correctly binding together a perceived object and its position, particularly in a multi-object scene. For example, if a scene containing a square to the left of a triangle is viewed, depictions of a square and a triangle are determined by the ventral stream (AIT), while their positions are determined by the dorsal stream (PP). The problem arises as the distributed cortical representation allows the scene to be interpreted either correctly with the square to the left of the triangle, or erroneously with the square to the right of the triangle. Furthermore, a representation of objects as a collection of features in AIT presents a similar problem when resolving the properties of an individual object amongst many. Consider figure 4, in which complex shapes in AIT are represented by model neurons, with colour represented separately. The forward network causes the neurons indicating the presence of a cross and a diamond to activate, but also the neurons coding for black and grey. The AIT representation is ambiguous, allowing the diamond to be incorrectly perceived as black, or correctly perceived as grey.

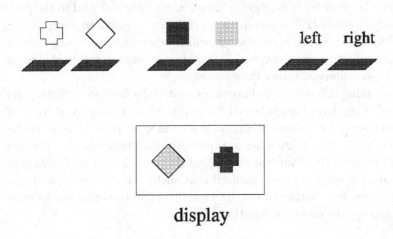

display

Fig. 4. Example of ambiguous representation of visual scene in AIT. When presented with the display of a grey diamond to the left of a black cross, neurons in AIT are activated for all the features present in the scene. This distributed representation requires binding to resolve.

In CLAM, this binding problem is resolved using a 'visual blackboard'[29] to tie together the distributed components of a scene. The blackboard itself is simply the early layers of the visual streams, where the layout of the neurons map topographically to the retina (retinotopic). As these areas are common to both the ventral and dorsal stream, interaction between them can occur.[5] Chelazzi and collaborators have demonstrated that when several features in AIT compete with each other, and one of them is task-relevant, then it will suppress the other features' activation. Subsequently feature-based activation is relayed to *all positions* in lower areas of visual cortex where it can interact with the visual stimulus information that is present there.[27] We have shown[22] that consistency checks can be performed by local cortical circuits. These local circuits have a higher activation if the locally present visual stimulus information matches the feature that corresponds to the feature-based attention activation, i.e. when locally bottom-up stimulus-driven information matches attention-driven top-down information. As we have demonstrated,[22] there are many more such local matches at the retinotopic position where the feature of interest resides, i.e. by matching top-down and bottom-up information we are able to isolate the retinotopic position of the relevant feature in low visual areas, where position information is present, unlike in AIT.

Once the retinotopic position is found, it can be transferred to the parietal cortex (area LIP) to prepare a saccade, or local information can be reprocessed, for example, to discover which other features belong to this particular object as demonstrated in.[30] This is an interpretation of binding as a two-step process, rather than as a state.[31]

In adopting this model, we have extrapolated the findings of Motter and Chelazzi. They have demonstrated the modulation of neuronal activity of neurons coding for a visual stimulus by factors external to their receptive field. Typically this external factor is interpreted as task-related activation originating from the temporal or prefrontal cortex. In our explanation of the binding process we have assumed that such activation goes to all positions in low-level cortical areas, because this is, in our opinion, the most parsimonious functional explanation of binding.

4. Results

An ANN with the following dimensions was created:

- V1: 16x16 (4 features: vertical, horizontal, forward-diagonal, backward-diagonal)

- V2: 15x15
- V4: 13x13
- PIT: 9x9
- AIT: 1x1 (4 features: square, horizontal cross, diamond, diagonal cross)

This network was then trained using backpropagation to associate V1 input patterns with their associated AIT shapes nodes. Each of the four shapes in AIT was presented to the network in every position of the central 100 squares (leaving a 3 neuron border to avoid edge artefacts). These 400 patterns were iteratively applied to the ANN in random order until the overall network error was less than 10^{-9} for all test patterns.

The trained ANN was then used to create a number of dynamic simulations. In all cases where a single object was applied as input and its associated shape was selected by external stimulation of the reverse network's corresponding AIT node, the activity in the disinhibition circuit showed the network correctly detected the object's location. This is not an interesting result, other than demonstrating the conversion from ANN to dynamic network is correct, as the network was trained from the application of these same single patterns. The more interesting cases are when multiple objects are presented to the network.

When multiple objects are applied, interference due to the overlapping receptive fields reduces the effectiveness of the network. To quantify the network's effectiveness, we discretised each layer of the disinhibition network into four equally sized quadrants (top left, top right, bottom left, bottom right). For the same quadrant in each layer of the disinhibition network, we summed the number of nodes with absolute activations above 0.05 (values below 0.05 were considered as noise). Using this method we recorded results when 2,3 or 4 non-overlapping shapes were applied as input in separate quadrants. In these tests the quadrant containing the searched for pattern was found using the method described above. Our results are presented below, and show that increasing the number of objects in the visual field of the network reduces the ability for the network to find the target. A neural mechanism to implement this check is on-going and will be developed within the implementation of the dorsal stream.

In cases where shapes overlapped (and to a lesser degree, where shapes were adjacent), the location of the object was impaired. Depending on the degree of overlap, some features of the target object were matched. It is hoped that future work on lateral inhibition within the disinhibition circuit will improve on this area.

Num. Shapes	Top Left	Top Right	Bottom Left	Bottom Right
2	23	8	12	11
3	23	11	14	12
4	23	10	16	12

Fig. 5. Dynamical network results. Numbers represent the median number of disinhibition circuits with outputs over 0.1. Trials were run with 2, 3 and 4 shapes in the visual field. Each shape occupied one of four quadrants: top left, top right, bottom left, bottom right. Trials were conducted so each quadrant was occupied in at least 8 trials for every 'number of shapes'. All tests were performed with non-overlapping shapes and the target object was always in the top left.

In figure 7 we show the result of our conversion of the ANN (figure 6) to the Wilson-Cowan model. The figures clearly demonstrate that the functionality of the ANN is transferred to the dynamical model. Using disinhibition circuits we are able to link the feedforward and feedback networks and model the interaction between them. With these networks we are now able, in principle, to model the experimental results discussed in this paper directly.

We can interpret both the enhancement of feedforward processing observed by Zhang and Luck and the influence of feature-based activation on locations where no visual stimulus is present as observed by Sàenz and Boynton. Presently we model the interaction between feedforward and feedback networks in the ventral stream by fields of disinhibition circuits. The disinhibition circuit enhances activation in the feedforward network if there is a corresponding match of the feedback network at a particular location. This is in line with the result obtained by Motter[32] who has observed a similar task-dependent modulation of neuronal activation in V4. Such an enhancement of activation can lead to faster processing and would explain the strengthening the P1/stimulus component of the attended features when the target is in simultaneous competition with distractors observed by Zhang and Luck.[20] Importantly, the feedback information also modulates neuronal activity where stimulus information is not present as observed by Sàenz et al,[19] which we interpret as being caused in response to the lack of position information in AIT: this is necessary to discover the retinotopic location.

The model was informed by experimental results obtained by Motter[32] and Chelazzi and collaborators[27] which demonstrated that the activity of neurons representing visual information in low level visual areas is modulated by task-related activation. As mentioned above, we extrapolated these results by hypothesising that this feature-based information goes ase-

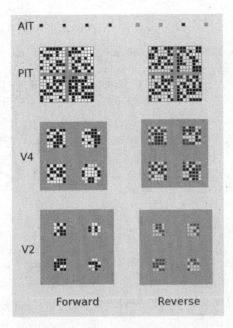

Fig. 6. The Artificial Neural Network. The forward network is on the left, showing neural activations propagating from four different objects presented to V1 (top). All four AIT neurons show positive activations, reflecting the presence of four different objects. To the right is the reverse network showing attention applied to the third object from the left. Corresponding activations in the lower layers show the object is located in the top-left quadrant. Black is strong positive activation, white strong negative activation. The grey background to each layer corresponds to no activation

lectively to every location in visual cortex and thus represents information about the identity of the feature at every location. At the time we proposed this mechanism, there was no experimental evidence for this extrapolation. In our opinion, the significance of the experimental work discussed in this paper[19,20] is that now, for the first time, there is. Zhang and Luck's work suggests that feature-based attention enhances feedforward processing in the hemisphere contralateral to where the task-relevant stimulus information is present. Boynton's work suggests that there is an influence of feature-based attention at locations where visual stimulus information is not even present.

5. Discussion

The model we presented in[22] is able to describe the experiments of Zhang and Luck, and Sàenz and Boynton. In particular the neuronal dynamics in

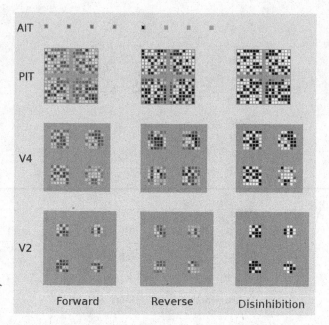

Fig. 7. The Dynamical Network. The neurodynamical simulation showing the forward network on the left, the reverse network in the middle and the disinhibition layers (for PIT, V4, V2) on the right. The dynamical network shows correlation between the forward network and disinhibition layers.

the different phases of the binding process can now be described accurately. The original model, in terms of Artificial Neural Networks (ANN's) was only to produce snapshots of these dynamics, since ANN's at best can only represent steady-state neuronal activity.[25] We have investigated the relationship between the activity of spiking neuronal populations, and established ways of converting ANN's into networks of neuronal populations.[25] In this paper we have demonstrated the first results of this conversion.

The upshot of our model is that we interpret the experiments as binding experiments, although they are not classical experimental binding paradigms. In the case of Zhang and Luck, the enhancement of feedforward processing in the contralateral hemisphere only takes place if the target and distractor stimuli are presented simultaneously. Our interpretation of these results is that when target and distractor dots are present simultaneously, only feature-based selection based on the identity of the target object can be used to perform the task, because target and distractor are present at the same location. This feature-based activation therefore enhances features of the corresponding identity at every location, and the neural mechanism that allow for this is exactly the feature-based attention required for binding.

There are many assumptions in our model which can be wrong: the interaction between feedforward and feedback may be implemented by gating networks which are not based on disinhibition as we have assumed, for example. The power of the model is that such assumptions can now be examined explicitly. We are currently experimenting with lateral connections that were not present in the original ANN model, for example.

Having a neurodynamical model of psychophysical experiments makes it possible, in principle, to predict the behavioural responses and imaging signals observed during the experiment. Tools are now starting to emerge which can convert neuronal model activity into local field potentials.[33] This raises the possibility of a more direct interaction between experiment and theory than is currently possible, which is an exciting prospect.

The model makes a number of explicit predictions. One of them is that binding is a two-step process. Binding of position to shape requires two large waves of activation: one from temporal to occipital regions, where local interactions decide the selection process and then a wave of activation from occipital regions to the parietal cortex where the outcome of the selection will be used to prepare a motor action (e.g. a saccade). It is our hope that these large-scale network interactions will be observable experimentally.

6. Conclusions

In this paper we have interpreted recent psychophysical experiments as providing direct evidence for the fact that feature-based attention influences low-level visual areas at all locations. Although this was hypothesised in a model of binding, experimental evidence was lacking so far. This novel interpretation of these experiments makes it possible to consider them as binding experiments. Such an interpretation is strongly suggested by the fact that a simultaneous presentation of target and distractor features is necessary to induce the feature-based feedback information.

At present our model stops just short of modelling the experimental results[2,3,19,20] directly. This is a matter of time: for the experimental paradigm of Sàenz et al[2,3,19] we need to implement a colour module in the dynamical model, for the results of Zhang and Luck[20] we need to include a motion module.

7. Future Work

Zhang and Luck[20] recently showed that feature-based attention modulates features even in the contralateral hemisphere from the object of interest by strengthening the P1/stimulus component of the attended features when the target is in simultaneous competition with distractors. Moreover, they demonstrated that the attentional neural modulation only occurs in instances of competition. Their study was similar to the Sàenz *et al* study described previously in this paper, but the target and distractor arrays were presented simultaneously or separately in different trials. They found similar results to Sàenz *et al*, but only when the target and distractor arrays were both present: without the competition of the distractor features there was no modulation of the neural trace. Unlike previous studies which have determined the need for competition for attentional modulation to be exhibited, Zhang and Luck measured the neural effect of attention in both competitive and non competitive scenarios, and hence claim their result unambiguously demonstrates the requirement of direct competition for feature-based attention to modulate neural behaviour. Our model should evolve to incorporate this important result.

An important extension of our model will be the inclusion of the dorsal stream. This is necessary to include the generation of saccades, so that behavioural data can be predicted by the model. It will also allow a refinement of a recently published model for global saliency (or 'pop-out'). In particular it will be possible to investigate the effect of target-distractor similarity.

8. Acknowledgements

The authors would like to thank The White Rose University Consortium for funding this research.

References

1. D. Walther, L. Itti, M. Riesenhuber, T. Poggio and C. Koch, Attentional selection for object recognition: A gentle way, in *BMCV '02: Proceedings of the Second International Workshop on Biologically Motivated Computer Vision*, (Springer-Verlag, London, UK, 2002).
2. M. Sàenz, G. T. Buracãs and G. M. Boynton, *Vision Research* **43**, 629 (2003).
3. G. M. Boynton, *Current Opinion in Neurobiology* **15**, 465 (2005).
4. M. M. Müller, S. Andersen, N. J. Trujillo, P. Valdés-Sosa, P. Malinowski and S. A. Hillyard, *Proceedings of the National Academy of Sciences* **103**, 14250 (2006).

5. F. van der Velde, M. de Kamps and G. T. van der Voort van der Kleij, *Neurocomputing* **58-60**, 607 (2004).
6. M. de Kamps, V. Baier, J. Drever, M. Dietz, L. Mösenlechner and F. van der Velde, *Neural Networks* **21**, 1164 (2008).
7. H. R. Wilson and J. D. Cowan, *Biological Cybernetics* **13**, 55 (1973).
8. R. Desimone and J. Duncan, *Annual Review Neuroscience* **18**, 193 (1995).
9. J. K. Tsotsos, *Brain & Behavioral Sciences* **13**, 423 (1990).
10. W. James, *The Principles of Psychology* (Henry Holt and Co., 1890).
11. A. B. Watson and J. A. Solomon, *Journal of the Optical Society of America* **14**, 2379 (1997).
12. T. Reynolds, J.H. Pasternak and R. Desimone, *Neuron* **26**, 703 (2000).
13. S. Treue and J. C. Martinez-Trujillo, *Nature* **399**, 575 (1999).
14. A. M. Treisman and G. Gelade, *Cognitive Psychology* **12**, 97 (1980).
15. J. C. Martinez-Trujillo and S. Treue, *Current Biology* **14**, 744 (2004).
16. J. H. R. Maunsell and S. Treue, *Trends in Neurosciences* **29**, 317 (2006).
17. M. A. Schoenfeld, C. Tempelmann, A. Martinez, J. M. Hopf, C. Sattler, H. J. Heinze and S. A. Hillyard, *Proceedings of the National Academy of Sciences* **100**, 11806 (2003).
18. J. Moran and R. Desimone, *Science* **229**, 782 (1985).
19. M. Sàenz, G. T. Buračas and G. M. Boynton, *Nature Neuroscience* **5**, 631 (2002).
20. W. Zhang and S. Luck, *Nature Neuroscience* **12**, 24 (2009).
21. M. Mishkin, L. G. Ungerleider and K. A. Macko, *Trends in Neurosciences* **6**, 414 (1983).
22. F. Van Der Velde and M. De Kamps, *Journal of Cognitive Neuroscience* **13**, 479 (2001).
23. C. Constantinidis and M. A. Steinmetz, *Journal of Neuroscience* **25**, 233 (2005).
24. L. C. Sincich and J. C. Horton, *Annual Review of Neuroscience* **28**, 303 (2005).
25. M. de Kamps and F. van der Velde, *Neural Networks* **14**, 941 (2001).
26. S. P. MacEvoy, T. R. Tucker and D. Fitzpatrick, *Nature Neuroscience* **12**, 637(April 2009).
27. L. Chelazzi, E. K. Miller, J. Duncan and R. Desimone, *Nature* **363**, 345 (1993).
28. T. P. Trappenberg, *Fundamentals of Computational Neuroscience* (Oxford University Press, 2002).
29. M. de Kamps and F. van der Velde, *Journal of Neural Engineering* **3**, R1 (2006).
30. M. de Kamps and F. van der Velde, *Neurocomputing* **38-40**, 523 (2001).
31. F. van der Velde and M. de Kamps, *Behavioral and Brain Sciences* **29**, 37 (2006).
32. B. C. Motter, *Journal of Neuroscience* **14**, 2178 (1994).
33. I. Bojak, T. F. Oostendorp, A. T. Reid and R. Kötter, *Brain Topography* **23**, 139 (2010).

MODEL SELECTION FOR EYE MOVEMENTS: ASSESSING THE ROLE OF ATTENTIONAL CUES IN INFANT LEARNING

DANIEL YUROVSKY

Department of Psychological and Brain Science, Indiana University,
1101 E 10th St., Bloomington, IN 47405, USA

RACHEL WU

Centre for Brain and Cognitive Development, Birkbeck,, University of London,
Malet Street, London, WC1E 7HX, UK

CHEN YU

Department of Psychological and Brain Science, Indiana University,
1101 E 10th St., Bloomington, IN 47405, USA

NATASHA Z. KIRKHAM

Centre for Brain and Cognitive Development, Birkbeck,, University of London,
Malet Street, London, WC1E 7HX, UK

LINDA B. SMITH

Department of Psychological and Brain Science, Indiana University,
1101 E 10th St., Bloomington, IN 47405, USA

A recent study[1] showed that different attention cues (social and non-social) produce qualitatively different learning effects. The mechanisms underlying such differences, however, were unclear. Here, we present a novel computational model of audio-visual learning combining two competing processes: habituation and association. The model's parameters were trained to best reproduce each infant's individual looking behavior from trial-to-trial in training and testing. We then isolated each infant's learning function to explain the variance found in preferential looking tests. The model allowed us to rigorously examine the relationship between the infants' looking behavior and their learning mechanisms. By condition, the model revealed that 8-month-olds learned faster from the social (i.e. face) than the non-social cue (i.e., flashing squares), as evidenced by the parameters of their learning functions. In general, the 4-month-olds learned more slowly than the 8-month-olds. The parameters for attention to the cue revealed that infants at both ages who weighted the social cue highly learned quickly. With non-social cues, 8-month-olds were impaired in learning, as the cue competed for attention with the target visual event Using explicit models to link looking and learning, we can draw firm conclusions about infants' cognitive development from eye-movement behavior.

1. Introduction

1.1. *Multimodal Relationships*

The infant's world is filled with sights and sounds that belong together (e.g., toys falling, people talking, cars driving). Linking these concurrent sights and sounds helps infants organize their cluttered multimodal world[2,3]. Moreover, tracking multimodal relationships (e.g., synced in tempo, motion, and location) helps infants learn about the events: One fundamental advantage of binding sights and sounds is that they allow for the prediction of future events. After learning information in two modalities (e.g., seeing and hearing a favorite toy dancing), it is useful for infants to remember the location of the toy when they only hear the toy's sound across the room. Tracking audio-visual information in this way can help infants organize events in spatial locations. Six-month-olds associate sounds to objects when they are perceived simultaneously in a particular location[4]. When presented with only the sound, infants look to the location where the object had previously appeared. This ability, referred to as spatial indexing, has been documented in infants as young as 3 months of age, with increasing reliability and flexibility over the first year of life[4,5].

1.2. *Social and Non-Social Cues*

The aforementioned research has established that infants distinguish and track multimodal events when presented in isolation (one multimodal event at a time). In noisy natural environments, unlike the laboratory setting, infants are often presented with multiple streams of cross-modal information. How do infants know which audio-visual event to bind? One way of knowing could be relying on attention cues. Since attending to appropriate events is a fundamental part of learning, infants can rely on attention cues to gain an advantage in learning relevant information. Cues can capture, direct, and sustain attention, though the quantitative and qualitative nature of this shifted attention can vary with each type of cue.

Both social and non-social cues shift infants' attention. Infants follow faces that look in a particular direction[6-8] or when flashing, dynamic shapes appear in a particular location[9-10]. Infants reach adult-levels of attention shifting with non-social cues in the periphery by 4 months of age[10]. With social cues, however, infants begin following eye gaze in simple naturalistic situations by 3 to 4 months (e.g., joint attention[6]) and show dramatically increased reliability by 6 to 8 months of age[8,11].

1.3. *Learning from Attention Cues*

How do different attention cues affect learning? In other words, how useful are these cues in helping infants' cognitive development? Wu and Kirkham[1] found that depth of learning audio-visual events from social and non-social attention cues was dependent on the age of the infant and the nature of the attention cue. This study measured gaze behavior of 4- and 8-month-old infants when they were presented with dynamic audio-visual events (i.e., cats moving to a *bloop* sound and dogs moving to a *boing* sound) in white frames in the corners of a black background. An object's appearance in a spatial location consistently predicted a location-specific sound. On every familiarization trial, infants were shown identical audio-visual events in two diagonally opposite corners of the screen (i.e., two valid binding locations). To test the effects of attentional cueing on audio-visual learning, either a social (i.e., a real face) or non-social (i.e., colorful flashes) cue shifted infants' attention to one of the two identical events on every trial. For the social cue, a face appeared, spoke to the infant, and turned to one of the lower corners containing an object. For the non-social cue, a red flashing square wrapped around the target frame appeared and disappeared at a regular interval (i.e., flashed continuously) throughout the familiarization trial. During the test trials, only the four blank frames were displayed on the screen while one of the sounds played (Figure 1).

Within one familiarization trial, two locations could have been associated with the sound, and across all familiarization trials, two locations were cued (one for each object type). The design of this paradigm allowed for the discrimination of two types of learning: 1) learning from attention cues, and 2) audio-visual learning. They measured where infants predicted the objects would appear. There were four possible learning outcomes: 1) Infants could predict that objects would appear in only cued locations (lower corners) regardless of multimodal information, 2) infants could predict that objects would appear in valid binding locations regardless of where they were cued, 3) infants could use both information from the attention cue and multimodal presentation by predicting objects would appear in cued correct object locations, or 4) infants could use neither set of information and look in incorrect frames or equally to all frames.

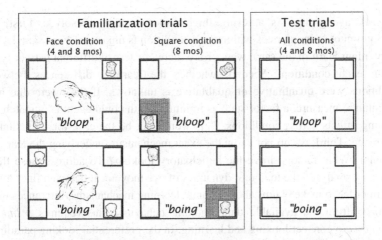

Fig. 1. Familiarization and test trials from the Face and Square cueing conditions from [1]. The stimuli were in full color; the frames were white and presented on a black background. The shaded areas represent red flashing squares.

Results showed that infants displayed qualitatively different looking patterns at test, despite fixating for equal time to the correct locations across different training conditions. Wu and Kirkham[1] showed that while both cues led infants to attend preferentially to cued locations during familiarization and test across all age groups, cross-modal contingencies were learned only by older infants exposed to social cues. Only 8-month-olds cued by the face during familiarization looked longer to *correct* cued object locations during test, whereas the 4-month-olds in the same condition anticipated events in both correct and incorrect cued locations, perhaps ignoring the multimodal information. The 8-month-olds cued with flashing squares (non-social cue) also looked longer to cued locations than to non-cued locations regardless of object–sound mappings. These findings suggest that specific multimodal learning is dependent on the nature of what orients attention as well as the age of the infant using the attention cue.

2. Microanalysis: A Model Selection Approach

2.1. *Motivation*

Using a preferential looking time method, Wu and Kirkham[1] demonstrated the impact of attention cues on learning during infancy. This paradigm used only a behavioral measure (i.e., looking time) and collapsed the data within a condition for each age group. As a result, three issues remain unresolved. First, the distribution of learning rates within each condition is unknown. For example, did every infant learn in the same way, or are there clusters of different learner types within each condition? Second, whether the learning differences between conditions were quantitative or qualitative is unknown. If they were due to a quantitative measure, a factor such as training length could eventually match the learning effects across conditions. This would not be the case for a qualitative difference. Third, we do not know the exact mechanisms underlying the learning behavior. What factors drove the anticipatory looking? To address these three issues, we analyzed the temporal dynamics of eye movement data at a finer level.

In order to make claims about infants' learning mechanisms, inferences must be made from the available data: looking behavior. This requires a *linking hypothesis* to connect looking and learning. In the preferential looking paradigm, Wu and Kirkham[1] implicitly committed to one such hypothesis: as infants learn about the associations between sounds and locations, they will prefer to fixate those locations when they hear the matching sounds. The same hypothesis used frequently in early word learning research[12]. Other infancy studies, focusing on other topics (e.g., visual perception[13]), however, sometimes adopt the opposite hypothesis: as infants learn more about an event, they preferentially fixate new locations to search for novel events (i.e., looking to the original event wanes, habituation). Moreover, these mechanisms that could drive infants' real-time looking behavior are complex. For example, infants' habituation profiles may be non-monotonic, with a preference first for familiarity and a later preference for novelty emerging as learning progresses[14,15]. This suggests two troubling implications for analysis of eye movements – one at the individual infant level, and one at the group level. First, if infants first show a familiarity preference and then a novelty preference over the course of learning, they may progress through a period of no preference in between. An infant who shows no preference, then, may in fact have learned an association. Second, if individual infants learn at different rates – and evidence suggests that they do[16] – then group analyses may average together data from infants who have a novelty preference with those who have a familiarity preference. A group null result thus becomes difficult to interpret[17,18]. We account for these factors in a model selection framework, using infant eye movements in the course of learning to demonstrate and interpret differential learning from attention cues.

2.2. Model Selection for Eye Movements

The main issue with using a linking hypothesis is initially choosing the appropriate one. As suggested by[19], this study relied on the data to specify the linking hypothesis. A model selection approach to this problem is a four-step procedure. First, we generated a formal description of the learning task. This included the input available to the infant on each trial of the experiment and the output categories (i.e., regions of interest) as they were measured in the original data analysis. Second, we defined a null model for the task. This null model was the function expected to generate eye movements for infants who did not learn about the input. Third, we defined a set of possible linking functions. The next section presents one principled way of generating a set of such functions (for an alternative, see Gilmore and Thomas[20]). Finally, we defined a method of selection, a way of determining which linking function was most likely to have generated each infant's recorded eye movements. For the selection, we used the Akaike Information Criterion (AIC)[21], a heuristic that trades off increasing the fit to data with increasing the number of parameters in the model. Other heuristics are possible, (e.g., BIC). Akaike's criterion, however, has been shown to have lower error when the true model is not among the set of candidates[22] – a situation very likely given the simplifying assumptions in our analysis. This issue will be further discussed in the context of specific models below.

The following sections review the four steps of the model selection framework for the cued attention task presented above, and demonstrate its utility for drawing inferences about infant learning at multiple levels.

3. Modeling the Cued Learning Task

3.1. Formalizing the Task

On each trial of the experiment, infants saw a black screen with four white-framed boxes, one in each corner of the screen. These four boxes, or locations (Loc_1, Loc_2, Loc_3, Loc_4), were defined as our regions of interest. On each trial, the model was asked to predict the duration of looking time to each of these four locations. For mathematical convenience, we used the log odds of looking to each location[23]. Using the odds ratio form of the exponentiated Luce choice axiom[24], we proposed that odds of looking to each location were the odds ratio of their theoretical activation functions (defined below).

$$OddsLook(Loc_i) = \frac{\exp Act(Loc_i)}{\sum_{j \neq i} \exp Act(Loc_j)} \qquad (1)$$

The four boxes, however, were unlikely to be equally interesting because objects appeared in two of the four boxes. We will refer to any box which contained an object as *salient*. Formally,

$$Salient(Loc) = \begin{cases} 1 & Loc\ contains\ an\ object \\ 0 & Otherwise \end{cases} \qquad (2)$$

In addition, one of the locations was *cued* – either by a centrally-located face (Face condition) or by a flashing square around the box (Square condition).

$$Cued(Loc) = \begin{cases} 1 & Loc\ was\ cued \\ 0 & Otherwise \end{cases} \qquad (3)$$

Finally, a sound was heard on each training trial. Since the sound was not a component of the visual display, we proposed that it did not have a direct effect on fixation patterns, but guided looking indirectly through sound-location associations. We return to the role of the sound on fixations in Step 3.

In contrast to the training trials, test trials contained neither objects nor visual cues, only white boxes and the sound. Because the test trials did not differ from the training trials in any other way and because the boxes were on screen in the presence of sounds for the same length of time as in training trials, we described both types of trials with the same formal vocabulary. The only difference was that the *salient* and *cued* functions always had the value '0' for all locations on the test trials.

3.2. A Null Model

After formalizing the structure of each trial, we defined a null model for the task. This null model defined the activation function (above) for infants for whom looking was not guided by learning. In the absence of learning, we suggest that looking was guided by two potential sources: 1) The on-screen cue's direction of attentional shift (*Cued*), and 2) the presence or absence of an object in each box (*Salient*). The null model was thus a function of these two factors:

$$Act(Loc) = c \times (Cued(Loc)) + s \times (Salient(Loc)) \qquad (4)$$

The constant c weighted the importance of the cue, and similarly, s weighted the importance of the salient objects.

3.3. *A Learning Model*

After defining the null model, we specified the linking function, which defined the activation function for infants whose gaze patterns were driven by their learning. First, we proposed that infants may have remembered which screen locations they frequently fixated. They may then have preferred not to fixate those locations on future trials (i.e., habituating to them). Efforts to characterize infant habituation functions[15,19,20] have modeled them with polynomial functions or bounded exponentials. Because habituation functions are non-monotonic[14], for simplicity we used polynomials of up to degree 2 (arbitrary orders are possible in· principle). Thus, we defined habituation to a screen location as a polynomial function of cumulative looking time to that location. Thus, the function could be increasing, decreasing, or both, and could be either linear or faster-than-linear. Formally, if N_h is the maximum order of the infant's habituation function,

$$Habit(c\_time_{Loc}) = \sum_{n=1}^{N_h} h_n \times c\_time_{Loc}{}^n \tag{5}$$

where h_n is the parameter of the nth term of the infant's habituation function. Parameters were selected by regression to best account for the infant's looking data. Then, model selection (below) was used to determine which order of habituation was appropriate for each individual infant.

Second, we proposed that infants may have learned the relationship between the sounds and the on-screen locations of the objects (in two locations) that were presented in synchrony. Binding the audio and visual events was of primary interest to Wu and Kirkham[1]. To determine whether infants learned this relationship, we formalized how this knowledge could drive looking. As with the habituation function above, we proposed that looking on a current trial was driven by a polynomial function of cumulative looking. However, in this case, we used cumulative looking to a location in the presence of the sound to indicate this type of learning. That is, the polynomial is a function of the subset of looking during which the association sound was heard. Equation 6 represents this dependency as a conditional probability notation. In addition, we again used up to second degree polynomials (though any order is possible in principle). Thus, if N_a is the maximum order of association for a given infant,

$$Assoc(c\_time_{Loc} \mid sound) = \sum_{n=1}^{N_a} h_a \times c\_time_{Loc \mid sound}^n \qquad (6)$$

In sum, the goal of the above models is to produce an explicit account of where infants should look on each trial given one of a set of possible models. Each of the models must predict the amount of time an infant will spend looking at each of the four possible screen locations on each trial. This amount is represented as a fraction of total looking time using a log odds representation. These fractions are then stored to represent cumulative looking time, which is the variable on which learning functions operate.

The models of learning used in this analysis are functionally similar to neurally inspired learning models[15], but are not intended to link directly to any brain structures. We take this approach primarily for efficiency and simplicity. The functions which are considered here are easy to parameterize, compare, and analyze, which are the questions of critical importance to this analysis. Tying these models to underlying neural mechanisms would be an interesting question for future research.

3.4. Selecting the Best Model

Up to this point, we have defined a set of possible learning models, as well as a null model for the task. In order to determine whether (and how) each infant learned, we only needed to determine which function was most likely to have generated the observed looking patterns. Therefore, we picked a criterion (Akaike Information Criterion[21]) to judge the correspondence between the model and the observed data. AIC trades off minimizing the divergence between predictions and observations (in the form of sum of squared errors) with increasing the complexity of the model. Intuitively, as the model becomes more complex (higher orders of association and habituation), it will produce an increasingly better fit to the data. As a result, however, there will be diminishing returns: eventually, the corresponding increase in goodness of fit for adding a new parameter will become small relative to the increase in model complexity. As per Occam's razor, we wanted the simplest model with a 'good enough' fit.

3.5. Model Training

After formalizing the learning task, defining a null model and a set of candidate learning models, and describing how to select among them, the next step was to fit the functions to each infant's looking behavior to find the most suitable one. Fitting functions is an optimization problem – a process of parameterizing the functions to fit the data.

The form of the *OddsLook* function supports easy parameter fitting via linear regression, for which a closed form solution is known. Thus, for each infant, parameters were selected for each function to best predict the data. Then, the most parsimonious of these models was selected with AIC. Because there was no principled reason to separate training trials from test trials, and because including training trials greatly increased the amount of data available, models were fit to the entire course of looking behavior during the experimental session for each infant.

4. Results and Discussion

We present the results in two steps. First, we walk through an in-depth analysis of the 8-month olds in the Face condition to show how the outcome of the model selection analysis can be interpreted. Second, we present a cross-condition comparison using the model selection framework. This analysis highlighted the differences between the experimental conditions, and allowed us to ask how learning differed across cue conditions and age groups.

4.1. *Data Analysis of 8 months Face Condition*

Data from 28 8-month-old infants were analyzed using the model selection framework described above. Infants were exposed to four blocks, each consisting of six training trials followed by one test trial. Over 28 trials, infants fixated each of the four locations for some length of time. Each model was required to fit this looking data. The large number of trials (training and test) per infant in these experimental sessions provided significantly more data than is typically used to assess learning via preferential looking analysis (only test trials).

To justify and draw conclusions from the modeling analysis, we first established that the models fit a significant proportion of each infant's looking data. The best model for each infant matched closely to that infant's actual data (mean Pearson's $r = .72$, $p < .001$, see Figure 2). Having confirmed that the chosen linking functions characterized each infant's looking data; we could draw further inferences from these functions.

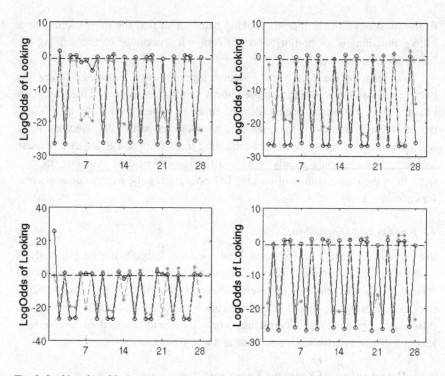

Fig. 2. Looking data (black circles) and model fits (gray circles) for one 8-month-old in the Face condition. The four graphs represent the four locations on each screen, and each data point represents log odds of looking on one trial. Marked trials on the x-axis indicate test trials.

Because each infant was modeled individually, we can determine whether or not each infant learned. As the main factor of interest is the nature of associations formed by the infants, we focused on parameters of infants' association functions (N_a). Of the 28 infants, 22 were found to have learned a relationship between sounds and screen locations ($N_a > 0$). Of these, the great majority learned at a faster-than-linear rate ($N_a > 1$, 17/22). Thus, multi-modal learning in this condition was both frequent and rapid. Moreover, if the model was correct, we expected to find a relationship between infants' looking preferences at test and the order of their association functions. Indeed, the strength of an infant's preference for the correct location at test correlated significantly with that infant's order of association ($r = .41$, $p < .05$). Figure 3 displays both the distribution of habituation and association orders, and the correlation between association and looking preference at test.

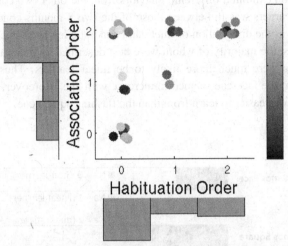

Fig. 3. A scatter plot of infant habituation and association orders. Association orders greater than zero imply that an infant learned the relationship between sounds and locations. When infants are ordered by the strength of their preference at test (lightest = strongest preference), this correlates with their order of association.

4.2. Comparison Across Conditions

The real power of the model selection framework is the leverage it provides for comparing across multiple conditions. We thus applied the same four-step procedure of the framework to each of the two other conditions – 4 months Face (i.e., face cue) and 8 months Square (i.e., flashing square cue). As in the previous condition, the most parsimonious model for each infant accounted for a significant proportion of the looking behavior ($r_4 = .68$, $p < .001$, $r_8 = .69$, $p < .001$). Therefore, we were licensed to make further inferences on the basis of the linking functions.

Analysis of the orders of association for the 8 months Face condition demonstrated that the vast majority of infants learned the multi-modal relationship, and that the majority of infants who learned did so at faster-than-linear rates. We compared this distribution of association orders to those found in the other two conditions. As can be seen in Figure 4, the distributions are different across conditions. Eight-month old infants cued with a flashing square instead of a face were much less likely to learn cross-modal contingencies ($N_a > 0$). In addition, infants who did learn the contingencies did so more slowly than those in the Face condition. The ratio of quadratic learners dropped from 3:1 (Face condition) to 2:1 (Flashing square condition). Four-month-olds in the

Face condition exhibited different behaviors from the other two conditions. The number of learners was in between those of the two 8 months conditions. More interesting was the distribution of linear and quadratic learners. In contrast to the 8-month-olds, the majority of whom were best described by quadratic functions, 4-month-olds were much more likely to be linear learners. Thus, the rate of learning from the face cue seemed to increase with age. Moreover, it seems that the face cue was easier to learn from than the flashing square cue.

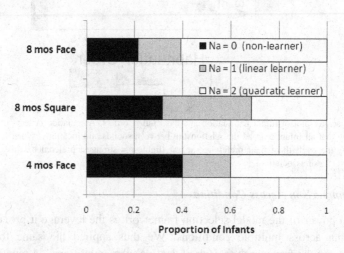

Fig. 4. Distribution of association order across conditions. Eight-month-olds learned more rapidly from the face than from the square, and 4-month-olds showed a different ratio of linear (N_a=1) to quadratic (N_a=2) learners than 8-month-olds.

For completeness, we performed a similar analysis for infants' habituation functions. Although habituation is not the question of primary interest in this analysis, it is worth making explicit we have included it as a mechanism which may have driven looking behavior. In fact, infants across all three conditions showed very similar habituation order distributions (Figure 5). Slightly less than half of the infants in each condition produced eye movements which implicated a habituation function. The rate of habituation (at least in terms of linear vs. quadratic) did not appear to differ across conditions or ages. Thus, although habituation is important for capturing some of the behavior in this task, it does not appear to be important for describing differences across cues. We thus focus further analysis on association orders.

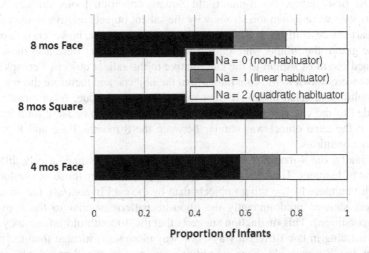

Fig. 5. Distribution of habituation order across conditions. Unlike the distribution of association orders across conditions (Figure 4), the habituation parameters were consistent across ages and cue types. Thus, habituation plays a role in directing eye movements in this task, but does not do so differently for different types of cues.

How did the learners in the different conditions learn? In addition to the learning rates found to best describe each infant, the models included weights for both cue and salience strength (eq. 4). We investigated the relationship between these parameters across conditions. Because the cue and object salience compete directly, we should expect a negative correlation between these two parameters across infants. The relationship of these parameters to learning rates, however, is not specified by the model's form. We thus investigate this relationship empirically. Did infants who learned have eye movements driven more by cues (face or square) or by object salience (object presence)? Figure 6 shows the cue and salience parameters for each infant (standardized to z-scores). Infants who did not learn ($N_a = 0$), linear learners ($N_a = 1$), and quadratic learners ($N_a = 2$) are represented by different markers. These distributions differed considerably across conditions.

In the 8 months Face condition, there was a clear separation between learners and non-learners. The successful learners were characterized by a strong preference for cue over salience. The infants whose looking was driven more by the cue than by the salient objects may have been more able to learn the relationship isolated by the cue. Thus, there was a strong positive correlation between the difference between cue and salience weights, and having a non-zero association order ($r = .395$, $p < .05$).

At first glance, the 8-month-old Square condition looks similar. Again, infants who were drawn too strongly by the salient objects relative to the cue did not learn successfully ($r = .440$, $p < .05$). A second cluster, however, is apparent on the graph: the infants who learned more slowly (linear) were also those who assigned the most weight to the cue relative to the salient objects. Perhaps these infants were drawn to the cue, rather than the objects, and therefore did not learn the multimodal relationship. If they were drawn to the cue, infants must have attended to the cue covertly (without fixating on the cue) because total looking time to the cued object was similar between the 8 months Face and 8 months Square conditions.

Finally, the 4-month-old Face condition showed two qualitatively different groups of learners. The linear learners were predominantly those whose looking was driven more by the salient objects than by the cue. In contrast, the quadratic learners showed predominantly the opposite pattern (similar to the 8 months Face condition). This distinction suggests that the 4-month-old infants may have been learning in two different ways, one way more sophisticated than the other. As in the 8-month-old Face condition, but not in the 8-month-old square condition, the best learning was exhibited by infants who attended predominantly to cued objects rather than to both objects. Nonetheless, some 4-month-olds cued by the face and some 8-month-olds cued by the square tended to ignore the cue and still learn the multimodal association. This alternative strategy perhaps requires more cognitive effort (learning associations in two locations) and more time. This analysis shows precisely why the model selection framework is powerful – it avoids the 'perils' of averaging across strategies[25].

In summary, we found that the weights of the two parameters in the learning function (*Cued* and *Salience*) were related to learning in both conditions for both age groups. In general, learners were most successful when they paid more attention to the cue than to the salient objects. However, the relationship was non-monotonic in the Square condition, with too much or too little attention to the cue leading to slower learning[26]. This result suggests a qualitative difference between the Face and Square conditions: infants may have processed the two cues differently. A crucial difference between the central social cue and the peripheral non-social cue is that the peripheral cue was wrapped around the target box. Perhaps this cue was harder to disengage from compared to the central cue, which occupied a separate spatial location from the cued event (for discussion, see Wu and Kirkham[1]). The linear learners in the Square condition may have been compelled to look at the correct location, but focused on the cue itself rather than the multi-modal relationship. If there was an increased focus on the cue, it must have been covert (without fixating on the cue) because total fixation length to the target object was similar between the two 8 months conditions[1].

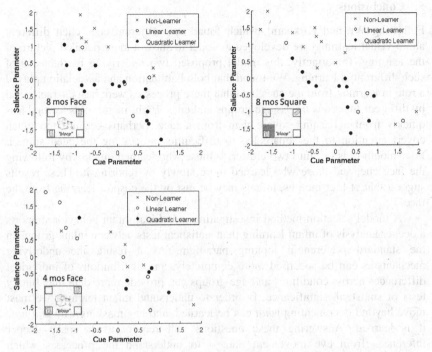

Fig. 6. Weights for *cued* and *salient* locations across conditions labeled by learning score. The negative slope is a direct consequence of our null function, but the relationship of the parameters to learning rates is not. In fact, weighting the cue over the salient locations led to better learning in both 8 months conditions, with an eventual decline in the face condition. Two distinct clusters of learners were found among the 4-month-olds.

Regarding the ability to disengage from the cue, the 4-month-olds who focused on the cued locations were the fastest to learn, perhaps engaging with the task most like the 8-month-olds. This notion suggests that more practice would allow more of these younger infants to exhibit successful learning. Combined with the results from the two 8 months conditions, these results suggest an optimal cue-weight parameter – a point of maximal return depending on the cue type and age of the infant. While 8-month-olds who focus too much on the cue do not learn as quickly, 4-month-olds are slower processors of complex scenes and thus need relatively higher cue weights. Alternatively, because infants have just started following social cues at this age[6], perhaps infants who did not learn from the cue do not yet know *how* to learn from this cue (i.e., did not follow the cue purposefully). Future research should identify the underlying reasons driving looking behavior between and within groups.

5. Conclusions

Following Wu and Kirkham[1], which found that different cues elicit different audio-visual learning, we developed a model to show a more detailed picture of the learning. Importantly, this model proposed two underlying mechanisms of such differential learning. We found that both habituation and association played a role in learning from the cues, and that these processes were best characterized by different functions across age groups and cues. Eight-month-olds learned less quickly from a flashing square than from a face, perhaps because too much covert attention to the square led to difficulties processing the cued stimuli. Four-month-olds fell into two clusters – those who learned quickly by following the face cue, and those who learned more slowly by ignoring it. These results suggest that at four months, infants may be just on the cusp of learning from the face.

A model selection method investigating individual infant behavior supports a deeper analysis of infant learning than statistical tests between infant groups in the standard preferential looking paradigm. As a result, the underlying mechanisms can be specified more completely, and distributions of individual differences across conditions and age groups can provide more data than binary tests of statistical significance. In order to understand infant learning we must move beyond documenting *what* can be learned, and begin asking *why and how* it is learned. Answering these questions will require us to make deeper inferences from eye movement data – to understand the processes which generate fixations and ultimately lead to learning. With the model selection framework, we can begin to unravel the contributions of internal and external drivers of this behavior. We can make eye movements make sense.

Acknowledgments

This work was supported by a NSF Graduate Research Fellowship to DY, a NIH Grant (R01HD056029) to CY, and a BPS Postgraduate Study Visits Award to RW. The authors would like to thank Shohei Hidaka for help developing the modeling methodology and Thomas Smith for data processing code.

References

1. R. Wu and N. Z. Kirkham, *J. Exp Child Psych.* **107**, 118 (2010).
2. L. E. Bahrick, In L. Nadel, *Encyclopedia of Cognitive Science* (Nature, 2004)
3. D. J. Lewkowicz, *Psych. Bull.* **126**, 281 (2000).
4. D. C. Richardson and N. Z. Kirkham, *J. of Exp. Psych.: Gen.* **133**, 46 (2004).
5. N. Z. Kirkham, D. C. Richardson, R. Wu, and S. P. Johnson, (under review).

6. G. Butterworth, in A. Slater and G. Bremner, *Theories of infant development* (Wiley Press, 2004).

7. B. M. Hood, J. D. Willen, and J. Driver, *Psych. Sci.* **9**, 131 (1998).

8. A. Senju and G. Csibra, *Curr. Bio.* **18**, 1 (2008).

9. M. H. Johnson, *Att. and Perf.* **15**, 291 (1994).

10. M. H. Johnson, M. I. Posner, and M. K. Rothbart, *J. of Cog. Neuro.* **3**, 335 (1991).

11. D. Poulin-Dubois, T. L. Demke, and K. M Olineck, in R. Flom, K. Lee, and D. Muir, *Gaze-following: Its Development and Significance* (Lawrence Erlbaum, 2007).

12. R. M. Golinkoff, K. Hirsh-Pasek, K. M. Cauley, and L. Gordon. *J. Child Lang.*: **14**, 23 (1987).

13. N. Z. Kirkham, J. A. Slemmer, and S. P. Johnson. *Cognition* **83**, B35 (2002).

14. M. A. Hunter and E. W. Ames. *Advances in Infancy Research* **5**, 69 (1998).

15. S. Sirois and D. Mareschal. *Trends. Cogn. Sci.* **6**, 293 (2002).

16. C. H. Cashon and L. B. Cohen, *Infancy* **1**, 429 (2000).

17. W. K. Estes, *Psychol. Bull.* **53**, 134 (1956).

18. D. Yurovsky, S. Hidaka, C. Yu, and L. B. Smith. *Proc. Cog. Sci.* (2011).

19. H. Thomas and R. O. Gilmore, *Psychol. Methods* **9**, 70 (2004).

20. R. O. Gilmore and H. Thomas, *Infant Behav. Dev.* **25**, 399 (2002).

21. H. Akaike, *IEEE T. Automat. Contr. Infancy* **AC-19**, 716 (1974).

22. Y. Yang, Biometrika. 92, 937 (2005)

23. D. Barr, *J. Mem. Lang.* **59**, 457 (2008).

24. R. D. Luce, *Individual Choice Behavior* (Wiley Press, 1959).

25. R. S. Siegler, *J. Exp. Psychol. Gen.* **116**, 250 (1987).

26. C. Kidd, S. T. Piantadosi, and R. N. Aslin, *Proc. Cog. Sci.* (2011).

THE IMPORTANCE OF LOW SPATIAL FREQUENCIES FOR CATEGORIZATION OF EMOTIONAL FACIAL EXPRESSIONS

L. LOPEZ[1], P. BONIN[2], N. VERMEULEN[3], A. MEOT[1] and M. MERMILLOD[1]

[1] 1Laboratoire de Psychologie Sociale et Cognitive, Clermont Université, Université Blaise Pascal, and Centre National de la Recherche Scientifique, UMR 6024, Clermont-Ferrand, France

[2] Université de Bourgogne, LEAD (UMR CNRS 5022), 21065 Dijon, France

[3] Université Catholique de Louvain and National Fund for Scientific Research, Psychology Department, B-1348 Louvain-la-Neuve, Belgium

The decomposition by the human visual system of visual scenes into a range of spatial frequencies is necessary for the categorization of the objects present in the visual scene. This decomposition of spatial frequencies may be particularly important for the processing of emotions. Experiments in the field of behavioral (Schyns & Oliva, 1999) and cognitive neuroscience (Vuilleumier, Armony, Driver, & Dolan, 2003) suggest that low spatial frequencies (LSF) are better than high spatial frequencies (HSF) for the categorization of emotional facial expressions (EFE). The aim of this study was to determine whether LSF information is more useful than HSF information for the categorization of emotions. We tested this hypothesis using artificial neural networks (ANN) subject to both unsupervised and supervised learning. The results indicated better emotion categorization with LSF information, thus suggesting that the HSF signal, which is also present in the BSF signal, acts as a source of noisy information during classification tasks in artificial neural systems.

1. Introduction

The human visual system decomposes spatial frequencies. This operation is necessary in order to categorize the objects present in the visual scene. LSF and HSF stimuli are processed by two different visual streams at the level of the lateral geniculate nucleus[1]. Magnocellular neurons in the dorsal visual stream primarily provide rapid but low spatial frequency cues which encode configural features as well as brightness and motion, while the parvocellular neurons of the ventral visual stream provide slower, but also higher spatial frequency, information (finer visual details) about local shape features, color, and texture[1]. This decomposition of spatial frequencies may be of crucial importance for the categorization of emotion. A functional magnetic resonance imaging experiment showed that the human visual system may use a subcortical pathway involving the superior colliculus, the lateral geniculate nucleus (LGN) and the amygdala when subjects process LSF pictures of faces depicting a fearful expression compared to LSF faces displaying a neutral expression. These results suggest that the information relative to threat may bypass the cortical streams by means of a subcortical pathway which transports the LSF information very quickly. These results could prove to be consistent with Ledoux's model[2] which suggests the existence of a direct subcortical stream which processes the LSF information from the visual scene from the LGN to the amydala. Overall, these results suggest that rapid access to LSF information may be of particular value for biological systems by assisting in the efficient categorization of EFE.

A number of different methods, including artificial neural networks (ANN), are described in the literature on the modeling of emotional facial expression categorization tasks[3-5]. The first step in developing a connectionist simulation of emotion categorization is to model the human visual system. Gabor filter banks constitute a biologically plausible perceptual model of vision which simulates V1 neuron receptive fields that are sensitive to different orientations and spatial frequency channels[34]. The statistical evaluation of the residual error between the difference in the response profiles of V1 simple cells and Gabor filters is not distinguishable from chance[6,7]. As a result, this model of vision has a remarkable biological plausibility[6,7] and is one of the most successful approaches to the processing of human facial recognition[8,4,5,9]. In this study, although we use Gabor filters, we implement these in the frequency domain by means of the modulus of the Discrete Fourier Transform (DFT), instead of in the spatial domain as in Dailey et al[4]. This is the main difference from the other models of the visual system used in previous simulations[8,4,5,9].

This visual data compression makes it possible for us to identify the quantity of energy associated with each spatial frequency and each orientation, independently of the spatial location of the wavelet. This is of value for two reasons: (i) performing Gabor filtering in the spatial domain results in a high dimensional perceptual vector (a vector size of 40,600 in Dailey et al.[4]) which necessitates a subsequent visual data compression step. During this step, some auhors have used a Principal Component Analysis[4] to reduce the perceptual space and then applied the ANN to the first 50 eigenvectors which make it possible to obtain efficient results in categorization tasks. Nevertheless, given the aim of this study, this procedure poses an important methodological problem. In effect, LSF information correlates highly with the first eigenvectors[10] and it is therefore possible that virtually all the eigenvectors are necessary in order to retain the HSF information. This result is problematic when investigating the role of spatial frequency channels. By using Gabor filter banks in the frequency domain, we avoid this kind of visual data compression by obtaining the quantity of energy associated with each spatial frequency and each orientation, independently of the spatial location of the wavelet. (ii) applying Gabor filters in the spectral domain renders the representation of the image (i.e., the output computed by the Gabor filters) phase-invariant, in a similar way to V1 complex cells[11]. In other words, our model of vision in which Gabor filters provide an average energy value for the entire image is holistic in nature. Although this method discards information about spatial locations, it has the advantage of retaining exactly the same amount of information, thus making it possible to compare the different SF channels in a reliable manner.

In this study, we performed two simulations. In the first of these, we used exactly the same database as Vuilleumier et al.[12] and performed unsupervised learning of the stimuli by means of a Self Organizing Map (SOM)[13]. The aim of the first simulation was to determine whether the greater efficiency of the LSF signal can be observed at a qualitative level on the basis of the output obtained using a small database. We designed Simulation 2 to generalize, in quantitative terms, the results obtained for the 6 basic EFE in Simulation 1 on the basis of a larger database, the *Karolinska Directed Emotional Faces*[14], and to identify the most efficient SF channels for the categorization of the primary emotions (fear, anger, sadness, surprise, happiness, disgust) and the neutral expression.

2. Simulation 1

2.1. *Stimuli*

The stimuli were the same as those used by Vuilleumier and colleagues[12]. These pictures, presented face on, corresponded to 160 human faces, i.e. 80 fearful and 80 neutral faces. Each image was defined on a gray scale and was centered in a 256 x 256 pixel frame for computational reasons relating to the symmetry of the rosette of Gabor wavelets applied to the image. The high-pass cutoff used for the LSF stimuli was >24 cycles/image and <6 cycles/image for the LSF stimuli. The mean brightness of the stimuli was 112, 118 and 115 on a 256 level gray-scale for the BSF, LSF and HSF images, respectively. These differences between experimental conditions are not significant and the stimuli were strictly identical to[12].

Fig. 1. Examples of stimuli from the database.
Top: left to right, fear BSF, LSF, HSF
Bottom: left to right, neutral BSF, LSF, HSF

2.2. Self-Organizing Map (SOM)

The SOM is a well-known data analysis tool for tasks such as data visualization and clustering[15]. This kind of ANN has been used for the modeling of different cognitive processes such as associative memory[13], the development of semantic maps[16], visuo-motor learning[17], as a method for reducing the input space in the field of emotion recognition[27] or in association with classification and statistical learning methods[28,29]. The SOM performs unsupervised learning that retains the topology of the high dimensional input space in the output space during the learning phase. There is no hidden layer since the weighting of the output neurons is directly affected by the input nodes. As it compresses information while preserving the most important topological and metric relationships of the primary data items, it can be thought of as producing some type of clustering of information.

The SOM usually consists of a regular, two-dimensional grid of neurons. Each neuron is fully connected to the input layer and is represented by a weight, or model vector, $\mathbf{m}_i = [m_{i1}, \ldots, m_{in}]$ where n is equal to the dimension of the input vector. In each training step, one vector $\mathbf{x}$ from the input data set is randomly chosen. The aim is to find the best-matching unit (BMU), denoted here by c, i.e. the neuron whose weight vector is closest to $\mathbf{x}$:

$$\| \mathbf{x} - \mathbf{m}_c \|^2 = \min_i \{ \| \mathbf{x} - \mathbf{m}_i \| \} \tag{1}$$

where $\|.\|$ is the distance measure.

After this step, the weight vectors of the BMU are updated. For a neuron i, the rule is:

$$\mathbf{m}_i\,(t+1) = \mathbf{m}_i\,(t) + \alpha\,(t).\,h_{ci}\,(t)\,[\mathbf{x}\,(t) - \mathbf{m}_i\,(t)] \qquad (2)$$

where t denotes time, α(t) the learning rate, h_{ci} (t) the neighborhood kernel around the BMU.

2.3. *Method*

For each image in the input data set, we applied Gabor receptive fields in the spectral domain. This method is equivalent to a convolution in the spatial domain. It is therefore possible to perform the filtering in the spectral domain by multiplying the spatial frequency information by the kernel of the Gabor function. To summarize, each image was first transferred into the Fourier domain and filtered by a set of Gabor filters, while the energy coefficients were determined by coding the local energy spectra. We applied 56 wavelets corresponding to eight different orientations (0, π/8, 2π/8, 3π/8, 4π/8, 5π/8, 6π/8, 7π/8), and seven different spatial frequency channels (the distance between two consecutive centers was increased by one octave per spatial frequency channel), with respect to biological data[11]. Therefore, each image was represented by 56 dimensional vectors. A Gabor filter was constructed using a Gaussian modulated by a complex exponential:

$$G\left(\mathbf{x},\mathbf{y},\mathbf{f}_c,\theta\right) = \frac{1}{2\pi\sigma_r\sigma_t}\,e^{-\frac{(\mathbf{x}.\mathbf{u})^2}{2\sigma_r^2}}\,e^{-\frac{(\mathbf{x}.\mathbf{u}_\perp)^2}{2\sigma_t^2}}\,e^{j2\pi\mathbf{x}\mathbf{f}_c}$$

$$(3)$$

With: $\left| \begin{matrix} \mathbf{x} = [x,y]^t, \mathbf{f}_c = [f_0\cos\theta, -f_0\sin\theta]^t \\ \mathbf{u} = [\cos\theta,\sin\theta]^t, \mathbf{u}_\perp = [\sin\theta,\cos\theta]^t \end{matrix} \right.$

$$(4)$$

where σ_r and σ_t in the Gaussian determine the spatial extent of the filter. The vector $\mathbf{f}_c$ with modulus $\mathbf{f}_0$ and direction θ describes the sine wave.

The output vectors extracted by Gabor filtering were then entered as input into the SOM. Two training phases were used. The first consisted of tuning the SOM to approximately the same space as the input data and the second of fine-tuning the map. The map used consisted of 900 neurons in a 30 X 30 lattice. For the first training phase, the number of iterations was 60 and the learning rate 0.5. The learning rate is defined by a Gaussian:

$$h_{ci}(t) = e^{-d_{ci}^2 \big/ 2\sigma_t^2}$$

$$(5)$$

where σ_t is the radius and decreases linearly from 8 to 2. For the second phase, the number of iterations was 225, the learning rate 0.05 and the radius decreased linearly from 2 to 1 as a function of the number of iterations. These values are the default parameters defined by the SOM toolbox[18] during map simulation. Thus, our simulation can be summarized in three steps:

- Transfer of each image in the input data set into the Fourier domain.
- Application of the Gabor filter bank in the spectral domain.
- Learning and categorization by the SOM.

We used the SOM toolbox[18] for map programming in the Matlab 7.9 environment.

Image   Fourier Transform   Gabor filtering

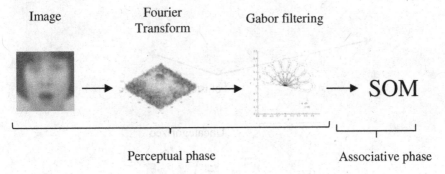

Perceptual phase   Associative phase

Fig. 2. Experimental procedure.

2.4. *Results*

The SOM permits us to visualize categorization in a two-dimensional space. One method of analysis frequently used for cluster visualization is the U-matrix projection which makes it possible to observe the distances between neurons. The clearer the neurons are, the closer they are (in terms of euclidian distances) and the more closely they correspond to the same emotional category. Conversely, the darker the neurons are, the further apart they are and the more likely they are to belong to separate emotional categories. Therefore, this technique makes it possible to visualize the borders between categories. The results of the U-matrix projection for the three conditions are as follows:

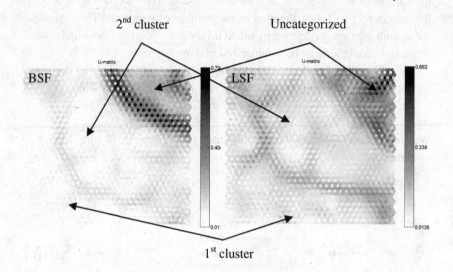

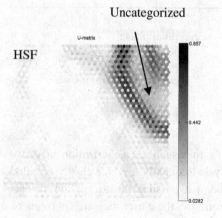

Fig. 3. U-matrix projection for the BSF,
LSF and HSF conditions.

For all the conditions, we observe a cluster of uncategorized images. In particular, we can note the formation of two well-defined clusters for the BSF and LSF conditions, while no clusters are formed for the HSF condition.

If we add the labels to the U-matrix for the BSF and LSF conditions, we obtain:

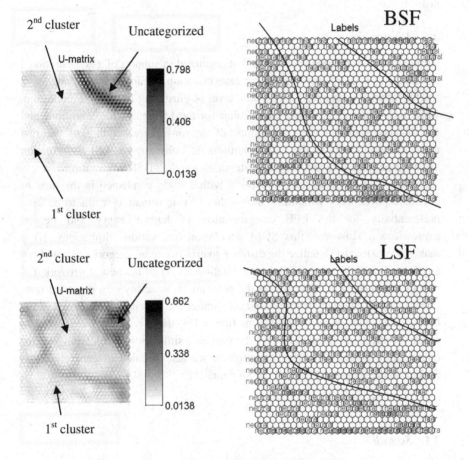

Fig. 4. U-matrix projection and labels for the BSF and LSF conditions.
BSF: BSF condition, U-matrix (left), label projection (right).
LSF: LSF condition, U-matrix (left), label projection (right).

We clearly observe that the SOM was able to categorize fear and the neutral expressions in the LSF and BSF conditions. In addition, the quantization error of the SOM for the LSF condition (0.29) was smaller than the quantization error for the HSF condition (0.33). The quantization error obtained for the BSF condition was 0.30 which is consistent with Mermillod and colleagues[32] who interpret the HSF signal as a noisy source of information for categorization tasks.

2.5. *Discussion*

Although this simulation provides a first argument in support of a computational advantage of LSF information for the categorization of EFE, this only applies to fearful faces. We observed a very low level of clustering in the HSF condition, while the clustering structure was similar for the LSF and BSF conditions and the distance between the two groups of neurons corresponding to the two emotions was larger in the LSF condition. In consequence, LSF information seems to be more efficient for EFE categorization than HSF information.

Overall, these results are consistent with a study conducted in the field of cognitive psychology which has shown that LSF information seems to be used preferentially for the EFE categorization of happy, angry and neutral expressions[19]. However, this SOM simulation has various limitations: (i) it makes it possible to visualize the distance matrix between categories but without any formal quantification of the categorization ability of the neural network, (ii) it does not make it possible to test the generalization ability of a powerful non-linear categorization algorithm based on parallel and distributed processes in the high-dimensional space of the Gabor filters. For these reasons, we decided to run a second experiment to extend the previous simulation to a learning vector quantization neural network. Furthermore, we also decided to generalize this finding to the 6 basic EFE in all the SF channels.

3. Simulation 2

3.1. *Stimuli*

The stimuli used came from the Karolinska Directed Emotional Faces (KDEF) database[14]. Among the 70 pictures constituting the database, 5 were removed because of bad lighting or low image quality. We then applied a Hann window identical to that used in Simulation 1. Each picture was converted to a gray-scale image centered in a 256 x 256 pixel frame. However, we also applied band-pass filters which increased by one octave between 2 consecutive filters: below 8

CpI; 8-16 CpI, 16-32 CpI, 32-64 CpI, above 64 CpI. The mean brightness was normalized to 118.71 for all images.

Fig. 5. Example of stimuli from the Karolinska Directed Emotional Faces database. From left to right: BSF faces, <8 CpI; 8-16 CpI, 16-32 CpI, 32-64 CpI and >64 CpI.

3.2. *Network*

A back-propagation neural network was used for simulations in hetero-associative mode similar to[4], i.e. each output vector generated by the Gabor wavelets for each of the images was associated with a specific code relating to an EFE category (1 0 0 0 0 0 0 for angry faces, 0 1 0 0 0 0 0 for disgust, 0 0 1 0 0 0 0 for fear, 0 0 0 1 0 0 0 for joy, 0 0 0 0 1 0 0 for neutrality, 0 0 0 0 0 1 0 for sadness and 0 0 0 0 0 0 1 for surprise). We normalized each of the energy vectors produced by the Gabor wavelets at the input to the network independently at a value of between 0 and 1 in order to avoid inducing any bias in favor of a spatial frequency or specific orientation. The network architecture consisted of 56 input units (the energy response of the Gabor wavelets), 42 hidden units and 7 output units (the category code for each category). The learning rate was fixed at 0.1 and the momentum at 0.9. The learning algorithm, the procedure and the learning parameters were selected to correspond to the parameters that have been most widely used in the literature as well as in previous simulations investigating this topic[30-32].

During the feed-forward phase, activation was rescaled by means of a sigmoid transfer function:

$$f(a) = \frac{1}{1+e^{-a}} \tag{6}$$

The input vector activation was then propagated through the network, layer-by-layer, until it reached the output layer. The supervised learning algorithm then computed the Sum of Squared Error (SSE):

$$E = \frac{1}{2} \sum_{p} \sum_{k} \left(t_{pk} - o_{pk} \right)^2$$

(7)

In this equation, p indexes the pattern in the training set, k indexes the output nodes, t_{pk} the desired output for the kth output node in the pth pattern, o_{pk} the observed output for the kth output node in the pth pattern.

Next, the error signal was computed using the standard back-propagation algorithm[27] and back-propagated through the network until convergence of the neural network.

3.3. *Procedure*

The overall procedure was the same as that used in Simulation 1. Only the learning phase and the test phase were different.

In the learning phase, each trial started with a random selection of 448 learning exemplars (64 faces out of 65 for the 7 EFE categories). The training phase then consisted of associating each of these 448 learning exemplars with the correct category code over 1000 iterations.

After the learning phase, we performed the test phase: the network was tested for its ability to generalize to the last actor on the last remaining exemplar. We recorded the value calculated at the output from the model after the corresponding energy vector of each of the EFE had been supplied at the input to the network. We then applied a "winner-take all" procedure to the observed output in order to determine the network's response to each EFE.

This training-test procedure was applied 100 times, with a new random selection of the learning and test faces on each trial in each network, in order to calculate a correct response percentage over 100 different trials. The dependent variable was the percentage of correct responses once this procedure had been run 100 times.

3.4. *Results*

We performed an ANOVA on the EFE category (joy, disgust, fear, anger, sadness, surprise and neutral) and X frequency channel (BSF; <8 CpI; 8-16 CpI; 16-32 CpI; 32-64 CpI; >64 CpI). First of all, the ANOVA showed a significant main effect of type of EFE ($F(6,3564) = 6.13$; MSE = 0.428; $p < 0.001$). A post-hoc Tukey test revealed that fearful and surprised faces were recognized significantly better than angry and happy faces. The differences between all the other EFE were not significant.

It also indicated a significant effect of spatial frequency channels ($F(5,594)$ = 53.9; MSE = 0.103; $p < 0.001$). This finding reveals that the categorization rate was better with LSF information than with HSF information.

We also found a significant interaction effect between SF channels and EFE ($F(30,3564) = 7.14$; MSE = 0.07; $p < 0.001$) which suggests that different EFE might have different diagnostic SF channels. For example, for the expressions of anger, disgust and surprise, the relevant spatial frequency was < 8 CpI, whereas for neutral and sad faces, we observed a better categorization rate at around 16-32 CpI.

We observed that all EFE resulted in reduced recognition rates above 32 CpI. In order to identify this effect, we performed exhaustive pair-wise comparisons between all SF channels on the basis of a post-hoc Tukey test. These pair-wise comparisons revealed that the two highest SF channels (32-64 CpI and above 64 CpI) produced categorization rates significantly below each of the other SF channels.

Table 1. Post-hoc Tukey test.

	BSF	< 8 CpI	8-16 CpI	16-32 CpI	32-64 CpI	> 64 CpI
BSF		0.420351	0.918217	0.998911	0.000020	0.000020
< 8 CpI	0.420351		0.953424	0.212609	0.000020	0.000020
8-16 CpI	0.918217	0.953424		0.736495	0.000020	0.000020
16-32 CpI	0.998911	0.212609	0.736495		0.000020	0.000020
32-64 CpI	0.000020	0.000020	0.000020	0.000020		0.000057
> 64 CpI	0.000020	0.000020	0.000020	0.000020	0.000057	

Moreover, there was no statistical difference between the three lower SF channels and there was no statistical difference between these and the BSF faces.

Table 2. Mean Correct Percentage for Each Emotion and Spatial Frequency Channel.

Emotion	Spatial frequency					
	BSF	< 8 CpI	8-16 CpI	16-32 CpI	32-64 CpI	> 64 CpI
Anger	93	96	96	94	84	57
Disgust	92	94	93	91	86	84
Fear	98	96	96	96	88	88
Happy	96	95	94	94	79	70
Neutral	90	96	95	99	79	84
Sad	92	94	97	98	91	63
Surprise	91	100	95	92	89	90
Overall average	93.14	95.86	95.14	94.86	85.14	76.57

3.5. *Discussion*

The results provided by Simulation 2 show that the LSF signal is sufficient for efficient EFE categorization. This main result obtained using a supervised learning procedure provides further confirmation of those obtained in Simulation 1 with unsupervised learning. Moreover, our categorization rate findings in general provide evidence in support of the data obtained in the literature using Gabor filters implemented in the spatial domain[8,4,5,9]. Indeed, in the same way as in Simulation 1, Simulation 2 revealed excellent categorization results with LSF information only. In fact, the correct categorization rate for all emotions with EFE filtered below 8 CpI was only 95.86%. More precisely, we found the best categorization rate to be around 8 CpI for anger, disgust and surprise and 16-32 CpI for sadness and the neutral categories. As in Simulation 1, we also observed a robust decrease in correct categorization rates above 32 CpI for all emotions. In conclusion, Simulation 2 confirms and extends, at the quantitative level, the results obtained in Simulation 1.

4. Conclusion

In both simulations, and in the case of both supervised and unsupervised learning, the main result is the finding that LSF is clearly superior to HSF information for the categorization and recognition of emotional facial expressions. This result is consistent with different behavioral studies [19], thus suggesting that the diagnostic scales relevant for each EFE might be similar in both human subjects and our current neural network simulation. This type of preferential link between LSF and the human fear system has also been observed at a psychological level using natural scene categories[33].

As stated in the Introduction, in the field of cognitive neuroscience, the results obtained by Vuilleumier et al.[12] suggest the existence of a direct subcortical pathway, as proposed in Ledoux's model[2], which is involved during the rapid processing of LSF components of fear-related stimuli. Although they do not constitute direct evidence, our results are consistent with this functional point of view. Emotion categorization is more efficient with the LSF than with the HSF signal. Therefore, a direct visual stream which processes the LSF signal very quickly could be the most accurate and the most efficient one for the categorization of stimuli related to fear[12] and possibly also other emotional expressions[20].

One possible explanation for the greater efficiency of the LSF signal over the HSF signal is that the LSF signal is very stable in terms of perceptual variability. Whereas HSF information corresponds to finer visual details[1], the LSF signal corresponds more to configural features which would be more stable at a perceptual level. This might explain the highly significant correlation that exists between the initial eigenvectors of a PCA and the LSF signal[10]. According to this point of view, the HSF signal would not be efficient for the categorization of emotions but could be relevant to other types of cognitive task, for example identifying an individual on the basis of an EFE.

In conclusion, we propose here a computational tool which makes it possible to examine new hypotheses about the functioning of the human perceptual and emotional system[35,36]. For example, one question that needs to be addressed in future studies would be to determine how the model performs with inverted faces. Since the Fourier transform is symmetrical, we should expect there to be no impairment (which is not the case in humans) of the neural network's performance when tested on inverted faces after being training on normal faces. However, the human perceptual system is obviously more complex than this model of facial recognition and we may assume that this disturbance might be the result of the stream of information provided by the dorsal pathway during binding. For instance, we can assume that the concept-specific responses obtained on the basis of single cell recording in the ventral pathway when coding conceptual information[37] could potentially be generalized on spatial invariance or spatial rotation but subsequently be disrupted after binding with spatial location information. This hypothesis, suggested by the current simulations and cognitive neuroscience data[37], has to be tested in further neuroimaging, computational and psychophysical experiments.

90

Acknowledgments

This work was supported by a Grant ANR-06-BLAN-0360-01 and ANR-BLAN08-1_353820 from the French National Research Agency (ANR) to Martial Mermillod.

Bibliography

1. Livingstone, M., & Hubel, D. (1988). Segregation of form, color, movement, and depth: anatomy, physiology, and perception. *Science, 240(4853),* 740-749.
2. Ledoux, J. (1996), The Emotional Brain: the mysterious underpinnings of emotional life, New York: Simon & Shuster.
3. Cohn, J., & Kanade, T. (2006). Use of automated facial image analysis for measurement of emotion expression. In J. A. Coan & J. B. Allen (Eds.), The handbook of emotion elicitation and assessment. New York, NY: Oxford University Press.
4. Dailey, M. N., Cottrell, G. W., Padgett, C., & Ralph, A. (2002). EMPATH: A neural network that categorizes facial expressions. Journal of Cognitive Neuroscience, 14 (8), 1158-1173.
5. Lucey, S., Ashraf, A. B., & Cohn, J. (2007). Investigating spontaneous facial action recognition through AAM representations of the face. In K. Kurihara (Ed.), Face recognition book (pp. 395-406). Mammendorf: Pro Literatur Verlag.
6. Jones, J. P., & Palmer, L. A. (1987). The two-dimensional spatial structure of simple receptive fields in cat striate cortex. Journal of Neurophysiology, 58 (6), 1187-1211.
7. Jones, J. P., Stepnoski, A., & Palmer, L. A. (1987). The two-dimensional spectral structure of simple receptive fields in cat striate cortex. Journal of Neurophysiology, 58 (6), 1212-1232.
8. Bartlett, M. S., Littlewort, G. C., Frank, M. G., Lainscsek, C., Fasel, I., & Movellan, J. R. (2006). Automatic recognition of facial actions in spontaneous expressions. Journal of Multimedia, 1 (6), 22-35.
9. Littlewort, G., Bartlett, M., Fasel, I., Susskind, J., & Movellan, J. (2006). Dynamics of facial expression extracted automatically from video. Image and Vision Computing, 24 (6), 615-625.
10. Abdi, H., Valentin, D., Edelman, B. E., & O'Toole, A. J. (1995). More about the difference between men and women: Evidence from linear neural networks and the principal component approach. Perception, 24 (5), 539-562.
11. De Valois, R. L., & De Valois, K. K. (1988). Spatial Vision. New York: Oxford University Press.

12. Vuilleumier, P., Armony, J. L., Driver, J., & Dolan, R. J. (2003). Distinct spatial frequency sensitivities for processing faces and emotional expressions. Nature Neuroscience, 6 (6), 624-631.
13. Kohonen, T. (1984) Self-Organization and Associative Memory. Springer Series Information Sciences, vol. 8, Springer, Berlin Heidelberg New York.
14. Lundqvist, D., Flykt, A., and Öhman, A. (1998), Karolinska Directed Emotional Faces, Stockholm: Karolinska Institute and Hospital, Section of Psychology.
15. Kohonen, T. (1997) Self-organizing maps.Springer, Berlin.
16. Ritter, H. and Kohonen, T. (1989) Self-organizing semantic maps. Biological Cybernetics, 61(4), 241-254.
17. Versino, C. and Gambardella, L. M. (1995) Learning the visuomotor coordination of a mobile robot by using the invertible Kohonen Map. From Natural to Artificial Neural Computation, 1084-1091.18. Vesanto, J., Himberg, J., Alhoniemi, E. and Parhankangas, J. (1999) Self-organizing map in Matlab: the SOM Toolbox. Proceedings of the Matlab DSP Conference, Espoo, Finland, 35-40.
19. Schyns, P. G., & Oliva, A. (1999). Dr. Angry and Mr. Smile: when categorization flexibly modifies the perception of faces in rapid visual presentations. Cognition, 69 (3), 243-265.
20. Yang, T.T., Menon, V., Eliez, S., Blasey, C., White, C.D., Reid, A.J., Gotlib, I.H., Reiss, A.L. (2002). Amygdalar activation associated with positive and negative facial expressions. Neuroreport, 13, 1737–1741.
21. French, R. M., Mermillod, M., Quinn, P. C., Chauvin, A., & Mareschal, D. (2002). The importance of starting blurry: Simulating improved basic-level category learning in infants due to weak visual acuity. Proceedings of the 24th Annual Conference of the Cognitive Science Society (pp. 322-327). Mahwah, NJ: Lawrence Erlbaum Associates.
22. Turkewitz, G., & Kenny, P. A. (1982). Limitations on input as a basis for neural organization and perceptual development: a preliminary theoretical statement. Developmental Psychobiology, 15 (4), 357-368.
23. Parker, D. M., Lishman, J. R., & Hughes, J. (1997). Evidence for the view that temporospatial integration in vision is temporally anisotropic. Perception, 26 (9), 1169-1180.
24. Schyns, P. G., & Oliva, A. (1994). From blobs to boundary edges: Evidence for time and spatial-scale-dependent scene recognition. Psychological Science, 5 (4), 195-200.
25. Mermillod, M., Guyader, N., & Chauvin, A. (2005a). The coarse-to-fine hypothesis revisited: evidence from neuro-computational modeling. Brain & Cognition, 57 (2), 151-157.
26. Mermillod, M., Guyader, N., & Chauvin, A. (2005b). Improving generalisation skills in a neural network on the basis of neurophysiological data. Brain & Cognition, 58 (2), 246-248.

27. Kumar, D., Rai, C. S., & Kumar, S. (2008). Dimensionality Reduction using SOM based. Journal of Multimedia, 3(1), 1-6.

28. Kumar, D., Rai, C. S., & Kumar, S. (2007). An Experimental Comparison of Unsupervised Learning Techniques for Face Recognition. International Journal of Computer And Information Science And Engineering, 1(3), 158-166.

29. Lawrence, S., Giles, C. L., & Tsoi, A. C. (1997). Face Recognition: A Convolutional Neural Network Approach. IEEE Transactions on Neural Networks, 8(1), 98-113.

30. Mermillod, M., Bonin, P., Mondillon, L., Alleysson, D., & Vermeulen, N. (2010). Coarse Scales are Sufficient for Efficient Categorization of Emotional Facial Expressions: Evidence from Neural Computation. Neurocomputing, 73, 2522-2531.

31. Mermillod, M., Vermeulen, N., Lundqvist, D., & Niedenthal, P.M. (2009). Neural Computation as a Tool to Differentiate Perceptual from Emotional Processes: The Case of Anger Superiority Effect. Cognition, 110 (3), 346-357.

32. Mermillod, M., Vuilleumier, P., Peyrin, C., Alleysson, D., & Marendaz, C. (2009). The Importance of Low Spatial Frequency Information For Recognizing Fearful Facial Expressions. Connection Science, 21 (1), 75-83.

33. Mermillod, M., Droit-Volet, S., Devaux, D., Schaefer, A., & Vermeulen, N. (in press). Are Coarse Scales Sufficient for Fast Detection of Visual Threat? Psychological Science.

34. Daugman, J. G. (1985). Uncertainty relation for resolution in space, spatial frequency, and orientation optimized by two-dimensional visual cortical filters. Journal of the Optical Society of America A, 2 (7), 1160-1169. .

35. Vermeulen, N., Godefroid, J., & Mermillod, M. (2009). Emotional Modulation of Attention: Fear Increases but Disgust Reduces the Attentional Blink. Plos One, 4(11), e7924.

36. Vermeulen, N., Mermillod, M., Godefroid, J., & Corneille, O. (2009). Unintended Embodiment of Concepts into Percepts: Sensory Activation Boosts Attention for Same-Modality Concepts in the Attentional Blink Paradigm. Cognition, 112, 467-472.

37. Quiroga, R.Q. Reddy, L. Kreiman, G. Koch, C. Fried, I. (2005). Invariant visual representation by single neurons in the human brain. *Nature, 435 (7045)*, 1102–1107.

MODELING SPEECH PERCEPTION WITH RESTRICTED BOLTZMANN MACHINES*

Michael Klein

Laboratoire de Psychologie Cognitive, CNRS & Aix-Marseille University
3, place Victor Hugo, Bat. 9, Case D, 13331 Marseille
E-mail: Michael.Q.Klein@gmail.com

Louis ten Bosch and Lou Boves

Center for Speech and Language Technology, Radboud University Nijmegen
Erasmusplein 1, 6525 HT Nijmegen
E-mail: {L.tenBosch,L.Boves }@let.ru.nl

Restricted Boltzmann Machines (RBMs) appear to be a good candidate to model information processing in the cerebral cortex, since they employ a simple unsupervised learning rule that can be applied to many domains and allows the training of multiple layers of representation. In this paper, we apply the RBM learning algorithm to speech perception. We show that RBMs can be used to achieve good performance in the recognition of isolated spoken digits using a multi-layer *deep belief network* (consisting of a number of stacked RBMs). This performance, however, appears to depend on the fine-tuning of weights with the supervised back-propagation algorithm. To investigate how central the role of back-propagation, we compare the performance of a number of deep-belief networks using fine-tuning with the performance of the same network architectures without fine-tuning. Furthermore, since one of the main strengths of RBMs is to build up multiple layers of representation, we combine the question of fine-tuning with the question of how beneficial additional layers are for the performance of the networks. To see whether the representations that emerge on higher levels make classification easier, we also apply a simple perception classification to the different levels of the deep-belief networks when it is trained without fine-tuning.

*This work was funded by the ACORNS grant and the O-Code grant of the European Union. We would like to thank Geoffrey Hinton and Simon Osindero for discussions and Jort Gemmeke for his normalized database of spoken English digits.

1. Introduction

Modeling speech perception[1-3] with artificial neural networks is a notoriously difficult task in itself. With the increasing body of knowledge about the neural computations in the brain,[4,5] the ambition to create models that are at least to some degree biologically plausible adds additional constraints and makes the endeavor even more challenging. The acquired cognitive representations involved in the perception of speech appear to be mainly cortical.[6,7] The learning method of the cortex, it seems, is of an unsupervised Hebbian-type.[8,9] Speech perception, however, requires the cortex to extract multiple levels of feature detecting neurons, which standard Hebbian learning seem to have difficulty in generating. This sort of hierarchical unsupervised learning can be performed by *Deep Belief Networks*,[10] an architecture consisting of multiple levels of Restricted Boltzmann Machines.[11] A Restricted Boltzmann Machines (or RBM) employs a simple unsupervised and correlation-based algorithm, that can be used to build up multiple layers of representations in an unsupervised manner. It has been successfully applied to several domains, most prominently to the recognition of handwritten digits.

This paper presents an investigation in the ability of the RBM algorithm and Deep Belief Networks to serve as a model of cortical processing of speech. Apart from demonstrating that RBMs are powerful enough to recognize speech well enough to be comparable to human performance, we are mainly interested in finding out how the performance is affected by the number of layers used in the deep-belief network. To do so, we use the design proposed by Hinton[10] and train a fully unsupervised deep-belief network in which the labels are integrated with a higher-level representation of input and used together to train the highest level of representation. We investigate the performance of this architecture with deep-belief networks of different depth: one layer, two layer, and three layer. After unsupervised training of the network, we fine-tune the connections with back-propagation, to see how far the performance can still be improved. We also run the back-propagation algorithms on these three architectures without prior training with the RBM algorithm to see whether the networks trained with the RBM algorithm first perform better than pure back-propagation networks. To gain additional insides in the representations that emerge from unsupervised training with the RBM algorithm, we also use the simple perceptron learning algorithm to categorize these representations. The purpose of this last set of simulations is to see whether the higher level representations are easier to be categorized.

2. Method

We will first present all the neural network algorithms used in the simulations reported in this paper. Then, we will give the details on the simulations we performed. Finally, we will describe the training data and how it is pre-processed before training.

2.1. *Neural Network Algorithms*

2.1.1. *Restricted Boltzmann Machines and Deep-Belief Networks*

In an RBM the units are binary and stochastic. Activation of a unit j is calculated by first computing the sum of its weighted input, including its bias b_j (equation 1), where x_i is the output of the unit i and w_{ij} is the weight between unit i and unit j.

$$z_j = b_j + \sum x_i w_{ij} \qquad (1)$$

From this sum, the probability of the unit j being 1 is computed with the logistic function (equation 2, Fig. 1).

$$prob(y_j = 1) = \frac{1}{1 + e^{-z_j}} \qquad (2)$$

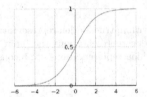

Fig. 1.   The logistic function.

Given this probability, activation is determined using a standard sampling procedure. In the simulations reported in this paper, we generate a random number between 0 and 1 and if this number is smaller than or equal to the probability of the unit, then the output of the unit is set to 1, otherwise to 0. We use the following (java) algorithm (where r.nextInt(100) generates a random natural number between 0 and 100):

```
random_number = ((float) r.nextInt(100)) /100;
if  (random_number <= probability) fire = 1;
```

Every unit in the input layer is connected to every unit in the hidden layer and each connections has a symmetrical weight (same value for bottom-up recognition as for top-down down generation) that changes during learning. There are no lateral connections between the units of a layer. In addition, every unit has a bias that also changes during learning. After random initialization of weights and biases (with random Gaussians around 0.1), an input vector is applied to the input layer and the hidden activations are computed from it. Then the input is reconstructed from the hidden representations by computing the downward activations. After that, a reconstructed hidden activation is computed from the reconstructed input (see Fig. 2).

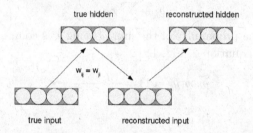

Fig. 2. The up and down algorithm: true hidden representations are generated from the true input. From the true hidden representations the input is reconstructed and from the reconstructed input the hidden representations are reconstructed.

Finally, the algorithm learns by increasing the weights by the correlation of the input and the hidden units' activation $< v_i h_j >_{data}$ minus the correlation of reconstructed input and hidden units $< v_i h_j >_{rcon}$ (equation 3)

$$\Delta w_{ij} = \epsilon(< v_i h_j >_{data} - < v_i h_j >_{rcon}) \tag{3}$$

Here is the implemented learning rule (in Java):

```java
for (i = 0; i < input_vector_length; i++)
    for (j = 0; j < hidden_vector_length; j++)
            weight[i][j] = weight[i][j] +
                alpha *
                ((visual_true[i] * hidden_true[j]) -
                (visual_rcon[i] * hidden_rcon[j]));
```

The weights of the input biases and hidden biases are changed accordingly. The learning rule is analogue since biases can be treated as weights of connections from units that are always 1. Here is the learning rule for input biases (in Java):

```java
for (i = 0; i < input_vector_length; i++)
                v_bias[i] = v_bias[i] +
                alpha *
                (visual_true[i] - visual_rcon[i]);
```

2.1.2. *Training a Deep-Belief Network*

To build up a fully unsupervised deep-belief network is done in several steps. First, an RBM is trained on the input data with the algorithms described above. Next, the weights of this networks are fixed. The input is then applied to this network with fixed weights and the output (at the hidden layer) serves as the input to the next RBM that is build on top of this one. This procedure continues until the desired depth of the overall neural model. Note, however, that to train a fully unsupervised deep-belief network, the final RBM does not only have the output of the pre-final RBM as input, but also the labels. To test such a model after training, the weights of the complete model have to be fixed. Then the input (but no labels) is presented to the network. Finally the activation of the labels are generated top-down from the top layer of the model.

Subsequently, such a network can be fine-tuned with the back-propagation algorithm (explained below). To do so, however, the top-layer of the deep-belief network will serve as the pre-final layer and the representations of the labels will serve as a top-layer

2.1.3. *Delta-Rule and Back-Propagation*

To fine-tune the weights of our deep-belief networks, we use the back-propagation algorithm. In some of the other tests reported in this paper, we will use a perceptron classification. A back-propagation network can be regarded as a multi-layer perceptron, or the perceptron as a special case (single-layer) of a back-propagation network. Therefore, we will treat both algorithms in this section.

The activation of a unit in both perceptron and back-propagation network is computed in the same manner as in the RBM (see equation 1). Also, the output of a unit j is computed with the logistic function analog to the probability of a unit being 1 in the RBM. However, since the output is not binary, there no sampling is necessary (equation 4.

$$O(y_j) = \frac{1}{1 + e^{-z_j}} \tag{4}$$

The computation of the error and the weight change for a perceptron is the same as for the final layer of a back-propagation network. In this kind of supervised learning, the output of the network y_k is subtracted from the desired output y_k^* to compute the error e_k (equation 5). The weight change Δw_{ik} is then calculated by multiplying e_k with the value of the input neuron x_i and the rate of change α (equation 6). Then Δw_{ik} is used to update the weight (equation 7).

$$e_k = y_k^* - y_k \tag{5}$$
$$\Delta w_{ik} = \alpha e_k x_i \tag{6}$$
$$w_{ik} \leftarrow w_{ik} + \Delta w_{ik} \tag{7}$$

Here is the code (java) for the update of the weights:

```java
for (int i = 0; i < networkWeights.LayerSize.getValue(in); i++)
{
    networkWeights.Weights[l].setValue(i, j,
      networkWeights.Weights[l].getValue(i, j)
    + alpha * layerError[out].getValue(j)
    * layerOutput[in].getValue(i));
}
```

The analogue code for the update of the biases is the following:

```
networkWeights.Biases[l].setValue(j,
  networkWeights.Biases[l].getValue(j)
  + alpha * layerError[out].getValue(j));
```

For the back-propagation network the training of the weights to the pre-final layers is somewhat more complicated. While the rule for the update of the weights can stay the same as in the perceptron and the final layer, the computation of the Δ is quite different. The only true error that we can observe, is of course at the output layer. To get an approximation of the error at the hidden layer, we simply distribute the error of an output unit j to all the hidden units that is it connected to, weighted by this connection (assuming that the contribution of this hidden unit to the error is proportional to its connection strength to that output unit). This principle is repeated for all hidden layers of the network. Equation 8 shows the computation of the error at the hidden layer.

$$e_j = y_j(1 - y_j) \sum_k e_k w_{jk} \tag{8}$$

The error e_j at unit j is the sum of errors e_k of units k to which this hidden unit is projecting, times the weight w_{jk} of the connections multiplied with the output of the unit y_j times $(1 - y_1)$.

Here is the code (java) for the computation of the error:

```
g = 0f;
for (int k = 0; k < networkWeights.LayerSize.getValue(out +1); k++)
{
    g = g + layerError[out+1].getValue(k)
        * networkWeights.Weights[out].getValue(j, k);
}

layerError[out].setValue(j,layerOutput[out].getValue(j)
    * (1 - layerOutput[out].getValue(j)) * g);
```

2.2. *Simulations*

2.2.1. *Unsupervised Deep-Belief Networks*

We constructed deep-belief networks with a several numbers of layer following the established method of Hinton.[10] We trained networks with one, two, or three layers and 800 units per layer using the RBM algorithm. Every layer was trained using 20 sweeps through the complete training set. Then the next layer was trained using the hidden representations of the previous layers as input to the next layer. The input to the top layer consisted not only of the 800 binary representations of the last hidden layer, but also of 11 binary representations of the 11 classes of spoken numbers, coded in the usual one-hot manner (see Fig. 3).

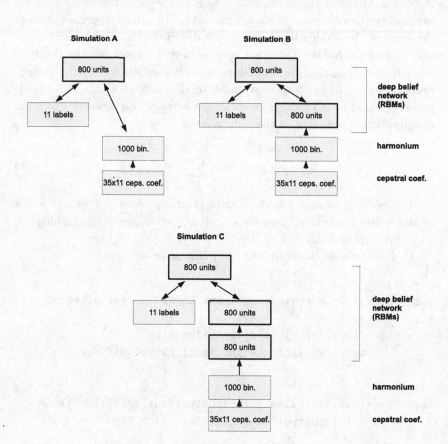

Fig. 3.   Deep-Belief Networks with 1 - 3 RBM layers.

2.2.2. *Fine-Tuning Deep-Belief Networks*

Next, we used the back-propagation of error algorithm to fine-tune the weights. We did this for all three architectures. Every architecture was fine-tuned using 20 sweeps through the complete data set.

2.2.3. *Back-Propagation Only*

As a control condition, we also trained the architectures described above with back-propagation alone (i.e., without any prior training with the RBM algorithm). Also in this case we used 20 sweeps through the complete data set.

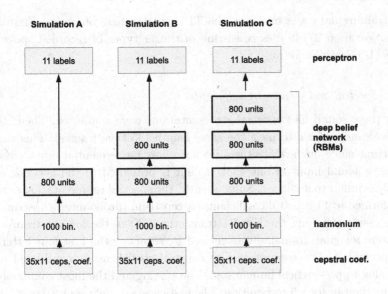

Fig. 4.   Perceptron classification of different levels of representation.

2.2.4. *Perceptron Classification*

Finally, to test the properties of the generated representations at the different levels, we used a single layer perceptron (delta-rule) to classify the representations that were obtained at the different levels into the desired 11 categories (Fig. 4). No back-propagation was used here to fine-tune the weights. The purpose of this test was to see whether the higher levels can be more easily categorized or whether categorization at those levels is harder. This test was done to test the importance of fine-tuning when several layers are employed.

As you can see in Fig. 4, for this test, we did not train a fully unsupervised deep-belief network, since we didn't use the labels as input to the final layer, but rather trained the layers without any reference to the labels and simply tried a supervised categorization of the representations that emerged on the different levels into the 11 categories.

2.3. *Training Material*

2.3.1. *Basic Sound Files*

The training data was based on the TIDigits database of spoken English digits. We used 27748 files consisting of the 11 types of recorded spoken digits (1-9, 'zero', and 'oh').

2.3.2. *Spectral and Cepstral Coefficients*

From these sound files spectral representations were computed. Then, all files were *normalized* to have the same length (35 time frames). This was important since our architectures do not allow for sequential input - the complete sound input of one spoken digit is presented to the network in parallel, similar to an image. Subsequently, the spectral representation were transformed to 11 cepstral coefficients. A cepstrum (pronounced /kpstrm/) is the result of taking the Fourier transform (FT) of the log spectrum as if it were a signal. Its name was derived by reversing the first four letters of "spectrum". The computation of cepstral coefficients is considered to be analog to pre-cortical human sound processing and the most commonly used method in speech recognition. The first cepstral coefficient (0) was not used during training, since we considered it to not carry too much relevant information relevant for the recognition of words.

2.3.3. *Harmonium Model*

Since RBMs use binary input, we transformed the 35 x 11 real values of the cepstral representations into 1000 binary values using a so-called *harmonium model*. The algorithm of the harmonium model works similar to the RBM algorithm (explained above). However, it starts with real valued input and generates binary higher-level representations. From these binary representations it tries to regenerate the real-valued input, therefore allowing it to generate a binary representation that codes the same information as the real-valued input.

3. Results

3.1. *Unsupervised Deep-Belief Networks*

3.1.1. *Single Layer*

Table 1. Error rates in % without fine tuning.

after epoch	3 layers	4 layers	5 layers
1	1.892	1.347	4.954
2	1.099	0.923	4.955
3	1.019	0.857	4.966
4	0.987	0.811	4.942
5	0.962	0.824	4.957
6	0.940	0.777	4.949
7	0.928	0.761	4.973
8	0.918	0.756	4.968
9	0.892	0.752	4.960
10	0.902	0.716	4.962
11	0.875	0.734	4.943
12	0.888	0.701	4.956
13	0.904	0.700	4.951
14	0.890	0.723	4.949
15	0.888	0.699	4.934
16	0.845	0.708	4.962
17	0.848	0.683	4.948
18	0.876	0.690	4.958
19	0.866	0.690	4.969
20	0.874	0.668	4.947

The single layer RBM was able to reduce the error to 1.82% within one training sweep. The performance continued to increase until the 16th sweep. Then the error stabilized at 0.85%.

The error rate is the error of all neurons at the output level, as defined in equation 9, averaged over the complete sweep (the whole set of training data).

$$E = \frac{1}{2} \sum_i e_i^2 \qquad (9)$$

3.1.2. *Two Layers*

The two layer deep-belief network outperformed the single layer RBM. It learned faster (error after one sweep is only 1.35%) and, when the error stabilizes around the 17th sweep, it has reached a lower error rate (0.68%).

3.1.3. *Three Layers*

The three layer deep-belief network performs clearly worse than the other two architectures. After the 1st sweep the error is at 4.95%, where it stays for the rest of the training.

3.2. *Fine-Tuning Deep-Belief Networks*

Table 2. Error rates in % after training with back-propagation.

after epoch	3 layers	4 layers	5 layers
1	0.324	0.669	8.248
2	0.233	0.437	8.248
3	0.196	0.321	8.248
4	0.166	0.231	8.248
5	0.124	0.190	8.248
6	0.092	0.142	8.248
7	0.068	0.120	8.248
8	0.055	0.107	8.248
9	0.041	0.084	8.248
10	0.032	0.080	8.248
11	0.019	0.066	8.248
12	0.012	0.056	8.248
13	0.006	0.036	8.248
14	0.003	0.021	8.248
15	0.001	0.016	8.248
16	0.001	0.012	8.248
17	0.001	0.006	8.248
18	0.001	0.003	8.248
19	0.001	0.002	8.248
20	0.001	0.002	8.248

3.2.1. *Single Layer*

Starting with an error of 0.85% after unsupervised training, one sweep of back-propagation reduces the error to 0.32%. The performance stabilizes around the 15th sweep with an error of around 0.001%. This is the simulation with the best performance.

3.2.2. *Two Layers*

The two layer architecture starts fine tuning with 0.68%. After one sweep of back-propagation the error is still around the same value (0.67%). The performance stabilizes around the 19th sweep with an error of around 0.002%. This is the simulation with the second best performance.

3.2.3. *Three Layers*

Interesting to see is the performance of the fine-tuned three layer deep-belief network. Starting with an error of 4.95%, the first sweep of back-propagation learning brings the error rate up (!) to 8.25% where it stays for the rest of the training.

3.3. *Back-Propagation Only*

Table 3. Error rates in % with back-propagation only.

after epoch	3 layers	4 layers	5 layers
1	0.872	7.838	7.973
2	0.351	8.209	8.247
3	0.257	8.248	8.248
4	0.217	8.247	8.248
5	0.175	8.248	8.248
6	0.174	8.248	8.248
7	0.150	8.248	8.248
8	0.123	8.248	8.248
9	0.121	8.248	8.248
10	0.114	8.248	8.248
11	0.095	8.248	8.248
12	0.083	8.248	8.248
13	0.078	8.248	8.248
14	0.079	8.248	8.248
15	0.067	8.248	8.248
16	0.064	8.248	8.248
17	0.069	8.248	8.248
18	0.060	8.248	8.248
19	0.045	8.248	8.248
20	0.043	8.248	8.248

3.3.1. *Single Layer*

While the fine-tuned RBM reaches an error of 0.001%, the error the network that only uses back-propagation is still at 0.043 at the end of the 20th sweep. Note, however, that altogether the fine-tuned RBM experiences twice as much training.

3.3.2. *Two Layers*

It's interesting to see that the two layer architecture stabilizes at an error of 8.25% after 3 sweeps and doesn't improve anymore. While this is not an impressive performance, it is still very high above chance level (91%).

3.3.3. *Three Layers*

Similar to the two layer architecture this one also quickly stabilizes at 8.25% and doesn't improve anymore.

3.4. *Perceptron Classification*

3.4.1. *Single Layer*

The perceptron classification using a single RBM after one training epoch (with the complete training set) yielded an error rate of 7.240% (the error rate being the number of incorrectly firing neurons as compared to overall neurons.).

3.4.2. *Two Layer*

Using a two layer deep belief network, the perceptron classification after one training epoch (with the complete training set) yielded an error rate of 10.956%.

3.4.3. *Three Layer*

The perceptron classification using a three layer deep belief network after one training epoch (with the complete training set) yielded an error rate of 13.918%.

4. Discussion

4.1. *Overall Performance*

This study demonstrates the ability of deep belief networks to recognize spoken digits. The overall performance of the one layer and two layer models with fine tuning is comparable to human performance. However, in contrast to most speech recognition algorithms, it is not dependent on a priori knowledge such as phonetic labels. This feature makes the approach very interesting as a cognitive model of speech perception. Note, however, that the task for the model is to recognize only 11 types or words and it receives a large amount of training (around 2500s item per category and sweep).

4.2. *Fine-Tuning*

Without fine-tuning, the performance of the model is still acceptable, but not as impressive. While this doesn't come as much of a surprise, there are a number of findings in this particular study that are worth mentioning. The first one being that without fine-tuning the two-layer deep believe network performs better than the single-layer RBM. After fine-tuning, however, it's the other way round. Further, while the single layer perceptron performs reasonable well, the two and three layer perceptrons appear to be stuck in some sort of local minimum. However, when the two-layer architecture is trained with the RBM algorithm beforehand, this does not occur. Although, in the case of the three layer architecture even the prior training with the RBM algorithm doesn't prevent this. In case of the three layer architecture, this also happens for the training with the RBM algorithm only. In sum it is fair to say, that the RBM algorithm with fine tuning performs better than back-propagation alone and can prevent the network from being stuck.

4.3. *Number of Layers*

It is interesting to observe that in the simulations using perceptron classification (without fine-tuning) the categorization performance appears to get worse, the more layers are added. This indicates that the performance of the deep belief network and its ability to use multiple layers of representation depends strongly on the fine-tuning and, therefore, on the back-propagation algorithm. This, however, is in contrast to the finding in section 3.1, where the two-layer deep-belief network clearly outperforms the single layer RBM. More research about this question is necessary.

4.4. Biological Plausibility

4.4.1. RBM and Deep-Belief Networks

While the fact that the RBM algorithm allows unsupervised learning of hierarchical representations makes the model appear biologically plausible, several reservations need to be mentioned at this point. The RBM learning algorithm is a type of correlation learning, very much like Hebbian learning, but unlike Hebbian learning, no direct evidence exists for the existence of the exact algorithm in the brain. Furthermore, the algorithm requires symmetrical connections between the input and the hidden layer. In neural network simulations, this is represented as a single value that is used for both bottom-up recognition and top-down generation. In the brain, on the other hand, this means that the strength of real bottom-up and top-down neural connections has to be symmetrical. There is no neurophysiological evidence supporting such an organization in the cortex. However, it has to be said that the brain must in some way be able to find a higher level coding of essential features that represent lower level activation and that is exactly the strength of the RBM algorithm. Another point that should be considered is that, as described in section 2.1.2, a deep belief network learns the layers subsequently and does not start the training of the next layer before the weights of the previous layers have finished training. Again, there is no biological evidence supporting this, although in itself it does not seem implausible.

4.4.2. Back-Propagation

While the biological plausibility of the back-propagation algorithm has often been questioned, it is not unreasonable to assume that top down information must play a role in shaping the representations on the lower levels. For example, if you take into account the role of a phoneme as the smallest meaning-distinguishing unit, it is clear that the fact that a distinction of sounds is relevant on a higher level has in some way be able to feed back to the lower levels. Another example that illustrated this point is the fact that the ability for phonetic distinctions disappear if these distinctions are not needed in the languages used in a person's environment, i.e., if a distinction is not needed on a higher level, it is no longer made on a lower level.

4.5. *Future Work*

The way the word recognition is implemented at this point, it is analogue to image recognition, using a static image-like cepstral representation of fixed length. To progress from here to more general speech input a dynamic input, such as conditional RBMs[12] would be necessary.

Also, it is not yet apparent what the different layers of the deep belief network represent. The great advantage of deep-belief networks is that they cannot only be used for recognition, but also for generation. In that sense it would be possible to generate cepstral output from selective representations at the different levels. However, unlike visual features of an image, partial cepstral representations are likely to be very hard to interpret.

References

1. J. L. McClelland and J. L. Elman, *Cognitive Psychology* **18**, 1 (1986).
2. A. Waibel, *Neural Computation* **1**, 39 (1989).
3. S. Grossberg, *Psychological Review* **107**, 735 (2000).
4. C. Koch, *The Biophysics of Computation: Information Processing in Single Neurons* (Oxford University Press, 1999).
5. K. Doya, *Neural Networks* **12**, 961 (1999).
6. C. Price, R. J. S. Wise, E. Wartburton, C.J.Moore, K. Patterson and D. Howard, *Brain* **119**, 919 (1996).
7. C. M. Wessinger, J. VanMeter, J. VanLare, J. Pekar and J. P. Rauschecker, *JCN* **13:1**, 1 (2001).
8. D. O. Hebb, *The Organization of Behaviour* (Wiley New York, 1949).
9. A. Artola, S. Brocher and W. Singer, *Nature* **347**, 69 (1990).
10. G. E. Hinton, S. Osindero and Y. W. Teh, *Neural Computation* **18**, 1527 (2006).
11. P. Smolensky, Information processing in dynamical systems: Foundations of harmony theory, in *Parallel Distributed Processing: Volume 1: Foundations*, eds. D. E. Rumelhart and J. L. McClelland (MIT Press, Cambridge, MA, 1986) pp. 194–281.
12. G. W. Taylor, G. E. Hinton and S. Roweis, Modeling human motion using binary latent variables, in *Advances in Neural Information Processing Systems*, (MIT Press, Cambridge, MA, 2007).

EARLY LANGUAGE AS MULTIMODAL LEARNING

Nadja Althaus[1,2,*] and Denis Mareschal[1]

[1] *Centre for Brain and Cognitive Development,*
Department of Psychological Science
Birkbeck, University of London

[2] *Department of Psychology,*
Oxford Brookes University
* E-mail: n.althaus@brookes.ac.uk

We introduce a model of word learning in infants based on cross-modal interactions. Our model employs an architecture consisting of two Self-organizing maps (SOMs), representing the visual and auditory modalities, which are connected by Hebbian links. In contrast to previous models using a similar architecture, our model employs active Hebbian connections which propagate activation between the visual and auditory maps during learning. Our results show that categorical perception emerges from these early audio-visual interactions in both domains. We argue that the learning mechanism introduced in our model could be behind the facilitation of infants categorization through verbal labelling reported in the literature.

1. Introduction

Research into the impact of verbal labelling on object categorization in infancy has provided evidence that novel labels facilitate category formation in infancy. Experimental work showed that infants may form categories in the presence of (consistent) novel labels which they do not form if the exemplars are provided in silence,[1-3] although contrasting findings have been reported as well.[4] Other studies have shown that labels may override visual category formation, causing infants to merge[5] or split[6] visual categories. The mechanism underlying these effects, however, is largely unknown. Althaus and Mareschal[7] found that providing labels directs infants attention to commonalities between category exemplars. To obtain a sound theory of how exactly labeling may be beneficial for category formation, it is necessary to investigate the learning mechanisms that may underlie category formation in the presence of labelling. In the following we introduce a novel model of the acquisition of word-object associations. In particular, we focus on audio-visual interactions that permit learning in each modality to influence learning in the other modality. We propose that the categorical perception effect which emerges in this cross-modal, interactive scenario, but not in a comparable non-interactive version of the model, is a potential candidate for the mechanism underlying the facilitation of categorization in infants.

A number of computational models have been proposed in the past to simulate learning at the interface between language and object processing. Several of these[8-10] have mainly provided evidence that the information available in the joint auditory and visual information streams infants typically perceive is sufficient for extracting word-object mappings, and that this multimodal information further allows better word segmentation/identification than the auditory input alone. Yu[9] has further provided a computational account of the impact of labeling on categorization. In his model, labels help to bootstrap categories by providing a way of identifying (potentially dissimilar) visual exemplars through label-co-occurrence. However, as all of these models employ computation-intensive statistical algorithms that need iterative access to the full data set, none of these approaches provide a plausible, mechanistic account of the interaction of labelling and categorization in infants.

Some connectionist approaches have gone further by using learning mechanisms that correspond more closely to the sort of processing that may occur in a neural system. For example, Schyns[11] modelled concept formation with a self-organizing map modified by the addition of a supervised naming mechanism. This way, the model integrated unsupervised self-organization processes with supervised learning, resulting in a prototype naming effect (the model produced the correct label faster for a category prototype than for exemplars distant from the category centroid). The model further demonstrated how hierarchical organization emerges in a top-down way (i.e. superordinate categories were learned first), and how differences in expertise in this context arose from different exposure.

Plunkett et al.[12] approached the word learning problem with a connectionist simulation. Their model was an autoencoder receiving images and labels as input. Both types of data were initially processed in separate pathways, and project onto separate set of output units (for which the target was to reconstruct the input pattern). However, both pathways met in a layer of hidden units, which therefore served to encode the image/label association. The model reproduced several important aspects of language acquisition in infants. Learning proceeded in a nonlinear fashion, resembling the vocabulary spurt observed in infants, as well as comprehension-production asymmetries: producing the correct image-output upon presentation of a label appeared easier to learn for the model than producing the correct label upon presentation of an image pattern. Furthermore the authors found that this cross-modal network learned the image categories faster than a unimodal version which did not involve any labelling. Clearly, the model was able to exploit the additional information given by the second modality.

Li et al.[13] introduced DevLex, a model consisting of two interconnected growing self-organizing maps, one for lexical-semantic information, and one for phonological information. Hebbian connections were formed between the maps such as to connect units that were co-activated. Thus the network learned, over time, to associate word forms with their semantic representation. Learning in this model consisted of two different learning modes – (1) Kohonen's (1982) self-organizing map (SOM) algorithm, and (2) a learning mode based on adaptive resonance theory (ART[14]). While the SOM mode was responsible for map organization, the ART mode was used for recruiting new network units to simulate vocabulary growth. Essentially, the model started out by learning in SOM mode, optimizing the topological organization of the existing units. This was followed by a gradual transition to ART mode, in which new units were recruited whenever the distance between input and map units failed to exceed a certain threshold. DevLex successfully simulated lexical confusion and age of acquisition effects (i.e. words learned early are processed more easily). Further, the model demonstrated that linguistic categories (nouns, verbs, adjectives and function words) can emerge in this form of learning, rather than having to be hard-wired into the system. An extension of this model was proposed by Li et al. (2007).[15] Working with classic self-organizing maps instead of the growing maps, and including an additional phonetic output map, this model was capable of simulating vocabulary spurt as well as frequency effects.

Mayor and Plunkett[16] introduced another dual-map model with Hebbian links. A visual map was trained with distortions of prototypical dot patterns. Simultaneously, an acoustic map was trained with speech samples. Model development included an early phase of synapto-genesis (i.e. increasing connectivity) and a later phase during which inactive Hebbian links were pruned away. While both maps essentially develop independently, joint attentional events train the Hebbian links between them: here, an object pattern is presented simultaneously with a matching acoustic label. The model demonstrated successfully that a high amount of joint attentional activity is beneficial for vocabulary growth. The authors argued further that taxonomic responding (i.e. the mapping of a label to all exemplars of an object's category, rather than just to the one exemplar) was an emergent property of the model. Taxonomic responding after just one object-label exposure was higher when the maps had developed independently for a longer period. This attributes a prominent role to the emergence of prelinguistic categorization without an early interaction with word learning.

A different approach, also using a self-organizing map, was taken up by Gliozzi et al.[17] who presented a model simulating the results from Plunkett et al. (2008).[5] In contrast to the multiple map approaches discussed above, this model only uses a single map which receives input from the two sensory domains. This model was specifically aimed at simulating the influences of labelling on categorization, by processing the label as the equivalent of an additional feature. Infants' categorization of the objects was measured by evaluating the distance between the test object and the best matching unit after presenting each training exemplar just once. The results mimicked the merging of visual categories that was found in the experiments with 10-month-olds.

Plebe et al.[18] introduced a further word learning model consisting of parallel visual and auditory hierarchies. The authors used stages of training to simulate development, incorporating incrementally more layers of the hierarchy in learning. Only in their last, linguistic, training phase are representations from the visual and auditory streams finally integrated. This stage-like process resulted in the emergence of fast-mapping at the time of integration.

In the following sections we introduce a new model to simulate the interaction between speech perception and object categorization. It is related to several of the above approaches in that it uses an interconnected pair of self-organizing maps, each of which represents a sensory domain (visual and auditory). In contrast to previous approaches, the focus here is on the interaction between the two maps. Specifically, we introduce a novel learning mechanism that is suitable for integrating cross-modal information, in the sense that representations in one modality can be influenced by the other modality. As will be seen, this mechanism supports the emergence of categorical perception in both domains.

2. The Model – Architecture, Learning and Training Data

2.1. *Model Overview*

The model we propose combines two self-organizing maps[19] which are connected by Hebbian links,[13,15,16] as schematically shown in Figure 1. The maps represent the auditory and visual domain, respectively, and are trained with input from that domain. The two maps are further fully connected by bidirectional Hebbian links, i.e. every unit in the visual map, M_{vis}, is connected to every unit in the auditory map, M_{aud}. The learning algorithm involves updating the map weights (i.e. weights from the input to the map units) as well as the Hebbian connections. Importantly, the Hebbian weights are active during learning: this means that map-weight update in each modality is not just based on the activation resulting from an input pattern in the same modality, but also incorporates activation resulting from propagation of activation from the other modality. This way, auditory development can influence visual development, and vice versa.

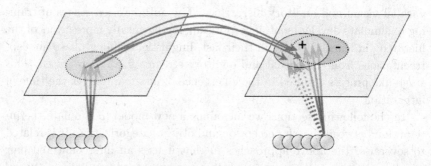

Fig. 1. Schematic model architecture, showing visual and auditory maps, input vectors, Hebbian connections, direct activation in the auditory map (left) and direct, as well as indirect activation in the visual map (right). For visibility, only cross-modal integration in one direction is shown. Plus and minus signs indicate enhancement and inhibition in the cross-modal learning mechanism.

2.2. *Training Data*

The visual stimuli represented geometrical surface-features measured from real objects. This kind of object representation has been used in other connectionist models of categorization,[20,21] and similarity measures across these dimensions have been found to reflect infants perception of the objects, as shown by their looking or object examination times.[22] Thus, toy objects from 11 categories were encoded using 18 different surface features. Each object was represented by an 18-dimensional vector of which each slot contained the (normalized) measured value of the corresponding surface feature. There were 8 objects from every category, resulting in a total of 88 object vectors. Word representations were kept as close to the acoustic wave form as possible, while also keeping the dimensionality of the resulting feature vectors low enough to make simulations computationally feasible. Therefore, a procedure similar to the one used by Mayor and Plunkett (2010)[16] was employed: Eight recordings of 11 bisyllabic nonsense words were made, corresponding to the eight instances of every object category in the visual data set. This introduced a natural variability in the auditory signal, similar to differences in utterances by human speakers. The recordings were then pre-processed with Matlab. Each recording was sampled using 5 hamming windows. The short-time Fourier transform (STFT) was warped onto a mel frequency scale. Using the mel frequency scale for stimulus encoding means that the power spectrum of a sound is based on frequency bands equally spaced in the mel scale, which allows for a representation of the sound signal that approaches more closely that of human auditory perception. The discrete cosine transform (DCT) was then used to convert the frequency-domain signal back to the time domain. The result was a set consisting of 65-dimensional vectors representing the individual recordings. All of these pre-processing steps were performed using the RASTAMAT package for speech processing.[23]

2.3. The Learning Mechanism

Input patterns were presented to the model pairwise, i.e. one visual and one (corresponding) auditory pattern. The presentation of an input pattern to each of the two maps resulted in a Gaussian "activation window": the best-matching unit (BMU) in the map was calculated as the unit whose associated weight vector was closest to the input vector, and a Gaussian with standard deviation σ, centred on the BMU, was used as a coefficient for calculating unit activation (Eq. 1). This activation pattern was termed the "direct activation" act_{dir}:

$$act_{dir}(k) = \mathcal{N}_{\sigma,BMU}(1 - \mathcal{D}_k), \qquad (1)$$

where $\mathcal{D}_k$ corresponds to the distance between the input vector and the vector of unit k. Activation was then propagated via the Hebbian links to the opposing map, resulting in an "indirect activation" pattern act_{ind} on this map:

$$act_{ind}(k) = \sum_{j=1}^{N} act_{dir}(j) * h_{j,k}, \tag{2}$$

where N is the number of units in the opposite map, and $h_{j,k}$ the strength of the Hebbian connection between units j and k. This way, each individual map had a direct and an indirect activation pattern, which were then combined into a joint activation pattern act_{joint} (Eq. 3):

$$act_{joint}(k) = (1 - \lambda) * \mathcal{N}_{BMU_{dir},\sigma}(k) + \lambda * \mathcal{N}_{BMU_{ind},\sigma}(k) \tag{3}$$

The parameter lambda controlled the impact of the cross-modal activation on learning in the individual maps. Map update was performed by moving the active units (according to the joint activation patterns) closer to the current input pattern:

$$w_k(t + 1) = w_k(t) + \eta * act_{joint}(k) * \mathcal{D}_k, \tag{4}$$

where $w_{k,t}$ refers to the map vector of unit k at time t. However, this cross-modal enhancement needs to be complemented by an inhibitory element, as will be shown in the results section. Units receiving both direct and indirect activation represent a history of similar objects having been paired with similar labels (and vice versa). Visual map units receiving only direct activation may be activated by objects that are visually similar to objects previously activating this unit, but labelled differently, and therefore less likely to belong to the category corresponding to that unit. The map vector should therefore be moved away from the present input pattern. The corresponding logic holds for auditory units only receiving direct input. Therefore, the combined weight update contained an inhibitory component:

$$w_k(t + 1) = w_k(t) + \eta \, act_{joint}(k)\mathcal{D}_k - \zeta[act_{dir}(k) - act_{joint}(k)]\mathcal{D}_k \tag{5}$$

Finally, the Hebbian weights were strengthened for co-activated units (in the joint pattern) according to Eq. 6.

$$h_{k,j}(t + 1) = h_{k,j}(t) + \kappa(act_{joint}(k) * act_{joint}(j)) \tag{6}$$

2.4. *Model Parameters*

As in Kohonen's (1992) algorithm, the present procedure incorporated several parameters. These were the neighborhood size σ, the learning rate η, the cross-modal integration coefficient λ, the inhibition coefficient ζ and the Hebbian update coefficient κ. While learning rate and neighborhood size decreased with time to enable learning first on a coarse, then on a finer scale, the other coefficients, which dealt with cross-modal integration, increased over time. This reflects the fact that as organization in the individual maps became more reliable, it could be exploited more and more for cross-modal integration.

3. Results

In order to evaluate the impact of early cross-modal interactions, we constructed two models for comparison. These were identical to the "interactive" target model (Model III) in all aspects, apart from the following: in the first, "non-interactive" model (Model I), the Hebbian weights were not active during learning, i.e. map update was solely based on direct activation ($\lambda = 0$), and hence there was no cross-modal interaction. In the second, "enhancement-only" (Model II) model, the Hebbians weights were active, causing cross-modal interactions, but learning was solely based on enhancement of activation, whereas the inhibitory component was not included in the map-update mechanism. Ten instances of all three models were trained for 450 epochs, using only "correct" word-object pairs. Performance was assessed with a number of metrics (partially adapted from Richardson and Thomas[24]) evaluating the topographic organization of the maps with regard to units which were BMUs for at least one training exemplar ("projections"). "Clustering" measured whether exemplars from one category were projected onto regions in close spatial proximity, but exemplars from different categories onto more distant regions: for each projection p, being the BMU for exemplar x, the 7 nearest units serving as projections of exemplars were found, and the Clustering metric indicates the proportion of those that were from the same category as x. Thus, the Clustering metric was 1 when the 8 exemplars from a category were mapped onto BMUs such that the distances between pairs of these BMUs were smaller than the distances to BMUs representing members of other categories. "Discrimination" assessed the granularity of categorization by dividing the number of projections existing for a category by the number of exemplars in the category. The "Mean Exemplar Distance" (MED) measured the average Euclidean distance between each pair of projections from one category. "Comprehension" measured the proportion of correct mappings of *words to objects*, and "Production" the proportion of correct mappings from *objects to words*. Figures 2, 3 and 4 show results for Models I-III, respectively. Figure 5 gives examples of the resulting map representation in the target model and the non-interactive version after 450 epochs of training.

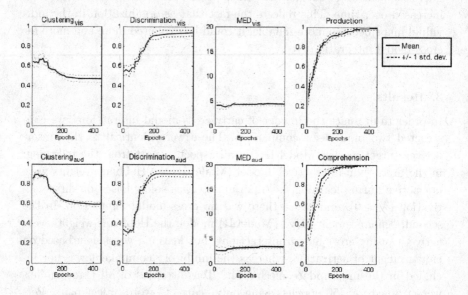

Fig. 2.   Results for non-interactive model (based on 10 simulations).

In Model I, where the maps developed independently and the Hebbian weights were trained in a passive way, development of cross-modal mappings appeared to be monotonous after the first 50 epochs, as shown by the steady increase in Production and Comprehension rates shown in Figure 2. Both measures reached 100% performance. At the same time, the model's discrimination ability increased throughout the learning phase, while Clustering decreased over the first 150 epochs before settling. The MED measure changed very little across those 450 epochs.

Model II, by contrast, exhibited a less straight-forward learning curve with regard to cross-modal connections (see Figure 3): Production and Comprehension rates increased steeply for about 180 epochs, as in Model I, but then became asymptotical and settled at a suboptimal level. The model also settled at lower Discrimination values than Model I.

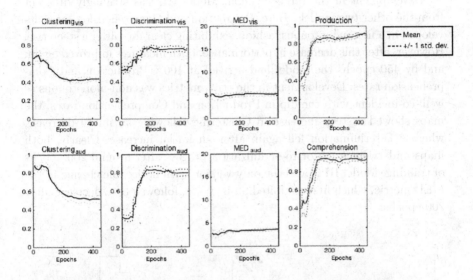

Fig. 3.   Results for enhancement-only model (based on 10 simulations).

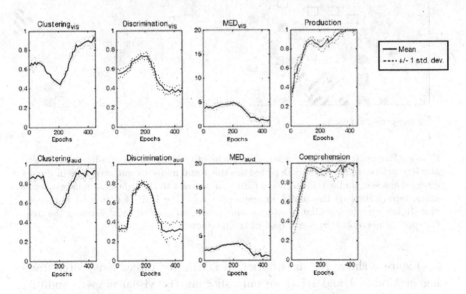

Fig. 4.   Results for interactive model, using enhancement and inhibition (based on 10 simulations).

Development in the target version, Model III, was strikingly different from the other two models. Here, Production and Comprehension rates developed in a non-monotonous fashion, exhibiting clear dips after a steep rise. However, after this decrease in performance, both measures improved again, and by 450 epochs the model had arrived at 100% Production and Comprehension rates. Development in the other metrics was non-monotonous as well: co-incident with the dip in Production and Comprehension rates, the maps showed a steep increase in Clustering following an initial decrease, whereas Discrimination fell again after an initial increase. Clearly, both maps underwent a major re-organization process after around 200 epochs of training. Model III is also the only version with noticeable change in the MED metric, which first exhibited an increase, followed by a decrease after 200 epochs.

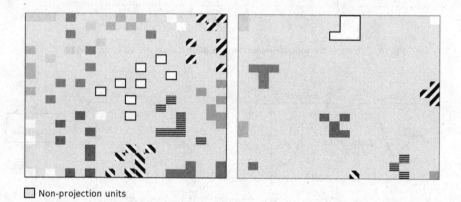

☐ Non-projection units

Fig. 5. Exemplar projections after 450 epochs of training in the non-interactive (left) and interactive (right) models. Depicted are the visual maps (overall structure in the auditory maps was similar). Patterned squares, in contrast to the light-gray non-projection units, represent projection units, or units that were the BMU for at least one exemplar. In both models, similar categories were projected onto adjacent areas in the map. Categorical perception only emerged in the interactive case.

Figure 5 shows the distribution of BMUs (or projections) after training in Models I and III (here only showing the visual maps – auditory maps were similar in terms of overall structure), illustrating how the representation of the input space differs as a result of the interactive learning mechanism. In both cases the map topography preserved similarities, with similar visual categories and similar-sounding words being projected onto units in close spatial proximity. In Model I, projections were almost equidistant, with spaces between projections of two members of the same category approximately as large as spaces between members of different categories. By contrast, the projections in Model III formed tight clusters, with larger spaces between projections of members from different categories.

4. Discussion

As our results show, early audio-visual interactions can have both beneficial and disruptive effects. Clearly, if the circumstances are not right, interaction can hinder development, as demonstrated in Model II, where the purely enhancement-based mechanism prevented cross-modal mappings from reaching 100% accuracy. However, Model III shows that the information present in the audio-visual signal can indeed be exploited to result in beneficial effects. Notably, the main target of our attention here is not the accuracy of cross-modal mappings. Achieving Comprehension and Production rates as high as in a non-interactive model is merely a prerequisite for attributing beneficial effects to cross-modal interactions. Instead, we were mainly interested in the *organization* of visual and auditory space in the two maps. Changes in the organization of the representation of visual space may explain the facilitation of (visual) category learning observed in infants. The superiority of Model III becomes clear when regarding Figure 5. As Model III develops a representation that forms tight clusters of exemplars from one category, while at the same time projecting different categories to spatially distant units in the map, a form of categorical perception emerges during development in this model.

As Figure 4 shows, the learning process involved a phase of "reorganization": up to a certain point, development was very similar in all metrics to the non-interactive model, i.e. Discrimination increased, and mapping quality improved. There was a turning point, however, from which Discrimination started to drop, and simultaneously a dip occurred in mapping performance. Close inspection of the training progress shows that this turning point coincided with the point at which $\lambda = .5$, i.e. where direct and indirect activation were weighted equally in calculating the joint activation. The outcome of the reorganization process was the tightening of category clusters, or categorical perception, in both domains.

The outcome observed in these simulations means that the interactive learning mechanism we introduced here has the potential of accounting for the impact of labelling on category learning in infants found in experimental work.[1-3,7] The combination of enhancement and inhibition used in the present learning mechanism apparently allowed the model to weight features in a way that puts a focus on commonalities between exemplars that occurred with similar input in the other modality, whereas differences are disregarded. Tighter clusters, as in Model III, make discrimination between categories easier, and thus may allow for a more robust rejection of non-category-members. If the information present in object-label pairings that occur in the infants environment is used in a similar way by the infants, then the facilitation of categorization in the presence of labels may be due to the formation of tighter category clusters. The model thus provides a plausible explanation for the looking behavior observed in experimental work with infants, where infants had a stronger novelty preference after learning a category in the presence of labels. An implication of this is that verbal labels may not just act as features similar to other visual features.[17] By contrast, the fact that labels are provided in a different modality from the remaining object information may be precisely what enables the facilitation effect.

Acknowledgements

This work was supported by European Commission Grant MESTCT-2005-020725 and ESRC Grant RES-000-22-3394.

References

1. S. Waxman and D. Markow, *Cognitive Psychology* **29**, 257 (1995).
2. A. Fulkerson and S. Waxman, *Cognition* **105**, 218 (2007).
3. A. Ferry, S. Hespos and S. Waxman, *Child Development* **81**, 472 (2010).
4. C. Robinson and V. Sloutsky, *Infancy* **11**, 233 (2007).
5. K. Plunkett, J. Hu and L. Cohen, *Cognition* **106**, 665 (2008).
6. N. Althaus and G. Westermann. Paper presented at the British Psychological Society Developmental Section Conference, Goldsmiths College, London, (2010).
7. N. Althaus and D. Mareschal. Poster presented at the XVIIth International Conference on Infant Studies, Baltimore, Maryland, (2010).
8. D. Roy and A. Pentland, *Cognitive Science* **26**, 113 (2002).
9. C. Yu, *Connection Science* **17**, 381 (2005).
10. C. Yu, D. Ballard and R. Aslin, *Cognitive Science* **29**, 961 (2005).
11. P. Schyns, *Cognitive Science* **15**, 461 (1991).
12. K. Plunkett, C. Sinha, M. Møller and O. Strandsby, *Connection Science* **4**, 293 (1992).
13. P. Li, I. Farkas and B. MacWhinney, *Neural Networks* **17**, 1345 (2004).
14. G. Carpenter and S. Grossberg, Adaptive resonance theory, in *The Handbook of Brain Theory and Neural Networks*, ed. M. Arbib (Cambridge,MA: MIT Press, 2003)

15. P. Li, X. Zhao and B. MacWhinney, *Cognitive Science* **31**, 581 (2007).
16. J. Mayor and K. Plunkett, *Psychological Review* **117**, 1 (2010).
17. V. Gliozzi, J. Mayor, J. Hu and K. Plunkett, *Cognitive Science* **33**, 709 (2009).
18. A. Plebe, M. Mazzone and V. D. L. Cruz, *Cognitive Computing* **2**, 217 (2010).
19. T. Kohonen, *Biological Cybernetics* **43**, 59 (1982).
20. D. Mareschal, R. French and P. Quinn, *Developmental Psychology* **36**, 635 (2000).
21. R. M. French, D. Mareschal, M. Mermillod and P. C. Quinn, *Journal of Experimental Psychology: General* **133**, 382 (2004).
22. D. Mareschal, D. Powell and A. Volein, *Journal of Experimental Child Psychology* **86**, 87 (2003).
23. D. P. W. Ellis, PLP and RASTA (and MFCC, and inversion) in Matlab (2005), http://www.ee.columbia.edu/ dpwe/resources/matlab/rastamat/.
24. F. Richardson and M. Thomas, *Developmental Science* **11**, 371 (2008).

FROM MOTHERESE TO ONE-WORD AND TWO-WORD CHILD LANGUAGE: A MULTIMODAL TEMPORAL CONNECTIONIST MODEL

ABEL NYAMAPFENE

College of Engineering, Mathematic and Physical Sciences, University of Exeter
North Park Rd, Exeter EX4 4QF, UK

In this paper Hebbian based cross-situational learning is incorporated into a temporal hypermap to enable it to model the acquisition of early child language from child directed speech (CDS). This model exhibits the same level of performance as an earlier non-temporal, localist, Hebbian based cross-situational model by the same author when recalling one-word utterances from associated extralinguistic information. However, the performance of the temporal model is markedly better than the non-temporal model when required to generate appropriate one-word utterances when fed with the extralinguistic information of multi-word utterances in the training corpus. Given that cognitive processes such as child language acquisition are inherently temporal in nature, this suggests that incorporating temporal processing in cognitive models may improve the performance of these models.

1. Introduction

It is generally accepted that child language acquisition normally takes place in the context of social interaction between a child and its caregivers[1]. Child language acquisition is a multimodal task in which different modalities such as perceptual entities, communicative intentions, and speech, are inextricably linked[2,3]. During the process of child language acquisition, the child learns to determine the entities the caregiver is speaking about, the conceptual relations between the objects in the environment as well as the caregiver's communicative intentions and associates these with the linguistic words uttered by the caregiver.

Within the context of social interaction, there are several factors that may help to facilitate the process of child language acquisition. For instance, early conversations between the infant and caregiver are normally restricted to familiar settings and to objects that are present thereby simplifying the process of word-meaning mapping[4]. Secondly, caregivers tend to speak to infants using simple, grammatically correct, short sentences that deal with the child's interests: actions, objects, people and events that are present in the 'here' and 'now'[1,2].

Thirdly, caregivers generally communicate with infants using a specially articulated version of normal speech known as "child directed speech" (CDS) or "motherese"[4,5].

CDS possesses features that may help the child to segment speech into words, phrases and sentences[1]. For instance, single-word utterances are quite frequent, and words are articulated clearly and slowly with distinct pauses between sentences. In addition, caregivers tend to repeat isolated phrases and words following the complete utterance. Consequently, CDS can be viewed as a highly specialised language with the necessary affective qualities to engage the child in language, and one which allows the child to remain focused on the provider of the input thereby maximising language learning[5].

Cross-situational learning[6], whereby infants acquire word-meaning associations by pairing individual spoken words with several co-occurring possible referents over a period of time and then statistically deciding on the most appropriate word-referent pair, has been proposed as a possible mechanism for child language acquisition[7]. Recently, a multimodal neural network that uses Hebbian learning[8] to acquire one-word child language from child directed speech (CDS) through cross-situational learning has been proposed[9]. This work improves on previous models of child language acquisition by Abidi and Ahmad[10] and Nyamapfene and Ahmad[11] in which the actual child language utterances were used to train the models. Such models seem to imply that the primary source of input for child language acquisition is the linguistic output of another child in the process of undergoing the same process. This is in contrast to the general view that the caregiver is the primary source of input during the process of child language acquisition.

In this paper the Hebbian based cross-situational learning proposed in Nyamapfene[9] has been incorporated into a multimodal temporal neural network. The result is a model that learns to acquire one-word and two-word child language from CDS in a gradual and continuous manner that emulates the process of child language acquisition in infants in the natural setting. The temporal neural network that has been used in this work is the temporal hypermap, a self-organising neural network that learns and recalls multiple sequences[12].

The transition of child language from the one-word stage to the two-word stage has previously been simulated using a gated multi-net architecture comprising a modified counterpropagation network and a temporal hypermap[13]. The modified counterpropagation network simulated child language at the one-word stage whilst the temporal hypermap simulated child language at the two-word stage. For each input encoding an event the child wished to speak about, the transition from one-word utterance to two-word utterance was determined probabilistically, with the likelihood for such a transition increasing as training progressed. Inhibitory links from the temporal hypermap to the counterpropagation network suppressed the counterpropagation network output whenever the temporal hypermap was active. This ensured that only one network was able to generate an output at any given instance.

The use of separate networks for the one-word stage and the two-word stage in the gated multi-net model suggests that these two stages are implemented by different brain networks in the developing child. However in the physical brain, the same set of neural networks is responsible for language processing. As the child's brain undergoes development, the networks implementing language processing progressively become better able to handle more complex language processing, hence the development from the one-word language stage to the two-word language stage. Since language is both multimodal and temporal, this developmental process is better modelled by multimodal temporal neural network architectures capable of adapting their structure to suit the structural and behavioural changes in the developmental data. The work reported in this paper extends the temporal hypermap to come up with a neural network meeting these requirements.

The rest of this paper is organised as follows: In the next section a brief overview of the Hebbian-based cross-situational model of child language acquisition from CDS is given. This is then followed by a review of the temporal hypermap in Section 3. In Section 4, the cross-situational concepts from the one-word child language acquisition model are combined with the temporal properties of the temporal hypermap to come up with a temporal neural network model that learns to acquire one-word and two-word child language from CDS. A brief overview of the CDS simulation data is also given. Section 5 discusses the simulations undertaken, including an analysis of the results of the simulations. Finally the paper concludes by summing up the contributions of the model to early child language research, and reveals ongoing work to further improve the model.

2. The One-Word Child Language Acquisition Model

As has been pointed out, during the process of child language acquisition, the child learns to determine the modal components of a caregiver's speech. These include the entities the caregiver is speaking about, the conceptual relations between the objects in the environment and the caregiver's communicative intentions. Nyamapfene[9] uses the term "extralinguistic components" to refer to the non-linguistic modal components of CDS speech. During this process, the child also learns to associate these modal components with the actual linguistic utterances made by the caregiver. For instance, the CDS utterance "more" made by the caregiver when giving the child an additional cookie may be analysed as follows: the utterance "more" is the actual spoken word; the communicative intention is "comment"; and the conceptual relation is "object recurrence". The actors in this scenario may be perceived to be the caregiver and the child, whilst the cookie is the object of the utterance. At a minimum, therefore, five sets of nodes are required in a neural model of child language acquisition, namely spoken word nodes, actor nodes, object nodes, conceptual relation nodes and communicative intention nodes.

Figure 1 shows the Hebbian-based cross-situational model of child language acquisition presented in Nyamapfene[9]. In this model Hebbian learning is used to update the weights between the activated modal nodes. The extent to which individual words in each CDS utterance co-occur with actors, objects, conceptual relations and inferred communicative intentions is established in an automatic, self-organising manner. The Hebbian weights are updated in accordance with the equation[14,15]:

$$\Delta w_{ij} = \varepsilon a_j \left(a_i - w_{ij} \right)$$

(1)

where Δw_{ij} denotes the change in weight from unit i to unit j, a_i and a_j denote the activation levels of units i and j respectively, and ε denotes the learning rate.

The term $\left(a_i - w_{ij} \right)$ ensures that weights do not grow without bound, thereby minimising the possibility of weight saturation. Eq.1 captures the conditional probability that a sending end node was active given that the receiving node was active[14,15] , i.e.

$$w_{ij} = P(a_i / a_j)$$

(2)

Consequently, whenever a given receiving node j is active, if a sending unit i also tends to be active, the interconnecting weight will tend to be high. In contrast, whenever a given receiving unit is active, if a sending node tends not to be active, the interconnecting weight between the two will tend to be low. In this way, the Hebbian learning yields weights that reflect conditional probabilities of activities, and in turn yield interconnecting weights that represent correlations in the environment. As reported in Nyamapfene[9], this model was able to recall virtually all the one-word utterances on which it had been trained (32 out of 33 utterances). However, the model could only generate appropriate one-word utterances in only 57 of the 84 extralinguistic data items associated with multi-word CDS utterances in the training dataset. In general a word may be used in more than one CDS utterance. This causes it to have a higher activation than more appropriate words used in the actual multi-word CDS utterance on which the model has been trained. A possible solution to this problem would be to restrict the search space for the winning word to the multi-word CDS sequences with the highest activation. This therefore requires the model to be based on a temporal neural network capable of sequential processing.

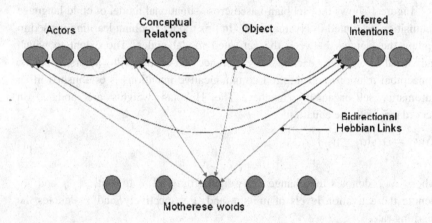

Fig. 1. The Hebbian-based cross-situational model of child language acquisition presented in Hebb[8]

3. The Temporal Hypermap

The temporal hypermap is a self-organising neural network that learns and recalls multiple sequences[12]. As shown in Figure 2, the temporal hypermap consists of a map whose neurons each have two sets of weights - context weights and pattern weights. Pattern weights encode sequence components whilst context weights encode the sequence identity. Associated with each neuron is a short term memory mechanism comprising of a tapped delay line and threshold logic units whose purpose is to encode the time varying context of the sequence component encoded by the neuron. Consecutive neurons in a sequence are linked to each other through Hebbian weights, and inhibitory links extend from each neuron to all the other neurons coming after it in the same sequence. The

Hebbian links preserve temporal order when spreading activation is used to recall a sequence whilst the inhibitory links preserve temporal order when fixed context information is used to recall an entire sequence.

A sequence is stored by applying its components to the temporal hypermap in their correct temporal order. Each temporal hypermap neuron encodes exactly one sequence item. This prevents ambiguity the retrieval of sequences in cases where identical pattern vectors are repeated in the same sequence or occur in other sequences. Each neuron has a responsibility variable that is set to one when the neuron is assigned to a sequence component; otherwise it remains reset at zero. When an input is applied, only those neurons with responsibility variables equal to zero are allowed to compete.

A winner-take-all mechanism is used to assign each sequence component to a free neuron as follows: On applying the context and weight vectors of a sequence component to the temporal hypermap, the network computes the context distances and pattern distances of all the unassigned neurons, i.e. those neurons in which the responsibility factor is set to zero. The context distance for a neuron is the Euclidean distance between the neuron's context weight vector and the input component context vector, whilst the pattern distance is the Euclidean distance between the neuron's pattern weight vector and the input component pattern vector. The product of these two distances gives the contextually weighted pattern distance for the neuron. The neuron with the smallest contextually weighted pattern distance is selected as the winner, and its context and pattern weights are set equal to the context and pattern vectors of the input sequence item respectively.

The inhibitory scheme for preserving temporal order during sequence recall through fixed context information operates as follows: When a context vector identifying a stored sequence is applied to the network, all the neurons belonging to the sequence are selected as winners. However, because of the inhibitory links, only the first neuron in the sequence is activated since it is the only one receiving no inhibitory signals from other neurons. In the next time-step when this neuron is deactivated, its inhibitory effect on all the other neurons is removed. The next neuron in the sequence is then activated since there is no longer any signal inhibiting it. This process of neuron activation and deactivation is repeated across the network, and in this way the sequence is reproduced in its correct temporal order. The inhibitory scheme is implemented as follows: When encoding a sequence item, all the neurons that have been used to encode previous components of the sequence – i.e. those neurons whose responsibility variable is set to one and whose context weight vectors match the sequence's context vector - extend inhibitory links to the current winning neuron. The lateral

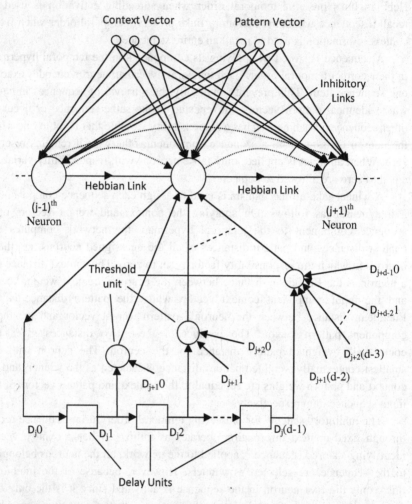

Fig 2. Temporal Hypermap Neuron and links to adjacent neurons. The current neuron is referred to by the subscript j, whilst the next neuron in the sequence is referred to by the subscript j+1, and the immediately prior neuron is referred to by the subscript j-1.

Hebbian weights between consecutive neurons in a sequence are set to a weight value of one using one-shot coding. Lateral weights between non-consecutive neurons are maintained at a value of zero. Spreading activation enables a sequence to be recalled beginning from a currently selected sequence item up to the end of the sequence as follows: Once a sequence item has been retrieved, the neuron is deactivated and generates a pulse which activates the next neuron via the unidirectional Hebbian connection. This process is repeated for each subsequent neuron in the sequence until the final neuron.

Each neuron has a tapped delay line whose length is set to one less the degree of the network. For instance, if the degree of the network is d, then each neuron will have a delay line with $d-1$ delay units. Each time an input pattern matches the pattern vector of a neuron, the neuron in question generates a pulse which is applied to the tapped delay line. This pulse propagates along the delay line for $d-1$ time-steps, after which it is cleared out of the delay line.

At the output of each delay unit is a tap that feeds into a threshold logic unit. There is one threshold logic unit for each delay tap position. As seen in Figure 1, the inputs to each threshold logic unit are the output of the tap position to which it is connected on its neuron's delay line as well as all the simultaneously active tap positions on later neurons in the sequence. For instance, the threshold logic unit connected to the output of the first delay unit in a neuron will also receive as input the non-delayed output of the next neuron in the sequence; the threshold unit connected to the output of the second delay unit on a neuron will have three inputs, namely the output of the second delay unit on the neuron, the output of the first delay output of the next neuron in the sequence, and finally the output of the second delay unit of the third consecutive neuron in the sequence.

The threshold level of each threshold logic unit is set equal to the number of inputs connected to the logic unit, which is one more than the delay tap position to which it is connected. In addition, the output of each threshold logic unit is scaled to give an output activation value equal to its threshold level. Consequently, when two or more threshold logic units are simultaneously activated in the temporal hypermap, the threshold logic unit with the highest threshold level wins the competition.

With regard to the use of partial subsequences to prompt the recall of a stored sequence, the winning threshold logic unit is the one encoding the shortest subsequence long enough to distinguish between stored sequence items responding to the inputted subsequence. When this threshold logic unit fires, its associated neuron also fires and generates an output and the rest of the sequence is then generated through spreading activation by means of the lateral Hebbian links.

4. The Temporal Hypermap Model of Child Language Acquisition from CDS

Bloom[3] suggests that when an infant hears a word (and perhaps a larger speech unit like a phrase or sentence), the word is entered in memory along with other perceptual and personal data that include the persons, objects, actions and relationships encountered during the speech episode. In addition, it is now generally accepted by child language researchers that single word utterances at the one-word stage convey a child's communicative intentions regarding the persons, objects and events in the child's environment, and the conceptual relationships between them[2,3].

At the two-word stage children appear to determine the most important words in a sentence and, almost all of the time, use them in the same order as an adult would[16]. In addition, as can be deduced from Brown's set of basic semantic relations[17], it appears that children at the two-word stage use word utterances for pretty much the same reasons and under almost the same circumstances as infants at the one word stage. Consequently, the five sets of nodes, namely spoken word nodes, actor nodes, object nodes, conceptual relation nodes and communicative intention nodes suffice to model both one-word and two-word child language acquisition.

4.1. *Temporal Hypermap Model Architecture*

The temporal hypermap has been modified as illustrated in Figure 3 to enable it to model the acquisition of child language from CDS. In the modified temporal hypermap, the pattern and context node vectors are replaced by spoken word, actor, object, conceptual relation and communicative intention modal vectors. An additional node vector, the "CDS utterance ID" vector has been incorporated to distinguish between different CDS utterances that have the same extralinguistic modal components.

After training, when extralinguistic information, excluding the CDS utterance ID, is applied to the temporal hypermap, it responds with an utterance, which corresponds to part or all of the CDS sequence associated with the inputted extralingusitic information. This is done through a two-stage competitive process. Given the extralinguistic information, the sequence with the highest activation response is identified. In this model, the activation response of a sequence to contextual information is defined as the average of all the individual activation of all the words in the sequence.

Once the sequence has been determined then the words making up the sequence are ranked in accordance with their individual activations. In one word utterance simulation, the word with the highest activation in the selected sequence is the one which is uttered. For two-word utterance simulation, the two words with the highest activation in the selected sequence are the words that are uttered. These words are uttered in accordance to their temporal order in the sequence.

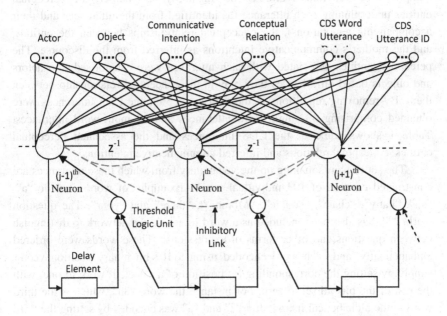

Fig. 3. Segment of a temporal hypermap that has been modified to enable it to model early child language acquisition from CDS - Details of the short-term memory mechanism (comprising the delay elements and threshold logic units) have been omitted for the sake of clarity.

4.2. Simulation Data

The data set used in the simulations described in this paper is derived from the child language acquisition data in the Bloom 1973 corpus[3]. This corpus is found in the Child Language Data Exchange System (CHILDES) corpora[18]. This is the same data used to simulate the model for one-word child language acquisition using CDS as input. Using the same dataset to test the temporal hypermap model of child language acquisition enables its performance at the one-word stage to be compared to the Hebbian based cross-situational model.

4.2.1. *Child-Directed Speech (CDS) Training Data*

The data set for training the network model and assessing its ability to generate child language utterances is taken from the earliest sample in the Bloom 1973 corpus, i.e. the sample taken at age "1 year 4 months and 21 days". This dataset comprises 195 utterances directed at Alison by her mother, the perceptual entities underpinning each utterance (as identified from the utterances and their accompanying annotations), the conceptual relationships between the entities, and the mother's communicative intentions as inferred from the discourse. The perceptual entities associated with each utterance were categorised into actors and objects based on the roles they play in the conceptual relationship between them. By removing repetitions in the dataset, 117 unique CDS utterances were obtained comprising 33 single word utterances and 84 multi-word utterances. Table 1 shows some of the CDS utterances and the associated perceptual entities, conceptual relations and inferred communicative intentions.

The set of words making up the vocabulary from which these utterances are constructed consists of 103 individual words. Examples of words include "a", "ah", "baby", "chair", "cookie", "Mommy", "there" and "your". The question mark, "?", has also been included as a word to enable the network to distinguish between questions and other forms of expressions. These words were ordered alphabetically, and each word encoded using a 103-bit binary position vector simply by setting the corresponding bit position of a selected word to one, with the rest of the bits all set to zero. For instance the word "ah", which is the third word in the alphabetical listing after "?" and "a" was encoded by setting the third bit of the 103-bit binary position vector to one with the rest of the bits all set to zero.

Thirty four entities making up the objects and actors were identified and the same positional coding used to encode spoken words was used to identify each entity. The same entity was used to represent both its singular and its plural form. For instance, the entity "cookie" is used to encode both a single cookie and multiple cookies. Similarly, thirty six conceptual relationships and fourteen communicative intentions were identified in the dataset, and these were encoded using the same positional coding scheme as for the word utterances and entities.

During training the CDS utterances, together with their associated extralinguistic information and CDS utterance identity vectors are simultaneously applied to the network. Only one pass is made through the dataset, beginning with the earliest recorded CDS utterance data to the most recent CDS utterance data. In this way the model is presented with the CDS data in much the same way as the child Alison encountered it.

Table 1. Some CDS Utterances from the Bloom 1973 Corpus along with their associated extralinguistic information

CDS Utterance	Actor	Object	Conceptual Relation	Communicative Intention
Up.	Alison	chair	person gets on chair	Request
There are no more cookies.	cookies	-	object disappearance	comment
Here's a cookie for you.	Cookie	Alison	give object to person	comment
Should we cover it up?	Alison and Mommy	jar	jar lid covers jar	Request
Chair .	chair	-	is-a	naming
Gone.	cookies	-	Object(s) disappearance	comment
The cookies are gone.	cookies	-	Object(s) disappearance	comment
There.	Top of chair	-	locate at a distance	Place location

5. Results and Discussion

This section presents a comparative assessment of the performance of the temporal hypermap model against the performance of the Hebbian-based cross-situational model. The emphasis of the discussion is on the differences in performance of the two models. The rationale for this is that these differences may shed light on the process of child language acquisition and help to further improve the modelling task.

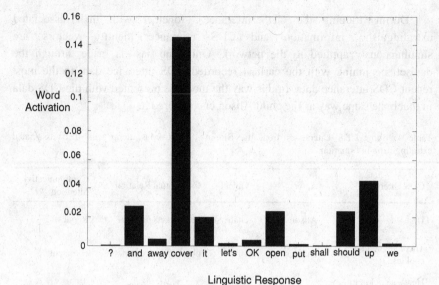

Fig. 4. Activation plot for all the words that responded with non-zero activation to the extralinguistic information comprising: communicative intention – *comment*, conceptual relation – *lid covers jar*, actors – *Alison and mom*, objects – *lid and jar*.

5.1. *Response of the Two Models to CDS Extralinguistic Data*

Both the temporal hypermap model and the Hebbian-based cross-situational model successfully recall each of the 33 single word CDS utterances in the training data. For both models, 32 of the utterances match exactly with the expected output. For instance, for the single word CDS input "up", each model correctly responds with the output "up". In the 33rd response, both models respond with "fell" instead of the expected word "down" when prompted with the extralinguistic information for describing a doll falling down from the chair.

Whilst the word "down" had been used in various other situations, the word "fell" had only been used in this particular instance. This is when Alison's mother is drawing Alison's attention to the fact that her doll has fallen from the chair on which it was placed to the ground. Alison's mother makes this sequence of four utterances, possibly accompanied by appropriate gestures:

1. Hey, look!
2. Your baby
3. Fell down
4. Down

In the output of both models, the word "fell" had the highest individual word activation (0.15654) and the word "down" had the second highest word activation (0.053253). In the case of the temporal hypermap model, the utterance "Fell down" had the highest sequence activation (0.10490) against a sequence activation of 0.053253 for "down". This is possibly due to the fact that whilst the word "down" had occurred in various other instances, the word "fell" had only occurred in this situation, and hence was viewed by both models as providing better discrimination. When considering the two-word output it is seen that the utterance "Fell down" is the most appropriate for the given extralinguistic information. Hence in this instance the temporal hypermap model successfully generates appropriate one-word and two-word utterances.

In the remaining 84 extra-linguistic inputs with multi-word CDS utterances, the Hebbian-based cross-situational model manages to generate 57 one-word utterances that may be regarded as equivalent, in a semantic sense, to the associated multi-word CDS expressions. For the remaining 27 extra-linguistic inputs the network generates single-word utterances that are difficult to classify as having the same meaning as the associated CDS multi-word utterances. In contrast, the temporal hypermap model manages to generate 64 one-word utterances that may be regarded as semantically equivalent to the associated multi-word CDS expressions with 20 failures. With regard to the generation of equivalent two-word utterances, the temporal hypermap model successfully generates 77 appropriate two-word utterances in their correct word order. This suggests that the two step algorithm used in the temporal hypermap model, whereby the word utterance with the highest activation is first determined through the winner take all (WTA) mechanism followed by the ranking of the words making up the utterance, may be more biased towards the recall of multi-word utterances than it is towards single word utterances.

An example of a linguistic response that can be regarded as appropriate is when the model in question simulates Alison's response to extra-linguistic response associated with CDS utterances made as Alison and her mother covered a jar with its lid. In this case, the extra-linguistic information presented to the network is as follows: communicative intention – *comment*, conceptual relation – *lid covers jar*, actors – *Alison and mom*, objects – *lid and jar*. Both models respond to this extra-linguistic information with the single word 'cover' - i.e. the word 'cover' gives the highest output activation to this extra-linguistic information. Although Alison never uses the word "cover" in her one-word utterances in the corpus, the word "cover" seems to be an appropriate one-word equivalent for the corresponding multi-word CDS expression: 'OK, let's cover it

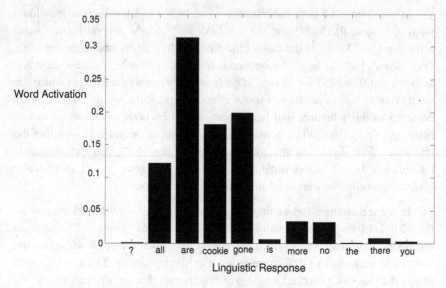

Fig. 5. Activation plot for all the words that responded with non-zero activation to the extralinguistic information comprising: communicative intention – *comment*, conceptual relation – *object disappearance*, actors – *cookies*, objects – *none*.

up and put it away' which emerges as the multi-word utterance with the highest activation in the temporal hypermap model.

Figure 4 shows all the words in the model that responded with non-zero activation to the extralinguistic information comprising: communicative intention – *comment*, conceptual relation – *lid covers jar*, actors – *Alison and mom*, objects – *lid and jar*. The two-word sequence generated by the temporal hypermap model is "cover up" which is appropriate.

An example of when the temporal hypermap model gives an appropriate one-word utterance response whilst the one-word child language acquisition model gives a one word utterance that that may be regarded as inappropriate is when extralinguistic information associated with CDS utterance "there are no more cookies" is presented to both models. The extra-linguistic information for this CDS utterance is: communicative intention – *comment*, conceptual relation – *object disappearance*, actors – *cookies*, objects – *none*. The temporal hypermap model responds to this extralinguistic information with the single word "gone" whilst the one-word child language acquisition model responds with the utterance 'are'.

Figure 5 shows all the words in the model that responded with non-zero activation to the extralinguistic information comprising: communicative intention – *comment*, conceptual relation – *object disappearance*, actors – *cookies*, objects – *none*. From Alison's one-word utterances, the correct response should have been 'gone', which is the second highest activation after 'are'. In the temporal hypermap model the utterance "gone" has the highest activation (0.1995) followed by the utterance "there are no more cookies" (0.1294). In this instance, it is apparent that the two step algorithm whereby the word utterance with the highest activation is first determined through the winner take all (WTA) mechanism followed by the ranking of the words making up the utterance performs better than the algorithm used by the one-word child language acquisition model which only uses the WTA mechanism to determine the word with the highest activation.

6. Conclusion and Future Work

In this paper a multimodal temporal neural network that learns through Hebbian learning has been used to model the acquisition of early child language from child directed speech (CDS) through cross-situational learning. When recalling one-word utterances, this multimodal temporal neural network model exhibits the same level of performance as the non-temporal Hebbian-based cross-situational model of one-word child language acquisition discussed in Nyamapfene[9]. However, the performance of the temporal model is markedly better than the non-temporal model when required to generate appropriate one-word utterances in place of multi-word utterances in the training corpus. This suggests that incorporating temporal processing in cognitive models may improve the performance of these models. This is an intuitive result given the inherent temporal nature of cognitive processes like child language acquisition. However, more experimental work still needs to be carried out to establish the validity of the model as a viable proof-of-concept cognitive model.

Currently, the ability of the temporal hypermap model of child language acquisition to generate appropriate two-word utterances given extralinguistic information is being assessed against typical two-word child utterances in the Bloom 1973 corpus. The model presented in this paper is localist in nature, with data being encoded using a simple positional binary encoding scheme. Although localist coding simplifies model design, it may lead to a model with poor generalisation. Consequently, an equivalent model based on distributed representation is currently being investigated.

References

1. P.A. de Villliers and J.G. de Villliers, *Early Language* (Havard University Press, Cambridge, 1979).
2. M. Small, *Cognitive Development* (San Diego: Harcourt Brace Jovanovich, 1990).
3. L. Bloom, *One word at a time: The use of single-word utterances before syntax* (The Hague: Mouton, 1973).
4. P.F. Dominey and C. Dodane, *Journal of Neurolinguistics,* **17**, 121(2004)
5. P. Matychuk, *Language Sciences* **27**, 301(2005).
6. J. M. Siskind, *Cognition* **61**, 39 (1996).
7. S. Pinker, *Learnability and cognition* (Cambridge, MA: MIT Press, 1989).
8. D.O. Hebb, *The Organisation of Behavior: A Neuropsychological Theory* (New York: Wiley, 1949).
9. A. Nyamapfene, *Connectionist Models of Behavior and Cognition II: Proceedings of the 11th Neural Computation and Psychology Workshop* (2009).
10. S. Abidi and K. Ahmad, *Journal of Information Science and Engineering* 13, 235 (1997).
11. A. Nyamapfene and K. Ahmad, *Proc. 20th IJCNN International Joint Conference on Neural Networks*, 783 (2007).
12. A. Nyamapfene, *International Journal of Computers and Applications*, 32, 2 (2010).
13. A. Nyamapfene and K. Ahmad, *Proc. IJCNN International Joint Conference on Neural Networks*, 1427 (2006).
14. D. E. Rumelhart and D. Zipser, Feature discovery by competitive learning. In *Parallel Distributed Processing: Explorations in the Microstructure of cognition, Volume 1: Foundations*, ed. D. E., Rumelhart and J. L. McClelland, and the PDP Research Group (Cambridge, MA: MIT Press, 1986).
15. Y. Munakata and J. Pfaffly, *Developmental Science* **7**, 141 (2004).
16. L.R. Gleitman. and E.L. Newport, The Invention of Language by Children: Environmental and Biological Influences on the Acquisition Language. In *Language: An Invitation to Cognitive Science*, ed. L.R. Gleitman and M Liberman (Cambridge, MA: MIT Press, 1995).
17. R. Brown, *A First Language: the early stages* (London: George Allen and Unwin, 1973).
18. B. MacWhinney, *The CHILDES project: Tools for Analyzing Talk.* 3rd edition (Mahwah, NJ: Lawrence Erlbaum Associates, 2000).

LEARNING THE VISUAL WORD CODE

T. HANNAGAN* and J. GRAINGER

Laboratoire de Psychologie Cognitive, Aix-Marseille University and CNRS,
Marseille, 13331, France
* E-mail: thom.hannagan@gmail.com
http://www.univ-provence.fr/gsite/document.php?project=lpc

Visual words are peculiar cognitive entities living under several apparently conflicting requirements. Although behavioural studies have taught us just how flexible visual word representations are in the brain, the trivial fact that we can distinguish between anagrams demands that these representations somehow carry letter order. In this chapter we present a connectionist network developed so as to test a simple hypothesis on the character of the orthographic code: that its flexibility is a by-product of location invariance. We then illustrate a more explanatory aspect of the modelling approach to gain some insights into the kind of code used by this location invariant network -how it actually keeps track of letter order. Implications for the field of visual word recognition and future research are discussed.

1. How do we represent words (and how can we know)?

How do we recognise visual words? From the Editor's foreword, one can appreciate that the modelling of visual processes —be it applied to generic object recognition or to face recognition— is an important theme in this volume. One window into visual representations has been provided by invariance. Since the mirror image of e.g. a cup is still a cup, it is reasonable to expect that neural representations for generic objects should be invariant with respect to mirror transformation —and for that matter also with respect to translation and rotation. Experimental studies have shown that this ideal expectation must be mitigated by our statistical experience of the environment. For instance turning upside-down an object that has a preferred side up hinders recognition, and the effect is even more pronounced for faces.[?] Invariance experiments have also manipulated constituent features, pointing in the case of faces to the importance of encoding not only local features, but also the global configuration between them.

Although these results can throw lights on the neural representations of objects and faces, visual words define a category of objects that further distinguishes itself at least in two immediate respects. For one thing in alphabetic languages words are built out of distinct and often disconnected letters which, for another, define an ordered set —e.g. anagrams "triangle" and "relating" have different meanings. Indeed visual words live at the intersection of different realms. They must carry order to provide a pathway to phonology and pronunciation, which is a sequential process, but are nevertheless visually displayed and usually recognised from a single ocular saccade [a],[?] in what appears to be a parallel process —although this idea has been challenged.[?]

What can invariance tell us about words? First, mirror images and rotations of word features are not generally invariant.—consider letters "b" and "d", or "p" and "q". Because children come to read already expert on object recognition, these letters basically force the system to selectively unlearn some mirror and rotation symmetries so as to maintain separate representations. Indeed there is ample evidence that young writers make many mirror errors at the letter and even at the word level.[?] In fact although this situation improves with experience, recent priming studies suggest that even the skilled reader still uses a remarkably late and loose discrimination strategy for these letters.[?] Brain imaging studies have also been recently carried out with rotated words in the plane.[?] Here the evidence is that rotation severely disrupts what is thought to be a parallel reading pathway of expert readers, subserved by an occipito-temporal region known as the Visual Word Form Area, and forcing a serial reading strategy that recruits a more dorsal pathway in the intraparietal cortex. It therefore appears that mirror and rotation invariance are limited as far as word representations are concerned, although perhaps less so at the letter level.

But invariance also plays a role in a more general issue that has been called the "hard problem" of visual word recognition: how to transform retinal imprints of letters to a word-centered orthographic code that carries position-in-word information.[?] In other words, how does the system achieve location (translation) invariance without losing information about letter order? One hypothesis put forward by Refs. [?] and [?] which is congruent with some of the previously reviewed findings for face recognition,

---

[a] For skilled readers and words of up to seven letters.

is that this is achieved through the encoding of the global configuration between letters. The simplest global configuration strategy would consist in keeping track, for every letter, of its position relative to all others. At an extreme this could be achieved simply by registering whether a letter stands left or right of another. The global configuration code for the word TIME might then simply consist of a set of statements such as T is on the left of I, T is on the left of M, T is on the left of E, ..., M is on the left of E. In a connectionist model, this would amount to defining units that would activate only when such letters are present in the correct order. This is known as the Open-Bigrams scheme.

Open-Bigrams promise to explain another phenomenon: the flexibility of the orthographic code. In recent years masked priming experiments have revealed that some transformations of a letter string (say GARDEN) that would have been commonly regarded as major disruptions, such as repeated deletions (GRDN), insertions (GARXXXDEN) or transpositions (GAE-DRN), seem in fact to produce very similar codes (see Ref. ? for a recent survey and modelling study). The web of relationships defined by Open-Bigrams would possess the right properties to account for masked priming data, as severe letter disruptions would still leave large parts of the web relatively unchanged. This is especially true when open-bigrams are implemented in a distributed way.[?] Although other schemes such as the overlap model or spatial coding can also explain these results, open-bigrams have received support from several recent brain studies. Neurons whose activities correlate with bigram frequency have been directly observed[b],[?] and there is a well-known area in the brain devoted to string encoding, the Visual Word Form Area,[?] which appears to be organised in a hierarchy involving an open-bigram level.[?]

In summary the orthographic code lives under tight, almost conflicting requirements: it must solve location invariance without losing letter order, and at the same time it should exhibit the distinct pattern of flexibility revealed by priming experiments. As we have seen one hypothesis is that the same scheme that solves location invariance would naturally produce flexibility —in other words flexibility would be a by-product of location invariance. In this paper we will first report how we used the connectionist modelling approach to test this hypothesis —an exploratory purpose, see

---

[b]Although these were not tested against open-bigram frequencies

Ref. ?. We will then describe another modelling endeavour: understanding the scheme that has been found by the network in order to solve location invariance —an explanatory purpose. Finally we will indicate future directions in our attempts at breaking the orthographic code.

2. Does location invariance imply flexibility?

Given its significance in cognition generally speaking, it should come as no surprise to the reader that invariance also has a fine history in connectionist modelling, playing a crucial role almost from the inception of the field.

Indeed invariance was first introduced as an argument against neural computation. In Minsky and Papert's famous Perceptron book,[?] the so-called "group invariance theorem" was instrumental in order to prove that perceptrons could not solve the X-or problem. This argument was later turned on this head to establish sufficient conditions on a feedforward network's connectivity that could guarantee any kind of invariance, for example invariance with respect to location.[?] Meanwhile the advent of the back-propagation algorithm[?] made it possible to address the question of how invariance could actually be learned in a multi-layered network: in particular Hinton showed that this learning algorithm could achieve satisfactory performances on a location invariance task.[?] Modified learning algorithms such as Tanprop[?] were also developed to enforce invariance to location or to any arbitrary transformation, although these algorithms required explicit prior knowledge of the invariant patterns to be learned. Other researchers investigated how neural networks could learn to self-organise in order to achieve invariance.[?]

Recently and quite relevant to the present work, Shillcock and Monaghan trained a backpropagation network to map location-specific letters into a location independent representation of the same letters.[?] For example, the network would learn to associate patterns WITH##, #WITH# and ##WITH (in which # represent blanks) to the common output WITH coded as a given letter identity at each of four possible positions (slot-coding).

The network shown in Figure 1 (top) represents an adaptation of Shillcock and Monaghan's modelling strategy. Dandurand *et al* trained a standard multi-layer perceptron network to map location-specific letter identi-

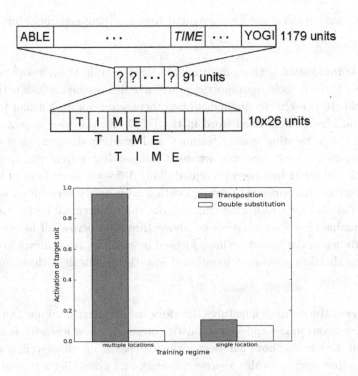

Fig. 1. Top: The feedforward network of Dandurand *et al* (DGD hereafter) maps location specific letter strings to location invariant word units through a hidden layer.[?] Letter inputs and word outputs (1179 English four letter words) are coded in a localist way (one unit for one entity). Training occurs in one of two regimes: word exemplars presented at multiple locations versus at a single location. Bottom: Transposition priming simulations. The network exhibits TL priming (for e.g. output unit TIME, a positive difference between the activity elicited for TMIE and for TXYE) only when trained at multiple locations.

ties onto location-invariant word representations.[?] Letter inputs and word outputs used localist codes (e.g. one word corresponds to exactly one unit in the network). The network was entirely feed-forward and consisted of an input layer of 260 units (26 letters x 10 locations), a single hidden layer of 91 units and an output layer of 1179 units (each corresponding to one English four letter word). Presentation of word e.g. TIME at central locations 4567 was achieved by setting the corresponding units to 1, while the other remained to 0. The signal was then propagated forward along connections whose weights w_{ji} were initially set at random, and at each level every unit i computed its activity A_i in the standard way, first by summing its incoming activity $Net_i = \sum_j w_{ji} A_j$ and then applying a sigmoid function $A_i = \frac{1}{1+\exp^{-Net_i}}$.

Backpropagation with momentum was used to train the network on all 1179 words until their corresponding output units reached a 0.99 activity threshold. It is useful to distinguish here between weak and strong forms of location invariance. Each word in the DGD network was presented at every possible location during training, and training stopped when each corresponding output unit was activated independently from the location at which the input had been presented. This defines a weak form of location invariance, as opposed to strong location invariance where not all words are seen at all locations during training, but the requirement on the target unit remains that its activation be above threshold across all locations[c]. Most studies in the literature have focused on weak location invariance,[?,?] although Hinton's previously mentioned investigation dealt with strong location invariance.[?]

Some of the network's features (feedforward architecture, input/output format, lexicon) might appear unrealistic considering how feedback is ubiquitous in the brain, how our best estimates based on single-cell studies clearly argue against localist representations[d], and given that a typical English reader's lexicon numbers tens of thousands of words. But simplification is an essential part of the modelling endeavour[?,?] and these simplifications were warranted considering the research question on which the authors focused. Indeed in order to investigate whether location invariance implied flexibility, the network was trained under two different regimes: input words presented at multiple locations or at single locations.

Dandurand *et al* considered two hallmarks of the flexibility observed in skilled readers: transposed-letter priming (TL) and relative-position priming (RP). TL priming covers the finding that primes obtained by transposing two letters in the target give more facilitation than those obtained by replacing two letters.[?,?,?] RP priming is the finding that primes obtained by removing or inserting some letters in the target while maintaining relative letter order are more effective than unrelated control primes.[?,?] The results presented in Figure 1 (bottom) show the average activity obtained for all

---

[c]we thank Colin Davis for pointing out this distinction
[d]see for instance Ref.? for a short review

words in the lexicon on a transposition and double substitution (RP conditions are not reported here for lack of space). Priming in this simple network is construed as the difference of activation elicited in the target unit by the prime and the control. For instance, the network would be said to show TL priming for the word TIME if the corresponding output unit had more activity for input TMIE than for TXYE. In support of the hypothesis being tested, the network was able to reproduce TL and RP priming only in the multiple location regime (difference between left bars in Figure 1, bottom). When training occurred at a single location the facilitation obtained for TL and RP primes diminished to the level of the control (difference between right bars in Figure 1, bottom).

This result might be intuitive considering that only in the multiple location regime was the network forced to acknowledge that a given letter seen at different locations *on different occasions* can be part of the same word. But although we have gained support for the idea that location invariance implies plausible flexible coding this leaves us with essentially no information as to the kind of coding scheme the network has developed, since many of them can accommodate TL and RP priming. For instance a letter-based account such as proposed in the overlap model[7] —where letter position-in-word is encoded as a probability density function over all positions— could easily accommodate these results, as would an open-bigram scheme with its web of diadic relationships. As of today it has generally been very difficult to tease coding schemes apart on the sole grounds of experimental priming results. How then can we hope to gain insights into the inner workings of this network? The issue is particularly salient since this class of network implements what is certainly one of the simplest possible trained model of visual word recognition, and understanding how it operates would appear to be a prerequisite to the study of more plausible models.

3. What is the coding scheme used by the network?

Characterizing the nature of operations and representations in trained networks has generally been a challenge for connectionism, and backpropagation networks constitute the example par excellence. Because activity patterns produced by this algorithm are very often distributed, by definition they usually won't comply to any one-to-one unit/entity correspondence, and will put on tougher resistance to inquiry. Although it is true that connectionist models are generally more opaque than for instance probabilistic ones[?] this is not to say that we are powerless when it comes to understanding these networks, and multiple techniques have been developed along the years. In fact the kind of multilayered feedforward perceptron network we are interested in here has been under investigation for many years. It turns out that in some circumstances network knowledge can be usefully visualised,[?] or extracted as rules operating over symbols.[?] However these studies did not deal with location invariant tasks. On the other hand all previous work on location invariance in backpropagation networks aimed at characterizing network performances rather than network knowledge.[?,?,?] Therefore the way location invariance is achieved in backpropagation networks has been essentially unknown until recently, and we now present some elements of answer selected from Ref. ?.

Before that, a brief word on representations. The term can be confusing because it has been used to refer sometimes to activity patterns and sometimes to weight patterns, two fundamentally distinct objects in the standard connectionist approach.[?] The former is supported by units and boils down to a vector of numbers while the latter is supported by connections and captured in a matrix of numbers. In this chapter we use the term "representation" in the first sense —for activity patterns supported by units— and when we refer to the information encoded in the connection weight matrices we will talk of network "knowledge". It is worth noting here that the dichotomy between vectors and matrices has once been argued to be a fundamental limitation which would always put for instance the compositional nature of language beyond the reach of connectionism[?] —because language requires associations between representations (matrices) to also serve as new representations (vectors) in a higher clause. This is relevant to our study because Fodor and Pylyshyn's worry has been proved wrong in several ways, one of which goes under the name of "holographic reduced representations"[?] and plays a critical role in the understanding of the network at hand.

How is location invariance achieved in this network? To answer this question we scrutinised its hidden layer, asking which patterns emerged upon presentation of different inputs and what were their relationships.[?] First and foremost, hidden representations for words were found to be densely distributed: approximately half of the hidden units were activated above .5 for any word. One way to analyze densely distributed patterns is through clustering techniques, such as the k-means algorithm.

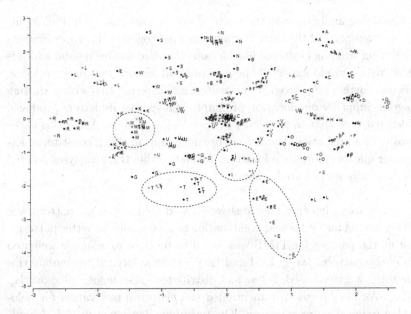

Fig. 2. Multi-dimensional scaling plot of hidden activity patterns evoked by single letter inputs seen at different locations. Letter categories are revealed by the fact that exemplars of the same letter cluster together (clusters for letter T, I, M and E are outlined). Within each cluster, letter exemplars show a proximity by location (the gradient of light-to-dark gray represents left-to-right locations).

Applying k-means to hidden representations evoked by single letter inputs across locations, we found that the network had formed well-defined letter categories during training. Of the 26 clusters identified by k-means 17 clusters were perfectly defined and the remainder had very little errors: across all clusters the average proportion of exemplars from the same letter was 98%. Indeed as the multidimentional scaling plot in Figure 2 illustrates, hidden representations for exemplars of the same letter were very similar and tightly clustered together. However these letter representations were not completely invariant with respect to location: representations for letter exemplars seen at nearby locations were more similar. This can be appreciated in Figure 2, where the gradient of gray stands for left-to-right locations, and points with the same shades of gray tend to be neighbours). We coined the term "semi-location invariant" to characterise the kind of letter representations achieved by this network.

Clustering analyses were then carried out for bigrams, with similar outcomes - exemplars of the same bigram clustered together. However bigrams seen during training clustered like bigrams that had not been seen, which is not what one would expect if the network had learned bigram knowledge. This was further supported by measurements showing that either shifting a bigram input by one location or simply transposing its letters produced hidden patterns that were equally distant to the original. Again this is the opposite of a prediction drawn from open-bigrams in which constituent letter order matters more than location. Taken together these analyses pointed to a decidedly letter-based scheme.

In fact using linear regressions we showed that any word pattern was well accounted for by a linear combination of its constituent letter patterns. That is, the pattern for TIME was found to be close to a simple weighted sum of the patterns for T, I, M and E. We then proceeded to emulate this code using a letter-based, linear and distributed code: holographic overlap coding. We have previously mentioned the historical motivation for holographic reduced representations. The technique developed in Ref. ? binds representations together using a circular convolution operator that leaves format unchanged —binding two vectors returns a vector, not a matrix. Building on a recent study that showed how this could be applied to string encoding,[?] we generated sets of letter and location vectors at random, and from then emulated the code for any arbitrary string using holographic operators. For instance the code for the word TIME seen at central locations was obtained in the following way:

$$\%\%\%TIME\%\%\% = T \otimes l_4 + I \otimes l_5 + M \otimes l_6 + E \otimes l_7 + 2\psi$$

Where l_i are location vectors with gaussian values previously generated at random but correlated by location, ψ is a vector common to all strings, and $\otimes$ is the circular convolution operator defined on two vectors X and Y by $(X \otimes Y)_i = \sum_{k=1}^{91} X_k * Y_{(i-k)mod(91)}$. Addition of the common ψ vector was prompted by the fact that in the network two unrelated strings still had non-zero similarities.

Computing similarities between string patterns generated in this way uncovered a surprisingly strong and useful correspondence with the network. The upper plot in Figure 3 shows the correlation between DGD and holographic coding on 475 string pairs drawn from various conditions (between letters, between or within words, and between anagrams). All similarities were high and regularly placed along the diagonal: first the relatively weak similarities between words, followed by within-string similarities, then by high similarities between letters seen at different locations, and finally by similarities between anagrams. DGD and holographic codes coincided very precisely, with a correlation coefficient of 0.98. In other words, the similarity between two strings is essentially the same in the network and in the code. This has practical importance because while the former consists of more than 100 000 connections and 1000+ units and was trained for numerous epochs using a complex learning algorithm, the latter only uses 26 letter vectors and 10 location vectors and does not require training.

But despite its success, this code leaves us with a very pressing interpretation issue. Indeed it is not the case that upon presentation of input e.g. TIME the network computes hidden activity patterns for T, I, M and E before summing them all together, as apparently described in the holographic code. Instead the code for TIME is produced directly from three elements: an input vector, a weight matrix (that registers connection weights between input and hidden layer), and an activation function. Any explanation for the coding scheme developed by this network should have something to say about these elements, and ideally it should articulate them explicitly.

Inspection of the input-to-hidden connection matrix pictured in Figure 3 (bottom) reveals an important fact about the network: the requirement for location invariance during training has produced a translation symmetry in network weights. That is, patterns in the matrix appear to repeat at regular intervals, every 26 locations. This translation symmetry is not entirely unexpected considering the previously mentioned theorem on invariance in feedforward networks,[?] which essentially states that under the assumption of closed layer topology, a sufficient condition for a given symmetry in network responses is that weights also follow this symmetry. But the present network does not conform to the somewhat implausible requirement on close layer topology, and it is not hand-wired. It is thus non-trivial that backpropagation has nevertheless driven network weights towards this particular solution. Crucially however, the translation symmetry achieved in this network is not perfect. This can be seen in Figure 3 (bottom), where the weight matrix is divided in 10 large chunks of 26 columns each: chunks

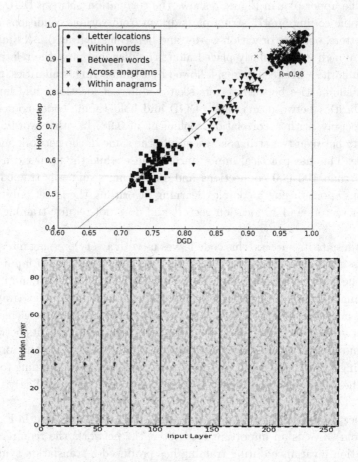

Fig. 3. Top: Network similarities (X-axis "DGD") plotted against holographic similarities (Y-axis "Holo. Overlap") on 475 pairs of letters strings. The very high correlation shows that network and codes define virtually the same topology on visual words. Bottom: Weight matrix between input and hidden units. Repeated weight patterns every 26 locations reveal that a broken translation symmetry has developed in network weights.

are not perfectly identical across the ten locations and nearby chunks are more similar than distant ones. Borrowing the term from physics where the concept has proved particularly useful, we will refer to this imperfect symmetry towards which the network has evolved as a "broken" translation symmetry in network weights.

When one further recalls that a single matrix column (one single vertical line in Figure 3, bottom) represents 91 weights from a given input unit to the hidden layer, pieces of the puzzle begin to come together. What we really do when we bind a holographic letter vector to a holographic location vector is to emulate a column in the weight matrix. Holographic letter/location bindings and matrix columns have exactly the same format: they are 91-dimensional vectors with a gaussian distribution centered on zero. The large overlap between holographic location vectors corresponds to the slightly broken symmetry in network weights. The act of summing holographic bindings together is just like computing the net input of the hidden layer: four weight columns are "enabled" by the localist input vector and activation flows to hidden units where it is summed. The holographic code for e.g. TIME is really the net input vector of hidden layer units — what we might call the hidden net vector. Although the application of a sigmoid activation function that ensues in the network is simply not captured by holographic codes, the fact that weights columns have a gaussian distribution centered on zero minimises discrepancies. This is because as a sum of weights centered on zero, most hidden net vector components are close to zero, where the sigmoid function happens to be close to linear.

With these insights in mind many phenomena in the network become clear. In particular we can now explain why exemplars of the same letter, bigram or any other string must cluster together: hidden net vectors produced by exemplars of a string are sums of more or less translated weight columns, which by virtue of the broken translation symmetry are very similar to one another. The same mechanism explains why location invariance implies flexibility: presenting a transposed prime or a relative position prime to the network boils down to using more or less translated weight columns, which will still give similar hidden net vectors and produce large activations in the target unit. On the contrary networks trained without invariance do not develop symmetrical weight columns: TL and RP primes are very disruptive because the weight columns being added do not overlap with those of the original. Given that this code is letter based and highly overlapping in nature, one might ask how the network still manages to distinguish between anagrams. Indeed the similarity between two centrally presented anagrams (for instance %%%TEAM%%% and %%%TAME%%%, crosses in Figure 3, top), was found to be quite large although still very significantly lower than the similarity between one anagram and its shifted version (%%%TEAM%%% and %%%%TEAM%%, diamonds in Figure 3, top). This suggests that despite large similarities in hidden layer representations, the network can make an efficient use of its set of hidden-to-output weights in order to distinguish between anagrams.

In short what might be called our "meta-modelling" approach using holographic coding was able to shed light on the coding scheme developed in the network, uncovering in the process a surprisingly acute correspondence. The main finding is that this backpropagation network solves the problem of location invariance by an overlapping and letter-based scheme that relies on broken symmetries in connection weights, a coding scheme that displays some hallmarks of the flexibility observed in humans.

4. Discussion and future directions

What are we to make of these results —how important are they for the field of visual word recognition? For instance can we conclude that the root of human orthographic flexibility is location invariance? Or that humans solve location invariance by way of a letter-based, overlapping coding scheme? Would answering "no" to the second question change our answer to the first?

To a large extent answering these questions requires to assess the importance of various elements in our modelling approach, such as input format, training base, network structure or learning algorithm. A brute-force strategy would be to systematically vary these elements and verify how results hold, but one can immediately see that the landscape of possibilities is daunting. Instead, one might resort to such guides as parsimony (which aspects of the model can be dispensed with?) or integrating more constraints from the behavioural and/or neural levels. As for parsimony one might wonder whether a network without a hidden layer would still be able to account for these results. Ref. ? showed that removing the hidden layer leads to failure on a basic word-non word discrimination task, where the original network succeeds. As for integrating new constraints we have now gathered evidence that improving on the number and lengths of words in the lexicon, or introducing more plausible letter visibility differences in the input, leaves the results presented here essentially unchanged. Taken together these investigations lend support to the notion that at least in these respects, the network studied in this chapter makes just the right simplifications.

However from a neural point of view one could argue that some constraints on connectivity should be acknowledged. Although connectionism does not claim any direct correspondence between single units and connections on the one hand, and single neurons and synapses on the other, it certainly is informed by the neural level and does posit some correspondence at some level of integration. Unit activations are usually construed as average activation rates among neural populations, and connections as the aggregated effect of synapses coming from inhibitory or excitatory neurons. Now as mentioned earlier the VWFA is a well circumscribed region in the brain that subserves the kind of location invariance string encoding we have studied, and it is thought to be connected in the same general way as the ventral visual pathway —hierarchically, and with limited receptive fields at any level. Would such modifications change anything to the coding scheme used in the network? We speculate they would.

For instance, one could design the network so that rather than "seeing" the entire input array, each hidden unit could only see a small window of two input locations. Then all other things being equal, a limited number of hidden units would be active for any word, and by construction each hidden unit activation would only depend on the activation of two contiguous letters, not four. During training many different bigrams would come to be seen at any two contiguous input locations, and we would then expect backpropagation to try and assign maximally distant activation values to the hidden unit these project to. Hidden units would then code for *location specific and contiguous bigrams*. Therefore location invariance would not obtain in the hidden layer itself: contrarily to the original network, exemplars sufficiently far away in the input layer would have completely orthogonal representations because they would not even activate the same hidden units. This would make the location invariant word recognition task more complicated to solve for the network, and adding more levels to the hierarchy might be in order. Each new layer in the hierarchy would simultaneously increase grain size and location invariance of the code, simplifying the task. Units in upper layers would end-up coding for location invariant letter combinations, and presumably those that are particularly informative in the language environment. Exemplars of the same word could then eventually activate a set of location invariant units coding for possibly non-contiguous letters in the word.

Although the above arguments hint that limited RFs and a more complex hierarchy would change the coding scheme, it is unclear whether it would jeopardise the result that location invariance implies flexibility, or for that matter the correspondence with holographic representations. It is possible that relying on a more coarse-grained code would in fact diminish the difference in flexibility observed across training regimes: this is because part of the flexibility would come from coding for letter combinations, and this does not depend on the regime but on network structure. Likewise the correspondence with holographic representations is not guaranteed to hold, but by design holographic representations can be composed in arbitrarily large structures that can be made as sparse as needed, and it is conceivable that representations in each layer of the hierarchy could correspond to levels in holographic structures. However for the correspondence to hold every new hidden layer would need to have the same format, and net inputs should not deviate significantly from a distribution centered on zero. In summary we think that making this network connectivity more plausible could completely modify the coding scheme, although it would not necessarily change the result that invariance implies flexibility, or that these networks can be usefully understood at the holographic level.

Finally it should be noted here that the idea to train a hierarchical network with limited RFs to perform location invariance is not new and has been explored both in the supervised and the unsupervised case. Ref. ? successfully trained a six layer feedforward network with backpropagation on a location invariant object recognition task. However the algorithm was supplemented by the authors who enforced invariance "by hand" during learning. The unsupervised alternative is provided by Visnet,[7] which is trained on a modified version of the hebb rule that integrates a memory trace. This network uses a very similar architecture except that it uses lateral inhibition within each layer. None of these hierarchical, limited RF alternatives for location invariant recognition has been applied to visual words[e] and we are currently investigating how the Visnet framework could be adapted to this purpose.[7]

---

[e]Although they have both been tested on letter recognition

5. Conclusion

In this chapter we have presented some work aimed at understanding the way humans represent written language. We have used the connectionist framework, and tried to introduce the unfamiliar reader along the way to some of the recurring strengths and issues of the field. We have also illustrated exploratory and explanatory instances of the modelling approach, and some new results obtained in the latter might have been of some interest to the expert connectionist. Finally taken together these studies show us how invariance can inform visual word recognition, and how it has been and continues to be a valid insight for cracking the orthographic code.

Acknowledgments

This work was conducted under the ERC#230313 grant awarded to Jonathan Grainger.

References

1. P. J. B. Hancock, V. Bruce and A. M. Burton, *Trends in Cognitive Sciences* **4**, 330 (2000).
2. K. Rayner, *Psychological Bulletin* **124**, 372 (1998).
3. C. Whitney, *Language and Cognitive Processes* (in press).
4. S. Dehaene, K. Nakamura, A. Jobert, C. Kuroki, S. Ogawa and L. Cohen, *Neuroimage* **49**, 1837 (2010).
5. N. Dunabeitia, J. A. an Molinaro and M. Carreiras, The recognition of mirror-letters and mirror-words: Insights from the masked priming paradigm. (2010), Talk presented at the 1st Joint EPS-SEPEX conference, Granada, Spain.
6. L. Cohen, S. Dehaene, F. Vinckier, A. Jobert and A. Montavont, *Neuroimage* **40**, 353 (2008).
7. J. Grainger, *Language and Cognitive Processes* **23**, 1 (2008).
8. J. Grainger and W. J. B. Van Heuven, *In P. Bonin (Ed.), Mental lexicon: "Some words to talk about words"* , 1 (2003).
9. C. Whitney, *Psychonomic Bulletin and Review* **8**, 221 (2001).
10. C. J. Davis, *Psychological Review* (in press).
11. T. Hannagan, E. Dupoux and A. Christophe, *Cognitive Science* (in press).
12. J. R. Binder, D. A. Medler, C. F. Westbury, E. Liebenthal and L. Buchanan, *Neuroimage* **33**, 739(Nov 2006).
13. L. Cohen and S. Dehaene, *NeuroImage* **22**, 466 (2004).
14. F. Vinckier, S. Dehaene, A. Jobert, J. Dubus, M. Sigman and L. Cohen, *Neuron* **55**, 143 (2007).
15. T. Stafford, What use are computational models of cognitive processes?, in *Connectionist Models of Behavior and Cognition II: Proceedings of the 11th*

Neural Computation and Psychology Workshop, eds. J. Mayor, N. Ruh and K. Plunkett (World Scientific.

16. M. Minsky and S. Papert, *Perceptrons* (The MIT Press, 1969).
17. J. Shawe-Taylor, *IEEE Transactions on Neural Networks* **4**, 816 (1993).
18. D. E. Rumelhart, G. E. Hinton and R. J. Williams, *Nature* **323**, 533 (1986).
19. G. E. Hinton, *Lecture Notes in Computer Science* , 1 (1987).
20. P. Simard, B. Victorri, Y. Le Cun and J. Denker, *Advances in neural information processing systems* 4 , 895 (1992).
21. R. C. Shillcock and P. Monaghan, *Neural Computation* **13**, 1171 (2001).
22. F. Dandurand, J. Grainger and S. Dufau, *Connection Science* (2010).
23. G. Wallis and E. T. Rolls, *Progress in Neurobiology* **51**, 167 (1997).
24. J. L. McClelland, *Topics in Cognitive Science* **1**, 11 (2009).
25. K. Plunkett, *Synthese* **129**, 185 (2001).
26. M. Perea and S. J. Lupker, *Memory and Cognition* **31**, 829 (2003a).
27. M. Perea and S. J. Lupker, *Journal of Memory and Language* **51**, 231 (2004).
28. S. Schoonbaert and J. Grainger, *Language and Cognitive Processes* **19**, 333 (2004).
29. J. Grainger, J. Granier, F. Farioli, E. Van Assche and W. Van Heuven, *Journal of Experimental Psychology: Human Perception and Performance* **32**, 865 (2006).
30. E. Van Assche and J. Grainger, *Journal of Experimental Psychology: Learning, Memory and Cognition* **32**, 399 (2006).
31. P. Gomez, R. Ratcliff and M. Perea, *Psychol Rev* **115**, 577 (2008).
32. T. L. Griffiths, N. Chater, C. Kemp, A. Perfors and J. B. Tenenbaum, *Trends in Cognitive Sciences* (in press).
33. T. Plate, J. Bert, J. Grace and P. Band, *Neural computation* **12**, 1337 (2000).
34. J. A. Alexander and M. C. Mozer, *Neural Networks* **12**, 479 (1999).
35. T. Hannagan, F. Dandurand and J. Grainger, *Neural Computation* (in press).
36. D. C. Plaut and J. L. McClelland, *Psychological Review* **117**, 284 (2010).
37. J. A. Fodor and Z. W. Pylyshyn, *Cognition* **28**, 3 (1988).
38. T. A. Plate, *IEEE Transactions on Neural Networks* **6**, 623 (1995).
39. F. Dandurand, T. Hannagan and J. Grainger, Neural networks for word recognition: Is a hidden layer necessary?, in *Proceedings of the Annual Conference of the Cognitive Science Society. Presented at the CogSci 2010, Portland, Oregon.*, in press.
40. M. C. Mozer, *Cambridge, MA: MIT Press* (1991).
41. T. Hannagan and J. Grainger (2010).

WHAT ARE THE FUNCTIONAL UNITS IN READING? EVIDENCE FOR STATISTICAL VARIATION INFLUENCING WORD PROCESSING

ALASTAIR C. SMITH

Department of Psychology, Lancaster University
Lancaster LA1 4YF, UK

PADRAIC MONAGHAN

Department of Psychology, Lancaster University
Lancaster LA1 4YF, UK

Computational models of reading have differed in terms of whether they propose a single route forming the mapping between orthography and phonology or whether there is a lexical/sublexical route distinction. A critical test of the architecture of the reading system is how it deals with multi-letter graphemes. Rastle and Coltheart (1998) found that the presence of digraphs in nonwords but not in words led to an increase in naming times, suggesting that nonwords were processed via a distinct sequential route to words. In contrast Pagliuca, Monaghan, and McIntosh (2008) implemented a single route model of reading and showed that under conditions of visual noise the presence of digraphs in words *did* have an effect on naming accuracy. In this study, we investigated whether such digraph effects could be found in both words and nonwords under conditions of visual noise. If so it would suggest that effects on words and nonwords are comparable. A single route connectionist model of reading showed greater accuracy for both words and nonwords containing digraphs. Experimental results showed participants were more accurate in recognising words if they contained digraphs. However contrary to model predictions they were less accurate in recognising nonwords containing digraphs compared to controls. We discuss the challenges faced by both theoretical perspectives in interpreting these findings and in light of a psycholinguistic grain size theory of reading.

1. Introduction

1.1. *Models of reading and functional units in reading*

There is a rich history of research using computational models in reading, and they have demonstrated profound insights into reading and reading disorders, illuminating the cognitive processes required to map written letters onto spoken words. Such models have been used to decide between competing theoretical accounts that differ in terms of the *mechanisms* implicated in mapping between representations, but also in terms of precisely what the relevant *representations* actually are within the reading system. The study reported in this paper combines computational modelling with a novel experimental paradigm to address each of these issues.

There are two proposed methods by which words may be identified. Either the word is identified holistically, as a single object, or it is identified by parts, whereby grain sizes smaller than the word are processed during word recognition. Such a debate has implications in both developmental and pedagogical domains, in terms of identifying potential sources of reading difficulties and monitoring reading acquisition, but also in terms of determining the appropriate grain size – letters, sets of letters, whole words – for training children to read most effectively.

There have been numerous computational models of reading created to improve understanding of the cognitive processes underlying our ability to map written words on to their spoken form. Models have differed in terms of whether they propose a single route forming the mapping[1-3] or whether there are two distinct routes[4-6], one involving sublexical mappings between letters and sets of letters and phonemes, the other mapping at the lexical level between written and spoken forms. Another issue at debate distinguishing different models of reading is whether in the architecture of the models the reading system operates serially left to right across the word or whether all letters in the word are simultaneously available. Different models have raised contrasting predictions regarding the functional units of the reading system with consensus remaining elusive.

There are a number of characteristics shared by dual-route models. The central unifying architectural feature is a lexical and sub-lexical route distinction. However in addition many also implement serial processing and explicit letter-grapheme relationships at either an input level or within the sub-lexical route. These two features are the prominent properties of the dual-route cascading model[4] and of more recent innovations that have adapted this modelling base incrementally[6]. In contrast, within single route models the reading system encodes the statistical relations, potentially at all levels of granularity, between patterns of letters and their pronunciation. Such models also tend to implement parallel processing of the visual input such that all letters in the words are simultaneously available[1-3]. The single-route architecture suggests that the functional units for reading will vary according to the useful statistical relations between letters and sounds, but that the word-level will not have a special architectural status independent from the sublexical mappings available within the vocabulary.

1.2. *Theories of grain-sizes in reading*

The link between variation in the functional units of reading and the statistical relations in letter sound mapping that emerges from single route models resonates with the Psycholinguistic Grain Size Theory of Ziegler and Goswami[7]. The theory describes the process of learning to read as acquiring the ability to find shared grain size in orthography and phonology. Grain sizes are therefore language specific, based on finding an efficient mapping between the two levels of representation. Ziegler and Goswami's theoretical model proposes that the extent to which letters map regularly and compositionally onto phonemes in words, determines the type of processing that occurs in the reading system.

In languages with shallow orthographies such as Spanish or Italian where letter to phoneme mappings are largely one to one, the grain size that emerges is small. However for languages where correct pronunciation of an individual letter is dependent upon its context, the grain size that develops is related to the context required for correct pronunciation. English has been termed "pseudo-regular"[2] in that it has examples of both componential and one-to-one mappings, and such variation should thus be reflected in varying grain size for different words.

The grapheme has received particular attention in recent years as a reflection of a potentially effective grain size in reading, and has been explicitly implemented as such in the sublexical route of dual route models[6] of reading. Graphemes are defined as written representation of phonemes, and in English they can thus be composed of single or multiple letters (such as the digraphs CH, SH, or TH; or the trigraphs, SSI in *mission*, or TCH, in *watch*). What evidence is there for the special status of graphemes in reading, and how does this relate to decisions about the architecture of the reading system?

1.3. *Rastle and Coltheart's (1998) analysis of grain size*

Rastle and Coltheart[8] tested the influence of graphemes on reading in the dual route cascading (DRC) model. In this model, the sublexical route processes letter by letter serially from left to right. Words are read by a combination of both the sublexical route and a lexical route, with explicit representations for each word. But nonwords are read exclusively by the sublexical route. If the DRC model is correct about the operation of the sublexical route, then nonwords containing pairs of letters that correspond to a single phoneme (i.e., digraphs), would result in a slowing of naming times. This was because in the model there is inhibition between phonemes generated by competing candidate graphemes. For the nonword *fooce*, for instance, the digraph "oo" competes with the single-letter grapheme "o" in terms of pronunciation, and also the digraph "ce", competes with the grapheme "c". The consequence is that in the model nonwords containing five letters but three graphemes (e.g., *fooce*) were read more slowly than nonwords containing five letters and five graphemes (e.g., *fruls*). A behavioural study confirmed this prediction. Participants read the three grapheme nonwords more slowly than five grapheme nonwords. They concluded that the DRC model's dual route mechanisms were confirmed – that for nonword reading, sublexical processing proceeds sequentially, with graphemes of different granularity competing in terms of pronunciation, indicating that the processing unit for reading is the letter – hence the competition between candidate combinations of letters, rather than naming time being positively correlated with the number of graphemes, this is dependent on the grapheme being the input level of representation for the sublexical reading system.

1.4. *Alternative perspectives on the grapheme grain size for reading*

The findings of Rastle and Coltheart[8] seem to be contradicted by a study investigating the granularity of representations used in reading in English[9]. In this alternative study, the performance of a computational model and behavioural studies testing reading under conditions of visual noise[9] seemed to indicate that the grapheme had a processing priority in reading for words.

Pagliuca, Monaghan, and McIntosh[9] tested a single route model based on Harm and Seidenberg's[6] connectionist model of reading. The model was trained to map between written and spoken forms of words for monosyllabic words in English. No explicit instruction was provided to the model in terms of how to solve this mapping, rather the model learned to exploit the useful regularities between certain patterns of letters and phonemes, which included letters, multi-word graphemes, and combinations of letters greater than graphemes, up to the whole word level. After training, the model was tested on two sets of five letter monosyllabic words, one containing digraphs in the initial word position, the other set containing no digraphs. When there was no impairment to the model's input, then no difference in reading the digraphs and non-digraphs was found. However, when the input of the model was impaired by reducing the activation across the word along a monotonic gradient from left to right, simulating noise added to the visual presentation of the word, then words beginning with digraphs were read more accurately by the model than control words.

The same sets of words were employed in a behavioural study in which visual noise was applied in a continuous gradient across the word such that the leftmost letters were most impaired – see Figure 3 for an example stimulus.

Pagliuca et al.[9] found that words containing digraphs were read more accurately than control words with no digraphs, confirming the predictions made by the model that digraphs were more robustly represented in the reading system than single letter graphemes.

Analysis of the model demonstrated that the advantage of digraphs for reading words was due to two input letter positions contributing to the activation of a single phoneme at the output, whereas for non-digraphs each letter only contributed to one phoneme's activation. Consequently, when noise was applied to the visual input, words containing digraphs were read more accurately because greater activity percolated through the model from these two positions.

The study by Pagliuca et al.[9] provided evidence consistent with the hypothesis that graphemes are indeed functional units within the reading system, indicating that the grain size for reading in English is adaptable according to the statistics of the letter-sound mapping. When multi-letter graphemes are available then these are encoded within the reading system, but when single-letter graphemes are present then the single letter is the granularity applied by the reading system. Furthermore, this adaptive granularity in the model's reading performance was due to encoding the useful levels of grain size in the mapping, rather than graphemes being explicitly encoded within the model.

1.5. *Resolving conflicting views on granularity*

The studies of Rastle and Coltheart[8] and Pagliuca et al.[9] therefore seem to present conflicting data on the representations used in the reading system, with consequences for different cognitive architectures for simulating human behaviour. However, there were a number of differences in the design of these studies that may have contributed to the difference in performance. First, the Rastle and Coltheart[8] study used nonwords, whereas the Pagliuca et al.[9] study tested word naming performance. Second, the Rastle and Coltheart[8] study tested presentations under normal conditions, whereas Pagliuca et al.[9] presented words under noise. We tested whether the model of Pagliuca et al.[9] would predict the same effects for nonwords as for words, and we also tested responses to both words and nonwords under noisy conditions in a behavioural study. If the nonword performance differed to words in the single-route model then this suggests that different mechanisms apply within the model for nonword reading, compared to word reading, with potentially different contributions of grain size variations. If the nonwords were similar to the words in the model, then this suggests that the critical difference is the additional stress on the reading system of adding noise to the visual input. This would then indicate that the effects of graphemes on reading are subtle and only observable for words when the reading system is placed under stress. A further aim of our study was to extend the naming study of Pagliuca et al.[9] to another aspect of lexical processing – a lexical decision task. This enables us to validate the task across different dependent variables associated with lexical access.

2. Modelling word processing under noise

2.1. *Method*

2.1.1. *Architecture*

The model used was based upon Harm and Seidenberg's[6] connectionist model of reading, and was the same as that used by Pagliuca et al.[9]. There were four layers of units in the model: an input orthographic layer, a hidden layer, an output phoneme layer, and an additional set of units producing phoneme attractor states.

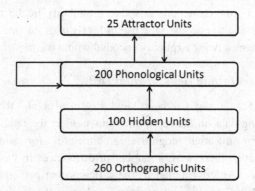

Fig. 1. Architecture of the model.

The orthographic layer contained 10 letter slots, each represented by 26 units, with each of the 26 units corresponding to a single letter. A letter was represented by activating the unit assigned to the letter in the given slot, with all other units in that slot having zero activation. Words were represented by contiguous letter slots in the input being activated. The first vowel of the word was placed in the fifth letter slot, with consonants preceding the vowel occupying letter slots to the immediate left of the vowel, and additional vowels and consonants following the first vowel occupying slots to the right of the first vowel.

The orthographic layer was fully connected to the hidden layer containing 100 units. These in turn were fully connected to the phonological output layer. This contained 8 phoneme slots with each phoneme represented in terms of 25 phonological features giving a total of 200 phonological units. There were two slots for the vowel, and three slots each for the onset and coda. The phonological units were self-connected (allowing basic dependencies between phonological features to be captured[6]) and connected to a set of 25 attractor units.

2.1.2. *Training and testing*

The model was trained on a corpus of 6229 monosyllabic words of length 1-10 letters extracted from the CELEX database. Frequencies were log compressed in the range [0.05,1], with values assigned to low frequency words capped at 0.05. The model was trained with a back-propagation learning algorithm[10] with a learning rate of 0.05. Initial connection weights were randomly assigned with mean 0, and variance 1. Training was capped at 5 millions cycles with words sampled randomly according to their frequency.

The stimuli used in testing consisted of four sets each containing 64 items. We selected words with digraphs in the onset, and control words with no digraphs, and also nonwords with digraphs in the onset, and a set of control nonwords with no digraphs. All stimuli were 5 letters in length and monosyllabic. The digraphs and the onsets of the control stimuli were the same as those used in Pagliuca et al.[9], the control words paired with SH digraph words began with the letters ST, control words paired with CH began with CR and control words paired with TH digraph words began with the letters TR. For the words, digraph and non-digraph stimuli were matched for same initial letter, unigram and bigram frequency, neighbourhood size, lexical frequency, body friends and body enemies (body friends are words with the same vowel and letters following the vowel with the same pronunciation of the vowel, whereas body enemies have similar spelling but different pronunciation), and partial view predictability (a measure of the likelihood of guessing a word given only part of the word was visible, when visibility is reduced from left to right across the word).

The nonwords were formed by switching onsets and rhymes within each word set, with changes in orthography mirrored in corresponding phonological target representations. The nonwords were controlled for the same variables as the words, except for lexical frequency. Due to the digraph TH mapping on to two possible phonetic representations 'D' and 'T', TH items within the digraph nonword stimuli set were recorded as correctly reproduced if either phonological representation was outputted by the model.

Each stimulus set was presented to the model under three conditions of noise: (1) Perfect input (no noise) in which the input orthographic representation was activated as it was during training; (2) Gradient noise, in which there was monotonically increasing activation from left to right, as used in Pagliuca et al.[9], such that the activation was most reduced in the left most occupied letter slot and at full activation in the rightmost occupied letter slot. The reduction in activation was set at 25% of initial noise in the leftmost letter slot; and finally (3) Uniform noise, where activation was uniformly reduced across all letter slots by 50% of the level used during training. This additional noise condition was included to test the generality of the visual noise impairment, or whether the digraph effect only emerged if the digraph letters were most affected.

2.2. Results and Discussion

Two values were recorded to monitor model performance. Accuracy of the model's performance was determined by taking the actual activation of the model's production for each phoneme slot in the output, and determining whether that activation pattern was closer to the target phoneme than to any other phoneme in the language. The model was judged to have named the stimulus correctly, if each phoneme slot was accurately reproduced. An additional, more sensitive measure was taken to be the Euclidean distance of the output from the intended target for each phoneme slot. We report both measures, but the t-test calculations were performed only on the Euclidean distance unless otherwise stated. There are many ways in which models' outputs are consulted to simulate behavioural responses to naming and lexical decision tasks (see Pagliuca et al.[9] for a review). Our intention in the dependent variable for the model was to provide a reflection of the accuracy with which the model represented the stimulus, and given the high correlation between lexical decision and naming accuracies and response times, we propose that this is a reasonable approximation to behavioural studies designed to elicit variance in ease of lexical access.

After training, the model performed with an accuracy of 99.9% on the training set of words. For the digraph and control word sets, accuracy was 100% - see Figure 2.

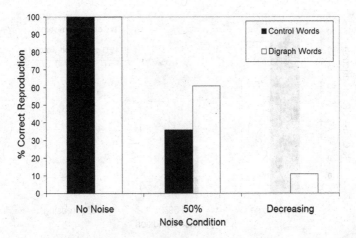

Fig. 2. Accuracy achieved by model in processing digraph and control words in perfect input, uniform noise and decreasing noise conditions

When uniform noise was applied across the inputs, digraph words were read with lower error, t(126) = 2.453, *p* < 0.01. This was also the case when decreasing noise was applied across the input, t(126) = 4.396, p < 0.01. This replicated and extended the findings of Pagliuca et al.[9], showing that digraph words were less prone to effects of noise than were non-digraph words. When error only across the word onsets was calculated, significant differences were again found between performance on the digraph and control word sets, in both the uniform t(126) = 4.876, p < 0.01, and decreasing t(126) = 10.668, p < 0.01, noise conditions.

The model's performance on nonword stimuli showed similar effects, see Figure 2. In the no noise condition, accuracy was high for both the digraph (84.4%) and control (92.2%) nonword sets, and at a level consonant with other models of nonword reading[1-5]. For uniform noise, just as for the words, digraph nonwords were read more accurately than control nonwords, t(126) = 3.355, p < 0.01, and this also pertained for the decreasing noise condition, t(126) = 2.495, p < 0.01.

The results show the model to be sensitive to the presence of digraphs in both words and nonwords under conditions of noise. The model predicts that reading of digraph words and nonwords should both show an advantage under noisy conditions. We tested this prediction in a behavioural study.

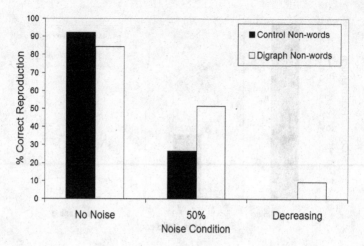

Fig. 3. Accuracy achieved by model in processing digraph and control nonwords in perfect input, uniform noise and decreasing noise conditions.

3. Testing word and nonword reading under noisy conditions

3.1. *Method*

3.1.1. *Participants*

15 university students aged 18-29, participated in the study. All were native English speakers and had normal or corrected-to-normal vision.

3.1.2. *Materials*

The same word and nonword sets as were applied to the model were used in the study. Stimuli were presented in dark grey text (Courier New 150) on a greyscale background (300 x 100 px). Random 2-dimensional digital pixel noise was applied across the word in a decreasing gradient from left to right, so that the initial letter was most impaired (an example is shown in Figure 3).

3.1.3. *Procedure*

Participants were instructed to perform a lexical decision on each stimulus by pressing appropriate response keys on a keyboard. A fixation cross on a 300 x 100px greyscale background with decreasing gradient noise was presented for 1000ms. Then the stimulus was presented for 250ms and followed by a mask of decreasing gradient noise for 500ms. The next fixation cross appeared after a further 2000ms. Stimuli were presented in randomised order.

Fig. 4. Example of stimuli used in behavioural experiment.

3.2. Results and Discussion

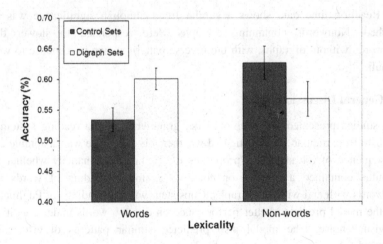

Fig. 5. Mean accuracy of response in lexical decision task for words and nonwords with and without digraphs in onset (error bars represent standard error).

In line with the model's prediction, words containing digraphs were responded to more accurately than control words, $t(14) = 3.254$, $p<0.01$. However, contrary to the model's prediction, nonwords containing digraphs were responded to less accurately than controls, $t(14) = 2.457$, $p<0.05$, see Figure 5.

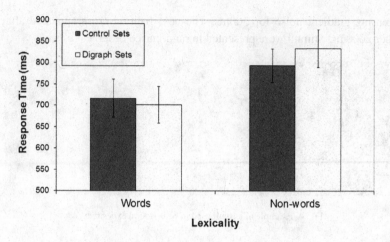

Fig. 6. Mean reaction time in lexical decision task for words and nonwords with and without digraphs in onset (error bars represent standard error).

Reaction time data shows a similar trend although significance was not reached. Nonwords containing digraphs were responded to slower than nonwords without digraphs, with the reverse pattern shown in response to word stimuli.

4. General Discussion

The studies presented here explored the granularity of the reading system in English. In particular we investigated whether this grain size was adaptable as a consequence of the statistical properties of the language, namely whether the stimulus contained a digraph or not. We examined reading of words and nonwords with and without digraphs. Consistent with the findings of Pagliuca et al.[9] the model predicted better performance on digraph words under conditions of visual noise. The model also predicted similar patterns of effects for nonwords.

In our behavioural study, we confirmed that words containing digraphs were identified with greater accuracy than controls when visual noise was applied in a decreasing gradient across the word. These lexical decision results confirmed the naming accuracy responses of Pagliuca et al.[9], and are consistent with the model's predictions. However, for lexical decision on nonwords, nonwords containing digraphs were identified with less accuracy than control nonwords under visual noise conditions, in contrast with the predictions of the model.

Such an effect is consistent with the results of Rastle and Coltheart[8], who found that digraph nonwords were named more slowly than non-digraph nonwords, thus the effect of digraphs may be different for words than for nonwords. The results are partially consistent with the dual-route view of the reading system – that digraphs interfere with production of phonology for nonwords. However, the effect of digraphs on word naming and lexical decision is inconsistent with this view. Also, there are potentially dissociations between the effect of digraphs for nonword naming compared to lexical decision in the predictions of the DRC model. The DRC model implements lexical decisions in terms of activation of the orthographic lexicon, thus orthography-phonology mappings are largely irrelevant for lexical decisions[4], so it remains an open question as to how and whether digraphs may influence lexical decision for nonwords.

We favour the view that the effects of digraphs for word reading are subtle and only observable under conditions of noise – when the reading system is placed under stress. Hence, digraph effects should be the same for words as for nonwords within a single reading system. Finding critical data to distinguish between DRC and single-route models of reading has proved challenging, but we have here discovered a task where different predictions are made by each model. Under conditions of noise, we anticipate that nonword *naming* will support only one of these architectures.

The inverse effect of digraphs for nonwords compared to words may then be due to the simultaneous presentation of word and nonword stimuli in a single study, using lexical decision. Digraph nonwords were treated as more "word-like" than control nonwords, resulting in reduced accuracy for the digraph nonwords. The intermixing of words and nonwords in a single study, and measurement of a rejection for the nonword stimuli may have resulted in an impure measure of digraphs on nonword reading. Investigating naming accuracy for nonwords only under conditions of visual noise is required to resolve this issue.

A digraph effect was present in both simulation and behavioural data for both words and nonwords. For the model, there was a strong prediction that digraphs are functional units for both word and nonword reading. In respect to the behavioural data, this prediction is borne out for words, but not yet for nonwords due to the potential difficulties of presenting both words and nonwords in the same study. However the presence of such an effect for words at least suggests that digraphs are functional units in reading and further indicates that the grain size for reading in English is adaptable according to statistics of the letter sound mapping, which provides interesting challenges to views on the independence of letter recognition[11], and demonstrates that word perception is affected by interdependencies between letters, resulting from letter-sound mapping statistics across the whole language. We have not yet firmly established the locus of digraph effects within the reading system – whether they are within one route of a dual route reading system, or whether they are hallmark features of a single route reading system responding to all the statistics mapping between sets of letters and phonemes. We have established, however, that digraphs have a prominent role in understanding the grain size of reading in English and in defining an adequate model of the reading system.

Acknowledgments

This work was supported by an Experimental Psychology Society studentship, awarded to the first author.

References

1. M. S. Seidenberg and J. L. McClelland, *Psychological Review.* **96**, 523-568 (1989).
2. D. C. Plaut, J. L. McClelland, M. S. Seidenberg and K. E. Patterson, *Psychological Review.* **103**, 56-115 (1996).
3. M. W. Harm and M. S. Seidenberg, *Psychological Review.* **163**, 491-528 (1999).
4. M. Coltheart, K. Rastle, C. Perry, R. Langdon and J. Ziegler, *Psychological Review.* **108**, 204-256 (2001).
5. M. Zorzi, G. Houghton, and B. Butterworth *Journal of Experimental Psychology: Human Perception and Performance.* **24**, 1131-1161 (1998).
6. C. Perry, J. C. Ziegler and M. Zorzi, *Psychological Review.* **114**, 273-315 (2007).
7. J. C. Ziegler and U. Goswami, *Psychological Bulletin.* **131**, 3-29 (2005).
8. K. Rastle and M. Coltheart, *Psychonomic Bulletin and Review.* **5**, 277-282 (1998).
9. G. Pagliuca, P. Monaghan and R. McIntosh, *Proceedings of the 30th Annual Conference of the Cognitive Science Society.* Mahwah, NJ: Lawrence Erlbaum. (2008).
10. D. E. Rumelhart, G. E. Hinton, and R. J. Williams, *Nature.* **323**, 533-536 (1986).
11. D. G. Pelli, B. Farrell and D. C. Moore, *Nature.* **423**, 752-756 (2003).

TESTING COMPUTATIONAL ACCOUNTS OF RESPONSE CONGRUENCY IN LEXICAL DECISION[*]

SEBASTIAN LOTH
COLIN J. DAVIS

*Department of Psychology, Royal Holloway, University of London
EGHAM, Surrey, TW20 0EX, United Kingdom*

Response congruency effects occur when responses to a target stimulus are faster and/or more accurate if the correct response to that target is the same as (what would be) the correct response to a preceding prime stimulus (relative to the situation where the correct response to the prime and target differs). Computational models of lexical access are challenged by recent findings of a response congruency effect in masked primed lexical decision. Two different types of models, the activation-based Spatial Coding Model and the probability-based Bayesian Reader are reviewed. We show that neither model accommodates the empirical data. However, replacing the homogeneous inhibition in the lexical component of the Spatial Coding model with selective inhibition enables the model to account for the response congruency effect while also providing an excellent account of other masked form priming data.

1. Introduction

In this chapter, we test two different computational models of visual word recognition in their capacity to predict a response congruency effect in masked primed lexical decision. The dataset shows that responses were facilitated when prime and target where of the same lexicality compared to trials where lexical state and response differed. One of these models, the Spatial Coding Model (SCM)[1], belongs to the general framework of competitive network models, in which the presentation of input stimuli leads to the activation of matching and partially matching lexical representations, and a competitive process driven by lateral inhibition selects the best-matching representation. The other model, the Bayesian Reader[2,3], embodies a different approach, based on Bayesian inference. The model combines prior information about the frequency of words with a series of noisy input samples in order to update posterior hypotheses about the identity of the word. In the case of lexical decision, the task which we focus on

[*] This work was supported by ESRC grant RES-000-22-3354

here, the Bayesian Reader integrates probabilities across the entire lexicon to evaluate the hypothesis that the stimulus is a word. It has been argued[2,3] that the Bayesian Reader offers a superior account of the evidence accumulation process in masked priming, although to date there has been less investigation of masked priming results with this model than with competitive network models such as the SCM.

One masked primed finding that has been simulated by the Bayesian Reader is the (absence of a) response congruency effect in lexical decision. In the following, we introduce the masked priming paradigm, provide an overview of response congruency effects in lexical decision, and then report simulations of response congruency data using both the SCM and the Bayesian Reader. To foreshadow our findings, we conclude that these data pose problems for current implementations of both models, but show that a modification of the lateral inhibition assumptions of the SCM enables this model to capture the findings well; adapting the Bayesian Reader to capture these data will require more fundamental modifications to the underlying assumptions of the model.

1.1. *Masked priming*

The masked priming paradigm is one of the most popular experimental methodologies used today. In this paradigm participants respond to a stimulus that is preceded by a briefly presented prime. Typically, the prime is masked by a preceding masking pattern and is followed by the target, which acts as a backward mask[4,5]. Also, the presentation duration is kept short (about 50 ms). As a result participants cannot report or consciously perceive the prime. Despite the brief and masked presentation a wealth of experimental results indicates a demonstrable effect of priming on cognition[6]. For example, the masked repetition priming effect refers to reaction times in a lexical decision task that are significantly faster when the prime is a lowercase version of the target (table – TABLE) compared to unrelated primes (drive – TABLE)[4]. Masked priming is used to investigate early processes of word recognition, e.g. orthographic priming effects can be shown in briefly presented masked primes but effects are not present in unmasked primes[7]. More specifically, response congruency is informative about the state of the lexicon after the prime stimulus has been processed up to an early stage.

In a masked primed lexical decision task the participants are asked to indicate whether the target is a word or a nonword[4]. If prime and target are of the same lexicality the responses are congruent (*nonword – NONWORD* or *word – WORD*, e.g. *quiet – CROWN*), otherwise they are incongruent (*word –*

NONWORD or *nonword* – *WORD*, e.g. *miytd* – *CROWN*). Congruent trials are usually associated with faster and more accurate responses than incongruent trials. Response congruency effects have been reported for various categorisation tasks, including number magnitude estimation[8,9] and valence categorisation[10].

Primes can be processed up to relatively high level where a semantic feature of the prime can influence the response towards the target[11]. This shows that specific information about the semantics of the prime was extracted by the participant. In contrast, a lexical decision task requires less specific processing. Hence, information about prime lexicality could be available earlier than information about a specific feature and could in turn influence the response to the target.

1.2. *Empirical evidence in masked primed lexical decision*

The empirical evidence for response congruency effects in masked primed lexical decision is mixed. Some studies have not found an effect[3,12,13]. Other studies have found a congruency effect[14-16]. In some cases[14] the primes and targets were repeated several times, which may enable a priming effect to emerge as a result of stimulus-response mapping rather than any bias in the evaluative process[17]. However, other studies controlled for stimulus-response mapping effects and nevertheless found a congruency effect in word and nonword targets[15]. In recent work[16] we have found that it is possible to manipulate the strength of the congruency effect, by choosing primes that are more or less wordlike. This finding provides an explanation of the previous mixed results. Congruency effects may not be apparent when word and nonword primes are not clearly differentiated with respect to wordlikeness (e.g., *share* and *shate* are quite similar in their global wordlikeness, even though they differ with respect to their lexical status). However, when primes are more straightforwardly informative (e.g., word primes like *share* versus nonword primes like *miytd*) a robust response congruency effect is found, and hence should be predicted by models when such stimuli are used.

2. Simulating response congruency effects with the SCM

Previous research has used the interactive activation model[18] to model a variety of masked priming effects in the lexical decision task[19-21]. The position-specific input coding scheme used by this model suffers from some shortcomings that prevent it from capturing a variety of masked form priming effects, e.g., those in which the prime is formed by transposing, adding or deleting letters of the target. However, recent work with the SCM[1] has shown that the substitution of a more flexible input coding scheme enables a competitive network model to provide an excellent account of masked form priming effects. We used the SCM to attempt to simulate response congruency effects in the lexical decision task.

2.1. *Lexical decisions in the spatial coding model*

Lexical decisions in the spatial coding model are based on the opponent process model[1,22]. In the opponent process model the *yes-* or the *no-*channel has to hit a threshold in order to trigger a response by the model. Both channels can inhibit each other. The information feeding into the *no-*channel is a non-specific signal that builds up as the decision process continues over time. The *yes-*channel receives input from the model's lexical level. In particular, it receives information about the summed lexical activation (a measure of the global "wordlikeness" of the stimulus). An additional potential source of input to the *yes-*channel is specific information about word identification events. The relative contribution of these two sources is assumed to be subject to strategic factors. For example, when the nonwords in an experiment are relatively un-wordlike (as was the case in the experiment simulated here) faster reaction times can be attained by placing a greater reliance on summed lexical activation than unique lexical identification[23].

The equations for updating activities in the two lexical decision channels are as follows:

$$\frac{d}{dt}YES = (1 - YES)\,ye\,s_{\text{in}} - (1 + YES)\lambda[NO]^+ \tag{1}$$

$$\frac{d}{dt}NO = (1 - NO)\,no_{\text{in}} - (1 + NO)\lambda[YES]^+ \tag{2}$$

where *YES* and *NO* represent the activities of the corresponding channels and the parameter λ weights the inhibitory signals exchanged between channels. The notation $[x]^+$ denotes a function that is 0 for $x<0$, and equal to x otherwise. The model outputs a decision as soon as one of the channel exceeds the response threshold, which was set at 0.8.

In equation (1), the expression yes_{in} is the input to the *Yes* channel, which is:

$$ye\,s_{\text{in}}(t) = y_{global}\,wordSum(t) + y_{id}\,ID \tag{3}$$

According to equation (3) there are two sources of input to the Yes channel. One of these is a global input, which is based on the total lexical activity generated by the stimulus (*wordSum(t)*). The other input represents the evidence for a unique lexical identification of the stimulus: if the stimulus has been identified, *ID*=1, otherwise *ID*=0. The latter input provides a more reliable basis for a *yes*-response; the global input, on the other hand, provides a fast, but not always reliable, indication of the likely lexical status of the stimulus. In the experiment of Loth and Davis [16] that we simulate here, the nonwords were relatively unwordlike (e.g., *miqxp*) and thus global lexical activity does provide a reliable index of lexical status. For that reason, the parameter weighting global lexical activity was increased from the default value of 0.4 assumed by Davis[1] to a value of 0.5. One consequence of this parameter choice is that lexical decisions for words are chiefly based on total lexical activity rather than the identification of a specific word, and thus the value of the parameter weighting unique lexical identification is somewhat arbitrary (here it was reduced to 0, although a similar pattern of results is obtained if this parameter is set at zero). Nevertheless, it can be noted that, on word trials, the activation of the target word node is the chief contributor to summed lexical activation.

In equation (2), the expression no_{in} is the input to the *No* channel, which is:

$$n\sigma_m(t) - n_{tecer}l_{\max(t)} \tag{4}$$

The term $l_{\max(t)}$ represents the maximum activity at the letter level at time t. This implies that the decision process starts as soon there is activity in the letter nodes (and not, for example, when the stimulus is a forward mask such as ######).

When simulating masked priming, it is assumed that the activity of the *yes*- and *no*-channels is reset at target onset, otherwise the initial decision bias due to the prime is difficult to overcome. Thus, the impact of the prime is limited to its effect on lexical activity (i.e., any "headstart" due to a prime has its locus at the lexical level rather than at the decision channels).

2.2. *Simulation*

We tested the SCM model using the same stimuli used by Loth and Davis[16] in which nonword stimuli were relatively un-wordlike and word stimuli were both high in frequency and orthographic typicality. Because the current implementation of the SCM is a deterministic model and our main interest is in reaction time, we confined the results reported here to reaction time and excluded error data from further discussion. The parameters for the simulation were identical to those in the published version of the model[1], except for the parameters that weight the inputs to the two channels implementing the lexical decision process. The global activity parameter was set to 0.5 (y_{global}=0.5), the unique lexical identification parameter was set to 0.0 (y_{id}=0.0), and the parameter weighting input to the *no*-channel was set to 0.22 (n_{letter} =0.22).

The results (see Table 1) indicate that there is no difference between the congruent and incongruent priming condition in word targets, but a facilitatory priming effect in nonword targets. Below we analyse these findings in more detail.

2.2.1. *Nonword targets*

Input stimuli that are un-wordlike nonwords produce negligible lexical activation in the model. Thus, when the trial consisted of a nonword prime followed by a nonword target there was very little input to the *yes*-channel, and hence relatively rapid *no* decisions. By contrast, when the prime was a high frequency word there was a much greater degree of lexical activation, resulting in a larger input to the *yes*-channel, which then inhibited the *no*-channel.

Table 1. Priming effects in empirical data[16], Spatial Coding Model (SCM)[1], the modified Spatial Coding Model and the Bayesian Reader (BR)[3]. Note, due to a stochastic element in BR each item was averaged across 50 simulations before contributing to the means[2].

	Words			Nonwords		
	Congruency			Congruency		
	inc	con	*effect*	inc	con	*effect*
Data	498	475	*23*	520	497	*23*
SCM	170	169	*1*	166	153	*13*
SI-SCM	169	155	*14*	166	154	*12*
BR	378	379	*-1*	558	562	*-4*

Reaction time in empirical data, the Spatial Coding Model and the Bayesian Reader in ms and cycles as a function of target lexicality and priming condition

Note: SCM = Spatial Coding Model[1], SI-SCM = selective inhibition SCM, BR = Bayesian Reader[3], inc = incongruent, con = congruent.

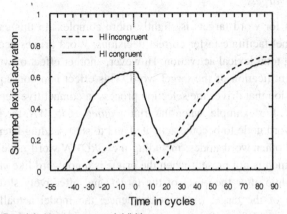

Panel A: Homogeneous inhibition

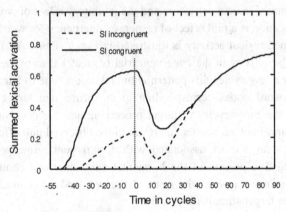

Panel B: Selective inhibition

Fig. 1. Comparison of summed lexical activity using homogeneous (Panel A) and selective inhibition (Panel B) in the SCM. The graphs show the processing of the example *miytd – CROWN* (incongruent) and *quiet – CROWN* (congruent). Negative cycles refer to prime presentation, cycle zero marks the target onset and positive cycles show target presentation.
Note: HI = homogeneous inhibition, SI = selective inhibition.

Consequently, *no* decisions were 13 cycles slower for nonword targets following word primes than for the same targets following nonword primes. The size and direction of this congruency effect is compatible with the results observed by Loth and Davis[16]

2.2.2. *Word targets*

The situation for word targets is slightly more complex. In this case, inputs to the *yes*-channel facilitate faster correct decisions. Word primes accomplish this by increasing total lexical activation. However, another effect of word primes is to inhibit identification of the target word. This effect is a consequence of the lateral inhibition that drives the selection process in competitive network models like the SCM. For example, when the trial is *quiet – CROWN*, the prime causes the *QUIET* word node to become activated and to start sending lateral inhibitory signals to all other word nodes, including the *CROWN* word node. This lateral inhibition, which is not present when the prime is a nonword like *miytd*, persists for a little while after the onset of the target, and effectively slows down the identification of the target. As a consequence, the model actually predicts a negative priming effect of response congruency on the speed of target word identification. In the simulation, the net effect of the facilitatory effect of word primes on summed lexical activation and the inhibitory effect of word primes on target identification is a null effect of response congruency for word targets. The flow of summed lexical activity is illustrated in Fig. 1 (Panel A). Directly after target onset the activity in the congruent trial is greater than in the incongruent trial, but after a few cycles this pattern is turned around due to lateral inhibition between the word nodes corresponding to the prime and target words. The advantage in the early cycles of target processing and the disadvantage in the later cycles cancel out each other and result in the observed null effect. Note that the greater lexical activity associated with a congruent prime prior to target onset (the negative portion of the horizontal axis) does not contribute to the ultimate decision because of the reset of the *yes*- and *no*-channels that takes place when the target stimulus is presented.

2.3. *Conclusion*

The SCM model predicts a congruency effect in nonword targets in line with empirical data. But in word targets the SCM fails, predicting a null effect where empirical data show a congruency effect.

3. Simulating response congruency effects with the Bayesian Reader

The Bayesian Reader is a computational model that can provide predictions for lexical decision[2] and masked primed lexical decision experiments[3]. The model evaluates a task specific hypothesis on the basis of accumulated noisy evidence at each time step.

3.1. *Overview of the Bayesian Reader*

In the Bayesian Reader model[3], lexical decision is based not on the identification of a single word, but on the overall evidence that the stimulus is word or a nonword. This process involves a comparison of two conditional probabilities: the probability that the stimulus is a word P(X|is a word) versus the probability that it is a nonword P(X|is a nonword), where X reflects the evidence from the input. As soon as one of these probabilities hits a threshold a response is triggered.

At the beginning of each trial the model is reset, so that the word priors reflect the respective word frequency. The letters of the input are represented by a position specific 26 element-vector. Hence, all representations of a letter string denote a point in an n-dimensional perceptual space, where n refers to the number of letters. Due to this mechanism the model can use a lexicon with words of a specific length. At each cycle, the model receives a sample of the stimulus, which reflects the stimulus plus Gaussian zero-centred noise. The mean location and standard error of the mean are updated with each new sample. According to the standard error, a probability density function for each word is computed, which forms an estimate on how widely dispersed the mean of the samples can be from the actual stimulus. Using this function the probability that the input was generated by a particular word P(I|W) is computed. P(I|W) is further multiplied with the respective prior probability and divided by the sum of all priors multiplied with their respective P(I|W)s. The result of that multiplication is the probability that a specific word forms the input P(W|I). The procedure so far will always result in the identification of a word that is close to the presented input, because P(W|I) reflects a relative probability. A transformation of all word probabilities and a probability for the stimulus being a nonword is required in order to compute P_{word}.

The probability that finally triggers a response is computed by assuming a virtual nonword and background nonwords. Specifically, the virtual nonword is positioned close to the input in perceptual space, but never closer to a word than a given nonword distance. The probability that the input matches one of those nonwords is computed in the same way as for words, since the equation is blind to the lexical status of letter strings, but also to whether the string pronounceable or legal. Finally, the probability that the stimulus is one of the letter strings that forms a word can be computed and this is P_{word} and $P_{nonword}$ is derived as $1-P_{word}$.

The processing for prime and targets does not differ. On target onset, the basis for drawing samples is exchanged for the target and the samples drawn from the prime are deleted, i.e. the final position in perceptual space that is generated by sampling from the input is defined by the target only. The contribution of the prime is reflected in the priors, which are updated continuously during the processing of prime and target.

If prime and target are orthographically related (e.g., brown – CROWN), the prime will have increased the priors of similar words and background nonwords (including CROWN). Hence, a priming effect is predicted. If prime and target are related by their response only (e.g., quiet – CROWN), the prime will not have altered the priors in the perceptual around the target. The influence of the priors around the prime in perceptual space is wiped out quickly, due to the multiplication with $P(I|W)$ that is reflecting an incompatibility with the current input. Finally, no priming effect is predicted.

Previous simulations of the Bayesian Reader have shown that it correctly predicts no prime congruency effect for the stimuli tested by Norris and Kinoshita[3]. In this context it was argued that the reason for this prediction is that the prime increases the evidence for words in a broad area of perceptual space, but does not alter the probability of a word or nonword response. However, it seemed plausible that the more informative primes used by Loth and Davis[16] might result in large differences in P_{word} for word versus nonword primes. This possibility was tested in the following simulation.

3.2. Simulation

The stimuli used in the simulation were the same as those used in the SCM simulation. Parameters were set to default level. The decision threshold for a word decision was set to 0.9 and for a nonword decision to 0.01, as in[3]. The Bayesian Reader has a stochastic element and hence each item is simulated 50 times and the mean reaction time of the correct responses is formed. A proportion out of these 50 trials may receive a false response and the model can predict error ratios[2], though here we focus on reaction times. The reaction times of the model do not show a congruency effect for either word or nonword targets, in contrast to the empirical data (see Table 1).

As noted above, it seemed plausible that the relatively informative primes used in this simulation would produce large differences in P_{word} for word versus nonword primes. In fact, this prediction was correct, but it did not result in a congruency effect. Although the model distinguishes between word and nonword primes, the early difference in P_{word} is wiped out with the onset of target processing. The Bayesian formulation requires that priors are multiplied by likelihoods for each hypothesis (i.e., for each word in the model's lexicon). At the moment of switching from prime to target the target's likelihood is zero and hence any priming effect preserved in the prior is wiped out by a multiplication with zero. Hence, there is no trace of the prime in the model and its contribution to the pooled probabilities is wiped out. It follows that the model cannot predict any priming effects (positive or negative) for primes that are (orthographically) unrelated to the target (i.e., primes and targets that share no letters). This prediction directly follows from the model's fundamental assumption about how information is integrated during masked priming. Thus, empirical data demonstrating a congruency effect for unrelated primes[15,16] challenge the basic assumptions of the Bayesian Reader model.

4. A modification of the SCM's lateral inhibition assumptions

The critical component that we have identified in the Spatial Coding model[1] is the lexicon and specifically the interplay of inhibition between word nodes. These processes are very similar to those in the interactive activation model[18] as outlined above. The purpose of inhibition is to foster a process that narrows activation from a number of words down to a single node. This aim can also be achieved by an alternative form of lateral inhibition called selective inhibition. We explain this mechanism in more detail in the following section, and also present simulation results showing how this form of inhibition can account for both response congruency effects and other critical masked priming data.

4.1. *Lateral inhibition in the SCM*

Simulations of the SCM reported in[1] followed the original IA model in assuming homogeneous inhibition between words of the same length[a]. That is, even though the word *QUIET* shares no letters with the word *CROWN*, activity in the *QUIET* word node inhibits the *CROWN* word node just as much as would activity in the *CLOWN* word node, or any other word node.

4.2. *An alternative to homogeneous inhibition*

The homogeneous lateral inhibition assumed in the IAM and in the SCM is not the only possibility. Selective inhibition has been employed in the SOLAR model[22] and in a modified version of the IA model[19]. According to selective inhibition, only word nodes that code orthographically overlapping words send inhibitory signals to each other. Thus, the *QUIET* word node would not inhibit

---

[a] Inhibition between words of different lengths is not homogeneous, because the SCM differs from IAM in implementing masking field principles, according to which the strength of inhibitory signals is greater for word nodes that code longer words.

the *CROWN* word node, and hence word primes would exert no inhibitory effect on the identification of unrelated target words.

4.3. *Implementation of selective inhibition*

There are various different ways in which the idea of selective inhibition might be implemented. The two chief problems are a) how to set the inhibitory weights, and b) the computational expense of assuming specific connection strengths for each pair of word nodes.

4.3.1. *Setting the strength of inhibitory connections*

In the SOLAR model[22] it was assumed that connection strengths are a continuous function of orthographic similarity (e.g., that *CLOWN* inhibits *CROWN* more than *CHAIN* inhibits *CROWN*). The model includes a learning algorithm that explains how lateral inhibitory connections could self-organise their weights. A simpler approach was taken by Davis and Lupker[19], who assumed binary inhibitory weights, and counted two words as orthographically overlapping if they shared at least one letter in the same position. For example, *AXLE* would receive inhibitory signals from word nodes like *ABLE*, *ARID* and *EXIT*, but not from word nodes like *DOOR* and *EMIT*. However, this position-specific approach is not consistent with the spatial coding model, and leads to some irregularities when words of different length are considered. For example, *LATE* and *PLATE* are relatively similar according the SCM's coding scheme, even though they do not share any letters in the same (absolute) position.

In the present implementation of selective inhibition we adopted aspects of both of the above approaches. As in Davis[22], spatial coding (rather than position-specific coding) was used to determine the degree of orthographic overlap between pairs of words. As in Davis and Lupker[19], we assumed binary inhibitory weights, i.e. two word nodes were either mutually inhibitory, or else they were independent (i.e., not linked by an inhibitory connection). Thus, whenever the overlap between two words exceeded a criterion match value there was a bidirectional inhibitory connection between the corresponding word nodes.

A match value is a measure of similarity between two given letter strings and ranges between 0.0 and 1.0. The more similar the two letter strings are the higher the match value is, with 1.0 marking equality (see Davis[1] for examples). We used a cutoff value of 0.3 to determine which pairs of nodes were mutually inhibitory. This implies that a word node like *CROWN* receives inhibitory connections from the *CLOWN*, *CHAIN*, *COW*, and *CLEAN* word nodes, but not from the *GROUP* word node. Most importantly, in the present context, there are no inhibitory connections between words that are strictly orthographically unrelated, such as *QUIET* and *CROWN*.

4.3.2. *Limiting the number of inhibitory connections*

The second problem that arises when implementing selective inhibition is specifically computational. A notable practical advantage of homogeneous inhibition is that the inhibitory signal to a word node can be determined by summing total word level activity and subtracting the activity of that node, so that it does not inhibit itself; the latter step can be conceptualised as a self-excitatory input. The implication is that non-selective inhibition can be implemented on the basis of summed activity without modelling any lateral inhibitory interactions. By contrast, to compute the inhibitory signal to a word node when selective inhibition is assumed necessitates multiplying each of the activities of other word nodes by the inhibitory connections that these word nodes send to the node in question. That is, computing all of the lateral inhibitory signals at each step requires $O(N^2)$ calculations, where N is the number of word nodes. In the brain, such calculations can be performed in parallel, and so the value of N does not affect the speed of processing. When implementing selective inhibition on a serial computer, however, processing speed becomes highly dependent on the value of N. In relatively small networks the time cost is manageable, but in more realistically sized networks it becomes impractical to fully implement selective inhibition. For example, the network used in the simulations here encodes a lexicon of over 30,000 words, and thus would require a lateral inhibitory matrix of approximately one billion connections.

In practice, the vast majority of all word nodes are not involved in the selection process on a given input trial. Those word nodes do not receive any activation and hence do not need to be exposed to inhibitory signals in order to ensure that only one word is identified. The word recognition process will not differ in its outcome if only those word nodes are taken into account that are similar to the input stimuli. This implies that a feasible way to solve the computational explosion caused by selective inhibition is to restrict the simulation on each trial to a subnetwork of critical nodes (i.e., those that will become active).

This idea was implemented as follows. In order to select the critical word nodes on each trial, match values were computed for each word node in the lexicon relative to the prime and target stimuli. Hence, each word node in the network had two values assigned to it (e.g., its match with the prime *quiet* and its match with the target *CROWN*). For selection purposes only the greater of the two values was taken into account, and the top 30 values were then used to select the critical word nodes. When the prime and the target are unrelated, as in the experiment simulated here, this process results in two clusters around the location of each stimulus in lexical space.

4.4. *Testing the selective inhibition SCM*

In order to test the selective inhibition SCM we conducted a number of simulations. The first simulation re-examined the response congruency effect to test whether the modification to lateral inhibition had had the desired effect of eliminating inhibition from unrelated word primes. The other simulations tested whether the modification to lateral inhibition had affected the SCM's ability to account for other masked priming data.

4.4.1. *Simulation of response congruency*

The simulation of response congruency effects used the same stimuli as in the previous simulations. The results of this simulation (see Table 1) indicate a response congruency effect of the same magnitude in word and nonword targets. This is in line with both experiments that reported such an effect[15,16].

As can be seen in the table, the switch to selective inhibition had no effect on nonword targets, which are not vulnerable to lexical inhibition. However, the switch to selective inhibition boosted the congruency effect for word targets from a null effect to a moderate facilitatory effect. In congruent word trials, the activity of the target word does not inhibit the word node that was activated by the prime, and this results in greater summed lexical activity in the selective inhibition SCM than in the homogeneous inhibition SCM. This is illustrated by comparing the graphs in Fig. 1. Both homogeneous (Panel A) and selective inhibition (Panel B) show an initial advantage in summed lexical activity in congruent compared to incongruent trials. But as a result of the modifications to lateral inhibition, the activity in the selective inhibition model does not drop as rapidly as in the homogeneous inhibition model, in which the prime and target are mutually inhibitory. The advantage of congruent over incongruent trials is therefore maintained for about 40 cycles after target onset in the selective inhibition model. At this point the activity of the prime has diminished as a result of spontaneous decay. Another reason for the difference between the accounts can be seen in the lexical identification functions for target words, which are indistinguishable in congruent and incongruent trials in selective inhibition. Since both word nodes do not interact, the modified version of the

SCM predicts that a target word is identified just as rapidly when preceded by an unrelated word prime or an unrelated nonword prime. This is illustrated in Fig. 1 (Panel B), where congruent and incongruent trials are almost perfectly overlapping after cycle 40 (at this point the activity in the prime has decayed). Using homogeneous inhibition (Panel A) the disadvantage in target identification is persistent for a substantial part of the lexical decision process.

The activity pattern in the incongruent trials is almost perfectly overlapping in Panel A and B in Fig. 1, because incongruent word trials involve only a single cluster of lexical activity where no difference between homogeneous and selective inhibition is expected.

In summary, immediate onset of activation in the target word node and a longer lasting activation in the prime enabled the modified version of the model to predict a congruency priming effect in word targets.

4.4.2. Simulation of other masked form priming data

The final set of simulations we conducted was a replication of the twenty masked priming simulations reported in Davis[1]; this set comprises 61 separate masked form priming effects, including conditions in which the prime is a) identical to the target, b) one or two letters different, c) a transposition neighbour, d) a subset of the target, or e) a superset of the target. The homogeneous SCM results in an excellent fit to the data, with a correlation of 0.95 between the predicted and observed priming effects. The selective inhibition SCM (using identical parameters to the original simulation) showed an equally good fit ($r = 0.95$). Thus, switching to selective inhibition eliminates the inhibitory effect of unrelated primes on target identification, but does not disrupt the ability of the model to capture priming effects due to related primes.

5. General Discussion

The results of the simulations show that neither the Spatial Coding model[1] nor the Bayesian Reader[3] predicts a response congruency effect in masked primed lexical decision. The empirical findings[15,16] indicate that such effects occur, given primes that are informative with respect to the lexical classification.

The Bayesian Reader cannot predict a response congruency effect due to the way the data are integrated within the model. The information gathered from the prime changes the priors, but not the probability for the target which remains at zero. When the target is presented the priors are multiplied with the zero probability of the target and the effect of the prime is wiped out. Without a fundamental modification the model cannot account for response congruency effects.

The Spatial Coding model assumes a lexical level of processing that is similar to that in the interactive activation model[18]. We have shown that the lexical component and specifically homogeneous inhibition prevents the model from predicting a response congruency priming effect. The same considerations apply to a number of other models, including the original interactive activation model and the multiple read-out model[23].

The introduction of selective inhibition enabled the SCM to correctly predict the response congruency effect. Instead of inhibiting all word nodes in the network, a word node in a model employing selective inhibition will only inhibit other word nodes that code orthographically similar words. The current implementation reduces the computational load by selecting the word nodes that will take part in the competition in advance which is in contrast to simulating a fixed number of connections as a function of the vocabulary size.

The introduction of selective inhibition did not impair the ability of the spatial coding model to predict a number of benchmark effects. Most of these effects concern primes and targets that are related to each other, e.g. share their outer letters or form anagrams of each other. This similarity locates them in close proximity in lexical space and hence the selective inhibition account does not differ from the homogeneous account in those cases.

6. Conclusions

We have shown that the homogeneous inhibition account cannot accommodate response congruency effects in masked primed lexical decision. A modification of the underlying lexical component to use selective inhibition allows the model to produce correct predictions while maintaining its ability to predict other well-established effects. This modification allowed the combination of a more economic computation with a greater scope of the model. The empirical data can be interpreted as evidence against the idea that reading a word causes inhibitory signals to be delivered to all other words, but rather activity is suppressed in a small number of similar words. This is seems to be more economic and plausible. Furthermore, we have shown that the Bayesian Reader model cannot predict a response congruency effect due to the way data are integrated over time.

References

1. C. J. Davis, *Psychol. Rev.* **117**, 713 (2010).
2. D. Norris, *Psychol. Rev.* **113**, 327 (2006).
3. D. Norris and S. Kinoshita, *J. Exp. Psychol. Gen.* **137**, 434 (2008).
4. K. I. Forster and C. Davis, *J. Exp. Psychol. Learn.* **10**, 680 (1984).
5. K. I. Forster, C. Davis, C. Schoknecht and R. Carter, *Q. J. Exp. Psychol.* **39A**, 211 (1987).
6. S. Kinoshita and S. J. Lupker, Eds., *Masked priming: The state of the art* (Psychology Press, New York and Hove, 2003).
7. G. W. Humphreys, P. T. Quinlan, L. J. Evett and D. Besner, in *Attention and Performance XII: The Psychology of Reading*, M. Coltheart, Ed. (Lawrence Erlbaum Associates, Hove and London (UK), Hillsdale (USA), 1987), pp. 106-125.
8. S. Dehaene et al., *Nature* **395**, 597 (1998).
9. L. Naccache and S. Dehaene, *Cognition* **80**, 215 (2001).
10. E. Chan, O. Ybarra and N. Schwarz, *J. Exp. Soc. Psychol.* **42**, 365 (2006).
11. M. Perea and A. Gotor, *Cognition* **62**, 223-240 (1997).
12. M. Perea, L. Fernández and E. Rosa, *Psicologica* **19**, 311 (1998).
13. M. Perea, P. Gómez and I. Fraga, *Psychon. B. Rev.* **17**, 369 (2010).
14. M. R. Klinger, P. C. Burton and G. S. Pitts, *J. Exp. Psychol. Learn.* **26**, 441 (2000).
15. A. M. Jacobs, J. Grainger and L. Ferrand, *Percept. Psychophys.* **57**, 1101 (1995).
16. S. Loth and C. J. Davis, in *London meeting of Experimental Psychology Society*, (London, 2010).
17. M. F. Damian, *J. Exp. Psychol. Human.* **27**, 154 (2001).
18. J. L. McClelland and D. E. Rumelhart, *Psychol. Rev.* **88**, 375 (1981).
19. C. J. Davis and S. J. Lupker, *J. Exp. Psychol. Human.* **32**, 668 (2006).
20. A. M. Jacobs, J. Grainger, *J. Exp. Psychol. Human.* **18**, 1174 (1992).
21. C. J. Davis, in *Masked priming: The state of the art*, Macquarie Monographs in Cognitive Science. S. Kinoshita, S. J. Lupker, Eds. (Psychology Press, New York and Hove, 2003), pp. 67-94.
22. C. J. Davis, thesis, University of New South Wales (1999).
23. J. Grainger and A. M. Jacobs, *Psychol. Rev.* **103**, 518 (1996).

SENTENCE COMPREHENSION AS MENTAL SIMULATION: AN INFORMATION-THEORETIC ANALYSIS AND A CONNECTIONIST MODEL

STEFAN L. FRANK

Department of Cognitive, Perceptual and Brain Sciences,
University College London,
London, United Kingdom
E-mail: s.frank@ucl.ac.uk

It has been argued that understanding a sentence comes down to mentally simulating the state-of-affairs described by the sentence. This paper presents a particular formalization of this idea and shows how it gives rise to measures of the amount of syntactic and semantic information conveyed by each word in a sentence. These information measures predict simulated word-processing times in a connectionist model of sentence comprehension.

1. Introduction

Generative language models, as defined in the field of Computational Linguistics, capture the occurrence statistics of linguistic forms. If the cognitive system is sensitive to such statistics, language models should be able to account for some aspect of human language processing. Indeed, language models give rise to formal measures of the amount of syntactic information conveyed by each word in a sentence, and it has been suggested that these information measures are related to cognitive processing effort.[1-3] The higher a word's information content, the more 'work' needs to be done to process the word, which would be apparent in, for example, prolonged reading times.

This information-theoretic view of sentence processing may seem at odds with the assumption that our experience with (and knowledge of) the *world*, rather than language, are central to language comprehension. As proponents of this 'embodied linguistics' would claim, the language-comprehension and perceptuomotor systems are deeply intertwined: To understand a sentence is to mentally simulate whatever situation the sentence states to be the case.[4] Consequently, processing difficulty should occur when this situation violates our expectations or experience regarding the way things happen in the world. Take, for example, these two sentences:

(1a) The boys searched for branches with which they went drumming.
(1b) The boys searched for bushes   with which they went drumming.

In an ERP experiment,[5] the N400 component on the sentence-final word was found to be larger in (1b) than in (1a), indicating relative comprehension difficulty in (1b). A possible explanation is that mentally simulating the described action is more difficult in (1b) than in (1a), because it makes no sense to try and drum with bushes whereas drumming with branches is possible (albeit somewhat unusual). It is therefore the sentence's meaning in relation to our knowledge of the world, and not our experience with linguistic forms, that is responsible for the N400 effect in this experiment.

The main objective of this paper is to show how the information-theoretic and mental-simulation views on language can be combined by extending the notion of word information to semantics (Sec. 2). Following this, Sec. 3 present a connectionist sentence-comprehension model that treats comprehension as mental simulation, that is, as the construction of a representation of the described situation. Syntactic and semantic word-information measures are defined within this modelling framework. In Sec. 4, the model's word-reading time predictions are compared to the information measures. Indeed, words take longer to process if they convey more information, be it semantic or syntactic. Sec. 5 discusses the implication of these findings for theories of language processing and acquisition, and Sec. 6 concludes.

2. Measuring word information

Formal measures of word information have only been proposed with respect to generative language models, in particular Probabilistic Context-Free Grammars.[1–3,6–10] By definition, a generative language model defines a probability distribution over sentences. As the words of a sentence are processed one at a time, this distribution changes. It is this fluctuation of sentence probabilities that gives rise to measures of word information. Since these sentence probabilities depend only on the statistics of linguistic *forms*, the information measures will be referred to as *syntactic*.

Alternatively, word information content can be defined with respect to the probabilities of different states of the world. When a sentence is processed incrementally, each word changes the probabilities of the states-of-affairs being described. Again, this leads to formalizations of word information. These information measures depend on knowledge of the *meaning* of language and will therefore be referred to as *semantic*.

Syntax and semantics are different sources of information. An orthogonal distinction is between different *measures* of information. Two such measures will be used here: *surprisal* and *entropy reduction*. As explained in more detail below, surprisal is a measure of the unexpectedness of a word's occurrence and entropy reduction quantifies the extent to which a word reduces the uncertainty about the upcoming material.

The remainder of this section explains and formalizes four types of information: syntactic surprisal, syntactic entropy reduction, semantic surprisal, and semantic entropy reduction.

2.1. *Syntactic information measures*

2.1.1. *Language model*

Let S denote the (possibly infinite) set of all complete sentences. An n-word sentence is a string of words $w_1, \ldots, w_n$, denoted $w_{1\ldots n}$ for short. A generative language model defines a probability distribution over S, such that $P(w_{1\ldots n}) = 0$ if $w_{1\ldots n} \in S$ is ungrammatical.

As a sentence is processed one word at a time, the sentence probabilities fluctuate. Let $P(w_{1\ldots n}|w_{1\ldots i})$ be the probability of sentence $w_{1\ldots n}$ given that the first i words (i.e., the string $w_{1\ldots i}$) have been seen so far. If $w_{1\ldots i}$ does not match the first i words of $w_{1\ldots n}$ (or if $n < i$) then $P(w_{1\ldots n}|w_{1\ldots i}) = 0$. Otherwise, $w_{1\ldots n}$ equals $w_{1\ldots i, i+1\ldots n}$, and, by definition of conditional probability,

$$P(w_{1\ldots n}|w_{1\ldots i}) = \frac{P(w_{1\ldots i, i+1\ldots n})}{P(w_{1\ldots i})}.$$

Here, the probability of the incomplete sentence $w_{1\ldots i}$ is the total probability of all sentences that begin with $w_{1\ldots i}$, that is,

$$P(w_{1\ldots i}) = \sum_{w_{1\ldots i, i+1\ldots n} \in S} P(w_{1\ldots i, i+1\ldots n}).$$

2.1.2. *Syntactic surprisal*

Linguistic expressions differ strongly in their occurrence frequencies. For one, idiomatic expressions are often more frequent than similar, non-idiomatic sentences. As a result, the word 'dogs' is more expected in the context of (2a) than in (2b):

(2a) It is raining   cats and dogs.
(2b) She is training cats and dogs.

Surprisal is a formal measure of the extent to which a word occurs unexpectedly. The syntactic surprisal of word w_{i+1} given the sentence-so-far $w_{1...i}$ is defined as the negative logarithm of the word's probability according to the language model:

$$s_{\text{syn}}(i+1) = -\log P(w_{i+1}|w_{1...i}) \qquad (1)$$
$$= \log P(w_{1...i}) - \log P(w_{1...i+1}).$$

It has been suggested that syntactic surprisal is indicative of cognitive processing effort and should therefore be predictive of word-reading time.[1,3] Indeed, reading times have repeatedly been shown to correlate positively with surprisal as estimated by a range of language models.[7–9,11,12]

2.1.3. *Syntactic entropy reduction*

Before a sentence has been fully processed, there may exist uncertainty about the upcoming words. This uncertainty usually (but not necessarily) decreases with each word that comes in. For example, after processing 'It is raining' it is uncertain if the sentence is over, if a connective (like 'and') will follow, or if the verb is used in the less frequent transitive sense, as in sentence (2a). Hence, there is quite some uncertainty about what will come next. Presumably, the amount of uncertainty is more or less the same after 'She is training'. Now assume that the next word turns out to be 'cats'. In (2a), the occurrence of 'cats' make it almost certain that the rest of the sentence will be 'and dogs', that is, uncertainty is reduced to nearly zero. In (2b), on the other hard, the occurrence of 'cats' is not very informative about what the next words will be, so much uncertainty remains.

Syntactic entropy is a formal measure of the uncertainty about the rest of the sentence. It equals the entropy of the probability distribution over all sentences in $\mathcal{S}$, which is defined as

$$H_{\text{syn}} = - \sum_{w_{1...n} \in \mathcal{S}} P(w_{1...n}) \log P(w_{1...n}).$$

When the sentence's first i words have been processed, and the sentence probabilities have changed accordingly, the entropy is

$$H_{\text{syn}}(i) = - \sum_{w_{1...n} \in \mathcal{S}} P(w_{1...n}|w_{1...i}) \log P(w_{1...n}|w_{1...i}). \qquad (2)$$

Note that entropy is minimal when all probabilities are zero[a] except for a single sentence $w_{1...n}$, which must then have a probability of one. In that case, there is certainty about the upcoming words. In contrast, uncertainty (and entropy) is maximal when all sentences have the same probability.

Processing word w_{i+1} reduces the entropy by

$$\Delta H_{\mathrm{syn}}(i+1) = H_{\mathrm{syn}}(i) - H_{\mathrm{syn}}(i+1).$$

This reduction in syntactic entropy due to processing a word has been argued to be a cognitively relevant measure of the amount of information conveyed[2,6] and has recently been shown to predict word-reading times independently of syntactic surprisal.[13,14]

2.2. Semantic information measures

2.2.1. World model

When defining the syntactic information measures above, the sentence-processing system's task was taken to be the identification of the incoming sentence. Likewise, the task of sentence *comprehension* is to identify the state-of-affairs that is asserted by the sentence. This requires knowledge of the many possible states of the world and their probabilities.

Let $\mathrm{sit}(w_{1...n})$ denote the situation described by sentence $w_{1...n}$ and $P(\mathrm{sit}(w_{1...n}))$ the probability of that situation. Situations can be combined using boolean operators. So, if p and q denote two situations then $\neg p$, $p \wedge q$ and $p \vee q$ are also situations. For example, if $p = \mathrm{sit}(it\ is\ raining)$ and $q = \mathrm{sit}(it\ is\ daytime)$ then $\neg p = \mathrm{sit}(it\ is\ not\ raining)$ and $p \wedge q = \mathrm{sit}(it\ is\ raining\ and\ it\ is\ daytime)$.

The situation described by an incomplete sentence, $\mathrm{sit}(w_{1...i})$, is defined as the disjunction of all situations described by sentences that start with $w_{1...i}$. So, $\mathrm{sit}(it\ is) = \mathrm{sit}(it\ is\ raining) \vee \mathrm{sit}(it\ is\ daytime) \vee \mathrm{sit}(it\ is\ freezing) \vee ....$[b]

---

[a]Strictly speaking, entropy is not defined when there is a zero probability because $\log(0)$ does not exist. However, when p goes to zero, $p\log(p) = 0$ in the limit. Therefore, we can take $0\log(0)$ to equal zero.

[b]This definition assumes that the sentence does not contain a negation. Without this assumption, $\mathrm{sit}(it\ is) = \mathrm{sit}(it\ is\ raining) \vee \mathrm{sit}(it\ is\ not\ raining) \vee ...$, which would be uninformative so sentence interpretation could not start until the sentence is over and it is sure the speaker will not suddenly exclaim '*Not!*'. In line with this assumption, experimental evidence[15] has indicated that negations are ignored initially and applied only after the negated statement has been mentally represented.

2.2.2. *Semantic surprisal*

Situations and events in the world differ in their (perceived) likelihood of occurrence. For example, according to our knowledge of the academia, the situation described in (3a) should be more probable than the one in (3b):

(3a) The brilliant paper was immediately accepted.
(3b) The terrible paper was immediately accepted.

Consequently, the word 'accepted' is more expected in (3a) than in (3b). Semantic surprisal quantifies the extent to which the incoming word led to the assertion of a situation that is unlikely to occur, given what was already learned from the sentence so far.

A sentence up to word w_i describes the situation $\mathrm{sit}(w_{1...i})$. The next word, w_{i+1}, changes the situation to $\mathrm{sit}(w_{1...i+1})$. The corresponding change in the situations' probabilities gives rise to a definition of the semantic surprisal of w_{i+1}, analogous to syntactic surprisal of Eq. 1:

$$s_{\mathrm{sem}}(i+1) = -\log P(\mathrm{sit}(w_{1...i+1})|\mathrm{sit}(w_{1...i}))$$
$$= \log P(\mathrm{sit}(w_{1...i})) - \log P(\mathrm{sit}(w_{1...i+1}))). \qquad (3)$$

Note that semantic surprisal is independent of the sentence probabilities. Only the probability of the described situation is relevant.

2.2.3. *Semantic entropy reduction*

Brilliant papers get accepted whereas the fate of a mediocre paper is unsure. Therefore, the uncertainty about the situation being communicated is higher in sentence fragment (4a) than in (4b).

(4a) The mediocre paper was immediately —
(4b) The brilliant paper was immediately —

When a sentence is complete (and unambiguous) there is no more uncertainty. Therefore, whether the next word of (4a) and (4b) turns out to be 'accepted' or 'rejected', it reduces uncertainty more strongly, and therefore conveys more semantic information, in (4a) than in (4b).

Semantic entropy quantifies the uncertainty about the described situation. It is not as easy to define as syntactic entropy; The main problem here is that the total probability over all situations is larger than 1 because situations are not mutually exclusive. For example, one situation may be that it is raining and another that it is daytime, and these can obviously occur simultaneously. As a result, the collection of situation probabilities does not form a probability distribution. Moreover, situations are not discrete entities like sentences: There seems to be uncountably infinite situations, whereas the number of sentences may be infinite but is at least countable. These two problems are circumvented here by only taking into account those situations that can be described by some sentence, and by normalizing probabilities to sum to 1:

$$P_{\text{norm}}(\text{sit}(w_{1...n})) = \frac{P(\text{sit}(w_{1...n}))}{\sum_{v_{1...n} \in \mathcal{S}} P(\text{sit}(v_{1...n}))}.$$

By analogy with syntactic entropy (Eq. 2), the semantic entropy after processing $w_{1...i}$ is

$$H_{\text{sem}}(i) = -\sum_{w_{1...n} \in \mathcal{S}} P_{\text{norm}}(\text{sit}(w_{1...n})|\text{sit}(w_{1...i})) \log P_{\text{norm}}(\text{sit}(w_{1...n})|\text{sit}(w_{1...i})),$$

$$(4)$$

making the semantic entropy reduction due to word w_{i+1}:

$$\Delta H_{\text{sem}}(i+1) = H_{\text{sem}}(i) - H_{\text{sem}}(i+1).$$

3. The sentence-comprehension model

This section presents a recent connectionist model of sentence comprehension[16] that implements language understanding as mental simulation. The model treats word-by-word processing of a sentence $w_{1...n}$ as the incremental construction of a representation of the described situation $\text{sit}(w_{1...n})$. As explained in detail below, probabilities of situations follow directly from the representations, making this framework ideally suited for incorporating semantic word-information measures and for studying their effect on sentence processing. A simple extension to the model makes it possible to obtain word-processing times, which are compared to word information.

3.1. *Microworld*

According to the mental-simulation view of language comprehension, understanding a sentence requires real-world knowledge and experience. To make world knowledge manageable for the model, it is restricted here to a small 'microworld'. The rest of this section presents the microworld and explains how states of the microworld are represented in the model. However, many details will be skipped since they can be found elsewhere.[16]

3.1.1. *Situations*

The microworld has only three inhabitants (sophia, heidi, and charlie) and four locations (bedroom, bathroom, street and playground. There also exist games and toys, like chess, hide&seek, ball, and puzzle. All in all, 44 different atomic situations can occur in the world. Examples are play(heidi,chess), win(sophia), and place(charlie,playground), which, respectively, refer to heidi playing chess, sophia winning, and charlie being in the playground. Atomic situations can be combined using the boolean operators of negation, conjunction, and disjunction, creating more complex situations such as play(heidi,chess) ∧ play(charlie,chess) ∧¬lose(heidi), which is the case when heidi does not lose a game of chess to charlie.

Some situations are more likely to occur than others. To name a few, heidi tends to win at hide&seek, sophia usually loses at chess, and charlie is most often in a different place than the girls. There are also hard constraints on possible situations, for instance, each of the three protagonists is always in exactly one place, the ball is only played with in outside locations, and someone has to play some game in order to win or lose.

3.1.2. *Representation*

Following a scheme originally developed for a model of story comprehension,[17] microworld situations are represented by vectors in a high-dimensional 'situation space'. A crucial property of these representations is that they are analogical, in the sense that relations among the vectors mirror relations among the represented situations. The same has been argued to hold for mental representations.[18]

The vectors for atomic situations follow from a large number of examples of microworld states. Each example shows which atomic situations are the case, and which are not, at one moment in microworld time. The probabilistic constraints on co-occurrences of situations, which are apparent from the examples, are extracted by a self-organizing network. Its output consists of one 150-dimensional vector $\mu(p) = (\mu_1(p), \ldots, \mu_{150}(p)) \in [0,1]^{150}$ for each atomic situation p. These situation vectors are such that approximate microworld probabilities follow directly. Probability estimates from situation vectors, called 'belief values', are denoted by the symbol τ:

$$\tau(p) = \frac{1}{150} \sum_j \mu_j(p) \qquad \approx P(p) \tag{5}$$

$$\tau(p \wedge q) = \frac{1}{150} \sum_j \mu_j(p)\mu_j(q) \approx P(p \wedge q). \tag{6}$$

From Eq. 5 and the fact that $P(\neg p) = 1 - P(p)$, it follows that $\mu(\neg p) = 1 - \mu(p)$. From Eq. 6 it follows that $\mu_j(p \wedge q) = \mu_j(p)\mu_j(q)$. By making use of the fact that $p \vee q \equiv \neg(\neg p \wedge \neg q)$, the vector representing the disjunction $p \vee q$ can also be constructed. In short, any complex situation can be represented by combining the 44 atomic situation vectors, and a vector's average element value is an estimate of the probability of the represented situation.

Another interesting and useful property of situation vectors is that probabilistic inference is performed by the representations themselves. The probability of any (atomic or complex) situation p given that q is the case, can be observed directly from $\mu(p)$ and $\mu(q)$:

$$P(p|q) = \frac{P(p \wedge q)}{P(q)} \approx \frac{\sum_j \mu_j(p)\mu_j(q)}{\sum_j \mu_j(q)} = \frac{\tau(p \wedge q)}{\tau(q)} = \tau(p|q).$$

This means that a representation of the fact that p is also a representation of anything that is implied by p. For example, if sophia is playing with the ball she cannot be in the bedroom, and indeed $\tau(\text{place}(\text{sophia},\text{bedroom})|\text{play}(\text{sophia},\text{ball})) \approx 0$. This property of direct inference, which distinguishes analogical from symbolic representations, is also present in mental representations: In one experiment,[19] participants who were told that *the pencil is in the cup* automatically and unconsciously formed a visual representation in which the pencil is in a vertical position, as opposed to when they heard that *the pencil is in the drawer*.

3.2. *Microlanguage*

Microworld situations are described by microlanguage sentences. Again, full details are published elsewhere[16] so they will not be presented here. The language has a vocabulary of 40 words, including (proper) nouns like *heidi, girl, playground,* and *chess*; verbs such as *beats, is,* and *played*; adverbs (*inside, outside*); and prepositions (*with, at, in*). These words can be combined to form 13,556 different sentences, each unambiguously referring to one (atomic or complex) microworld situation. A few examples are presented in Table 1.

Table 1. Examples of microlanguage sentences and corresponding situations. c = charlie; h = heidi; s = sophia.

Sentence	Situation
charlie plays chess	play(c, chess)
chess is played by charlie	play(c, chess)
girl plays chess	play(h, chess) ∨ play(s, chess)
sophia plays with ball in playground	play(s, ball) ∧ place(s, playground)
chess is lost by heidi	lose(h) ∧ play(h, chess)
charlie wins outside	win(c) ∧ (place(c, street) ∨ place(c, playground))
sophia beats charlie at hide-and-seek	win(s) ∧ lose(c) ∧ play(s, hide&seek)

3.3. The model

3.3.1. Architecture

The sentence-comprehension model is a Simple Recurrent Network (SRN)[20] that takes as input a microlanguage sentence, one word at a time, and is trained to give as output the vector representing the corresponding situation. As shown in Fig. 1, the network has a standard three-layer architecture, with 40 input units (one for each word in the microlanguage), 120 hidden (i.e., recurrent) units, and 150 output units (corresponding to the 150 dimensions of situation space).

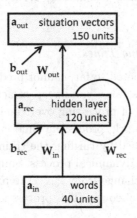

Fig. 1. Architecture of the sentence-comprehension network.

To process the word occurring at sentence position $i + 1$, the common SRN equations are:

$$\mathbf{a}_{rec}(i+1) = f(\mathbf{W}_{rec}\mathbf{a}_{rec}(i) + \mathbf{W}_{in}\mathbf{a}_{in}(i+1) + \mathbf{b}_{rec})$$
$$\mathbf{a}_{out}(i+1) = f(\mathbf{W}_{out}\mathbf{a}_{rec}(i+1) + \mathbf{b}_{out}), \tag{7}$$

where $\mathbf{W}$ are connection weight matrices; $\mathbf{b}$ are bias vectors; $f(\mathbf{x})$ is the logistic function; and $\mathbf{a}_{in}(i+1)$ is the input vector that forms a localist encoding of word w_{i+1}. The sentence-comprehension model follows these equations except that, after training, $\mathbf{a}_{out}(i+1)$ is computed differently, as explained in Sec. 3.3.3 below. When a sentence that describes microworld situation p has been processed, the output vector $\mathbf{a}_{out}$ ideally equals p's vector representation $\mu(p)$.

3.3.2. Network Training

Training examples were randomly sampled from all 13,556 microlanguage sentences, with shorter sentences having a larger sampling probability. Each sampled sentence was presented to the network, one word at a time. At each word, the target output was the vector representing the situation described by the complete sentence, and network weights and biases were updated accordingly using the standard backpropagation algorithm. Training stopped when the squared error between targets $\mu(\text{sit}(w_{1...n}))$ and actual outputs $\mathbf{a}_{out}(n)$, over all microlanguage sentences $w_{1...n}$, was down to 2% of the pre-training error. It took approximately 1.4 million training sentences to reach that criterion.

3.3.3. Obtaining Processing Times

The original model, presented so far, cannot predict reading times because processing a word always takes one sweep of activation through the network: There is no notion of processing over time. To extract reading-time predictions from the network, processing time must be made to vary over words. This is accomplished by turning the trained network's output vector update (Eq. 7) into a dynamical process. Simply stated, processing the word at $i+1$ involves a change from $\mathbf{a}_{out}(i)$ to $\mathbf{a}_{out}(i+1)$ over continuous time t rather than instantaneously. This process follows a simple differential equation:

$$\frac{d\mathbf{a}_{out}}{dt} = \mathbf{a}_{out} - f(\mathbf{W}_{out}\mathbf{a}_{rec}(i+1) + \mathbf{b}_{out}), \tag{8}$$

where the initial value of $\mathbf{a}_{out}$ equals $\mathbf{a}_{out}(i)$, and $\mathbf{a}_{out}(0)$ is set to the unit vector, which conveys no information about the state of the microworld because $\tau(p|\mathbf{1}) = \tau(p)$ for any p.

According to Eq. 8, the output vector $\mathbf{a}_{out}$ moves over processing time towards $f(\mathbf{W}_{out}\mathbf{a}_{rec}(i+1) + \mathbf{b}_{out})$ which equals $\mathbf{a}_{out}(i+1)$ of Eq. 7. The processes converges when $\mathbf{a}_{out}$ no longer changes, that is, when $d\mathbf{a}_{out}/dt = 0$. This is only the case when $\mathbf{a}_{out} = \mathbf{a}_{out}(i+1)$. Hence, after convergence, the output vector equals the output of the standard SRN (see Eq. 7). However, convergence is asymptotic so $d\mathbf{a}_{out}/dt$ never quite reaches 0. For this reason, the process is halted when the rate of change in $\mathbf{a}_{out}$ drops below a certain threshold:

$$|d\mathbf{a}_{out}/dt| < \max\{0.1 \times |\mathbf{a}_{out}|, 10^{-8}\}, \tag{9}$$

where $|\mathbf{x}|$ denotes the euclidean length of vector $\mathbf{x}$. So, word processing stops when the amount of change in $\mathbf{a}_{out}$ is less than 10% of the length of $\mathbf{a}_{out}$ itself, or smaller than 10^{-8}, whatever comes first. The amount of time t required to reach the stopping criterion of Eq. 9 is the simulated reading time on word w_{i+1}.

3.4. Measures of Word Information

The model's reading-time predictions are compared to measures of word information. The current framework allows for definitions of both syntactic and semantic information, both in terms of surprisal and in terms of entropy reduction.

3.4.1. Syntactic Information

The probabilities $P(w_{i+1}|w_{1...i})$ and $P(w_{1...n}|w_{1...i})$, from the definitions of syntactic surprisal (Eq. 1) and entropy (Eq. 2), are estimated directly from the frequencies with which sentences were sampled for training. This gives

$$s_{syn}(i+1) = \log(\text{freq}(w_{1...i})) - \log(\text{freq}(w_{1...i+1}))$$

$$H_{syn}(i) = -\sum_{w_{1...i,i+1...n} \in \mathcal{S}} \frac{\text{freq}(w_{1...i,i+1...n})}{\text{freq}(w_{1...i})} \log \frac{\text{freq}(w_{1...i,i+1...n})}{\text{freq}(w_{1...i})},$$

where $\text{freq}(w_{1...n})$ is the number of times sentence $w_{1...n}$ was sampled for training, and $\text{freq}(w_{1...i})$ is the total sampling frequency of sentences that begin with $w_{1...i}$.

3.4.2. Semantic Information

The computation of semantic surprisal (see Eq. 3) requires an estimate of $P(\text{sit}(w_{1...i}))$, the probability of situations described by sentences that start with $w_{1...i}$. Since the set of sentence/semantics-pairs in the microlanguage is known, determining $\text{sit}(w_{1...i})$ is straightforward: It is the disjunction of $\text{sit}(w_{1...n})$ over all sentences $w_{1...n}$ that start with $w_{1...i}$. The probability of $\text{sit}(w_{1...i})$ is estimated by its belief value, which follows from its vector representation:

$$P(\text{sit}(w_{1...i})) \approx \tau(\text{sit}(w_{1...i})) = \frac{1}{150} \sum_j \mu_j(\text{sit}(w_{1...i})).$$

To obtain measures of semantic entropy (Eq. 4), estimates of $P_{\text{norm}}(\text{sit}(w_{1...n})|\text{sit}(w_{1...i}))$ are needed. Let Z denote the set of microworld situations that can be described by some microlanguage sentence. The belief value for each such situation $z \in Z$ is $\tau(z)$. When the sentence-so-far $w_{1...i}$ has been processed, the belief values are $\tau(z|\text{sit}(w_{1...i}))$. These belief values are made to sum to 1, turning them into a proper probability distribution:

$$P_{\text{norm}}(\text{sit}(w_{1...n})|\text{sit}(w_{1...i})) \approx \tau_{\text{norm}}(\text{sit}(w_{1...n})|\text{sit}(w_{1...i}))$$
$$= \frac{\tau(\text{sit}(w_{1...n})|\text{sit}(w_{1...i}))}{\sum_{z \in Z} \tau(z|\text{sit}(w_{1...i}))}.$$

4. Experiments and Results

Everything is now in place to investigate the relation between the four word-information measures and the model's word-processing times. First, for each of the 84,321 word tokens in the 13,556 microlanguage sentences, surprisal and entropy reduction were computed with respect to both syntax and semantics. Next, the trained network received all sentences and processed them one word at a time, yielding a processing time for each word token.

Although all sentences are different, many are identical up to a certain word. The information measures and processing times are also identical up to that word, so many data points occur multiple times. All these copies were removed from the analysis, leaving a total of 15,873 data points.

The predictive value of the four information measures is determined by regressing the word-processing times on these measures. In addition, the position of the word in the sentence is included as a predictor. The pairwise correlations between these five predictors are shown in Table 2.

Table 3 presents the result of a stepwise regression analysis in which the predictor with the highest additional explanatory value was added at each step. The table shows both the predictor's coefficient and the fraction of variance explained (R^2) over and above what is accounted for by the predictors already in the model. Each addition resulted in a highly significant ($p < 10^{-8}$) increase in regression model fit.

Table 2. Matrix of correlation coefficients between predictors.

	ΔH_{syn}	s_{sem}	ΔH_{sem}	Position
s_{syn}	.95	.09	.21	−.03
ΔH_{syn}		.08	.21	−.07
s_{sem}			.42	.28
ΔH_{sem}				.13

Table 3. Regression analysis results. Factors are in order of inclusion in the regression model.

Predictor	Coefficient	R^2
s_{sem}	0.04	.310
ΔH_{sem}	0.64	.082
s_{syn}	0.12	.026
Position	0.08	.011
ΔH_{syn}	0.20	.001

By far the largest contribution to explained variance (31.0%) comes from semantic surprisal: A word takes longer to process if it makes the sentence describe a less likely situation. Semantic entropy reduction comprises the second largest contribution (8.2%): A word takes longer to process if it more strongly reduces the uncertainty about the situation being described. Syntactic information measures explain little (2.8% in total), but significant, additional variance in word-processing time. The effect of syntactic entropy reduction is particularly weak (just over 0.1%) but considering the high correlation with syntactic surprisal[c] (see Table 2) the additional variance explained by syntactic entropy reduction could only be very small. In total, 43.01% of variance in processing time is accounted for by the five predictors. The four word-information measures together account for 41.96%.

There is still 56.99% of variance in processing time unaccounted for. In order to investigate to what extent this may be due to imperfections in the SRN's output, the dynamical process of Eq. 8 was run once more but this time on the correct situation vectors $\mu(\text{sit}(w_{1...i}))$ rather than the network outputs $\mathbf{a}_{\text{out}}(i)$. As shown in Table 4, this increases the fraction of total

---

[c]The strong correlation between syntactic surprisal and syntactic entropy reduction seems to be an artifact of the artificial nature of the language. On a corpus of newspaper texts, the correlation between the two information measures was found[13] to be only around .25.

variance accounted for to as much as 83.68%, suggesting that a large part of the variance that is not accounted for in Table 3 is indeed caused by noise in the network's output.

Table 4. Regression analysis results when using correct situation vectors instead of network outputs. Factors are in order of inclusion in the regression model.

Predictor	Coefficient	R^2
s_{sem}	0.50	.758
ΔH_{sem}	4.66	.075
Position	0.30	.003
ΔH_{syn}	0.34	.001
s_{syn}	0.30	.000

5. Discussion

The sentence-comprehension model implements the mental-simulation theory of language understanding, in the sense that the comprehension process results in a non-linguistic, analogical representation of the situation described by the sentence. This representation is constructed incrementally: It is continuously updated as the sentence's words come in one by one. The incorporation of the incoming word into the current representation continues until the representation's rate of change drops below a threshold level. Consequently, more time is required if the word signals a greater change in the situation being described. As such, it may not come as a surprise that processing times correlate with formal measures of semantic information content: Words that convey much information are precisely those that have a large impact on the described situation.

Nevertheless, the current findings have implications for theories about the role of formal notions of information in cognition. Both surprisal and entropy reduction have been claimed to quantify amount of information and as such were assumed to predict word-reading times. However, this does not explain *why* information content would be related to processing time. The fact that surprisal and entropy reduction have independent effects on human word-reading times[13,14] would seem to indicate that there are two distinct cognitive processes or representations involved, one explaining the effect of surprisal and the other that of entropy reduction. The current finding, however, suggest an alternative: The only relevant comprehension processes is the revision of a single mental representation. Surprisal and entropy reduction merely form two complementary quantifications of the extent of this revision. The fact that they are formal measures of information does not give them any special cognitive status. Although language understanding can be viewed as information processing, information-theoretic concepts do not necessarily correspond to psycholinguistic reality.

In addition to semantic information, other factors were found to affect word-processing time. First, the word's position in the sentence had a positive effect. This contradicts experimental findings which have shown that reading speeds up over the course of a sentence.[8] Hence, the model cannot explain this effect of word position. Possibly, the construction of a mental simulation is not responsible for faster reading at later words.

Second, it is of some psycholinguistic interest that syntactic surprisal and syntactic entropy reduction accounted for some of the variance in word-processing time. Again, the relation was positive: words that convey more syntactic information are processed more slowly. Somehow, the network has become sensitive to the statistical patterns in the microlanguage and is thereby able to account (at least to some extent) for the effects of syntactic information on cognitive processing effort, which have been found in human reading-time data. When word-processing times were obtained by using the correct situation vectors rather than the network outputs, the effect of syntactic information all but disappeared: As can be seen in Table 4, the total R^2 associated with syntactic information is now only 0.001. The effect of syntactic surprisal is no longer significant ($p > .9$). This suggests that the relation between syntactic information and processing time is not just a fluke of the particular microlanguage and microworld, but originates from the network that learns to map the sentences to the corresponding situation vectors. Interestingly, this task does not require any syntactic knowledge, that is, knowledge of sentences probabilities is not needed for learning the form-meaning mapping. The finding that syntactic knowledge nevertheless affects word-processing times therefore suggests that learning the meaning of language can result in the acquisition of syntax as a side effect.

6. Conclusion

It was shown how cognitively relevant definitions of syntactic information can be extended to semantics. All it takes is a shift in focus from the statistics of the language (syntactic patterns) to the statistics of the world (semantic patterns). A connectionist sentence-comprehension model, rooted in ideas from Embodied Linguistics, predicted that words that convey more information take longer to process, irrespective of the information source (linguistic knowledge or world knowledge) and information measure (surprisal or entropy reduction). This constitutes a first step towards a more computationally developed theory of Embodied Linguistics, in which the incorporation of world knowledge into the definition of information provides a more sound formal basis to the notion of mental simulation.

Acknowledgements

This research was supported by grant 277-70-006 of the Netherlands Organization for Scientific Research (NWO). I am grateful to Michael Klein and Eddy Davelaar for commenting on an earlier version of this paper.

References

1. J. Hale, A probabilistic Early parser as a psycholinguistic model, in *Proceedings of the Second Meeting of the North American Chapter of the Association for Computational Linguistics*, (Pittsburgh, PA: Association for Computational Linguistics, 2001) pp. 159–166.
2. J. Hale, *Journal of Psycholinguistic Research* **32**, 101 (2003).
3. R. Levy, *Cognition* **106**, 1126 (2008).
4. R. Zwaan, Experiential traces and mental simulations in language comprehension, in *Symbols, embodiment, and meaning: debates on meaning and cognition*, eds. M. D. Vega, A. M. Glenberg and A. C. Graesser (Oxford, UK: Oxford University Press, 2008) pp. 165–180.
5. D. J. Chwilla, H. H. J. Kolk and C. T. W. M. Vissers, *Brain Research* **1183**, 109 (2007).
6. J. Hale, *Cognitive Science* **30**, 643 (2006).
7. M. F. Boston, J. Hale, U. Patil, R. Kliegl and S. Vasishth, *Journal of Eye Movement Research* **2**, 1 (2008).
8. V. Demberg and F. Keller, *Cognition* **109**, 193 (2008).
9. B. Roark, A. Bachrach, C. Cardenas and C. Pallier, Deriving lexical and syntactic expectation-based measures for psycholinguistic modeling via incremental top-down parsing, in *Proceedings of the 2009 Conference on Empirical Methods in Natural Language Processing*, (Association for Computational Linguistics, Singapore, 2009) pp. 324–333.
10. H. Brouwer, H. Fitz and J. Hoeks, Modeling the noun phrase versus sentence coordination ambiguity in Dutch: Evidence from surprisal theory, in *Proceedings of the 2010 Workshop on Cognitive Modeling and Computational Linguistics*, (Association for Computational Linguistics, Uppsala, Sweden, 2010) pp. 72–80.
11. S. L. Frank, Surprisal-based comparison between a symbolic and a connectionist model of sentence processing, in *Proceedings of the 31st Annual Con-*

ference of the Cognitive Science Society, eds. N. A. Taatgen and H. van Rijn (Austin, TX: Cognitive Science Society, 2009) pp. 1139–1144.

12. N. J. Smith and R. Levy, Optimal processing times in reading: a formal model and empirical investigation, in *Proceedings of the 30th Annual Conference of the Cognitive Science Society*, eds. B. C. Love, K. McRae and V. M. Sloutsky (Austin, TX: Cognitive Science Society, 2008) pp. 595–600.

13. S. L. Frank, Uncertainty reduction as a measure of cognitive processing effort, in *Proceedings of the 2010 Workshop on Cognitive Modeling and Computational Linguistics*, (Association for Computational Linguistics, Uppsala, Sweden, 2010) pp. 81–89.

14. S. Wu, A. Bachrach, C. Cardenas and W. Schuler, Complexity metrics in an incremental right-corner parser, in *Proceedings of the 48th Annual Meeting of the Association for Computational Linguistics*, (Association for Computational Linguistics, Uppsala, Sweden, 2010) pp. 1189–1198.

15. B. Kaup, R. H. Yaxley, C. J. Madden, R. A. Zwaan and J. Lüdtke, *Quarterly Journal of Experimental Psychology* **60**, 976 (2007).

16. S. L. Frank, W. F. M. Haselager and I. Van Rooij, *Cognition* **110**, 358 (2009).

17. S. L. Frank, M. Koppen, L. G. M. Noordman and W. Vonk, *Cognitive Science* **27**, 875 (2003).

18. L. W. Barsalou, *Behavioral and Brain Sciences* **22**, 577 (1999).

19. R. A. Stanfield and R. A. Zwaan, *Psychological Science* **12**, 153 (2001).

20. J. L. Elman, *Cognitive Science* **14**, 179 (1990).

MODELLING FREE RECALL – A COMBINED ACTIVATION-BUFFER AND DISTRIBUTED-CONTEXT MODEL

ANAT ELHALAL

School of Psychology, BirkbeckCollege, University of London, UK

MARIUS USHER

Department of Psychology, Tel Aviv University, Israel and School of Psychology, Birkbeck College, University of London, UK

A computational model of free recall is described, extending previous models by including both an activation buffer (Davelaar *et al.*, 2005) and a distributed changing context representation (Howard and Kahana, 1999, 2002). The model was used to simulate published free-recall data, and to make new predictions for the role of context in continuous distractor free recall. A faster contextual change is predicted to cause a shift from primacy to recency, in comparison to a slower contextual change. An experiment was carried out, and results are consistent with this prediction.

1. Introduction

Contemporary computational models of memory use "context" in order to differentiate between episodic and semantic knowledge[1]. However, little is known of the cognitive representation and dynamic processes of context. Here a computational model for free recall is presented, in an attempt to bring together two main computational modelling frameworks in the field: an activation buffer component[1-3], and TCM - Temporal Context Model[4-6]. The model we develop is a hybrid, which shares components with both the dual memory model of free recall – the capacity limited activation buffer and with the temporal context model – the gradually changing context. The model is then used to investigate the role of context in free recall.

We start with a recap of the dual activation-context model, followed by a description of the new hybrid model's processes and components. Following, simulation results of various manipulations are presented: basic serial position effects in immediate and continuous-distractor free recall (in short; IFR and CD, respectively), as well as data from semantic similarity manipulation and amnesic patients. Next, a new prediction, on the effects of contextual change on serial position functions is presented and supported by experimental data.

1.1. *Dual activation buffer model*

The dual activation-context model[1] is comprised of two layers: a localistic lexical layer, which is interconnected with a localistic context layer. Each lexical unit represents a word. In a simulation of studying a list of words, lexical units receive input sequentially. They remain active after stimulus offset due to self-excitation. Each lexical unit sends inhibition to all other lexical units. The balance between the self-excitation and global inhibition limits the number of co-active lexical units. The outcome is a competitive buffer mechanism in which newly presented items compete to replace older items whose activation levels are lower (the addition of buffer noise makes this process probabilistic). The active lexical units, thus, form a short-term buffer. Episodic learning takes place between active items in the buffer, and the currently active context unit. The context drifts in a random-walk manner along a linear axis (a single unit is active in the context layer at each time step). Retrieval starts by unloading the active items from the buffer. This is followed by an associative retrieval process from long-term memory, in which items compete for retrieval by their episodic strength: the relative selection probability depends on items' connection to the retrieval time context. During retrieval the context continues drifting by the random-walk, enabling the selection of other items.

This model can explain a vast amount of free-recall findings, including: short- and long-term serial position curves; short- and long-term lag-CRP (Conditional Response Probabilities); negative recency in final free recall; neuropsychological patients' dissociations between immediate and continuous distractor free recall, and differential effect of proactive interference on immediate and continuous-distractor free recall. Nevertheless, a few findings were found challenging to simulate, and will be used as benchmark data for the hybrid buffer-distributed-context model. First, the Davelaar *et al.* 2005 model[1] predicted a smaller recency effect than that reported in the literature. A richer context representation could overcome this. Second, primacy in the model is simulated in a somewhat artificial way, by resetting the retrieval time context to the start of the list context after half of the retrieval attempts. Third, the model did not account fully for the effect of semantic relatedness in the continuous-distractor task[7].

1.2. *Distributed context*

It is suggested that a distributed context representation could aid overcome these difficulties, while being more biologically plausible. In the hereby proposed model, an activation buffer (similar to the Davelaar *et al.* model) is linked with a neural network implementation of a TCM-like temporal context layer[4]. A distributed context is also more biologically plausible than a linear random walk context. A distributed context is the main component of the TCM model, in which context changes due to pre-experimental context of the words presented in the experiment, which represents semantic information related to these words. The context component in the current model is inspired by TCM, but also includes a second random change source, which represents changes in the environment which do not depend on the experimental material (as in random context models[8]).

2. The model

A hybrid model combining the activation buffer[1] and a neural network implementation of a TCM[4] style context is hereby presented. Such a model could possibly benefit from the two approaches, and simulate a larger body of evidence than each one of them separately.

2.1 Model components

The hybrid model is comprised of a localistic lexical layer, whose active units are considered to correspond to an activation buffer (bottom layer of Figure 1), and a context layer (middle layer of Figure 1). The context representation is distributed, and is implemented as a vector which changes with time; two sources drive this change: the pre-experimental context of the currently active lexical unit (as in TCM), and random noise. The pre-experimental context represents the effect of semantic information on the current context (vector illustrated at top of Figure 1), while the random change in the context represents the influence of factors external to the experiment material itself, such as random thoughts and environmental influences.

A third component is the connectivity matrix between the lexical and context layers. Episodic Hebbian learning takes place at encoding, via strengthening connections between active units in the two layers. These connections later drive retrieval. They also form the experimental (or episodic) context for the presented items, and are used to update the context in the case of a successful retrieval.

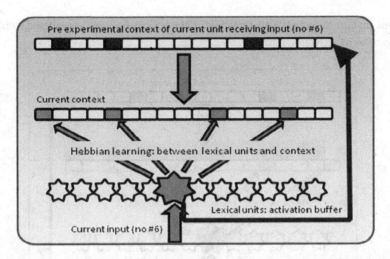

Fig. 1. Main components of the model: a lexical layer (bottom) is interconnected to a sparse context layer (middle). For example, if item number 6 is activated, Learning takes place between this item and active context units. This item also induces a context change by adding related semantic information to the context. This is represented by the item's pre-experimental context (vector illustrated at the top of drawing).

2.1. The encoding stage

At encoding (Figure 2), input is clamped on the lexical units (bottom layer), sequentially, one at a time, for T time-steps each. Studying a list is simulated by activating a few units (usually 12) consecutively. The currently activated lexical unit triggers its pre-experimental context (top vector, represents semantic memory, for example, the word "apple" could remind of being hungry), which is added to the present context (middle layer) along with random noise. The K-most-active context units remain active, while the rest are set to zero (K-winner take all activation rule[9]). Active lexical items get associated with active context units, via a Hebbian learning rule.

2.1.1. The lexical layer (activation buffer)

The lexical layer is comprised of 40 units, out of which twelve serve as list items, and have pre-experimental context. When implementing continuous distractor free recall, twelve more units serve as distractors (distractors have no pre-experimental context).

During a simulation of list presentation, lexical units are activated sequentially by clamping each unit for a "sensory" input for T = 80 time steps.

Units that are active above a threshold in the lexical layer are considered to be in a short term activation buffer.

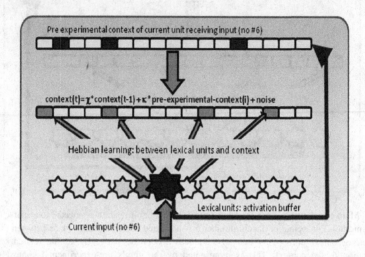

Fig. 2. Encoding: Item no 6 is currently clamped to the input (some distractor units, or previously presented items, are still active in the buffer). The unit's activation activates its pre-experimental context that leads to context update. Hebbian learning then takes place between the item and the new active context units.

Units are connected to themselves via self-excitation, to maintain activity after input offset. They are also negatively connected to all other units in the layer, to create global inhibition. The balance between the magnitude of the self excitation and global inhibition creates a limited capacity buffer. When a certain number of items are co-active, input to the next item will make its activation rise, and so cause the activation of the weakest item to diminish through global inhibition. The new item would eventually replace the weakest item in the buffer. Buffer dynamics are controlled by the following equation:

$$x_i(t) = \lambda x_i(t-1) + (1-\lambda)(\alpha F(x_i(t)) - \beta \sum F(x_j(t)) + I_i(t) + \xi) \tag{1}$$

where $F(x) = x/(1+x)$ for $x>0$, and 0 otherwise. $x_i(t)$: activation of lexical item i at time t. All activations are set to zero at the beginning of a simulation. λ a time constant, controlling the amount of change in each time step; α the self excitation parameter; β the global inhibition parameter;. $I_i(t)$: the sensory input to unit i at time t. The input is clamped to each list (or distractor) unit for **T** time steps. Input is zero for all other items. ξ Gaussian noise, with zero mean.. Values of buffer parameters were derived from past explorations[10].

The buffer dynamics are illustrated in Figure 3. Only few items can be co-active in the buffer, due to the dynamics between self excitation and global inhibition. When a new item is activated, it replaces the weakest item in the buffer, usually the oldest one, unless due to buffer noise. A distractor task is simulated by clamping input on "irrelevant" items, which do not participate in the later retrieval process. The rise of these items in the buffer replaces previous activations, and therefore simulates the flush of the short-term buffer by the distractor task.

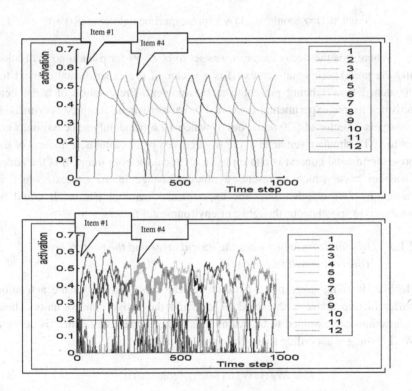

Fig. 3. Buffer dynamics (activation level vs. time step) in a simulation of list presentation. Top: simulation without buffer noise (artificial situation) bottom: buffer dynamics with noise. In both panels it can be seen that the input to item no. 4 (bold line) causes item no. 1 to leave the buffer. The vertical line at 0.2 is the buffer threshold.

214

2.1.2. *The context layer*

The context layer is comprised of 500 units, out of which 10% are active at any time ("K winner take all" with K=50). At the beginning of a simulation the activation of all context units is initialised to random small numbers, which are slightly higher than the steady state values to reflect the assumption that at the beginning of the list context is distinctive from the learning time context, due to the vast contextual change from rest to study.

The context is updated with random noise, and current active item's pre-experimental context, by the following equation:

$$\text{context}(t) = \chi * \text{context}(t-1) + \kappa * \text{pre-experimental-context}(i) + \eta \qquad (2)$$

Where χ is the decay factor, κ was set to be $(1-\chi)$ for pseudo-normalisation and the pre-experimental-context(i) is a vector of pre-experimental context for the item i that is being presented at the moment. Presentation of a list item activates its pre-experimental context. For each list item, the pre-experimental-context is a vector of 500 units, out of which 10% (randomly selected) units are set to 1. To simulate semantic similarity between pairs of items, a fraction of the pre-experimental context is chosen to be identical for both items. η is the added Gaussian noise which represents a random change in the context, which is caused by factors other than the experimental material per se. It could be attributed to spontaneous thoughts, or environmental factors.

2.1.3. *Hebbian learning between the lexical layer and the context layer (the connectivity matrix W)*

Hebbian learning takes place between lexical units that are in the activation buffer (active above a threshold of φ_1), and the active context units. These connections are assumed to be symmetrical. The connectivity matrix is denoted W. Learning is according to the following equation:

$$W_i(t) = W_i(t-1) + \varepsilon * (s_i * \text{context}(t)) \qquad (3)$$

Where s_i is the integral over the item activation (above threshold) since the last W update, and ε is the learning rate.

2.2. *The Retrieval Stage*

At retrieval (Figure 4), the lexical units compete for selection. Retrieval starts with unloading of active items from the buffer, and continues with episodic retrieval which is driven by the context layer and its connections with the lexical layer. There are 40 retrieval attempts; each attempt can either be successful or unsuccessful, following the principles of the SAM model (Search for Associative Memory[11]). The relative selection probabilities depend on the amount of activation each lexical unit receives from the current context.

$$P^{sel}_i = \exp(W_i \cdot context/\rho)/\Sigma_j \exp(W_j \cdot context/\rho) \tag{4}$$

P^{sel}_i is the selection probability, which depends on the item episodic encoding strength. ρ is the process "temperature". It controls the relationship between bigger episodic strengths, to larger probabilities of selection ("softmax" equation). The probability of selection is calculated for each lexical item, one of which is selected randomly according to its probability. Non-list items can also be selected (distractors or lexical units which were not activated at encoding by the input), and the result will be a non-successful retrieval attempt. Once an item is selected, it goes through a probabilistic recovery process, according to the following equation:

$$P^{rec}_i = 1/(1 + \exp(\varphi_2 - W_i \cdot context/\tau)) \tag{5}$$

Where P^{rec}_i is the recovery probability, φ_2 and τ are the recovery thresholds. (As in the SAM model, once an item has been retrieved, it cannot be retrieved again.).

The context keeps changing at retrieval. In the case of an item being retrieved, both its pre-experimental and experimental contexts are added to the current context, in addition to random noise.

$$context(t) = \chi \cdot context(t-1) + \kappa \cdot pre\text{-}experimental\text{-}context(i) + \tag{6}$$
$$(1-\chi-\kappa) \cdot experimental\text{-}context(i) + \eta$$

216

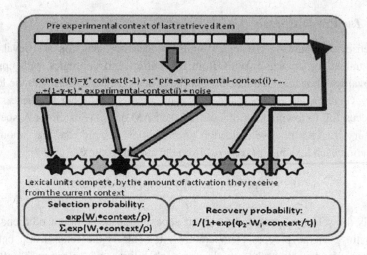

Fig. 4. Retrieval is context driven. Activation is sent from the current context to the lexical units. The units then compete for selection, by the softmax function. The selected item goes through a recovery process. If the retrieval attempt is successful, the pre-experimental-context of the item, as well as the experimental-context are added to the current context.

Where experimental-context: is the activation sent from the item to context units, i.e. the corresponding row from the W matrix. The pre-experimental and experimental context can be seen as contributions from semantic memories (pre-experimental context) and episodic memories (experimental context, which is stored in the connections between the items activated during the experiment and the context units). If no item is retrieved in the current attempt, noise only will be added to the context.

Additional details regarding the model processes can be found online at: www.bbk.ac.uk/psyc/staff/academic/musher/documents/ncpw12/model.pdf.

3. Simulations results

The model was used to simulate published data, as well as new experimental results. For initial validation, the model was first used to simulate basic serial position and lag-CRP curves. Following, benchmark data sets that proved challenging for previous models were simulated.

3.1. Basic simulations – serial position and lag-CRP in immediate free recall and continuous distractor free recall

Immediate and continuous-distractor free recall were simulated using the model. Results (see Figure 5, Figure 6) show good resemblance to reported data in the literature[12], as well to data from an experiment carried out in our lab[13].

The model serial position curves (Figure 5) show similar patterns to data, both for immediate and continuous-distractor free recall (in short, CD). For both tasks the model produces the typical bow shape curve with recency and primacy. The recency however is due to different processes in the two tasks. In continuous-distractor free recall (bottom of Figure 5) recency is a result of contextual similarity of the retrieval time context to the encoding context of the last items in the list, which results in a "J" shaped curve – the last item always has the highest probability of recall. Probability goes down the more remote the encoding time from the retrieval time context (similarity decays in an exponential way as in the TCM model). In immediate free recall, however, recency is further enhanced by retrieval of active items from the buffer. In addition to higher probability of recall for the last items (in comparison to CD), the shape of the graph is different – "S" shaped (or sigmoid). Due to noise in the buffer, the last item does not always have the highest probability of recall, hence the flattening of probability of recall for the few last items (Usher et al., 2008).

Primacy on the other hand is a result of the same process for both immediate and continuous distractor free recall, and therefore has the same shape. Primacy in the current model is simulated as initialisation of the context layer to slightly higher values than the rest of the simulation (steady state values). It is assumed that the beginning of the list context is distinctive from the learning time context, due to the vast contextual change from rest to study. This was enough to enable the model to predict primacy.

Next, the conditional response probabilities functions (or lag-CRP[15]) will be examined. Lag-CRP curves (Figure 6) show that the model, similar to participants, tends to retrieve items from nearby serial positions, and that this tendency is larger for forward than for backward transitions. As in TCM, this asymmetry is due to the contribution of the pre-experimental context, which enhances the contextual similarity to items presented later but not earlier in time.

218

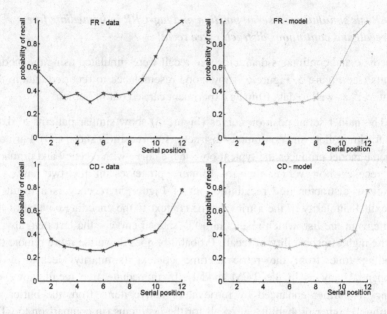

Fig. 5. Serial position curves for immediate free recall (up) and continuous distractor free recall (bottom). Left: free recall data from our lab[13]; Right: model simulation results.

As in the serial position curves, there is a difference between the graphs for the tasks of immediate and continuous-distractor free recall. In CD, the lag-CRP is a result of contextual similarity only, while in immediate free recall retrieval from the buffer enhances the contribution of the +/- 1 lags, as these are the most common distances between items that co-exist in the active buffer. The current model results reproduce the dissociations between immediate free-recall and CD discussed in Davelaar *et al*[1].

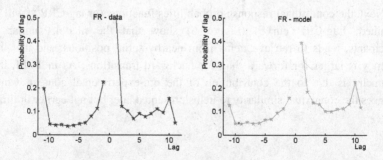

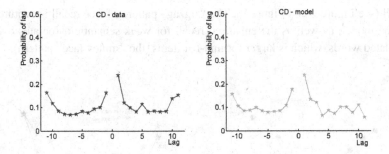

Fig. 6. Lag recency curves for immediate (up) and continuous distractor (bottom) free recall. Left: free-recall data from our lab[13]; Right: model simulations results.

3.2. Semantic similarity

The model was used to simulate the effect of semantic similarity on free recall reported by Davelaar et al.[7]. In the study participants perform free recall for lists of words comprised of pairs of weak associates, using a similar paradigm to Glanzer and Schwartz[16]. For example: light, candle, sleep, blanket, spider, snake, heavy, stone, street, curb, hotter, boil. Enhanced probability of recall is observed for the weak associates lists in comparison to control lists of unrelated words, both in immediate and continuous distractor free recall. In addition, a "zigzag" pattern appears in immediate free recall, with improved recall for the second member of every pair (see Figure 7, left). In continuous distractor free recall a different pattern emerges – improved probability of recall for mid-list items, but less so for the primacy/recency items (a "smiley face" shape, see Figure 8, right).

The model by Davelaar et al.[7] was able to simulate the effect in immediate free recall. In addition to the activation buffer dynamics of the Davelaar et al.[1] model, the buffer units also send small excitatory input to similar units (which represent semantic associations). These connections help the second member of a pair of associates to survive the buffer competition for a longer time, and therefore get better encoded. However, the above mechanism was not sufficient to explain the differential advantage of weak associates in continuous distractor task (the "smiley face" shape in Figure 9, right).

To be able to account for both the immediate and continuous distractor free recall data, in the current (hybrid) model weak associates are represented as items which have similar pre-experimental context. 50% of the pre-experimental context vector units were chosen as identical for each pair. Simulation results show resemblance to data both for immediate and continuous-distractor free recall (see Figure 7 and Figure 8). The "zigzag" pattern of free recall is captured by the model, as well as the enhanced recall for weak semantic associates over unrelated words, which is larger for mid-list items (the "smiley face" pattern).

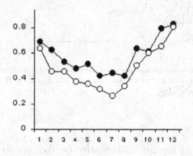 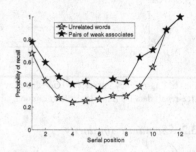

Fig. 7. Serial position curves for immediate free recall of a list of weak semantic associates vs. unrelated words. Left: data from Davelaar et al.[7]. Right: model results. Black: weak semantic associates, white: unrelated words.

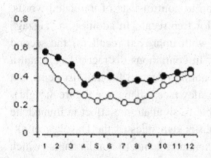 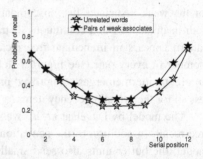

Fig. 8. Serial position curves for continuous distractor free recall of a list of weak semantic associates vs. unrelated words. Left: data from Davelaar et al.[7]. Right: model results. Black: weak semantic associates, white: unrelated words.

The model accounts for the CD data, as the mechanisms for recency and primacy play a more prominent role than the mechanism for semantic similarity. Therefore, the serial position curves for weak associates list and the unrelated words list converge at the primacy and recency parts, but not in the middle of the list.

3.3 Amnesic syndrome

Amnesic patients' memory is impaired for all serial positions of immediate and continuous distractor free recall, except for the recency items in immediate free recall[17]. This neuropsychological dissociation serves as important evidence for the existence of a short term store, which is intact in these patients. In order to simulate the amnesic syndrome, the lexical layer was partially disconnected from the context layer, to represent hippocampal damage. This was done by randomly setting a certain percentage of the connections between the context layer and the lexical layer connections (the W matrix) to zero. Different rates of damage were simulated; results shown are with 70% of the connections set to zero. The model results show good resemblance to experimental data (Figure 9 and Figure 10), with overall impairment of recall, except for the recency items (last 3) in

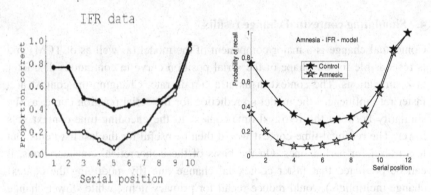

Fig. 9. Serial position curves for immediate free recall of amnesic patients. Left: data from Davelaar et al.[1] (reprinted from Carlesimo et al., [17]), Right: model results. White: amnesic patients, black: control group.

In immediate free recall, retrieval from the buffer is not affected by the lesioned episodic learning, resulting in an intact recency effect. Interfering with episodic learning makes probability of recall for all pre-recency items lower, but saves the relative advantage of the primacy items, as they have stronger connections to the context layer relative to the mid-list items, even after the "lesion".

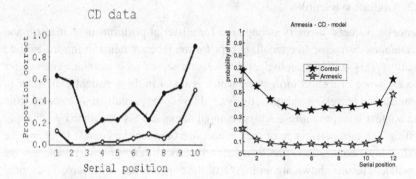

Fig. 10. Serial position curves for continuous distractor free recall of amnesic patients. Left: data from Davelaar et al.[1] (reprinted from Carlesimo et al.[17]), Right: model results. White: amnesic patients, black: control group.

4. Simulating contextual change results

Contextual change is a major component of the model (as well as of TCM) and is responsible for the shape of the serial position curve in continuous distractor task simulations. The context drifts at a certain rate. Changing the context at a faster rate influences the model's prediction for the serial position curve, as the similarity between the retrieval-time-context to the encoding-time-context gets lower. The retrieval-time-context would then be useful for the last list items, but less useful for earlier ones. On the basis of these theoretical considerations, it can be predicted that faster contextual change rate (by modifying the context change multipliers) would reduce recall for primacy items, while slower change rate would reduce the advantage of the recency items. This has been formally demonstrated in a model-simulation (Figure 11, left), to be discussed later (together with the experimental results). It can be seen that when context changes slower, the probability to recall recency items (black markers) is reduced, while faster context change reduces the probability to recall primacy items (white markers).

An experiment was carried out to test this prediction. Pictures were presented in the background of the classic continuous distractor free recall task[18]. In CD, distractors appear before and after every word presentation and are believed to flush short term memory activations. CD was chosen for this experiment as participants can only rely on long term - context dependent - memory for recall. Highly familiar pictures were added to the background of the CD display, in attempt to manipulate participants' contextual change, word by word. Participants were instructed to pay attention to the words and the distractor task, but were not instructed to memorise the background pictures. Therefore the background pictures are considered as part of the encoding context. In the fast contextual change condition the background pictures changed with every word presentation, while in the slow contextual change condition the same background picture stayed throughout an entire list. By manipulating the rate of background change, the participants' context is assumed to change faster or slower within a list, and influence the resulting serial position curves. (Further details regarding the experiment design and results can be found at: www.bbk.ac.uk/psyc/staff/academic/musher/documents/ncpw12/experiment.pdf. The experimental results (figure 11, right) support the hypothesis that in the constant picture condition the recency is reduced, and the primacy is enhanced, in comparison to the changing pictures condition; although, small, the difference proved statistically significant. The experimental results support the model predictions; hence the context component of the model may be a truthful representation of human context.

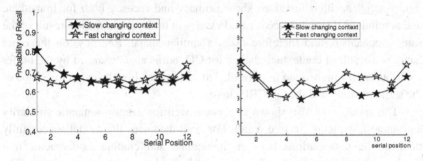

Fig. 11. Serial position curves for a model simulation, in which the parameters that affect the speed of contextual change are manipulated (left), and experimental data (right) comparing recall with a slow (black) and fast (white) changing context.

The parameters used in the simulation results illustrated in Figure 11 (left) are different than those used in previous simulations, to fit experimental data. First, the data overall shows a much flatter serial position curve than usual. To account for this, context noise level in the model was lowered. The implication of reduced context noise is a decrease in the difference between the context in which different items are encoded, and therefore less contrast/preference at retrieval for items whose context is more similar to the encoding time context.

However, a similar cross-over between the "fast" and "slow" context curves is obtained using the original parameters among many other possible choices of parameters. The cross-over is a result of the difference in context change rate and the competitive/relative nature of the retrieval process. When context changes slower than some baseline, the end-of-list context would be a better retrieval cue for the first list items than the baseline. As a result, primacy is enhanced at the expense of recency in that condition. Similarly, when context changes faster than the baseline, the end-of-list context would be a better retrieval cue for the last list items than the baseline. As a result recency is enhanced on the expense of primacy in that condition. Therefore, comparing a fast changing context condition with a slow changing context condition is predicted to generate an interaction.

5. Discussion

A new neurocomputational model that combines the components of an activation buffer and TCM-like context mechanism was developed. The model was used to simulate serial position and lag-CRP curves for immediate and continuous-distractor free recall of published data as well as new experimental results. The model serial position functions show primacy and recency both for immediate and continuous-distractor free recall. Primacy in both paradigms is a result of the same mechanism, and therefore takes a similar shape. Recency, on the other hand, is a result of contextual change for CD, but is also enhanced by the buffer contribution for immediate free recall. This difference is reflected at the shape of the serial position and the lag-CRP curves.

This model was also shown to account well for data on semantic similarity and amnesic patients' in free recall. For both data sets, the model successfully predicts the dissociations between immediate and continuous-distractor free recall, which are believed to be mediated by a short term memory store. The contribution of the buffer component of the model could explain these differences for two qualitatively and quantitatively different data sets. The model also enhances and modifies the dual model account of free recall. For example, the primacy mechanism of the dual model[1,7] predicted primacy in CD as reset of the context layer to its state at the beginning of the encoding phase after half of the retrieval attempts. Although participants do sometimes show such a transition during recall, this approach is arguably artificial (it is not explained how the model remembers the start context). In the hybrid model primacy was simulated in a different way; it is assumed that the beginning of the list context is distinctive, due to the vast contextual change from rest to study. To reflect this fact, the start context was initialised to slightly higher values than the steady state ones. This was enough to enable the model to simulate primacy.

A new prediction was derived from the model, for the way in which a different rate of contextual change affects the shape of the serial position and the lag-CRP curves. This prediction was supported by new experimental results. Specifically it was predicted that changing the pictures at the background of the CD task would create a faster change in the context, in comparison to a constant picture condition. This faster change causes a larger contextual similarity of the retrieval time context to the last items, but a smaller contextual similarity to the first ones, in comparison to the slower context change. These effects were found in the experimental serial position curves – in the changing pictures condition, memory for the last items is better than the constant picture condition, whereas the opposite is true for the first list items.

These experimental results also highlight two characteristics of context change. First, the change can be manipulated by factors other than the experimental (to-be-remembered) material alone, and second, the rate of the change can be influenced by an experimental manipulation. Therefore, the approach chosen for the context representation in the current model seems the most intuitive – a mental state which changes along many dimensions, and is affected by the experimental material, as well as factors external to the experiment. The context could possibly be even more powerful with different components changing in different rates, such as the new TCM variant – CMR, in which the context representation is fragmented[6].

Acknowledgements

Anat Elhalal was supported by Birkbeck School of Psychology and the Overseas Research Students Award Scheme (ORSAS). We also wish to thank Eddy Davelaar for very helpful discussions on the model and the experimental study.

References

1. E. J. Davelaar, Y. Goshen-Gottstein, A. Ashkenazi, H. J. Haarmann and M. Usher, *Psychological Review*, **112**, 3 (2005).
2. E. J. Davelaar and M. Usher, *Connectionist models of cognition and perception: proceedings of the seventh neural computation and psychology workshop,* eds. J. A. Bullinaria and W. Lowe (Singapore: World Scientific, 2002).
3. H. J. Haarmann and M. Usher, *Psychonomic Bulletin and Review*, **8**, 568 (2001).
4. M. W. Howard and M. J. Kahana, *Journal of Mathematical Psychology*, **46**, 299 (2002).

5. P. B.Sederberg, M. W. Howard and M. J. Kahana, *Psychological review*, **115**, 893 (2008).
6. S. M.Polyn, K. A. Norman and M. J. Kahana, *Psychological review*, **116**, 129 (2009).
7. E. J. Davelaar, H. J. Haarmann, Y. Goshen-Gottstein and M. Usher, *Memory & Cognition*, **34**, 323 (2006).
8. G. J. Mensink and J. G. W. Raaijmakers, *Psychological Review*, **95**, 434 (1988).
9. R. C. O'Reilly and Y. Munakata, *Computational explorations in cognitive neuroscience: Understanding the mind by simulating the brain.* (Cambridge, MA: MIT Press, 2000).
10. E. J. Davelaar, *Unpublished doctoral dissertation* (University of London, 2003).
11. J. G. W. Raaijmakers and R. M. Shiffrin, *Psychological Review*, **88**, 93 (1981).
12. M. W. Howard and M. J. Kahana, *Journal of Experimental Psychology: Learning, Memory, and Cognition*, **25**, 923 (1999).
13. A. Elhalal, *Unpublished doctoral dissertation* (University of London, 2009).
14. M. Usher, E. J. Davelaar, H. J. Haarmann and Y. Goshen-Gottstein, *Psychological Review*, **115**, 1108 (2008).
15. M. J. Kahana,. *Memory and Cognition*, **2**, 103 (1996).
16. M. Glanzer and A. Schwartz, *Journal of Verbal Learning & Verbal Behavior*, **10**, 194 (1971).
17. G. A. Carlesimo, G. A. Marfia, A. Loasses and C. Caltagirone, *Neuropsychologia*, **34**, 177 (1996).
18. R. A. Bjork and W. B. Whitten, *Cognitive Psychology*, **6**, 173 (1974).

INFERENCE, ONTOLOGIES AND THE PUMP OF THOUGHT

ANDRZEJ WICHERT

IST - Technical University of Lisboa,
2780 990 Porto Salvo, Portugal
andreas.wichert@ist.utl.pt
web.tagus.ist.utl.pt/~andreas.wichert/

The pump of thought model[1] is a theoretical cell assembly model that explains how thoughts represented by assemblies can be propagated and changed by the brain. The process of human problem solving is described by this model as the transformation of thoughts through a sequence of assemblies. Activation of a critical number of neurons within the assembly leads to the activation of the entire assembly, so that manipulations on the representation of a complex object are performed. Thoughts can be represented by verbal rules. Verbal rules are based on discrete features[2] and allow the representation of symbolic rules. A symbolic rule contains several if-patterns and one or more then-patterns. A pattern in the context corresponds to a set of features. The similarity between rules is defined as a function of the features they have in common. A rule can establish a new assertion by the then part (its conclusion) whenever the if part (its premise) is true. We present a straightforward transformation from the symbolic rules into a distributed representation by associative memory with practical examples (diagnostic systems). Problem solving by cell assemblies is modelled by an associative memory with feedback connections.

1. Introduction

In this work we examine how the human problem-solving can be realized by the human brain. Human problem-solving algorithms are studied in Artificial Intelligence and Cognitive Psychology. The key idea behind these algorithms is the symbolic representation of the domain in which the problems are solved. Symbols in this context are used to denote or refer to something other than themselves namely other things in the world (according to the pioneering work of Tarski[3-5]). Symbols do not, by themselves, represent any utilizable knowledge. For example, they cannot be used for a definition of similarity criteria between themselves. They are defined by their occurrence in a structure and by a formal language, which manipulates these structures.[6–9] We try to build a bridge between the symbolical representation and neural assembly theory. The neural assembly theory was introduced by Donald Hebb.[10] He proposed a connection between the structures found in the nervous system and those involved in high-level cognition such as problem solving. An assembly of neurons acts as a closed system, and can therefore represent a complex object. Activation of some neurons of the assembly leads to the activation of the entire assembly, so that manipulation on the representation of a complex objects can be performed.[11,12] The pump of thought model[1,13,14] is a theoretical assembly model that explains how thoughts represented by assemblies can be propagated and changed by the human brain. The process of human problem solving is described by this model as the transformation of thoughts through a sequence of assemblies.[14,15] Thoughts can be represented by verbal categories. Verbal categories are based on discrete features[2,16] and allow the representation of symbolic rules. The associative memory with feedback connections offers a self-contained architecture for the pump of thought model.

Unlike common approaches the question and the answer vectors of our model represent the same address space. This means that a particular feature is represented by the same position in both the question and the answer vectors. During the inference, the conclusion of the occurring features is determined. Furthermore, there can be hierarchical chains; a conclusion can also be a feature of a premise that causes other conclusions. During the inference the short-term memory is initialized with the present feature. The newly obtained conclusions are added to the short-term memory through the feedback connections. This procedure is repeated until the short-term memory does not change. Our model is well suited to represent hierarchical compositional relationships between knowledge and its representation by the human brain. It explains by practial examples, how cell assemblies act as building blocks of cortical representations.

2. Neural assemblies

The Lernmatrix, also simply called "associative memory", was developed by Steinbuch in 1958 as a biologically inspired model from the effort to explain the psychological phenomenon of conditioning .[17,18] The Lernmatrix[17–22] is composed of a cluster of units. Each unit represents a simple model of a real biological neuron. The Lernmatrix was introduced by Steinbuch, whose goal was to produce a network that could use a binary version of Hebb learning to form associations between pairs of binary vectors. Each unit is composed of weights, which correspond to the synapses in the real neuron. They are described by w_{ij} in Figure 1. T is the threshold of the unit. We call the Lernmatrix simply "associative memory" if no confusion with other models is possible.[23,24] The biological and mathematical aspects of the Lernmatrix were studied by G. Palm.[14,22,25,26] It was shown that Donald Hebb's hypothesis of cell assemblies as a biological model of internal representation of events and situations in the cerebral cortex corresponds to the formal Lernmatrix model.

The patterns that are stored in the Lernmatrix are represented by binary vectors. The presence of a feature is indicated by a 'one' component of the vector, its absence through a 'zero' component of the vector. A pair of these vectors is associated and the process of storing these associations in the associative memory is called learning. The first vector $\vec{x}$ is called the *question* vector and the second $\vec{y}$, the *answer* vector. After learning, the *question* vector is presented to the associative memory and the *answer* vector is determined.

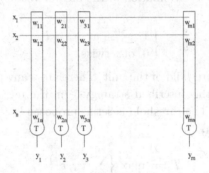

Fig. 1. The Lernmatrix is composed of a set of units which represent a simple model of a real biological neuron. The unit is composed of weights that correspond to the synapses and dendrites in the real neuron. They are described by w_{ij} in this figure. T is the threshold of the unit.

This process is called association*.

Learning In the initialization phase of the associative memory, no information is stored. Because the information is represented in weights, they are all initially set to zero. In the learning phase, pairs of binary vector

---

*In the literature, a distinction between heteroassociation and autoassociation is often made. An autoassociation is present when the answer vector represents the reconstruction of a faulty question vector. A heteroassociation is present if both vectors are different.

are associated. Let $\vec{x}$ be the question vector and $\vec{y}$ the answer vector, the learning rule is:

$$w_{ij}^{new} = \begin{cases} 1 & if \quad y_i \cdot x_j = 1 \\ w_{ij}^{old} & \text{otherwise} \end{cases} \tag{1}$$

This rule is called the binary Hebbian rule.[14] Every time a pair of binary vectors is stored, this rule is used.

Retrieval In the *one-step* retrieval phase of the associative memory, a fault tolerant answering mechanism recalls the appropriate answer vector for a question vector $\vec{x}$. For the presented question vector $\vec{x}$, the most similar learned $\vec{x}^l$ question vector regarding the Hamming distance is determined and the appropriate answer vector $\vec{y}$ is identified. For the retrieval rule, the knowledge about the correlation of the components is sufficient. The retrieval rule for the determination of the answer vector $\vec{y}$ is:

$$y_i = \begin{cases} 1 & \sum_{j=1}^{n} w_{ij} x_j \geq T \\ 0 & \text{otherwise.} \end{cases} \tag{2}$$

where T is the threshold of the unit. There are many possibilities for its determination. For the described strategy $\geq$ in the retrieval equation can be replaced with $=$. The threshold is set as proposed by[27] to the maximum of the sums $\sum_{j=1}^{n} w_{ij} x_j$:

$$T := \max_{1 \leq i \leq m} \left\{ \sum_{j=1}^{n} w_{ij} x_j \right\}. \tag{3}$$

Only the units which are maximal correlated with the question vector are set to one.

3. Representation

Lernmatrix models cell neural assemblies, which are the building blocks of cortical representations. Cell assemblies should represent objects and abstract entities of thought. How can we model this form of representation by a Lernmatrix? Objects can be described by a set of discrete features, such as red, round and sweet .[2,16] The similarity between them can be defined as a function of the features they have in common .[28,29] An object is judged to belong to a verbal category to the extent that its features are predicted by the verbal category.[30] The similarity of a category C and of a feature set F is given by the following formula, which is inspired by the contrast model of Tversky ,[2,31,32]

$$Sim(C, F) = \frac{|C \cap F|}{|C|} \in [0, 1] \qquad (4)$$

$|C|$ is the number of the prototypical features that define the category a. The present features are counted and normalized so that the value can be compared. For example, the category *bird* is defined by the following features: flies, sings, lays eggs, nests in trees, eats insects. The category *bat* is defined by the following features: flies, gives milk, eats insects. The following features are present: flies and gives milk.

$$Sim(\mathbf{bird}, present features) = \frac{1}{5}$$

$$Sim(\mathbf{bat}, present features) = \frac{2}{3}$$

This is a very simple form of representation. The set of features can be represented by a binary vector in which the positions represent different features. For each category a binary vector can be defined. This would lead to a grand mother coding in which each neuron represents a category.[33,34] Recently[35] suggested related form of representation for an auto-associative memory. Feature sets describing categories are stored in an auto-associative memory. Overlaps between stored patterns correspond to overlaps between categories. Nested category hierarchies can be represented by subsets of overlapping features. A hierarchy level is defined as a maximal set of objects paired with the maximal set of features they share. They characterize the objects in terms of shared features. In the next section we will present an inference model that is based on cell assemblies.[36]

4. Inference

The 'pump of thought' model is related to the production systems theory which is a psychological model of actual human problem-solving behavior.[9,37–39] Human problem-solving can be described by a problem-behavior graph constructed from a protocol of the person talking aloud, mentioning moves considered and aspects of the situation. According to the resulting theory, problems are solved by searching in a problem space whose state includes the initial situation and the desired situation.[9,37,40] The short-term memory is limited to holding the temporary state. Progressive depending and local focusing leads to a depth-first search.[9] This process can be described by the production system theory. Production systems are composed of if-then rules which are also called productions. A rule[41–43] contains several if-patterns and one or more then-patterns. Problems without side effects of actions can be described by deduction systems which are a subgroup of production systems.[41] In deduction systems the premise specifies combinations of assertions, by which a new assertion of the conclusion is directly deduced. This new assertion is added to the working memory. Deduction systems do not need strategies for conflict resolution because every rule presumably produces reasonable assertions and there is no harm in firing all triggered rules. Example of deduction systems are semantic nets, ontologies and diagnostic systems. Ontology is the representation of knowledge by a set of categories and the relationships between them. It is used to reason about the properties of that domain, and may be used to describe the domain. Simple if then rules can be represented by features and categories. The knowledge that describes the relationship between features and categories is represented by a knowledge base in the form

- $B \wedge C \wedge D$ then A
- $F \vee H \vee I$ then E.

The category A is described by the features B and C and D. The category E is described by features F or H or I . The number of the features is not fixed During the inference features specify the categories that are deduced. A knowledge base is a set of such rules. As an example we present a compendium of six rules concerning problems with the oil of a car expert system:

(1) oil lamp lights during driving round a bend **or** oil lamp lights during braking **then** cable of the oil pressure lamp is loose
(2) driving round a bend **and** problems with oil **then** oil lamp lights during driving round a bend
(3) braking **and** problems with oil **then** oil lamp lights during braking
(4) oil lamp goes out after some time **and** problems with oil **and** during idling **then** oil pressure too low
(5) problems with oil **and** during idling **then** oil level too low
(6) oil lamp lights up **then** problems with oil

For clarity we can replace the names of features and categories by symbols, each symbol representing a name, for example B representing "oil lamp lights during driving round a bend":

(1) B ∨ C then A
(2) D ∧ F then B
(3) E ∧ F then C
(4) H ∧ F ∧ I then G
(5) F ∧ I then J
(6) K then F

It should be noted, that a particular category can be also a feature that describes other categories. The representation of the logical relationship defined by these rules requires an extension to the basic graph model known as AND/OR graph. AND/OR graphs are an important tool for describing the search space generated by expert systems and logical theorem provers.[43] We can represent the set of rules (for example describing an ontology) by a directed AND/OR graph. In figure 2 we see the representation of the six rules.

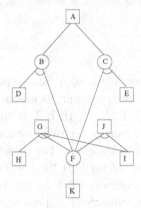

Fig. 2. Representation of six rules by a directed AND/OR graph. The 'and' rules are indicated by an arc between the links connecting the nodes indicating the manifestations.

Such a graph can be represented by an associative memory with feedback connections. The architecture of pump of thought corresponds to a long-term memory represented by an associative memory and short-term memory representing the state during the inference, see Figure 3.

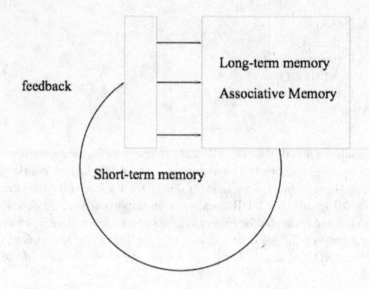

Fig. 3. The architecture of pump of thought corresponds an associative memory with feed-back connections.

5. Architecture

Binary vectors can represent features. A 'one' represents a feature at the corresponding position of a binary vector; its absence is denoted by a 'zero'. The feature set A, B, C, D, E, F, G, H, I, J, K (defined in the preceding section) is represented by a binary vector of dimension 11, no distinction between categories and features is made. The presence of features C and E is represented by the binary vector [0 0 1 0 1 0 0 0 0 0 0]. After learning using the Equation 1, the categories can be determined by the inference with the aid of associative memory. The present features represented by the question vector $\vec{x}$ are presented to the associative memory and the categories are identified by the retrieval rule which determines the answer vector $\vec{y}$ with the aid of the following retrieval rule:

$$y_i = \mu(z_i) \tag{5}$$

with

$$z_i = \frac{\sum_{j=1}^n w_{ij} x_j - 1}{\sum_{j=1}^n w_{ij}} \qquad (6)$$

corresponding to Equation 4 and

$$\mu(z_i) = \begin{cases} 1 \ if \begin{cases} z_i > 0 \quad and \quad T_i = 1 \text{ for or rules} \\ z_i = 1 \quad and \quad T_i = 0 \text{ for and rules} \end{cases} \\ 0 \ else \end{cases} \qquad (7)$$

The short-term memory, which is initialized with the initial state description, is represented by the row buffer (short-term memory) on the left side of the associative memory, see Figure 4. The features of the short-term memory are presented to the associative memory, which determines the categories by using the retrieval rule to perform an inference step. The determined categories are transported from the buffer below the units (column buffer) via the feedback connections to the short-term memory. The short-term memory is updated and the procedure is repeated until the short-term memory does not change, i.e. the number of features in it does not grow.

We demonstrate this procedure with the following example. The features 'oil lamp lights up' and 'braking' are present (represented in our symbol notation by K and E). The short-term memory is initialized with $/K, E/$, see figure 5 (i). In the first inference step, F is deduced; the short-term memory is now $/K, E, F/$, see figure 5 (ii). The features of the short-term memory are presented to the associative memory and, in the following inference, C and F are deduced, see figure 5 (iii). The short-term memory is then updated to $/K, E, F, C/$. In the next inference steps, C, F and A are deduced. A is deduced, because $A \Rightarrow B \vee C$ is an 'or' rule as indicated by the threshold value of the corresponding unit, see figure 5 (iv). The inference procedure is completed because no new features are determined in the following inference step. In our example the category A would correspond to 'the cable of the oil pressure lamp is loose'.

5.1. *Probabilistic inference*

An object is judged to belong to a verbal category to the extent that its features are predicted by the verbal category.[30] If some features are not present for a complete definition of a category the results of Equation 4 are below 1 and above zero. During probabilistic inference the Equation 7 is

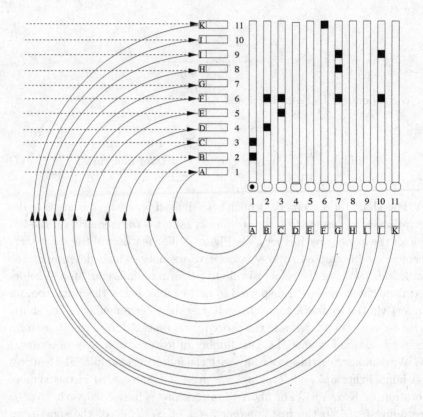

Fig. 4. The architecture of our inference system is composed of associative memory with feedback connections.[22,44] The rule A $\Rightarrow$ B $\vee$ C is represented by the first unit; that it is an 'or' rule is indicated by a one in its threshold (represented in this figure by a black dot). The associative memory forms the long-term memory; the short-term memory that is initialized with the initial state description is represented by the row buffer on the left side of the associative memory. The features of the short-term memory are presented to the associative memory, which determines the categories by using the retrieval rule. The determined categories are transported from the buffer below the units (column buffer) via the feedback connections to the short-term memory.

changed into

$$\mu(z_i) = \begin{cases} 1 \; if \begin{cases} z_i > 0 \quad and \quad T_i = 1 \text{ for or rules} \\ z_i = p \quad and \quad T_i = 0 \text{ for and rules} \end{cases} \\ 0 \; else \end{cases} \tag{8}$$

The inference process is started with $p = 1$. If no categories are deduced, p is lowered by a small rate factor c, such as $c = 0.1$ leading to $p = 0.9$ and the inference process is repeated. The p values are lowered, until some

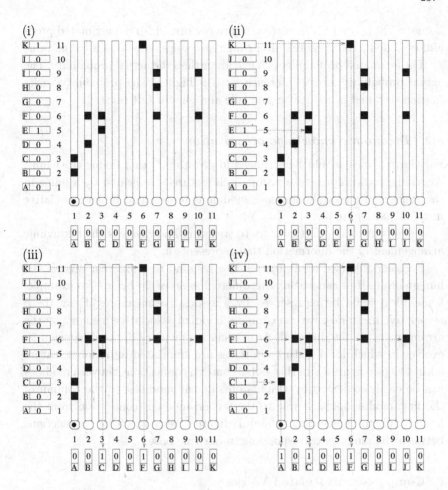

Fig. 5.   (i) The features 'oil lamp lights up' and 'braking' are represented in our symbol notation by K and E respectively. The short-term memory is initialized with $/K, E/$. (ii) In the first inference step, F is deduced. The activation of the units is indicated by the buffer below the units and should be not confused with the 'or' rule indication of a one in the threshold (represented by a black dot). iii) The short-term memory is now $/K, E, F/$. The features of the short-term memory are presented to the associative memory, and C and F are deduced in the following inference. (iv) The short-term memory is now updated to $/K, E, F, C/$. In the next inference step, C, F and A are deduced. A is deduced, because $A \Rightarrow B \vee C$ is an 'or' rule as indicated by the threshold value *one* of the corresponding unit (represented by a black dot).

categories are deduced or p value approaches 0. If categories are deduced, the short-term memory is updated and the procedure is repeated until the short-term memory does not change, i.e. the number of features in it does not grow. Supposed t inference steps are performed, so the estimated probability of deduced categories after t inference steps corresponds to the value p^t. The estimated probability is much lower then the actual probability. The actual probability after t inference steps is higher. The probability varies in each step and is $z(i)$ for an and rule and one for OR rules.

5.2. *Taxonomic knowledge organization*

For clarity, rules should be arranged in groups[45,46] that define taxonomy. A module could represent a group, each feature is indicated by a name in the context of a module and each module is represented by an associative memory (see figure 6).

One of the most effective ways to structure knowledge is the taxonomic arrangement of the information that represents it.[47]

Each module (see figure 6) could correspond to a different area of the human brain. How can we link this different areas of the brain? For example, 5 modules would be represented by 5 associative memories. From the 5 associative memories, we can compose a global associative memory by the arrangement on the diagonal. An associative memory of the dimension 30 evolves in which local feature addresses are translated into global feature addresses (see figure 7). In this global context, connections between modules can be easily indicated by weights outside the modules, in the column of the first module and the row to the second module (connection from the first module to the second module). In figure 7 we can see three connections between the modules corresponding to our rule base.

6. Comparison to Related Works

In distributed representations, concepts are represented as distributed patterns.[14,23,48,49] Distributed representation enables vector completion.[14,50] The vectors may represent pictures or features. Aleksander and Morton suggest the usage of icons for the representation of states.[51] Icons are pictures which cannot be broken into meaningful pieces and can be processed by a neural state machine. Vectors composed of features were used by Steinbuch[18] for weather prediction and medical diagnosis with an associative memory. Since then, feature representation has been widely used. A "present" feature is indicated by a "one" at a certain position.[52]

DSCP is the distributed connectionist production system.[53,54] A production rule of a DCPS consist of a premise and a conclusion. A premise is described by two triples and these triples are matched against the working

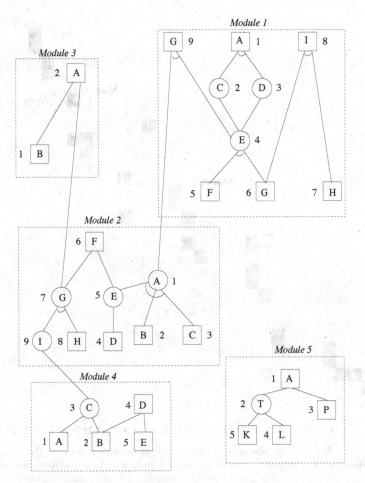

Fig. 6. Representation of 16 rules arranged in five modules by two directed AND/OR graphs. A name and a number in the context of a module indicate each feature. Each module is represented by an associative memory. The number of a feature indicates the position in the corresponding vector. A disorder that is defined in a certain module can cause a manifestation in other modules. This relation corresponds to connections between modules. The 'and' rules are indicated by an arc between the links connecting the nodes, which indicate the manifestations.

memory. A conclusion consists of commands for adding and deleting triples of the working memory. The rules are represented by a subpopulation of units in the rule space. The working memory is also represented by a subpopulation of units in the working memory space. The system operates as a Boltzman machine, finding a rule that matches the state of the working memory by simulated annealing.

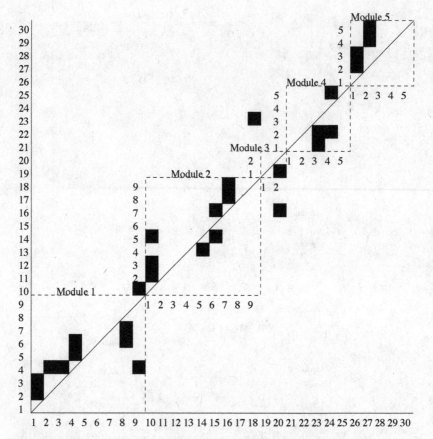

Fig. 7. The five modules are represented by five associative memories. By arranging them diagonal, we compose a global associative memory. An associative memory of dimension 30 evolves. In this global context, connections between modules can be easily indicated by weights depicted outside the modules. Connection from the first to the second module is indicated by the weights in the column of the first module and the row of the second module. In this figure we can see three connections between the modules.

Neuro-Soar is an attempt to show that the system SOAR can be implemented by neural networks.[55] The atomic part of the model is the graph representation which is interpreted as a neural network. Objects are represented by graphs, binding by edges of the graph. Productions are also represented by graphs, just like the elements of working memory. A production fires if the graph representing the precondition, and the graph representing the working memory elements match together. However, there is no possibility in this model to represent the problem space or to perform a search.

Another hybrid problem solving approach through associative memories which solves some planing tasks, is described in.[56,57]

Hierarchical categorization was proposed by taxonomical arrangement of verbal categories represented by different associative memories.[34].

In our proposed approach the question and the answer vectors of our model represent the same address space of one associative memory, making the model much simpler in description. However negation can not be interpreted by our model, only represented by a corresponding feature name.

7. Conclusion

We described the theoretical pump of thought model by an associative memory with feed-back connections. The representation of knowledge is based on a straightforward transformation from the symbolic rules into a representation by associative memory. Another way to look at the same transformation is the representation by directed AND/OR graphs of the search space generated by the inference system. Unlike the approaches[16,18,34] the question and the answer vectors of the associative memory represent the same address space, no distinction between categories and features is made. This means that a particular feature is represented by the same position in both the question and the answer vectors. It should be noted that both vectors have the same dimension n.

During the inference the short-term memory is initialized with the present features. It is then presented to the associative memory, which determines the categories by the retrieval rule. In the retrieval step the answer vector is calculated. The newly obtained categories are added to the short-term memory through the feedback connections. The categories are represented by units (one-of n code, grandmother coding). Each time a new feature is learned, the address space grows and a new unit is introduced. This procedure is repeated until the short-term memory does not change, i.e. the number of features does not grow. A breadth-first search in the directed AND/OR graph is executed. The number of inference cycles made by the associative memory with feedback connections corresponds to the maximum depth of the represented graphs.

References

1. V. Braitenberg, *Vehicles: Experiments in Synthetic Psychology* (The MIT Press, 1984).
2. A. Tversky, *Psychological Review* **84**, 327 (1977).
3. A. Tarski, *Philos. and Phenom. Res.* **4**, 241 (1944).

242

4. A. Tarski, *Logic, Semantics,Metamathematics* (Oxford University Press, London, 1956).
5. A. Tarski, *Pisma logiczno-filozoficzne. Prawda* (Wydawnictwo Naukowe PWN, Warszawa, 1995).
6. H. A. Simon, *The Science of the Artificial* (The MIT Press, 1969).
7. H. A. Simon, *Models of my Life* (Basic Books, New York, 1991).
8. A. Newell, *Physical symbol sytems* (Norman, 1981).
9. A. Newell, *Unified Theories of Cognition* (Harvard University Press, 1990).
10. D. Hebb, *The organization of behavior* (John Wiley, New York, 1949).
11. D. Hebb, *Textbook of psychology* (Sanders, Philadelphia London Toronto, 1958).
12. G. Palm, *Hippocampus* **3**, 219 (1993).
13. V. Braitenberg, *Gehirngespinste, Neuroanatomie für kybernetisch Interessierte* (Springer-Verlag, 1973).
14. G. Palm, *Neural Assemblies, an Alternative Approach to Artificial Intelligence* (Springer-Verlag, 1982).
15. V. Braitenberg, Cell assemblies in the cerebral cortex, in *Theoretical Approaches to Complex Systems*, eds. R. Heim and G.Palm (Springer-Verlag, 1978) pp. 171–188.
16. J. McClelland and D. Rumelhart, *Journal of Experimental Psychology: General* **114**, 159 (1985).
17. K. Steinbuch, *Kybernetik* **1**, 36 (1961).
18. K. Steinbuch, *Automat und Mensch*, fourth edn. (Springer-Verlag, 1971).
19. R. Hecht-Nielsen, *Neurocomputing* (Addison-Wesley, 1989).
20. T. Kohonen, *Self-Organization and Associative Menory*, 3 edn. (Springer-Verlag, 1989).
21. J. Hertz, A. Krogh and R. G. Palmer, *Introduction to the Theory of Neural Computation* (Addison-Wesley, 1991).
22. G. Palm, Assoziatives Gedächtnis und Gehirntheorie, in *Gehirn und Kognition*, (Spektrum der Wissenschaft, 1990) pp. 164–174.
23. J. A. Anderson, *An Introduction to Neural Networks* (The MIT Press, 1995).
24. D. H. Ballard, *An Introduction to Natural Computation* (The MIT Press, 1997).
25. E. Fransén, Biophysical simulation of cortical associative memory, PhD thesis, Stockhokms Universitet, (Dept. of Numerical Analysis and Computing Science Royal Institute of Technology, S-100 44 Stockholm, Sweden, 1996).
26. T. Wennekers, *Synchronisation und Assoziation in Neuronalen Netzen* (Shaker Verlag, Aachen, 1999).
27. G. Palm, F. Schwenker, F. Sommer and A. Strey, Neural associative memories, in *Associative Processing and Processors*, eds. A. Krikelis and C. Weems (IEEE Press, 1997) pp. 307–325.
28. D. N. Osherson, Probability judgment, in *Thinking*, eds. E. E. Smith and D. N. Osherson (MIT Press, 1995) pp. 35–75, second edn.
29. R. Sun, A two-level hybrid architecture for structuring knowledge for commonsense reasoning, in *Computational Architectures Integrating Neural and Symbolic Processing*, eds. R. Sun and L. A. Bookman (Kluwer Academic Publishers, 1995) pp. 247–182.

30. D. N. Osherson, *Journal of Mathematical Psychology* **31**, 93 (1987).
31. E. E. Smith, Concepts and categorization, in *Thinking*, eds. E. E. Smith and D. N. Osherson (MIT Press, 1995) pp. 3–33, second edn.
32. K. Opwis and R. Plötzner, *Kognitive Psychologie mit dem Computer* (Spektrum Akademischer Verlag, Heidelberg Berlin Oxford, 1996).
33. A. Wichert, Hierarchical categorization, in *Ninth Midwest Artificial Intelligence and Cognitive Science Conference*, ed. M. W. Evens (AAAI Press, 1998).
34. A. Wichert, *Expert Systems with Application* **19**, 149 (2000).
35. T. Wennekers, *Journal of Cognitive Computation* **1**, 128 (2009).
36. A. Wichert, *Neurocomputing* **69**, 810 (2006).
37. A. Newell and H. Simon, *Human Problem Solving* (Prentice-Hall, 1972).
38. J. Anderson, *The Architecture of Cognition* (Harvard University Press, 1983).
39. P. Klahr and D. Waterman, *Expert Systems: Techniques, Tools and Applications* (Addison-Wesley, 1986).
40. J. R. Anderson, *Cognitive Psychology and its Implications*, fourth edn. (W. H. Freeman and Company, 1995).
41. P. H. Winston, *Artificial Intelligence*, third edn. (Addison-Wesley, 1992).
42. S. J. Russell and P. Norvig, *Artificial intelligemce: a modern approach* (Prentice-Hall, 1995).
43. G. F. Luger and W. A. Stubblefield, *Artificial Intelligence, Structures and Strategies for Complex Problem Solving*, third edn. (Addison-Wesley, 1998).
44. G. Palm, F. Schwenker and A. Bibbig, Theorie Neuronaler Netze 1 Skript zur Vorlesung, (1992), University of Ulm, Department of Neural Information Processing.
45. J. Aikins, *Artificial Intelligence* **20**, 163 (1986).
46. G. Kahn, A. Kepner and J. Pepper, Test: a model-driven application shell, in *National Conference on Artificial Intelligence*, 1987.
47. H. L. Resnikoff, *The Illusion of Reality* (Springer-Verlag, 1989).
48. J. McClelland, D. E. Rumelhart and G. Hinton, The appeal of parallel distributed processing, in *Parallel Distributed Processing: Explorations in the Microstructure of Cognition. Volume 1: Foundations*, eds. D. E. Rumelhart and J. L. McClelland (The MIT Press, 1986) pp. 3–44.
49. R. Miikkulainen, *Subsymbolic Natural Language Processing: An Integrated Model of Scripts, Lexicon and Memory* (The MIT Press, 1993).
50. P. S. Churchland and T. J. Sejnowski, *The Computational Brain* (The MIT Press, 1994).
51. I. Aleksander and H. Morton, *Neurons and Symbols, the Stuff that Mind is made of* (Chapman and Hall, 1993).
52. J. McClelland and A. Kawamoto, Mechanisms of sentence processing: Assigning roles to constituents of sentences, in *Parallel Distributed Processing*, eds. J. McClelland and D. Rumelhart (The MIT Press, 1986) pp. 272–325.
53. G. Touretzky, D.S. amd Hinton, Symbols among the neurons: Details of a connectionist inference architecture, in *Proceedings of the Eighth International Joint Conference on Artificial Intelligence*, (Morgan Kaufman, San Mateo, CA, 1985).

54. G. Touretzky, D.S. amd Hinton, *Cognitive Science* **12**, 423 (1988).
55. B. Cho, P. Rosenbloom and C. Dolan, Neuro-soar: A neural-network architecture for goal-oriented behavior, in *Proceedings of Thirteenth Annual Conference of Cognitive Science Society*, (Lawrence Erlbaum Associates, Chicago, IL, 1991).
56. A. Wichert, *Connection Science* **13** (2001).
57. A. Wichert, *Cognitive Systems Research* **6**, 111 (2005).

MODELLING CORRELATIONS IN "RESPONSE INHIBITION"

RICHARD P. COOPER

Department of Psychological Sciences, Birkbeck, University of London
Malet Street, London, WC1E 7HX, United Kingdom

EDDY J. DAVELAAR

Department of Psychological Sciences, Birkbeck, University of London
Malet Street, London, WC1E 7HX, United Kingdom

"Response inhibition" is argued by many authors to be a general cognitive control process or function that is invoked in situations where it is necessary to avoid producing an habitual or prepotent response. Individual differences in the efficacy of this function are consequently held to underlie individual differences in performance on tasks that are thought to rely on the function. This position is supported by empirical studies which have reported mild but reliable correlations across subjects in performance on response inhibition tasks such as Stroop colour-naming and the stop-signal task. This paper investigates the computational basis of response inhibition by exploring potential common mechanisms within existing computational models of the Stroop and stop-signal tasks. It is argued that mechanisms such as lateral inhibition, which are shared by the models and which might be thought to relate to the response inhibition construct, cannot account for the observed behavioural correlations. Instead, it is suggested that such correlations are likely to arise from a computational process of attentional bias.

1. Introduction

In much everyday behaviour, and in many psychological tasks, it is necessary to resist temptation or to avoid producing a response that is primed by the environment or irrelevant tasks. Consider the well-known Stroop colour-naming task, where the subject is required to name the colour of the ink in which a word is printed. On so-called incongruent trials, where the word is the name of one colour but it is printed in a second colour, (e.g., the word RED printed in green ink) then subjects must actively or deliberately resist the temptation to read the word if they are to successfully name the ink colour.

It is commonly argued that the ability to inhibit a prepotent response is facilitated by a cognitive control process referred to as response inhibition. Response inhibition is not intended to be a task-specific construct limited to (for example) the Stroop task. Rather, it is held to be one of several general "executive" processes that contribute to the control of behaviour across a range of tasks. According to this line of thinking, individual differences in performance on tasks such as Stroop are held to reflect individual differences in the efficacy of response inhibition.

There is substantial behavioural and neuroscience evidence, as well as good theoretical reasons, for supposing that response inhibition is a task-general control function. Consider first the theoretical perspective. A general mechanism of response inhibition fits well within the influential supervisory system/contention scheduling framework of the control of thought and action of Norman and Shallice[1]. On this account, a system for the control of routine or well-learned behaviours, contention scheduling, is modulated by a deliberative system, the supervisory system, when routine behaviour is inappropriate and must be overridden. Contention scheduling is capable of generating the prepotent response whatever the situation. If this is not appropriate, as in incongruent trials of the Stroop task, the supervisory system must override contention scheduling. A plausible way for this to be operationalised is in terms of response inhibition acting as a sub-function of the supervisory system.

Behaviourally, as indicated above, response inhibition is generally considered to be evidenced in tasks where an established or habitual response must be suppressed or inhibited, possibly in favour of a less frequent response. This occurs in the colour-naming condition of the Stroop task, but also in anti-saccade tasks, where the subject must avoid making an eye-movement to a distracting stimulus[2], in go/no-go and stop-signal tasks, where the subject is normally required to produce some kind of response unless a low-frequency event co-occurs with, or immediately follows, the stimulus[3]. Broad neuropsychological support for the concept comes from patients who exhibit utilisation behaviour[4] and anarchic hand syndrome[5]. Such patients have difficulty inhibiting environmentally-appropriate behaviours. More specific neuropsychological support may be adduced from deficits in the behavioural tasks mentioned above following focal frontal brain injury or disease[6,7]. Finally, neuroimaging studies of tasks such as the stop-signal task suggest a common response inhibition mechanism, localised cortically within right inferior frontal gyrus and subcortically within the basal ganglia[8,9].

Another source of behavioural evidence for the task-general nature of response inhibition comes from a large individual differences study of Miyake, Friedman and colleagues[10]. In this study, 137 subjects completed a battery of 14 tasks, three of which were argued, on a priori grounds, to specifically require response inhibition. Subsequent factor analysis of subject performance across the tasks supported this view, with performance on the response inhibition tasks being related to a single factor that differentiated those tasks from others in the study, which were held to primarily tap other executive functions (namely the functions of set-shifting and memory monitoring and updating).

The three response inhibition tasks of Miyake et al.[10] were: a) a forced-choice decision variant of the stop-signal task; b) the Stroop colour naming task; and c) an anti-saccade task. Our focus in this paper is on the first two, and so we describe these in detail.

In Miyake et al.'s stop-signal task, subjects were required to indicate with a button press whether a (visually presented) word was or was not an animal name. The first block of 48 trials were all "go" trials. These were used to establish a mean response time for each subject. One quarter of the trials in the second block (of 192 trials) were stop trials. In these trials, a beep was sounded shortly after presentation of the word (225ms prior to the subject's mean response time, as determined in block 1), and subjects were required to withhold their response. The dependent measure was the proportion of stop trials on which a response was given. In the well-known Stroop colour naming task, subjects were presented with a "word" written in one of six colours. They were required to name the colour of the stimulus word. On neutral trials the word was a string of asterisk symbols while on incongruent trials it was the name of another colour. The dependent variable was the difference in mean response times for incongruent and neutral trials.

For our purposes, the critical result of this individual differences study was a mild but significant positive correlation ($r \approx 0.20$) between performance on the stop-signal task and the Stroop task (and in fact between all pairs of response inhibition tasks). In general, this correlation was stronger than that between any single response inhibition task and any of the non-response inhibition tasks explored in the study. This result was replicated in a subsequent study with 220 subjects which used the same tasks but slightly different dependent measures[11].

The studies of Miyake, Friedman and colleagues appear to provide strong support for the response inhibition construct and for its variability across individuals. However, interpretations of the results are limited by the correlational nature of the experimental designs. These studies do not provide a mechanistic account of response inhibition as it might manifest itself in the various tasks. Yet if response inhibition is a cognitive control process that plays a causal role in the performance of the Stroop and stop-signal tasks (amongst others), then that process should be shared by computational accounts of these tasks. Moreover if the efficacy of response inhibition can vary across individuals, then that process should be parameterised in the computational accounts. Lastly, if pair-wise correlations in performance of the tasks are to be attributed at least in part to the efficacy of response inhibition, then varying the response inhibition parameter in the computational accounts should also result in pair-wise correlations.

The purpose of the work presented here is to begin to address this limitation of the existing empirical work by exploring potential common mechanisms within established process models of two of Miyake et al.'s response inhibition tasks. We focus on models of the stop-signal task and the Stroop task because there are established models of each task (due to Boucher et al.[12] and Cohen & Huston[13], respectively) and those models bear at least a superficial similarity. This superficial similarity offers the possibility of relating the models to each other and thereby identifying a shared response inhibition mechanism. As should be clear from the above argumentation, for such a mechanism to be explanatorily adequate it must be parameterisable, with the observed behavioural correlations between tasks arising in part from variation in a shared parameter. To foreshadow, simulation findings derived from reimplementations of the existing published models suggest that directly shared parameters fail to yield the required correlation in performance. However, an appropriate correlation is forthcoming if attentional biasing mechanisms are yoked. Unfortunately, attentional biasing is not normally related conceptually to response inhibition. We conclude that either a) response inhibition is not the mechanism underlying the behavioural correlation in these tasks, or b) one or both of the accepted models is in need of updating.

2. The Stop-Signal Task

2.1. *The Model*

Early work with the stop-signal task demonstrated that subject behaviour could be well accounted for by a race model consisting of two stochastic processes, a "go" process which is slow to activate but has a head start, and a "stop" process which is faster to activate but starts late[3]. Successful performance on a stop trial requires that the stop process reach threshold before the go process. Boucher et al.[12] note that despite this model's strengths, it is inconsistent with neural evidence of an interaction between stop and go processes. They present their interactive race model, an update of the original model in which the stop and go processes compete through mutual lateral inhibition.

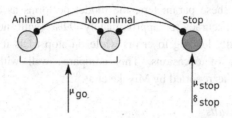

Fig. 1. The interactive race model of the stop signal task. On any one trial, either the animal or the nonanimal node receives activation from a semantic categorisation process. The strength of this activation is given by the parameter μ_{go}. On "stop" trials, the stop node also receives activation, though this activation is delayed relative to the activation from the semantic categorisation process. The parameter μ_{stop} is the strength of the stop process while the delay is δ_{stop}.

In order to explore the computational basis of response inhibition we have developed a reimplementation of this model within the context of Miyake et al.'s semantic categorisation variant of the stop-signal task. The model, shown in Figure 1, is extremely simple. It consists of just three nodes: one for each of the two responses and one for the stop process. Processing in the model is cyclic with each node operating as a leaky competing accumulator[14]. On each cycle, the activation of a node is increased by an amount proportional to its external input, less an amount proportional to the activation of its competitors (corresponding to lateral inhibition), less an amount proportional to its current activation (its leakage), plus normally distributed random noise. Parameters control the contributions of the various sources to this accumulation. For default behaviour we assume ballpark parameters scaled from those of Boucher et al. to give a response threshold of 1.0. Thus, we assume lateral inhibition, β, of 0.025 between all pairs of nodes, leakage of 0.0 (i.e., the accumulators do not leak), and the standard deviation of noise, σ, of 0.025 units per cycle.

In addition, it is assumed that on any trial external input to one of the response nodes (animal or non-animal) is provided by a semantic categorisation process (which is not modelled). The level of input is controlled by the parameter μ_{go}, set in the basic model to 0.005 units per cycle. It is assumed that the other response node receives zero external input. On stop trials it is assumed that at some point during the trial external input is provided to the stop node. The level of this input is μ_{stop}, set to 0.030 units per cycle. Finally, we assume that the delay between input to the response nodes and input to the stop node is 250 cycles. This delay is the sum of the actual delay between presentation of word and stop stimuli (referred to as SSD), and the time to initiate the stop process, μ_{stop}. With these parameters, the model performs as desired – on go trials its response accuracy is approximately 99% (with noise and lateral inhibition occasionally leading to error) while on stop trials it fails to stop on approximately 65% of occasions. This compares well with mean subject performance of 67% as reported by Miyake et al.[10].

2.2. *Simulation Results*

An initial set of simulation studies was performed to determine the relation between the model's performance and the key parameters that could reasonably be argued to vary across individuals, that is: μ_{go}, μ_{stop}, β (lateral inhibition), and δ_{stop}. In order to determine the effect of these key parameters on the proportion of stop errors each of them was varied about a "default" value (the value given in section 2.1), with all other parameters fixed at their default values. Figure 2 summarises the results, based on 100 blocks per parameter, each of 100 trials.

As can be seen from the figure, there is a slight non-monotonic relation between β (lateral inhibition) and the model's performance, with fewer stop errors at intermediate values. Increasing μ_{stop} also reduces stop errors, though here the relation is monotonic and the explanation is relatively straightforward: with stronger excitation of the stop node it is more likely to reach threshold on stop trials before one of the go nodes. Stop errors correlate positively with μ_{go} and δ_{stop}. In both cases the effect of the parameter is transparent. With faster excitation of the go process or with greater delay, the stop process has less chance of reaching threshold before the relevant go process. Consequently stop errors are more likely.

Relating the results to the concept of response inhibition, it appears that "good inhibitors" are those who either have: a) near optimal levels of lateral inhibition; b) slow go processes or short stop process delays; or c) fast stop processes. Miyake et al. (2000) do not report the behavioural data that would help to discriminate between these options.

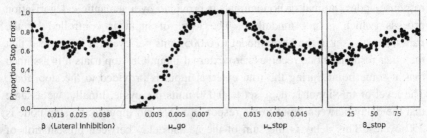

Fig. 2. Effects of varying key parameters on the proportion of stop errors produced by the interactive race model of the stop-signal task.

3. The Stroop Task

3.1. *The Model*

Many models have been developed of the Stroop task. We focus on the well-known model of Cohen and Huston[13], as its principal functional mechanism, interactive activation, is shared with Boucher et al.'s interactive race model. The model, shown in Figure 3, consists of four sets of nodes, with nodes within each set competing for activation through lateral inhibition. There are two task demand nodes, three word input nodes, three colour input nodes, and two response nodes. One task demand node corresponds to the colour naming task while the other corresponds to the word reading task. The colour naming task demand node is connected to all colour input nodes, while the word reading node is connected to all word input nodes. Colour input nodes and word input nodes are each connected to one response node. Crucially, the connections from word inputs to response nodes are stronger than those from colour inputs to response nodes. This is justified on the grounds that word reading is the more practiced of the two tasks. As in the stop-signal model, the operation of the network is cyclic with activation accumulating over time. However, the accumulation functions differ. For the Stroop model activation accumulates according to the logistic function of the time-averaged input to a node. (See Cohen & Huston[13], for details.)

Processing on any given trial occurs in two stages. First, input is provided to

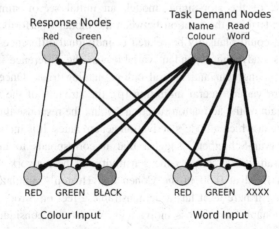

Fig. 3. The Stroop model of Cohen and Huston[13].

one of the task demand nodes (based on the task instructions). This causes that node to become active and the other task demand unit (through lateral inhibition) to become depressed. As a task demand unit becomes active, it excites the input nodes to which it is connected, raising the resting activation of either the colour input nodes or the word input nodes. The network settles into this temporary state, which, it is assumed, corresponds to a subject who is prepared for either a colour naming or word reading Stroop trial. Input is then provided to one colour input node and one word input node. If, for example, the trial was to name the colour of the word "RED" printed in green ink, then input would be provided to the GREEN colour node and the RED word node. In this case the colour nodes would already be moderately activated, and so the additional input to one colour node would tend to excite the appropriate response node (i.e. GREEN). At the same time, the less active word node for RED would also be receiving input and this would be tending to excite the RED response node. Hence both response nodes will receive excitation, and the balance of this excitation, plus the degree of lateral inhibition between the response nodes, will determine how quickly either response node reaches threshold.

As is clear from the architecture, there is no dedicated mechanism or parameter for response inhibition. Thus, verbal descriptions of performance on the Stroop task are at odds with the computational details of the models. Nevertheless, what may be interpreted as response inhibition may well have a different label at the computational level.

3.2. Simulation Results

As in the case of the stop-signal model, an initial set of simulations was performed to determine the relation between the model's performance and key parameters that could plausibly be related to individual differences. Paralleling Miyake et al.'s study, the dependent variable was the difference in processing time between incongruent and neutral colour naming trials. Once again, four parameters were varied: lateral inhibition (β), the strength of the task demand units (μ), the gain of the activation function (γ) and the response threshold (τ). γ controls the rate at which a node's activation accumulates. It is included because Cohen and Servan-Schreiber[15] suggest that it corresponds to an attentional modulation parameter. τ controls the sensitivity of the network to produce a response. It is fixed at 0.60 in the Cohen and Huston[13] simulations, but we consider varying it here as it has a demonstrable affect on Stroop interference and might reasonable vary across individuals. We do not consider varying the weights from input nodes to response nodes, as these are intended to capture

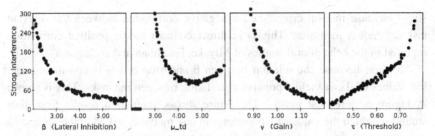

Fig. 4. Effects of varying key parameters on the difference in processing time for correct incongruent and neutral colour naming trials produced by the interactive activation model of the Stroop task.

learned contingencies which, while possibly varying across individuals, should not vary systematically with any specific executive function.

The results of these four sets of simulations are summarised in Figure 4. The model is more complex than the stop-signal model, and consequently the relations between the parameters and the relevant dependent measure – Stroop interference – are less perspicuous. Nevertheless, three of the four relations are monotonic, with Stroop interference correlating negatively with β (lateral inhibition) and γ (gain), and positively with τ (threshold). That is, "good inhibitors" correspond in the Stroop model to individuals with high lateral inhibition, optimal task demand weight, high gain or low threshold.

4. Yoked Simulation Studies

Recall the purpose of considering the effects of the various parameters on the performance of the two models: we are concerned with understanding the source of common variance in the tasks to which the models relate. It is hypothesised that this might be achieved by identifying a parameter that could plausibly vary across individuals and, in so doing, could underlie the observed behavioural correlation between Stroop colour naming interference and stop-signal errors.

We are now in a position to consider candidate parameters. For example, both models share a mechanism of lateral inhibition, and pre-theoretically one could suggest that it is this mechanism, and individual differences in the shared parameter β, that underlies the behavioural correlation. The left-most panels of Figures 2 and 4 suggest that this is implausible. The issue is not the absolute size of the parameter's default value (0.025 for the stop-signal model and 3.0 for the Stroop model). One can envisage re-engineering the models so that lateral inhibition in both is of a similar magnitude. The issue is that relatively high values of β lead to a reduction in Stroop interference together with, if anything, a slight increase in stop errors, i.e., a negative correlation between the relevant task dependent measures. This is in direct contrast to the positive correlation reported in the behavioural studies of Miyake, Friedman and colleagues[10,11].

In fact, because the relation between β and stop errors is non-monotonic, low values of β can yield a positive correlation between the tasks. This is shown in Figure 5 (left-most panel). The figure shows simulation results from four studies in which the value of a parameter in one model is yoked to the value of a corresponding parameter in the other model. In all four cases the relevant parameter values vary across the full ranges explored in Figures 2 and 4. Thus, the data in the left-most panel was generated by random sampling a dummy variable uniformly distributed between 0.0 to 1.0, and mapping the value of this onto a) the interval 0.00 to 0.05 to give a value of β for the stop-signal model, and b) the interval 2.0 to 6.0 to give a yoked value of β for the Stroop model. This procedure was repeated 100 times for four pairs of parameters, yielding the four scatter-plots in Figure 5.

From the figure we may immediately rule out several potential factors underlying the observed correlation between performance on the tasks and hence several candidates for the response inhibition function. The key parameter shared by the models – lateral inhibition (β) – does not produce correlations of the appropriate form. Hence, it would seem that individual differences in this parameter cannot underlie the observed correlations. Equally, as shown by the second plot in Figure 5, yoking the strength of the go process and the strength of task demand weights – an account not immediately related to any conceptual mechanism of response inhibition but one which, nevertheless, relates two parameters with similar functionality – fails to yield a positive correlation between the relevant dependent measures.

The desired positive correlation is shown, however, in the two right-most plots of Figure 5. Thus, the models predict that performance on the two tasks

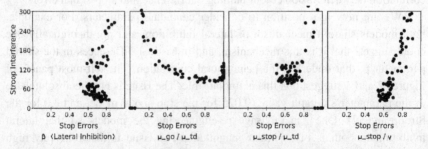

Fig. 5. Effects of varying key parameters in a yoked fashion on the correlation between Stroop interference and the proportion of stop errors produced by the two models.

will correlate positively if: a) the strength of the stop process and the strength of task demand weights are (positively) correlated (third panel of Figure 5); or b) the strength of the stop process and the gain in the Stroop model are (positively) correlated (fourth panel of Figure 5). There is no a priori reason to suppose the latter, but the former is plausible as both parameters concern the strength of deliberative or attentional bias. Thus, these simulation results fail to provide support for the idea that the positive behavioural correlation between Stroop interference and stop-signal errors is due to a shared mechanism of response inhibition. Rather, they suggest that the correlation arises because subjects who are able to provide stronger activation to the stop process in the stop-signal task are also able to provide stronger attentional bias to the colour naming task in Stroop. This suggestion is backed up by the right-most plot which shows a positive correlation resulting from yoking μ_{stop} and γ (gain). Recall that γ was also associated (positively) with attentional bias by Cohen and Servan-Schreiber[15].

5. Discussion and Conclusion

Recently we[16] considered closed-form approximations to the same two models discussed here. We demonstrated that the explanation of the behavioural correlation in terms of a shared process of response inhibition is suspect, and an attentional biasing account was proposed as a plausible alternative. The simulation results reported here corroborate both of these conclusions.

Our suggestion of attentional biasing, rather than response inhibition, as the locus of shared variability on the tasks resonates with the approach to response conflict management of Botvinick et al.[17]. They demonstrate, within the context of three models including the Cohen and Huston Stroop model, how trial-by-trial regularities in behaviour might be accounted for in terms of a mechanism of conflict monitoring which measures the degree of conflict in the network's output nodes and modulates attentional bias, increasing it under conditions of high conflict and decreasing it under conditions of low conflict. Thus, rather than addressing response competition through response inhibition, Botvinick et al.[17] do so through attentional biasing.

We are reluctant to fully endorse this account, however. Critically, the account is not fully consistent with the results of Miyake et al.[10], who hold that while stop-signal errors and Stroop interference are dependent upon response inhibition, these measures are also *not* dependent on two other putative executive functions – task shifting and memory monitoring and updating. Thus, if we are to account for the behavioural correlation between these tasks in terms of attentional bias, it is also necessary to show that attentional bias does not systematically affect behaviour on the other tasks of Miyake et al. which were held to tap these other two functions and not to tap response inhibition. Here there is reason to be cautious. Gilbert and Shallice[18] consider performance on a task switching variant of the Stroop task in which subjects switch between colour naming and word reading. They model the critical behavioural affects by using essentially the same mechanism proposed here (i.e., by biasing task demand units) in exactly the same model (the Cohen and Huston model). Yet these are effects that, on the decomposition of Miyake and colleagues, should be explained in terms of a distinct task shifting function. Moreover in the study of Miyake et al.[10] all correlations between putative task shifting tasks and putative response inhibition tasks were non-significant.

The concept of response inhibition held by Miyake et al.[10] to underlie good performance in the stop-signal and Stroop tasks was also held to underlie good performance in the anti-saccade task. Thus, a fuller analysis of response inhibition requires also consideration of process models of the anti-saccade task. This remains to be attempted. We would hypothesise, however, that performance in this task will also correlate with an attentional bias parameter.

Returning to the two models considered here, it should also be noted that while they share principles of interactive activation, there are also major differences between them. For example, different equations govern the accumulation of activation in each model. Whether these differences are substantive or cosmetic remains to be demonstrated. However, these differences really only serve to reinforce a more general conclusion, namely, that until we have unified process models of the various putative separable executive functions, any theoretical account of their supposed unity and diversity is incomplete. By extrapolation, to understand the executive functions which underlie the battery of tasks used by Miyake et al.[10], we need to develop, within a single unified framework, models of all of those tasks. Such models must, of course, demonstrate the hypothesised shared mechanisms. Only then can we be confident that we have a plausible account of the various executive functions that contribute to the control of complex behaviour. This is, of course, one of Newell's arguments for the utility of Unified Theories of Cognition (Newell[19]).

Acknowledgments

We are grateful to Marius Usher and several anonymous referees for comments on earlier drafts of this chapter.

References

1. Norman, D.A. & Shallice, T. (1986). Attention to action: willed and automatic control of behaviour. In R. Davidson, G. Schwartz, and D. Shapiro (eds.) *Consciousness and Self Regulation, Volume 4*, pp. 1–18. Plenum: NY.
2. Everling, S., & Fischer, B. (1998). The antisaccade: a review of basic research and clinical studies. *Neuropsychologia, 36*(9), 885-899.
3. Logan, G. D., & Cowan, W. B. (1984). On the ability to inhibit thought and action: A theory of an act of control. *Psychological Review, 91*(3), 295-327.
4. Boccardi, E., Sala, S. D., Motto, C., & Spinnler, H. (2002). Utilisation Behaviour Consequent to Bilateral SMA Softening. *Cortex, 38*(3), 289-308.
5. Marchetti, C., & Della Sala, S. (1998). Disentangling the Alien and Anarchic Hand. *Cognitive Neuropsychiatry, 3*(3), 191-207.
6. Aron, A. R., Fletcher, P. C., Bullmore, E. T., Sahakian, B. J., & Robbins, T. W. (2003). Stop-signal inhibition disrupted by damage to right inferior frontal gyrus in humans. *Naure Neuroscience, 6*(2), 115-116.
7. Gauggel, S., Rieger, M., & Feghoff, T. (2004). Inhibition of ongoing responses in patients with Parkinson's disease. *Journal of Neurology, Neurosurgery & Psychiatry, 75*(4), 539-544.
8. Aron, A. R., Robbins, T. W., & Poldrack, R. A. (2004). Inhibition and the right inferior frontal cortex. *Trends in Cognitive Sciences, 8*(4), 170-177.
9. Chambers, C. D., Garavan, H., & Bellgrove, M. A. (2009). Insights into the neural basis of response inhibition from cognitive and clinical neuroscience. *Neuroscience & Biobehavioral Reviews, 33*(5), 631-646.
10. Miyake, A., Friedman, N. P., Emerson, M. J., Witzki, A. H., Howerter, A., & Wager T. D. (2000). The unity and diversity of Executive Functions and their contributions to complex "Frontal Lobe" tasks: A latent variable analysis. *Cognitive Psychology, 41*(1), 49-100.
11. Friedman, N. P., & Miyake, A. (2004). The relations among inhibition and interference control functions: A latent variable analysis. *Journal of Experimental Psychology: General, 133*(1), 101-135.
12. Boucher, L., Palmeri, T. J., Logan, G. D., & Schall, J. D. (2007). Inhibitory control in mind and brain: An interactive race model of countermanding saccades. *Psychological Review, 114*(2), 376-397.
13. Cohen, J. D. & Huston, T. A. (1994). Progress in the use of interactive models for understanding attention and performance. In *Attention and performance 15: Conscious and nonconscious information processing*. C. Umiltà & M. Moscovitch (Eds) (pp. 453-476). Cambridge, MA, US: The MIT Press.
14. Usher, M., & McClelland, J. L. (2001). The time course of perceptual choice: The leaky, competing accumulator model. *Psychological Review, 108*, 550–592.

15. Cohen, J. D., & Servan-Schreiber, D. (1992). Context, cortex, and dopamine: A connectionist approach to behavior and biology in schizophrenia. *Psychological Review*, *99*, 45–77.

16. Davelaar, E. J., & Cooper, R. P. (2010). Modelling the correlation between two putative inhibition tasks: An analytic approach. In Catrambone, R., & Ohlsson, S. (Eds.), *Proceedings of the 32nd Annual Conference of the Cognitive Science Society*. Cognitive Science Society Incorporated, Portland, OR, USA.

17. Botvinick, M.M. Braver, T.S., Barch, D.M., Carter, C.S. & Cohen, J.D. (2001). Conflict monitoring and cognitive control. *Psychological Review*, *108*, 624–652.

18. Gilbert, S. J., & Shallice, T. (2002). Task Switching: A PDP Model. *Cognitive Psychology*, *44*(3), 297-337.

19. Newell, A. (1990). *Unified Theories of Cognition*. Harvard University Press, Cambridge, MA.

A FIRST APPROACH TO AN ARTIFICIAL NETWORKED COGNITIVE CONTROL SYSTEM BASED ON THE SHARED CIRCUITS MODEL OF SOCIOCOGNITIVE CAPACITIES

A. SÁNCHEZ BOZA[a]* and R. HABER GUERRA[ab]

[a] Centre for Automation and Robotics, Spanish National Research Council,
Ctra. Campo Real km. 0,200, Arganda del Rey, Madrid 28500, Spain
[b] Escuela Politécnica Superior, Universidad Autónoma de Madrid,
Calle Francisco Tomás y Valiente 11, Madrid 28049, Spain
* E-mail: alfonso.sanchez@car.upm-csic.es
www.iai.csic.es

The top priority in high-performance manufacturing processes is the development of a new generation of control systems to enable faster, more efficient manufacturing by means of cooperative, self-organized, self-optimized behaviour. Some natural cognitive systems display effective behaviour through perception, action, deliberation, communication, and interaction with other individuals and with the environment. An artificial cognitive control architecture is presented which is based on the shared circuits model (SCM) of sociocognitive skills proposed by Hurley.[1] The proposal consists of a five-layer architecture in which the SCM approach is used to emulate such sociocognitive skills as imitation, deliberation, and mindreading. In Hurley's approach, these capacities can be enabled by mechanisms of control, mirroring the actions of others, and simulation. A control system thus designed should be capable of responding efficiently and robustly to the problems it is set. In the present implementation, the original SCM approach was enriched and modified in the light of constructive suggestions and evaluations in the literature. With these modifications, SCM served as the foundation for the design of a networked control architecture for application to an industrial case study – a high-performance drilling process. Experiments demonstrated that the proposed artificial cognitive control system can deal with nonlinearities and uncertainties in the drilling process, providing a good transient response and good error-based performance indices.

1. Introduction

The effective behaviour of a natural cognitive system is achieved through perception, action, deliberation, communication, and interaction with other individuals and with the environment. The flexibility of such a system which allows it to deal with the unexpected[2] comes from its capacity to *reason* in different ways, using large quantities of knowledge which it has appropriately represented in advance. In addition, by learning from experience it can improve how it operates, explain itself and accept new directives, be aware of its own behaviour and reflect on its capabilities, and respond robustly to unexpected changes.

A broad variety of strategies have been applied in order to partially or fully emulate cognitive capacities in computational architectures. Each has been based on a different conception of the nature of cognitive capacity, of what comprises a cognitive system, and of how to analyze and synthesize such a system.[3,4]

Meanwhile of course, there are thousands of complex systems and processes waiting for *intelligent solutions* in order to be able to respond adequately to disturbances and uncertainties. In the present century, manufacturing in particular has become a clear example of a dynamic social and technical system operating in a turbulent environment characterized by continuous changes at all levels, from the overall manufacturing system network to individual factories, production systems, technical processes, machines, and components.

The present work is based on the shared circuits model (SCM)[1] approach, taking this model as the foundation for designing an artificial cognitive control system that emulates imitation, deliberation, and mindreading processes in a software architecture built around computationally efficient algorithms. In Hurley's approach, these skills are taken to be achievable through control mechanisms, through mirroring of the actions of others, and through simulation. They are incorporated into an artificial cognitive control system designed to respond efficiently and robustly in the presence of nonlinearities, disturbances, and uncertainties.

The rest of this article is organized into a further three sections. Section 2 explains how SCM is enriched to provide the computational solution represented by the modified shared circuits model (MSCM) – a model which implements an artificial cognitive control system. Section 3 presents a first implementation of MSCM applied to the control of a high-performance drilling process. Finally, the conclusions are presented in Sec. 4.

2. An Architecture for Artificial Cognitive Control Based on the Shared Circuits Model of Sociocognitive Skills

Using a layered structure, SCM describes how certain human skills (imitation, deliberation, and mindreading) are deployed thanks to subpersonal mechanisms of control, mirroring, and simulation. The brain is envisaged as

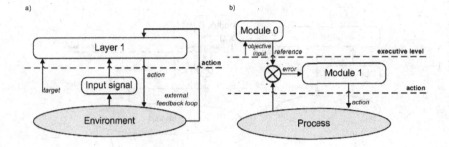

Fig. 1. (a) Model-based control in SCM. (b) An MSCM closed-loop control mechanism.

making use of inverse models to estimate the motor plan that will achieve a goal in a given context, but also of forward models to anticipate the perceivable effects of motor plans in order to improve response efficiency.

The basis of MSCM is a modular architecture that is a translation of SCM's layered structure, designed to have the functionality of an artificial cognitive control system. The modules use inverse and forward models of the process to control that process and anticipate the effects of their control, respectively. The following subsections will describe MSCM's functionality together with the corresponding improvements that needed to be incorporated into the original SCM.

2.1. *Imitation through simulative mirroring*

There are two mechanisms in SCM with which an individual's action is performed.

Layer 1 implements a model-based control that estimates the motor plan needed to achieve a goal. Inputs are mapped to outputs by means of instrumental relationships. In MSCM's Systems Theory and Computational Science perspective, its *module 1* is equivalent to SCM's layer 1. This module is represented by a controller and an optimization and adjustment process to enable this controller to adapt to new environmental conditions. It performs instrumental associations, similar to the closed-loop control systems that have been extensively used since the early 20th century (Fig. 1).

Given this kind of control system and the characteristics of the SCM proposal, the controlled process is equipped with feedback with the purpose of (i) avoiding the current output delaying the following input, (ii) precluding comparator overshoot when changes are sudden, and above all (iii) balancing out the influence of disturbances on the overall system. The

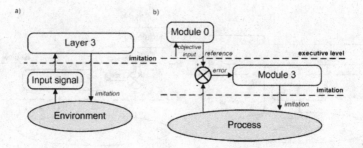

Fig. 2.   (a) SCM mirroring for priming, emulation, and imitation. (b) MSCM mechanism for an imitation process.

information in the feedback depends both on the system's own output and on exogenous events (which are often considered disturbances).

On the other hand, in SCM an agent may mirror an action that she [a] has observed to be successful in others for a particular objective if she considers that she herself has not yet learned a successful action for that objective. Then *layer 3* of SCM acts by imitating the input it receives. Module 3 in MSCM simulates this functionality, but now an error signal (*error*) of the difference between the output and a reference triggers an action mirroring the behaviour of other agents. Module 3 applies a set of inverse models to *error* as input to yield an imitative output action (Fig. 2b). This set of models maintained by module 3 constitutes a common repository shared by all the agents, and is enriched and modified by those agent-observed relationships that prove successful. In particular, each agent adds relationships or behaviours that it observes to be successful to a knowledge base that is accessed by other agents, thus leading to the sharing of these imitative actions.

Learning in MSCM consists of incorporating successful imitative knowledge from module 3's knowledge base into the initial knowledge base of instrumental associations managed by module 1. MSCM also includes an optimization and adjustment procedure based on a set of forward models handled by module 2, as will be shown below. This module also has an anticipative stage that attempts to speed up the control process by anticipating changes in the reference system.

---

[a] Following Hurley's usage in her original paper, we shall use the feminine pronoun to refer to the agent but without implying any loss of generality.

Module 4, analogous to *layer 4*, is responsible for inhibiting the previous modules, allowing the agent to distinguish between information from self and from others. But the SCM approach does not consider the temporal sequence defining when the different layers are to act, and neither does it provide relevant information about the performance of the agent. For this reason, *module a* is introduced into MSCM to estimate a performance index or figure of merit. This performance index is used in deciding when each module is to act and which combination of modules to run at each instant, depending on whether or not they improve that figure of merit. Module 4 also uses this index to decide when to perform optimization and learning.

In the present work, the system uses a performance index or figure of merit J to evaluate its own behaviour. This performance index J is calculated from partial figures of merit or weights chosen by a selector J_s according to whatever the current goals are. Since no such mechanism is described in SCM, in MSCM it was necessary to include an objectives manager (*module 0*, see Figs. 2 and 8). The function of this module is to handle a variety – technical, production, economic, etc. – of objectives, providing a set of reference signals and their corresponding partial figures of merit J_i that modules 1 and 3 will use to achieve those objectives. The weights J_i evaluate how well the objectives are being achieved.

2.2. *Deliberation using prediction of effects*

In SCM, deliberation is a cognitive skill that improves the prediction of an action's effects. Its *layer 2* adds a predictive mechanism to *layer 1* to speed up and smooth out the response, since the feedback mechanism of *layer 1* can slow operation down or destabilize the response (Fig. 3).

The predictive mechanism consists of an inner loop to predict inputs on the basis of layer 1's output. *Module 2* of MSCM has the same functionality as SCM's layer 2, incorporating a set of forward models on whose basis, given a control signal, a future output is generated. A criticism expressed by Behrendt is that it is too soon to predict the effect of an action on the environment when the action has never been observed before, as the SCM approach assumes.[5] Also, Makino posited that in order to achieve mindreading (one of the properties whose enablement SCM describes) one needs to develop a predictive model of the observation of one's own movements.[6]

A major feature of MSCM is that it attempts to take into account the actual characteristics of the environment, i.e., the exogenous input and/or the influence of noise and disturbances in the controlled process, generated by external variables that are not contemplated in its description (such as

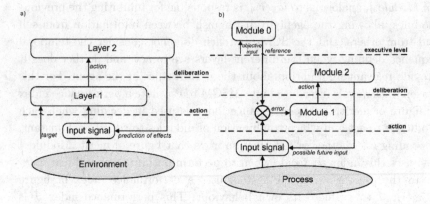

Fig. 3. (a) SCM simulates the prediction of effects. (b) The MSCM mechanism for a simulative prediction of effects for improved control.

environmental features: external temperature, vibrations, etc.). An artificial mechanism is introduced to update the inverse models used by module 1 and forward models used by module 2 if the noise is significant, that is, if it exceeds a certain threshold. This mechanism is implemented by a process that observes the new effects and learns to incorporate them into these models.

Makino also notes that SCM does not specify when the operation of layer 2 should be inhibited. For this reason, from a computation science perspective, it is necessary to define and implement some mechanism to decide whether or not to perform action, imitation, or deliberation. Thus, in close analogy to SCM's layer 4, MSCM's *module 4* in our proposal performs executive functions in the system, being the module responsible for managing the aforementioned decisions. Makino suggests that inhibition depends on failure monitoring. Our interpretation of this type of monitoring is that there is failure if, in the deliberation stage, the prediction (represented by the aforementioned performance index J as a figure of merit) of the effect of the action using module 2 is reported as being unsuccessful, i.e., that this action does not comply with the control objective. The kind of inhibition that characterizes the deliberation, action, and imitation cycle is described in Sec. 2.4.

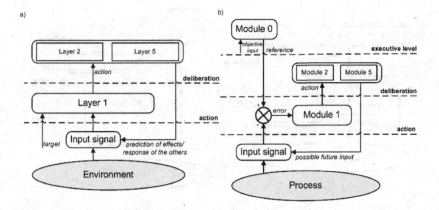

Fig. 4.   (a) SCM counterfactual input simulation for layer 1 control. (b) MSCM counterfactual input simulation for module 1 control.

2.3. *Mindreading by evaluating the response to the environment*

In SCM, mindreading is an important cognitive skill because it enables an agent to take others' responses into account in order to elaborate her own response. To this end, in SCM *layer 5* is responsible for emulating an exogenous input or disturbance. This mode of operation provides information on how the agent's possible acts may influence the acts of others. But SCM does not describe a process for emulating the reaction of other agents taking into account information on the environment. Hence, MSCM's *module 5* enriches SCM's *layer 5* by defining and managing a set of forward models $\underline{D}$ that associate the action generated by the system with the possible, or counterfactual, inputs, i.e., the reaction of others (fig. 4).

When this simulation is executed, the actual process is replaced by one of the models of the set that gives a prediction of which disturbances would occur. The system thus envisages the exogenous input that would result if the action were performed, enhancing the architecture's enactive qualities. But we believe that, contrary to what is proposed in SCM, it has to be module 4 that decides whether to inhibit the operation of module 5, instead of this being a decision of module 5 itself. The reason is that, taking the framework of the SCM description into account, the system as a whole (not just module 5) is enabled to deliberate about the possible strategies that others may enact using module 3 (not inhibited by module

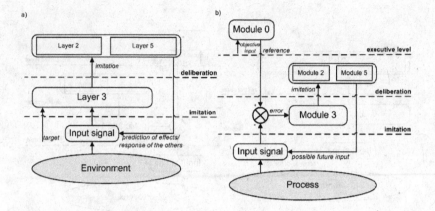

Fig. 5. (a) SCM counterfactual input simulation enabling strategic deliberation. (b) The MSCM solution for the same purpose.

4), and incorporating the deliberation that takes place thanks to the role of module 2 (Fig. 5).

2.4. Development of cognitive skills through interaction between modules

The orientation of MSCM is towards the control of complex processes. For this purpose, a temporal sequence of module functioning needs to be defined since there is no such sequence described in the SCM proposal. As mentioned above, in SCM the cognitive capacities of deliberation, imitation, and mindreading are enabled by the interaction between layers, and, analogously, in MSCM the relationships and interactions between modules make it possible to artificially emulate those cognitive capacities. The description of layer interactions is, however, one of the main weaknesses of the SCM approach, and, in order to develop a computational framework for the design of control systems, it will be necessary to address module interactions.

SCM just outlines these interactions, neglecting the temporal issues underlying how the layers operate. We took into account the commentaries of other authors to elaborate a temporal pattern that clarifies how and when the MSCM system is to act. For example, Carpendale and Lewis pointed out from their analysis of SCM that the model offers no evident mechanism whereby an action can be comprehended solely through the imitation process.[7]

With the SCM approach, an agent can make sensorimotor associations of her facial movements as being her own on the basis of indirect observations (in a mirror, for instance), enabling the imitation mechanism. This case is used in SCM to reach the conclusion that some correspondences between input and output are innate, while others are acquired (such as those in front of a mirror) and imitated [1, p. 14]. This leads us to posit that the starting point has to be some innate knowledge, although Hurley does not commit herself to establishing which correspondences are innate, acquired, or both [1, p. 14].

Hence in MSCM, if the result of evaluating the set of possible innate or already-acquired actions is unsatisfactory, the action leading to the objective is imitated. If this action is satisfactory, the agent learns by incorporating the action into the set of instrumental associations used in module 1 control. Otherwise, module 1 acquires new knowledge by means of an optimization process: as an interaction algorithm that is described below, module 1 is optimized if there is noise in excess, giving the system the capacity to adapt in the presence of significant environmental noise and to evolve by taking environmental changes into account. This optimization process is the mechanism of last resort because it is more costly than copying an observed association.

The actual models involved in this process are: the set of forward models handled by module 5 to simulate the counterfactual effects of actions taken by the system; a set of forward models used to simulate the effects, available for module 2, and to optimize the set of inverse models of module 1; and the set of inverse models for imitation, available for module 3.

An artificial cognitive control system can be designed following the scheme of Fig. 6. In this iterative procedure, the evaluation of whether or not there is excessive noise is determined relative to a given threshold.

In order to carry out this process, the modules are connected as was shown above in this section. The main feature to note is that module 4 is responsible for governing the action, imitation, and learning cycle according to the success of the control as given by the error found in its implementation.

3. An Implementation of a Basic Configuration of MSCM to Control a High-Performance Drilling Process

The modification of SCM – MSCM – is oriented to control. At this stage of the project, as a proof of concept case study, a basic configuration of an MSCM architecture was implemented to control a particular complex

(1) Deliberate on the possible actions to carry out by means of the interaction of modules 1, 2, and 5.

(2) If an action leads to success, execute it.

   (a) If noise surpasses the threshold, module 2 learns the new effects that have resulted.

(3) Otherwise,

   (a) If noise surpasses the threshold, go to (3.iii.A).

   (b) Otherwise,

      i. Deliberate on the possible actions of others (imitative actions) by means of the interaction of modules 2, 3, and 5.

      ii. If an imitative action leads to success, execute it.

         A. Learn this action by incorporating the corresponding instrumental association into module 1's private set of forward models.

      iii. Otherwise,

         A. Through an optimization process, acquire a new action using the process model handled by module 2 whose results are handled by the said optimization process in module 1.

         B. Execute a new action by means of the operation of module 1.

Fig. 6. Algorithm of the system's action, imitation, and learning cycle.

industrial process – high-performance drilling. Drilling is one of the most intensively used processes in the manufacture of vehicle and aircraft parts, and of molds and dies in general. The aim of the present work was to demonstrate that MSCM provides the theoretical framework needed to design an artificial cognitive control system.

The role played by the internal models in the MSCM approach opens up the possibility of using the design method provided by the Internal Model Control (IMC) paradigm of Control Theory. Indeed, to implement MSCM one has an extensive choice provided by Control Theory, Artificial Intelligence and its techniques, Computer Science, Systems Theory, and Information Theory. In the present case, we exploit the advantages of neurofuzzy systems. This kind of system combines the semantic transparency of fuzzy systems[8] with the learning ability of artificial neural networks. The resulting capacities of incorporating experience, of learning, and of adaptation and self-adjustment[9] are in line with those of MSCM for emulating the sociocognitive experiences of imitation, deliberation, and mindreading. For this proof-of-concept configuration, artificial neural networks were used to obtain good (forward and inverse) models of the process. In the future, optimization processes will be included which will also use artificial neural networks to improve and adjust the models online (i.e., while the control process is running), adapting and modifying the system's initial knowledge base.

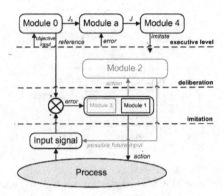

Fig. 7. Diagram of the basic MSCM configuration applied to the action stage of the control process.

In this basic configuration, module 1 implements a fuzzy controller, and modules 2 and 3, from a control theory perspective, follow the fundamental scheme of a closed-loop control system. They have forward models (handled in module 3, as was mentioned above). Indeed, this is how the IMC paradigm establishes a control design strategy which explicitly uses a model of the process.[10] This is very similar to the role assigned to the forward and inverse models in MSCM, which are essential for implementing modules 2 and 3. Learning processes are not yet implemented at this stage of the project.

Module 4 uses the module interaction algorithm (see subsec. 2.4) to decide which module is to act. Module 0 receives the main objective and translates it into a reference value. In the present case study, the reference is the drilling force. If the control action provided by module 1 is successful as given by the performance index J, or from its deliberation using module 2, that action is performed (Fig. 7). Otherwise, module 3 (which handles the inverse model) takes an input (e.g., the difference between the reference and the value that results from taking another difference between the process output and the direct model output or *possible future input*) and implements the imitation stage (Fig. 8). In both cases, before executing these stages, their effects are deliberated using the prediction mechanism provided by module 2 to check whether they are successful, and if so to execute them (Figs. 6 and 9).

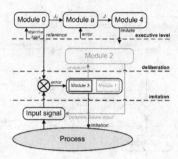

Fig. 8. Diagram of the basic MSCM configuration applied to the imitation stage of the control process.

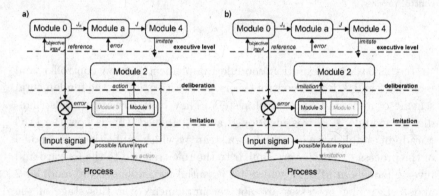

Fig. 9. Diagram of the basic MSCM configuration applied to the deliberation stage in (a) action and (b) imitation.

The modules are independent of each other. Hence, not only can they be developed and improved separately, but the different computational modules can be situated in different computers as independent servers, or several in one computer. In this latter case, another program must be responsible for connecting their input and output, taking signals from module 4 to enable or disable the other modules (see Sec. 3.2).

Indeed, Linear and Nonlinear Control Theory provides one with many strategies that can be used in the modules of the MSCM by establishing analogies between the roles of the modules and control paradigms. A comparative study of resemblances to some common control strategies such as feedforward control, adaptive control, predictive control, and robust control, to cite only a few, would go beyond the scope of the present article.

3.1. *Performance Index Computation*

A performance index is a single measure of a system's performance designed to recognize the responses that are deemed to be important in terms of time and error as against some pre-defined reference. Complex control systems require sophisticated performance criteria to optimize their performance subject to certain given constraints. The indices that are used are essentially error-based criteria (i.e., they are based on the deviation of the process's output relative to the reference).

The SCM approach does not address temporal issues affecting the operation of the different layers. In the present work, however, the module that handles the function of layer 4 is equipped with executive functions to determine the sequence of functioning modules. It is also very important to provide relevant information about the performance of the agent. To this end, module a in MSCM estimates a performance index or figure of merit. This is an essential module because the performance index that it calculates is used in deciding which modules should act and in which combination, and which modules should not run.

There are many performance indices J_i (IAE, $ITAE$, IAU, ...), each designed to measure the attainment of one or several objectives. For example, $ITAE$ is used in drilling processes to define whether the objectives of maximizing tool life and productivity are attained in those processes. ITAE is the *integral of time multiplied by the absolute error*:

$$ITAE = \int_0^\infty t|e(t)|dt$$

where $e(t)$ is the error of the input signal relative to a reference at instant t.

In the present work, the system utilizes a global performance index or figure of merit J to assess its own behaviour. This index is calculated by weighting the figures of merit J_i (such as $ITAE$) by a weight vector J_s according to different given objectives.

In the preliminary version whose test is reported here (see sec. 3.2), we only used $ITAE$ as performance index (thus $J = ITAE$), with the objectives of maximizing tool life and productivity.

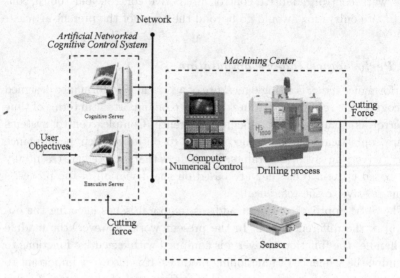

Fig. 10. An MSCM control architecture implemented in a real-world process.

3.2. *Simulation results for the drilling process*

The experimental data were obtained from a simulation of a cast-iron drilling process. Two variables were taken into account in this process: the force on the piece along the Z-axis, and the tool feed rate. The nominal operating conditions were a spindle speed of 870 rpm, an initial feed rate of 100 mm/min, and a cutting depth of 15 mm.

Networked control is implemented as distributed over two machines: one receives the user's targets and the values measured by the sensors, and performs executive functions; the other emulates cognitive processes (Fig. 10). The machines communicate through the intermediary communications system *Ice* [b]. In this way, the communications are transparent to the network's characteristics and to the machines that perform these processes.

The main goal is to obtain a good transient response without overshoot, using the cutting parameters provided by the manufacturer for this combination of tool and workpiece material. In this case, a cutting force of 1000 N has to be maintained throughout the process. A random noise was introduced into the simulation to bring it closer to a real process. For this

---

[b]http://www.zeroc.com/ice.html

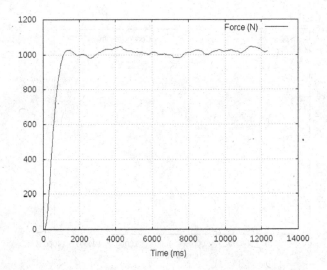

Fig. 11. Resultant force of the control actions of the preliminary MSCM implementation.

reason, one observes peaks around this 1000 N reference value (Fig. 11).

Switching between modules is enabled when the transition zone observed in the plot of the force (in Fig. 11 from 0 to 1 s approx.) has passed and the force is in the stationary region of the drilling process – specifically at 4 s. If not dealt with suitably, this switching between modules could lead to sudden sharp control responses that might break the tool or the piece. In the physiological context, the brain responds smoothly to different stimuli: its neural network responds linearly, even if single neurons have responded to varying synaptic inputs with unreliable spikes, i.e., overall it responds in a filtered manner.[11] Therefore, MSCM uses a low-pass filter when module 4 switches between module 1's action and module 3's imitative action. This smoothness of response can be appreciated at 4 or 6 s, for example, in the plot of the spindle speed control response (Fig. 12).

4. Conclusion

We have presented a first approach to designing an artificial cognitive control system based on the conceptual framework given by the shared circuits model (SCM) approach to emulating sociocognitive skills. The SCM approach was enriched and improved in the light of recent advances in this

274

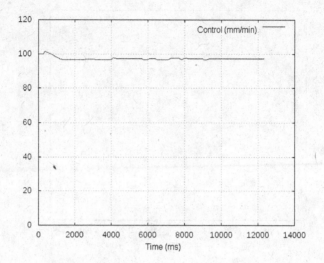

Fig. 12. Control action (feed rate) provided to the drilling process by the preliminary MSCM implementation.

field. Other work in this field and the authors' own previous contributions have played a major part in this project. The modified SCM (MSCM) is designed from a Systems Theory and Computer Science perspective. The conceptual scheme consists of a translation from SCM's layers to modules in MSCM, with the sequence of operation of the modules described in this article. The suggested procedure allows the activity of a combination of modules or of a single module alone. In sum, MSCM is a development of the SCM approach aimed at deriving a computational solution to complex control problems.

Another contribution of MSCM is towards enabling more efficient and faster manufacturing through cooperative, self-organized, self-optimized behaviour by process control systems. The intention with this work is to contribute to the advance in artificial intelligent systems from mechanisms of imitation towards comprehension of the evolution of the human mind.

Theoretically, MSCM provides an alternative conceptual framework for control tasks to be performed in the efficient, robust fashion that characterizes human cognitive processes. Basically MSCM translates the process of imitative learning described by SCM into the transfer of information between actions to imitate (handled by module 3) and the agent's own knowledge (handled by module 1). Module 1 also includes a process that is not considered in SCM – one of optimization and adjustment to implement a new action. It is indispensable to have a module (*module a* in this work) that monitors the behaviour of the overall artificial cognitive control system on the basis of some performance index. This information is used by module 4 to select which modules are to act in the control process.

Another aspect was that SCM does not provide the necessary bases for the management of objectives. Thus, it was necessary to add a module responsible for this task. Likewise, the procedure of how the layers function is insufficiently specified in SCM, so that it was also necessary to establish a sequence of operation. For example, module 2 can run before the action is performed in order to evaluate or deliberate on different possible actions, depending on whether or not the agent's action (implemented by module 1) has been successful.

As a proof of concept of the proposed approach, a preliminary artificial cognitive control system was implemented for the regulation of drilling force as a case study of a manufacturing process. This simplified implementation of the MSCM approach demonstrated its viability from the computation science and control system perspective. In addition, the modular architecture of the proposal facilitates the system's future improvement and modification. The following steps in our implementation of MSCM are to develop a module 0 that is responsible for managing and coordinating objectives. Part of our ongoing work concerns the optimization and learning processes, and their inclusion in the implementation. Another task is to incorporate communication mechanisms with other companion machines in order for them to share information.

Acknowledgements

This work was supported by DPI2008-01978 *Networked cognitive control system for high-performance machining processes* (COGNETCON) of the Spanish Ministry of Science and Innovation.

References

1. S. Hurley, *Behavioral and Brain Sciences* **31**, 1 (2008).
2. D. Vernon, G. Metta and G. Sandini, *IEEE Transactions on Evolutionary Computation* **11**, 151 (2007).
3. Z. Pylyshyn, *Computation and cognition: Toward a foundation for cognitive science* 1984.
4. L. B. Thelen, E. Smith, *A Dynamic Systems Approach to the Development of Cognition and Action* (MA: MIT Press, Cambridge, 1994).

5. R.-P. Behrendt, *Behavioral and Brain Sciences* **31**, 22 (2008).
6. T. Makino, *Behavioral and Brain Sciences* **31**, 32 (2008).
7. J. Carpendale and C. Lewis, *Behavioral and Brain Sciences* **31**, 23 (2008).
8. R. Precup, M. Tomescu, S. Preitl, E. Petriu, S. Kilyeni and C. Barbulescu, Stability analysis approach to a class of fuzzy controlled nonlinear time-varying systems, in *IEEE EUROCON 2009, EUROCON 2009*, (St. Petersburg, 2009).
9. T. Fukuda and N. Kubota, *Proceedings of the IEEE* **87**, 1448 (1999).
10. G. C. Goodwin, *Control system design* (Prentice Hall, Englewood Cliffs, NJ., 2001).
11. T. Sasaki, R. Kimura, M. Tsukamoto, N. Matsuki and Y. Ikegaya, *Journal of Physiology* **574**, 195 (2006).

DIGITAL TYPOLOGY MODELLING OF COGNITIVE ABILITIES[*]

AGNÈS GARLETTI[†]

Départment of Languages' Didactic, Université du Maine, Avenue Olivier Messiaen Le Mans, 72085, France

This article links a Typology of Cognitive Abilities with computer action formats to reach later cognitive remediation. For that, it is necessary to instrument a didactic and evaluative on-line teacher in his/her perception activity of the student's cognitive processes. This instrument is on-line questionnaires which bring on items of written comprehension for a student of French as a Foreign Language.

1. Introduction

The aim of our research is to create a Digital typology modelling of cognitive abilities. To create this Digital typology modelling of cognitive abilities, we link a Typology of Cognitive Abilities that we define with psychomotor operations to computer action formats. This Typology of Cognitive Abilities only concerns the reading of written texts from a student who is taking an on-line course on French as a Foreign Language. Our works are theoretical. To take into account the reality of the background, it is important to question the student of French as a Foreign Language on his/her cognitive processes. For that, we instrument an on-line teacher whose role is to follow the student, with didactic and evaluative questionnaires. These questionnaires will help the on-line teacher with his/her perception activity of the cognitive processes of the student in written comprehension tasks.

For this, we created four on-line courses on written communication in French as a Foreign Language. The seven modules of the four on-line courses must help the student reach the level B1 of the Common European Framework of Reference (CEFR). There are thematic modules which will be on a Moodle platform e-learning of the University of the Maine.

---

[*] This work is supported by University of the Maine (Le Mans, France) and by University of Rome Tre (Rome, Italy).
[†] Work partially supported by Vinci grant of the French Italian University.

We studied one activity of written comprehension for each module. There are seven activities of written comprehension with fifty nine items. From these fifty nine items we created seven questionnaires on cognitive processes which can be used to do items. The questionnaires will be experimented by foreign students of the University of the Maine.

Firstly, we present a theoretical contribution to define and evaluate the competence to communicate in language and the cognitive processes on a Digital Learning Environment. Afterwards we show the three stages to create a Digital Typology modelling of cognitive abilities.

2. From the Competence to the Cognitive Processes: Defining and Evaluating on a Digital Learning Environment

Before speaking of the evaluation of the cognitive processes, it seems important to us to place this specific evaluation in context. This context is the evaluation of the competence to communication in languages in Digital Learning Environments.

2.1. Defining the Competence to Communicate in Language

Firstly, we choose to shortly define the concept of competence in order to progress towards a definition of the competence to communicate in language according to certain communicative patterns and Beacco's pattern[1].

According to Roegiers[2] the competence is "the possibility, for an individual, to mobilize with an internalized manner an integrated set of resources to solve a family of situations-problems". Scallon specifies that the resources "are constituted of internal or external to the subject knowledge, know-how and know-being"[3]. Moreover, the interdependent elements of these resources become integrate-knowledge[2,3]. The use of the integrate-knowledge in a new situation becomes a transfer-knowledge[3,4].

We adopt the definition used by Beacco[1] which took again the following definition. The competence to communicate in language includes "the capacities of language or the required aptitudes for the realisation of a text in a situation of determined interaction"[5]. We specify these capacities of language or required aptitudes according to communicative patterns and to complete these patterns with Beacco's four competences of the organisation of languages communicative teachings[1].

Certain communicative patterns take into account[1]:
- The linguistic component which is constituted by the coded elements of the language and requires that the learner masters the language system.

- The sociolinguistic component which is the skill to use language according to the characteristics of the cultural or socio-cultural context.
- The discursive component which deals with the formal knowledge of the discourses in their linguistic characteristics.
- The strategic component which is cognitive and organizes the discursive behaviours.

Beacco's communicative patterns specify the discursive and the strategic components and add an intercultural dimension[1]:

- The discursive component takes into account the discursive gender and the discursive index.
- The strategic component can be psycho-cognitive strategies as those used in reception, in production, in interaction or meta-cognitive strategies as those used in mediation.
- The formal competences are the facts to master the linguistic forms.
- The cultural and intercultural competences include the ethnolinguistics' component (the "verbal live together"), the action-related component (the "know how to act"), the relational component (to know how to manage the interactions), the interpretative component (to give meaning and to realize what is unknown in another society) and the intercultural component (to use positive attitudes with the difference).

2.2. *Evaluating on Digital Learning Environments and more precisely on Moodle Platform*

This competence to communicate in language can be evaluated in Digital Learning Environments. According to Laurier there are four types of tests to evaluate the competence[6].

Firstly the computer test is a test in which the administration and correction are automated. The advantages of the computer test are the capacity to treat the data, to individualize the administration and to establish the learner's score. But the computer tests are similar to the paper-pen tests. Moreover, it is difficult to treat open questions with the computer test.

Secondly the adaptive test is a test which level of difficulty of the administered tasks varies according to the learner's performance. The adaptable test enables an individualized evaluation to place the learners on an ability scale even if they have not done the same tasks and to reduce the duration of the test.

Thirdly the continuing measurement can be:

- A test which builds the learner's profile and makes a diagnosis from several abilities[7].

- A test which enables to find the deficiencies with an adaptable procedure and a hierarchical content[8].
- Multidimensional patterns which enable to take account for complex learnings.
- A procedure which enables to take frequent information and to verify the mastery of complex abilities.

Fourthly the intelligent measurement wants to introduce a detailed analysis of answers within the context of the artificial intelligence researches.

More precisely Springer offers four procedures to evaluate the learner's activity on a Moodle platform[9]:

- The test module offers standardized on-line exercises with automatic answers.
- The courses management suggests the recording and the following of the users' activity, the reports of activities and the details of the users' actions on forums for example. It is the following of the student's activity in the tracking.
- The Workshop module enables a peers' evaluation or a self-evaluation.
- The Poll module offers a vote on a subject with the students' feedbacks.

If we put in relation the four procedures to evaluate the student's activity according to Springer[9] with these four types of tests to evaluate the competence[6], we can see that the test module is a computer test and that the courses management, the workshop module and the poll module are continuing measurements.

2.3. *Defining and Evaluating the Cognitive Processes*

For Legendre, the cognitive process or the cognitive strategy is an "intellectual technique chosen by a person as being the more favourable to a problem resolution"[4]. Romainville specifies the terms "intellectual technique" by a conscious and intentional "set of procedures" used to reach a goal[10]. Our cognitive strategy was a strategy of written comprehension. But few written production strategies are used because our written comprehension activities on Moodle platform asked the student to write the answer.

For us, evaluating the cognitive strategies means that we studied the student's degree using a panel of cognitive strategies at the appropriate time. It is the fact to evaluate a strategic behaviour[3]. Scallon speaks about "inferring one strategy or strategies"[3].

We inferred or evaluated cognitive strategies in a formative way and in a continuing measurement. We searched to take frequent information to verify the degree of using the cognitive strategies to do a written reception item.

Our questionnaires on cognitive strategies were a new instrument to the on-line tutor to follow the student's cognitive activities in written comprehension.

There were three stages to create a Digital typology modelling of cognitive abilities in written comprehension:
1. Linking of language abilities and learning tasks to cognitive operations.
2. Naming of cognitive processes with an instrument to help the on-line teacher in his/her perception activity
3. Linking cognitive abilities and psychomotor operations to computer action formats.

3. How to Obtain Cognitive Abilities?

3.1. *The First Hypothesis*

Firstly we refer to the evaluative context that Springer relates in a diagram entitled *Complexité de l'évaluation en langue*, in digital environments of learning. The social actor's ability to communicate with language depends on four entities including the cognitive and language abilities and the individual tasks[9]. So, we can say that if we link a language ability and learning tasks to cognitive operations, then we can obtain cognitive abilities.

3.2. *The Method to Obtain Cognitive Abilities*

The method firstly consisted in describing the language abilities in learning tasks[11] such as to identify, to associate, to choose, to find an identical expression, to condense, to extract, etc. Secondly, we associated each learning task with a cognitive operation of Bloom's Taxonomy of Educational Objective[12]. If we take the learning task "to associate", we find one definition of it in terms of cognitive operation according to Bloom. The definitions are the concern of the knowledge category and more precisely of the knowledge of classification sub-category. This learning task is defined as to classify, categorize "to structure better and schematize the phenomena". Thirdly, we put in relation the definition of the learning task in terms of Bloom's cognitive operation found with a new definition often in terms of cognitive operation of the New Taxonomy of Educational Objective of Marzano and Kendall[13] to precise it. If we take again the learning task "to associate", we specify Bloom's first definition in two ways according to Marzano and Kendall. The first leaning task "to associate" comes on the knowledge utilization category whereas the second learning task "to associate" comes on the retrieval category. Such as for Bloom, for Marzano and Kendall, we search the under-categories and then, we define the learning task "to associate" in two ways, "to make a specific decision or [...] a decision regarding the generalization or principle" and to recognize organizing ideas in "identifying accurate statements about generalizations and principles". The comparison between Bloom's definition and Marzano and Kendall's definition enabled to find an adequate action verb in the graphic help-memory of Bloom Taxonomy[14]. For the learning task "to associate", we found the action verb "to link up". So the association between this learning task, "to associate" and this action verb "to link up" constituted a cognitive ability. And with this comparison of cognitive operations for a learning task, we could define this cognitive ability in two ways to know its meaning.

3.3. *The Result: A Typology of Cognitive Abilities*

The result was a typology of cognitive abilities. This typology of cognitive abilities included 25 cognitive abilities with firstly the 23 cognitive abilities of written comprehension and secondly the 2 cognitive abilities of written production.

In written comprehension, we obtained:

- Eleven varied categories to identify elements such as to define, to name and memorize, to memorize, to select, to convert, to sum up, to detect, to re-know and distinguish, to infer and to examine.
- Two categories to link elements.
- Two categories to choose elements.
- One category to interpret elements.
- One category to resume elements.
- One category to extract elements.
- Two categories to discriminate or decompose elements.
- One category to classify elements.
- Two categories to arrange or regroup elements.

These categories are organized in function of Bloom's cognitive scale from the knowledge to the analysis.

Table 1. Cognitive abilities' categories about identifying elements.

Cognitive abilities	Cognitive operations according to Bloom (1969)	Cognitive operations according to Marzano and Kendall (2007)	Numbers of items
1- To identify/ 7to define	- Knowledge / Knowledge of terminology	- Retrieval / Recalling Information	67
	- "find the signification of a word"	- To "recall about a specific vocabulary term"	
2- To identify/ to give a name and memorize	- Knowledge / Knowledge of particular facts	- Retrieval / Recognizing Information	32
	- To give a name and memorize (to remember and identify an indication, a denomination)	- To "identify accurate statements regarding terms, facts and time sequence"	
3- To identify/ to memorize	- Knowledge / Knowledge of classifications	- Comprehension / Integrating Information	41
	- « to delimit the covered field by » the part of a given type of document which has been treated previously	- To identify "the essential versus non essential elements of specific details"	
4- To identify/ to select (1)	- Knowledge / Knowledge of classifications	- Comprehension / Integrating Information	38
	- « to delimit the covered field by » the part of a headline, by the instructions of a given type of document	- To identify "the essential versus nonessential elements of specific details"	
5- To identify/ to convert (1)	- Comprehension / Transposition of a symbolic form to another form	- Comprehension / Integrating Information	5
	a/ - to transpose a visual symbol under a verbal form	- To identify "essential versus non essential elements"	1
	b/ - to transpose a verbal form under a visual symbol	- To « represent the major aspects of details in [...] abstract form"	4
6- To identify/ to convert (2)	- Comprehension / Transposition of a symbolic form to another form	- Comprehension / Symbolizing Information	6
	a/ - to transpose a visual symbol under a symbolic form	To « represent the major aspects of details in [...] abstract form"	1
	b/ - to transpose a symbolic form under a verbal form	To « represent the major aspects of details in [...] abstract form"	5
7- To identify/ to sum up	- Comprehension / Transposition of a level of abstraction to another	- Comprehension / Symbolizing Information	6
	a/ - "to transpose a long communication into a shorter or a more abstract account"	To « represent the major aspects of details in [...] abstract form"	3
	b/ - to transpose a symbolic form into a shorter verbal or a more abstract account	To « represent the major aspects of details in [...] abstract form"	3
8- To identify/to detect	- Analysis / recognize and classify the elements	- Analysis / Matching Information	7
	- To identify and distinguish elements	- To identify "how specific details are similar or different"	
9- To identify/ to select (2)	- Analysis / recognize and classify the elements	- Analysis / Classifying Information	8
	- To recognize and distinguish elements which have a signification, a sign in common	- To identify subordinate categories for a generalization	
10- To identify/to infer	- Analysis / Analysis of a series of data extracted from a document	- Analysis / Generalizing With Information	1
	- "To distinguish the title of a headline of the arguments which support it"	- To construct and to defend "new generalizations and principles based on already known details"	
11- To identify/ to examine	- Analysis / "to determine the main relations between the elements"	- Analysis / Matching Information	4
	- "To analyse the connections between the elements in an argumentation"	- To identify " how specific details are similar or different"	
Total			215

Table 2. Other cognitive abilities' categories in written comprehension.

Cognitive abilities	Cognitive operations according to Bloom (1969)	Cognitive operations according to Marzano and Kendall (2007)	Numbers of items
12- To associate/ to link up (1)	- Knowledge / Knowledge of classifications	- Knowledge Utilization / Decision Making with Information	1
	- To classify, categorize "to structure better and schematize the phenomena"	- "to make a specific decision or [...] a decision regarding the generalization or principle"	
13- To associate/ to ink up (2)	- Knowledge / Knowledge of classifications	- Retrieval / Recognizing Information	79
	- To classify, categorize "to structure better and schematize the phenomena"	- To recognize organizing ideas in "identifying accurate statements about generalizations and principles"	
14- To choose/ to select (1)	- Knowledge / Knowledge of principles and laws	- Retrieval / Executing Mental Procedures	1
	- To make "the choice of a line of action"	- To "perform or execute [...] without significant error"	
15- To choose/ to select (2)	- Knowledge / Knowledge of principles and laws	Knowledge Utilization / Decision Making with Information	13
	- To make "the choice of a line of action"	- "to make a specific decision or [...] a decision regarding the generalization or principle"	
16- To find an identical expression/ to interpret	- Comprehension / "to transpose each of the main parties» and « to understand the connection between the various parts and dispose them mentally in a new order"	- Comprehension / Integrating Mental Procedures	6
	- "To understand the topic of a work", to understand the sense of various types of data	- To identify and to articulate "the various steps of that skill or process as well as the order of those steps and the logic of that order"	
17- To condense/ to sum up	- Comprehension / "to understand the connection between the various parts and dispose them mentally in a new order"	- Comprehension / Integrating Information (Organizing ideas)	3
	- "Ability to understand and to interpret the elements with more and more acuteness and clarity"	- To identify "the defining characteristics of a generalisation or a principle"	
18 – To extract/to detect	- Analysis / To recognize and classify the elements	- Analysis / Matching Information	53
	- To identify and distinguish elements	- To identify "how specific details are similar or different"	
19- To distinguish/ to discriminate	- Analysis / "Analysis which distinguishes the main parties of the argumentation"	- Analysis / Matching Information	12
	- "to analyse the connections between elements" textual "according to their presentation " iconographic [...] to distinguish those which support it from those which do not support it"	- To identify "the manner in which a [...] fact [...] is similar to, or yet different from, related structures."	
20- To distinguish/ to decompose	- Analysis / to recognize and classify the elements	- Analysis / Classifying Information	11
	- To decompose a given type of document in definite parts	- To identify subordinate categories for a generalization	
21- To class/ to classify	- Analysis / to determine the relations between the elements	- Analysis / Classifying Information	6
	- "to analyse the connections between the elements in an argumentation"	- To identify "super ordinate and subordinate categories for a generalization or a principle"	
22- To regroup/ to order	- Analysis / "analysis of structure and organization of a communication"	- Analysis / Classifying Information	1
	- to put arguments in order	- To identify "super ordinate and subordinate categories for a generalization or a principle"	

23- To regroup/ to regroup	- Analysis / "to determine the main relations between the elements"	- Analysis / Classifying Information	18
	- "to analyse the connections between the elements in an argumentation"	- To identify "the super ordinate category to which specific details belong"	
Total			204
Total number of items in written comprehension			419

Table 3. Repartition of Cognitive abilities' categories in written comprehension according to the level of cognition.

Cognitive abilities' categories Level of cognition	Identifying elements	Others categories of written reception	Total number of items in written reception
Down level	195	103	299
Analysis	20	101	121
Total number of items in written reception	215	204	420

We can see that the number of items about the 11 categories *identifying elements* is the most important with 215 items. If we take again Bloom's scale, the cognitive abilities of down level that is to say "to identify/to define", "to identify/to select", "to identify/to memorize", "to identify/to name and memorize" include 178 items.

In the other categories of written comprehension, there are 204 items with an almost equal part to the cognitive down level such as 103 items and the analysis level such as 101 items.

Table 4. Cognitive abilities' categories in written production.

Cognitive abilities	Cognitive operations according to Bloom (1969)	Cognitive operations according to Marzano and Kendall (2007)	Numbers of items
24- To reproduce/ to use by imitation	- Application / Use of specialized knowledge acquired during the training	- Knowledge Utilization / Problem Solving With Information	53
	- To use a written account, a written information by imitation from a written stimulus	- To use "his or her knowledge of details to solve a specific problem or solve a problem regarding the details"	
25- To formulate/to produce	- Synthesis / to use a particular means of expression with its forms and its conventions	- Knowledge Utilization / Problem Solving With Information	19
	- To write out from constraint deriving from written stimulus	- To accomplish "a goal for which obstacles or limiting conditions exist"	
Total number of items in written production			72
Total number of items in written comprehension and production			491

These categories are organized in function of Bloom's cognitive scale from the knowledge to the analysis.

In written production, we obtained:

- One category to use by imitation elements.
- One category to produce elements from written stimuli.

These two categories of written production aimed at restoring the learner's written comprehension. The first category is in relation with the application field and second category is with the synthesis field.

In the two categories of written production, using elements by imitation is the most representative category with 53 items out of 72 items.

The second stage is to create an instrument to help the on-line teacher in his/her perception activity to visualize the student's cognitive activity.

4. How to Visualize the Student's Cognitive Activity?

4.1. *The Second Hypothesis*

Secondly we thought that there is a gap to visualize the student's cognitive activity in Digital Learning Environments. So, the digital environment of learning *Croisières* takes into account the cognitive strategies' concept in the development of a situation of learning regulation activity[15]. But the processes of visualisation are not sufficient to detect the student's cognitive processes which cause a blockage. The learning cognitive activities appear inaccessible to the tutor's perception even in the tracking[16]. So if we create an instrument to help the on-line teacher in his/her perception activity to evaluate the cognitive processes then, he/she can visualize the student's cognitive activity.

4.2. *The Method to Instrument the On-Line Teacher*

The method consisted in taking again the cognitive abilities and their definition according to Bloom's Taxonomy of Educational Objectives[12] and Marzano and Kendall's New Taxonomy of Educational Objectives[13]. With the action verbs of each cognitive ability[14] and their definition, we could name each cognitive strategy or cognitive process and their degree of use by the student. And then we gave a scale to the student in order to ask him what the degree of use of the cognitive process is.

4.3. The Result: Seven questionnaires on cognitive processes

We created seven qualitative questionnaires on cognitive processes of written comprehension. The Table 5 sums up the names given to the cognitive processes which are linked to the two categories of cognitive abilities *To associate/to link up*.

Table 5. A summary of cognitive processes' names for two categories of cognitive abilities

Cognitive abilities	To name cognitive abilities in the questionnaires to the learner	Numbers of items
12- To associate/to link up (1)	- I link the meaning of a drawing to a text on a stereotype.	1
13- To associate/to link up (2)	- I link the meaning of important words of the order to the part/parts of the text to be treated.	55
	- I link each symbol's part to be treated to the adequate part of the requests' table.	2
	- I link X to "Y" concept.	18
	- I link X to Y.	4
Total number of items		80

The third stage was to create a digital typology modelling of cognitive abilities.

5. How to Obtain a Digital Typology Modelling of Cognitive Abilities?

5.1. The Third Hypothesis

We want to show that if the mental practice - which is based on the mental image, notably visual and kinaesthetic[17] - is associated with the physical practice then the effects produced in the improvement of the produced performance will be superior[18]. So if the typology modelling of cognitive abilities is associated with the psychomotor field and computer action formats, then we can obtain a Digital Typology Modelling of Cognitive Abilities.

5.2. The Method to Create a Digital Typology Modelling of Cognitive Abilities

The method consisted in taking our first typology of cognitive abilities and to add to each cognitive ability the definition of psychomotor operation according to Marzano and Kendall. With this new definition, we found a computer action format to connect and we connected it to a cognitive ability. The computer action format could include one or several combinations of computer tasks.

Table 6. A Digital Typology Modelling of Cognitive Abilities identifying elements.

Cognitive abilities	Psychomotor operations According to Marzano and Kendall	Computer formats of action	Numbers of items
1- To identify/to define	To describe "the general nature and purpose of a psychomotor skill" in "generating basic information".	To write a basic definition.	67
2- To identify/to give a name and memorize	To validate "the accuracy statements about psychomotor skill or process".	To click on the right statement.	32
3- To identify/ to memorize	To describe "the logic of the major aspects of a psychomotor process".	To write the significant steps to memorize something in a logical manner.	41
4- To Identify/ to select (1)	To describe "the logic of the steps involved in a psychomotor skill".	To draw a table with essential and non essential details in a logical manner.	38
5- To identify/ to convert (1)	To represent "the component parts of a psychomotor process" which is a symbolic form in a linguistic form.	To write the different component parts of an abstract form.	5
6- To identify/ to convert (2)	To represent "the component parts of a psychomotor process" which verbal form in a non linguistic or abstract form".	To draw the different component parts of a linguistic form.	6
7- To identify/ to sum up	To represent "the component parts of a psychomotor process" which is a long communication in a shorter linguistic form.	To write a shorter linguistic document from a long communication.	3
	To represent "the component parts of a psychomotor process" which is symbolic in "a more abstract or shorter account".	To draw or to write a shorter account from a symbolic form.	3
8- To identify/ to detect	To identify "how psychomotor processes are similar and different".	To draw a table with similar and different elements and to copy/paste the elements in the table.	7
9- To identify/ to select (2)	To identify "superordinate and subordinate categories for a psychomotor process".	To click on a list of subordinate elements for a category.	8
10- To identify/to infer	To construct and defend "new generalizations and principles based on information about specific psychomotor process".	To slide/to put the elements in a table and to write or to click on their general idea.	1
11- To identify/ to examine	To identify "how psychomotor processes are similar and different" from their main relations.	To write the main relations and connections between elements.	4
Total number of items			215

5.3. *The Result: A Digital Typology Modelling of Cognitive Abilities*

The result was a digital typology modelling of cognitive abilities which can be used by the on-line teacher or the conceptor of educative resources to create new digital tasks to help the student during his/her learning to understand what cognitive strategies could be used to succeed in a written comprehension task. The student's answers to these written reception tasks will help the on-line teacher in his perception activity.

Table 7. A Digital Typology Modelling of Cognitive Abilities about other cognitive abilities' categories.

Cognitive abilities	Psychomotor operations According to Marzano and Kendall	Computer formats of action	Numbers of items
12- To associate/ to link up (1)	To use "his/her knowledge of a psychomotor process to make a specific decision" or to make "a decision regarding the psychomotor process".	To slide/to put the elements in a table, to draw, to write, etc. and to link the elements.	1
13- To associate/ to link up (2)	To validate "the accuracy of statements about psychomotor processes".	To link the elements.	79
14- To choose/ to select (1)	To perform "the psychomotor process without significant error".	To write, to click on the right elements.	1
15- To choose/ to select (2)	To use "his/her knowledge of a psychomotor process to make a specific decision" or to make "a decision regarding the psychomotor process".	To slide/to put the elements in a table, to draw, to write, etc. and to click on the well considered elements.	13
16- To find an identical expression/to interpret	To describe "the logic of the major aspects of a psychomotor process" to interpret and to find an identical expression.	To draw a table with the varied expressions and to link the identical expressions.	6
17- To condense/ to sum up	To describe "the logic of the major aspects of a psychomotor process" and to clearly understand the elements to sum up.	To draw a table with the written document and the main elements and then to give a number to the same ideas.	3
18- To extract/to detect	To identify "how psychomotor processes are similar and different" to extract the well considered elements.	To draw a table with the element to take in his/her answer and the other elements and then, to write his/her answer with sliding/putting the well considered elements at the right place.	53
19- To distinguish/ to discriminate	To identify "how psychomotor processes are similar and different" according to the possible connections between the elements.	To draw a table and to write why there are connections or not between the similar elements.	12
20- To distinguish/ to decompose	To identify "superordinate and subordinate categories for a psychomotor process" to find the different parts of a document.	To cut/to slide the different parts of a document at the well considered place.	11
21- To Class/to classify	To identify "superordinate and subordinate categories for a psychomotor process" to analyze the relation between the element.	To draw a table with the elements and to write the connections between the elements and then, to copy/paste the elements at the right place.	6
22- To regroup/ to order	To identify "superordinate and subordinate categories for a psychomotor process" to order the elements.	To draw a table with the elements and to write the connections between the elements and then, to copy/put the elements at the right place and with a number.	1
23- To regroup /to regroup	To identify "superordinate and subordinate categories for a psychomotor process" to regroup the elements.	To draw a diagram with the elements and to write the connections between the elements of a group and then, to copy/put the elements at the right place in a diagram.	18
Total number of items			204

Table 8. A Digital Typology Modelling of Cognitive Abilities about written production.

Cognitive abilities	Psychomotor operations According to Marzano and Kendall	Computer formats of action	Numbers of items
24- To reproduce/ to use by imitation	To use "his/her skill at or understanding of a psychomotor process to solve a specific problem or solve a problem regarding the psychomotor process" to reproduce information.	To copy/paste the terms and the expression to give an answer.	53
25- To formulate/ to produce	To use "his/her skill at or understanding of a psychomotor process to solve a specific problem or solve a problem regarding the psychomotor process" to write his/her answer from constraints.	To write and to copy/paste the elements which are given.	19
Total number of items in written production			72

For the Digital Typology Modelling of Cognitive Abilities in written production, this work only takes into account the cognitive abilities which are used to answer a task of written comprehension. This work is also to be specified.

6. Conclusion

To conclude our 3 stages to create the digital typology modelling of cognitive abilities aim at 3 uses:

• To help the student understand what kind of cognitive strategies can be used to succeed in a task and to know his/her learning cognitive profile.

• To help the on-line teacher visualize the cognitive process of the student.

• To help the on-line teacher and the conceptor do digital activities of cognitive remediation.

References

1. J.-C. Beacco, L'approche par compétences dans l'enseignement des langues, Les Editions Didier, Paris (2007).
2. X. Roegiers, Une pédagogie de l'intégration : compétences et intégration des acquis dans l'enseignement, De Boeck Université, Bruxelles (2000).
3. G. Scallon, L'évaluation des apprentissages dans une approche par compétences, De Boeck Université, Bruxelles (2004).
4. R. Legendre, Dictionnaire actuelle de l'éducation, Guérin, Montréal (1993).
5. J. Dolz and J.-P. Bronckart, "La notion de compétence", in J. Dolz and E. Ollagnier (dir.): L'Énigme de la compétence en éducation, De Boeck, Bruxelles (2000).

6. M. Laurier, "Méthodologie d'évaluation dans des contextes d'apprentissage des langues assistés par les environnements informatiques multimédias", in T. Chanier, M. Pothier (Dir.), "Hypermedia et apprentissage des langues", études de linguistique appliquée (éla), 110, 247-255 (1998).

7. M. Laurier, "Using the Information Curve to Assess Language CAT Efficiency", in A. Cumming et R. Berwick (dir.), *Validation in Language Testing*, Clevedon, UK : Multilingual Matters. 111-123 (1996).

8. G. Trentin, "Computerized Adaptive Tests and Formative Assessment", Journal of Educational Multimedia and Hypermedia, vol 6, 2, 201-220 (1997).

9. C. Springer, "Evaluer les apprentissages dans les environnements numériques", [online], http://www.scribd.com/doc/8696921/2009-Evaluer-les-apprentissages (2009).

10. M. Romainville, *Savoir parler de ses méthodes : métacognition et performance à l'université*, De Boeck-Wesmael (1993).

11. D. Lussier, *Evaluer les apprentissages dans une approche communicative*, Hachette, coll. F/Autoformation, Paris (1992).

12. B. Bloom *and al.*, *Taxonomie des objectifs pédagogiques, tome 1. domaine cognitif.*, Les Entreprises Education Nouvelle, Inc., Montréal (1969).

13. R. J. Marzano and J. S. Kendall, *The New Taxonomy of Educational Objectives*, Corwin Press (2007).

14. F. Guité, *Aide-mémoire graphique*, [online], http://www.opossum.ca/guitef/archives/003601.html (2007).

15. P. Teutsch, J.-F. Bourdet and O. Gueye, "Perception de la situation d'apprentissage par le tuteur en ligne", [online], http://hal.archives-ouvertes.fr/docs/00/02/75/16/PDF/Teutsch_Bourdet.pdf (2004).

16. E. Villoit-Leclerq, P. Dessus, "Les contraintes de l'activité de tutorat à distance. Supervision et contrôle de situations dynamiques", [online], http://hal.archives-ouvertes.fr/docs/00/41/14/40/PDF/eiah09.pdf (2009).

17. M. Cadopi and A. Ille, "Rôle des représentations cognitives dans les activités physiques à dominante morphocinétique chez l'enfant et l'adolescent", in *Développement psychomoteur de l'enfant et pratiques physiques et sportives*, Editions «Revues E.P.S», 149-164, Paris (1999).

18. T. S. Weinberg, *The relationship between mental preparation strategies and motor performance: a review and critique*, Quest, 33, 195-213 (1981).

USING ENRICHED SEMANTIC REPRESENTATIONS IN PREDICTIONS OF HUMAN BRAIN ACTIVITY

JOSEPH P. LEVY

Department of Psychology, Roehampton University, Holybourne Avenue, London, SW15 4JD, UK

JOHN A. BULLINARIA

School of Computer Science, University of Birmingham, Edgbaston, Birmingham, B15 2TT, UK

There have been many different theoretical proposals for ways of representing word meaning in a distributed fashion. We ourselves have put forward a framework for expressing aspects of lexical semantics in terms of patterns of word co-occurrences measured in large linguistic corpora. Recent advances in the modelling of fMRI measures of brain activity have started to examine patterns of activation across the cortex rather than averaging activity across a sub-volume. Mitchell et al.[11] have shown that simple linear models can successfully predict fMRI data from patterns of word co-occurrence for a task where participants mentally generate properties for presented word-picture pairs. Using their MRI data, we replicate their models and extend them to use our independently optimised co-occurrence patterns to demonstrate that enriched representations of word/concept meaning produce significantly better predictions of brain activity. We also explore several aspects of the parameter space underlying the supervised learning techniques used in these models.

1. Introduction

There have been many suggestions for methods of representing word or concept meaning in terms of a distributed pattern of feature values[9,14]. Some of these reflect linguistic intuitions of participants (or experimenters/modellers) and others measure the distributions of words in language corpora. One of the challenges in the field is to test whether a particular scheme for semantic representation can explain or predict human behaviour better than another scheme. Recent work by Mitchell, Shinkareva, Carlson, Malave, Mason & Just[11] has shown that the co-occurrence statistics for a small hand-picked set of verbs can be used to predict functional brain imaging data at a level well above chance. In this paper, using the brain imaging data they have generously made public, we compare their results with the performance of their method using our own co-occurrence statistics that have been independently optimised.

Magnetic resonance imaging (MRI) is a form of spectroscopy that can produce high-resolution 3-dimensional images of materials including the anatomy of the brain. This technique can be extended to produce images that reflect blood deoxygenation in the brain where the strength of the "blood oxygen level dependant" or BOLD signal is measured for subvolumes or "voxels" of brain tissue of around 3-5mm-cubed and assumed to correlate with neural activation. The functional (fMRI) signal can usually only be measured relative to a resting or contrasting state and is small and noisy. The usual and highly successful method of analysing fMRI data is the so-called mass-univariate approach where a map is produced of the inferential statistic for each voxel produced by a linear statistical model of the predictors in an experiment. With appropriate adjustments for multiple comparisons, this approach allows a map to be produced showing areas of the brain sensitive to the experimental prediction or for a prediction that a particular area is sensitive to the experimental contrast to be statistically tested. However, the method ignores the possibility that what may be interesting in the data is the *pattern* of activation across individual voxels rather than the level of activation of a voxel or its mean across voxels. Mitchell et al's work is an example of this increasingly popular use of BOLD signal voxel patterns.

As reviewed by Naselaris et al.[12], these pattern analysis techniques have the potential for wide application in cognitive neuroscience. Here, we explore the possible ways of analysing the encoding of lexical or conceptual meaning in the brain. Specifically, we test the efficiency of different linear mappings from putative semantic representations to patterns of brain activation. In general, this allows us to identify distinct brain areas whose activity can be predicted by a particular representational scheme, but here we concentrate on comparing the encoding accuracy of linear computational models built using two different kinds of lexical co-occurrence vectors. The eventual aim is to test the validity of different ways in which neural computational models represent word or conceptual meaning by using measures derived from brain physiology.

In the following section we describe the Mitchell et al. model in more detail, and discuss the key performance measures we employ. Then we outline our own approach to corpus derived semantic representations, and present the parameter optimisation process involved in using them effectively. The comparative results for the key tasks in the Mitchell et al. study are then presented for both regularised and unregularised models, and the effect of varying the training data set size is explored. The paper ends with our conclusions and some discussion.

2. Description of the Computational/Statistical Model

Mitchell et al. asked participants to mentally generate properties for 60 previously studied simultaneously presented word-picture pairs of concrete entities, such as vehicles or animals (e.g., *cat*, *cow*, *train*, *airplane*), whilst lying in an fMRI scanner. Each word-picture pair was presented on 6 different occasions. The scanner data yielded vectors of BOLD activation (relative to a baseline) across the voxels for all the grey matter in the brain being scanned. Feature selection was achieved by choosing the 500 voxels whose values were most *stable* across the 6 repeats for each word (measured by averaging the pairwise correlations between the 60-item vectors produced for each of the presentations of the 60 words for each voxel). The BOLD signal values were then averaged across the repeats for each word and normalised to produce vectors of 500 continuous values for each of the 60 words.

Mitchell et al. hand-picked 25 verbs whose co-occurrences with the nouns in question could be expected to distinguish the patterns of usage and hence meaning of the nouns. The co-occurrences were measured in the 1 trillion word Google corpus to yield an 25-dimensional vector representing word/concept meaning.

To train a model to predict brain activation from word meaning, 58 of the 60 words were used to fit a linear regression model predicting each of the 500 most stable voxels for those 58 words from the 25 feature co-occurrence vectors. The models were then tested on their ability to predict the activation of the two held-out words. The model was deemed to have a correct prediction if the sum of the distances between measured and predicted brain activation was smaller for the correct mapping of input vector to output vector compared to the incorrect mapping. The process was then repeated until all the 1770 combinations of training set and test set had been trained and tested and the success of the model expressed as the mean binary scores.

The exercise produced highly statistically significant results as measured against a distribution of randomly permuted models. As such, it is an important demonstration that a distributed pattern known to reflect some of the properties of a stimulus (the 25 co-occurrence features) can be used to make statistical predictions of putative measurements of brain activity.

Mitchell et al. speculate that a richer representation of word meaning might yield better results in their models. They have generously made their data available [http://www.cs.cmu.edu/~tom/science2008/index.html] and we describe here how we have replicated their work and extended it to use our semantic representations. This advances their work by using vectors that can be shown to have better semantic distinctiveness and are general to all words of a reasonable frequency in the corpus we used to generate the vectors. However, these advantages for the input features of the model are offset by the practical considerations of increasing the dimensionality of the input from 25 to tens of thousands, which results in much slower computation of the linear models and the need for regularisation to prevent overfitting.

Following Mitchell et al., we used MATLAB to compute multiple linear regression models to predict each output voxel value from the values of all input features. This is equivalent to computing a multiple regression for each output voxel consisting of a linear combination of predictors from the input feature values. These computations are conveniently expressed as the minimisation of the sum-squared output error E of the model over a set of training items i:

$$E = \sum_i |m_i - v_i|^2, \quad m_i = Wf_i$$

where f_i is the vector of features, v_i is the vector of voxels, and m_i is the vector of model outputs, for word i. The matrix W of model weights/coefficients can be computed easily using standard matrix pseudoinversion techniques. Mitchell et al. report results from models that used their 25 input features and the 500 most stable voxels across the training set. We attempted to exactly replicate their model and also investigated the effects of varying the number of voxels used and the dimensionality of our own input vectors when they were used.

Regularisation techniques help avoid the overfitting of a model when the ratio of predictors to data points is high. The standard approach is to add a term proportional to the sum of the squares of the model coefficients W to the sum-squared error term E that is being minimised by least-squares learning. This penalises model complexity and helps avoid the fitting of the model to noise rather than true data, and is equivalent to ridge regression. We report later on the optimisation of the parameter that multiplies the regularisation term.

The aim is to test generalisation, i.e. how well the model outputs m_i match the actual voxel patterns v_i for unseen input words i. Following Mitchell et al., we measure this similarity using the cosine $\cos(m_i, v_i)$ between the relevant vectors. For small data sets (such as the 60 words here) a cross-validation approach is appropriate: withhold each possible pair of words (i, j) from training and for each withheld word i determine whether the model output is more similar to the corresponding voxel pattern or the voxel pattern of the other withheld word, i.e. whether $\cos(m_i, v_i) > \cos(m_i, v_j)$. That gives 59 tests for each word, and the model performance is the average number of correct matches over the 3540 tests (which we shall call *Perf*). This *Perf* is the cross-validated estimate of the average probability p that the model output for a given word is closer to the correct word target output than that of another word. It can therefore be used to estimate the expected average performance on harder tasks, such as leaving N words out of training and seeing how often the correct word is closest (i.e. probability p^{N-1}) or where the correct word ranks in closeness among the other N-1 words (i.e. position $1+(1-p)(N-1)$). Mitchell et al. actually combined the cosine similarities for each word pair, i.e. tested whether the pair total $\cos(m_i, v_i) + \cos(m_j, v_j) > \cos(m_i, v_j) + \cos(m_j, v_i)$, and took their performance to be the average number of those correct matches over the 1770 word pairs (which we shall call *PairPerf*). If the semantic features were random, both performance measures would be 0.5, and for totally successful models both would be 1.0. For intermediate levels, however, *PairPerf* will generally be higher than *Perf*. Permutation tests show empirically that the 0.05 significance level falls at 0.58 for *Perf* and 0.62 for *PairPerf*.

3. Features Used in the Modelling

We aim to compare the hand-picked 25 feature set used by Mitchell et al. with our own much larger feature vectors. One way to judge whether it is likely that our feature set will perform better in predicting fMRI data from a task that taps lexical/semantic judgments is to perform an unsupervised cluster analysis on the two sets of vectors for each of the 60 words used by Mitchell et al. The word-picture pairs describe 5 instances each of 12 conceptual categories (e.g., animals, plants, tools, buildings) and so it should be possible to see some of this category structure in the cluster analysis.

The purity P_r of a cluster r is simply the fraction of its members that belong to the most represented class. Then the overall purity P of clustering is the weighted average of the individual cluster purities P_r. Formally

$$P = \sum_{r=1}^{k} \frac{n_r}{n} P_r, \qquad P_r = \frac{1}{n_r} \max_c \left(n_r^c \right)$$

where n_r and n_r^c are the numbers of words in the relevant clusters and classes, with r labelling the k clusters, and c labelling the classes[15]. Applying the CLUTO Clustering Toolkit[7] with cosine distance and default parameters shows the 25 dimensional features they use to have a purity of 0.47, and the 500 most stable voxels give purities 0.53, 0.42, 0.45, 0.47, 0.45, 0.43, 0.37, 0.33, 0.38 (mean 0.43) for the nine participants.

It is known that optimised corpus-derived semantic representations can achieve perfect purity (1.00) for un-ambiguous concrete nouns[2], so it makes good sense to explore whether using such representations can improve the results in the Mitchell et al. study. We have previously carried out a systematic exploration of how to generate the best semantic representations and found that simply computing vectors of probabilities that words occur next to each other in large corpora, and calculating point-wise mutual information (PMI)[10] leads to vectors that perform well across a range of tasks[1]. It is that type of semantic representation, derived from the two billion word ukWaC corpus[4], that was used to explore clustering ability and achieved perfect purity in some cases[2]. Using such vectors with 10,000 components achieves cluster purity of 0.83 on the 60 Mitchell et al. words. This is still not perfect, and it is clear that such corpus derived vectors never can work well for all words[1,2,5,8], but the improved clustering over the Mitchell et al. features suggests that they are worth testing in the Mitchell et al. model. It might then be expected that, although more computationally expensive, our vectors may be able to predict fMRI data more successfully.

4. Parameter Optimisation

We began our experiments with an exact replication of the Mitchell et al. study, which involved computing the voxel stability values using only the 58 training set items so there could be no issue of non-independence in using the test items during training. However, simply computing the most stable voxels across the entire 60 member training + testing set once for all models, instead of once for each of the 1770 training sets, actually proved to have very little effect on the resulting performance, and allowed massive improvements in computing time, so that approach was followed for the remainder of this study.

We surveyed the different mean performance results for both the *PairPerf* and *Perf* criteria for all 1770 combinations of 58 item training sets and 2 item test sets for a large range of values for the regularisation parameter, the number of frequency-sorted corpus components (for our input features) and the number of stability-sorted voxels. This allowed us to identify near optimal parameter values for both types of input vectors. Each point in the following graphs shows the mean performance over the 9 participants and thus summarises 9 x 1770 = 15,930 trained models.

It is interesting to see how performance changes as the size of the input feature set increases and this is shown in Figure 1 where performance is plotted against number of input components (ordered by associated word frequency in the ukWaC corpus) for different numbers of stability-sorted voxels. Performance peaks at around 10,000 components for both the *PairPerf* and *Perf* criteria. This

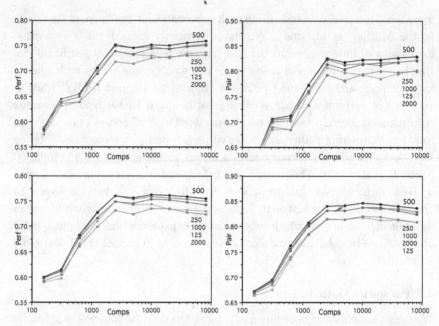

Fig. 1. Performance using our vectors as a function of number of corpus components: *Perf* (left) and *PairPerf* (right), regularization parameter 0 (upper) and 10,000 (lower). Individual lines correspond to different numbers of voxels as indicated by the line labels.

pattern is familiar for this kind of corpus-derived representation – the increased information from more components is eventually out-weighed by the noise that comes from poorer estimates of co-occurrence probabilities for lower frequency words[1,2]. These graphs also show that for these data, averaged over the 9 participants, 500 voxels is consistently the best performing number of voxels.

Figure 2 shows that for our 10,000 component input vectors, performance peaks at a regularisation parameter of around 100 for the *Perf* criterion and 300 for the *PairPerf* criterion, and remains fairly level for higher values. It also shows more clearly how the performance falls off for more or fewer than 500 voxels. However, we have observed that for individual participants with the most stable voxels (perhaps simply due to not moving whilst in the scanner as noted by Mitchell et al.), larger numbers of voxels are advantageous and that leads to different optimal regularisation parameters.

For fair comparison, we also checked the optimisation of parameters for the Mitchell et al. study. Figure 3 shows that for the 25 input features used by Mitchell et al., optimal performance was obtained for a regularisation parameter of 1 and 500 voxels. Choosing optimal parameters for such models should really

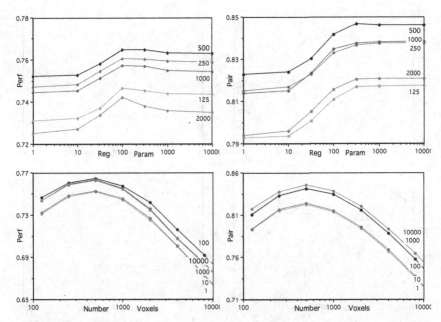

Fig. 2. Optimization of performance using our 10000 components corpus vectors: *Perf* (left) and *PairPerf* (right), regularization parameter (upper) and number of voxels (lower). Individual lines correspond to different numbers of voxels (upper) or regularization parameter (lower) as indicated by the line labels. [Note the differing vertical-axis scales.]

be done using an independent validation set, but with only nine participants of rather variable performance, that was not feasible. It is clear that for these experiments, regularisation makes little difference to the success of the trained models for this task. This might be expected for the low dimensional Mitchell et al. features, and Mitchell et al. did not use regularisation, but we were surprised that our much larger vectors didn't benefit more from its use. For all the comparative studies we used 500 voxels which appears close to optimal on average for both types of input features, and was used in the original Mitchell et al. study. Performance was tested without regularisation, and with regularisation parameter of 1 for the Mitchell et al. features (where there appears to be a consistent peak) and of 10,000 for our 10,000 dimensional corpus features (which is perhaps not optimal, but safely in the flat region of the performance graphs).

Figures 1, 2 and 3 also show how the Mitchell et al. *PairPerf* success measure produces slightly better results than the *Perf* measure across all model parameters. Such a difference is to be expected from a simple consideration of

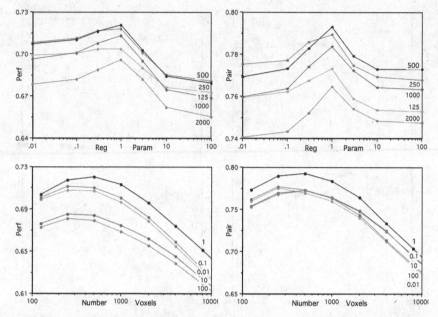

Fig. 3. Optimization of performance using the Mitchell et al. features: *Perf* (left) and *PairPerf* (right), regularization parameter (upper) and number of voxels (lower). Individual lines correspond to different numbers of voxels (upper) or regularization parameter (lower).

combining pairs of values from a roughly Gaussian distribution of cosine differences $\cos(m_i, v_i) - \cos(m_i, v_j)$. However, the nature of the model outputs can lead to the individual cosine differences in the pairs of combined values being anti-correlated, and that can lead to surprising advantages to the *PairPerf* measure. We therefore present both the *Perf* results (that are sure to be free from such artifacts) and *PairPerf* (for comparison purposes).

5. Comparative Results

Now that we have some confidence that we have near optimal values for the main parameters for each of the two different kinds of input features, we can compare performance across the 9 individual participants with and without regularisation. Table 1 shows the results for the individual participants for the *PairPerf* criterion as used by Mitchell et al.: for the 25 dimensional Mitchell et al. feature set, with no regularisation and with regularisation parameter 1, and for our 10,000 component corpus vectors, with no regularisation and with regularisation parameter 10,000. For all cases, 500 voxels were used. Column 2

Table 1. Results for each participant from the original paper by Mitchell et al.[11] (Science), our replication, and for the regularised (with reg) and non-regularised (no reg) models using Mitchell et al. (M. et al.) or Bullinaria & Levy (B & L) features for the *PairPerf* success criterion.

P	Science	Replication	M. et al. no reg	M. et al. with reg	B & L no reg	B & L with reg
1	0.83	0.83	0.83	0.84	0.91	0.92
2	0.85	0.85	0.84	0.80	0.78	0.80
3	0.76	0.77	0.78	0.78	0.82	0.85
4	0.78	0.79	0.79	0.82	0.89	0.91
5	0.82	0.82	0.81	0.84	0.78	0.83
6	0.73	0.73	0.71	0.76	0.79	0.83
7	0.78	0.78	0.78	0.78	0.85	0.87
8	0.72	0.72	0.71	0.76	0.70	0.73
9	0.68	0.68	0.69	0.76	0.87	0.88
mean	0.77	0.77	0.77	0.79	0.82	0.85

shows the original results published by Mitchell et al., and column 3 is our replication of what they did. There are small differences that are presumably due to variations in the rounding errors coming from different implementations. Column 4 is the same but with the voxel stability computed just once for the full set of 60 words, rather than for each of the 1770 training sets of 58 words. The differences are slightly larger here, but the mean is the same, which is our justification for using this computationally more efficient approach for the remainder of this study. Column 6 shows the equivalent for our input features. Finally, columns 5 and 7 are the regularised versions corresponding to columns 4 and 6. We tested statistical significance throughout using paired t-tests with one-tailed p-values. In all cases, the statistically significant results are also significant using Wilcoxon non-parametric tests. Our vectors show a modest improvement over those of Mitchell et al. for most participants for both non-regularised ($t(8) = 2.123$, $p < 0.05$) and regularised ($t(8) = 2.877$ $p < 0.05$) conditions. Regularisation appears to make a slight improvement for both feature sets.

Table 2 show the comparison in performance between the input features sets using the *Perf* success criterion. There is again an apparent small advantage for regularisation and statistically significant improvements for our features set over the Mitchell et al. set ($t(8) = 2.111$, $p < 0.05$ for the non-regularised cases and $t(8) = 2.564$, $p < 0.05$ for the regularised cases).

Table 2: Results for each participant for non-regularised and regularised versions of each type of input feature for the *Perf* success criterion.

P	M et al. no reg	M et al. with reg	B & L no reg	B & L with reg
1	0.77	0.76	0.84	0.84
2	0.76	0.73	0.72	0.72
3	0.71	0.71	0.74	0.76
4	0.73	0.76	0.81	0.83
5	0.73	0.75	0.71	0.74
6	0.66	0.70	0.73	0.74
7	0.72	0.70	0.79	0.79
8	0.67	0.69	0.65	0.65
9	0.63	0.69	0.79	0.79
mean	**0.71**	**0.72**	**0.75**	**0.76**

The advantages of our feature vectors are that they did not need to be generated specifically for this task and they are general to a very wide range of possible words. However, the difference in performance over the Mitchell et al. vectors is rather modest, especially given the computational expense of using 10,000 features rather than 25. To test whether this might be due to a ceiling effect of the fMRI data for this particular task, we progressively increased the difficulty of the task. Figure 4 compares results when the size of the training + test set was successively reduced from 60 words to randomly selected subsets of the original word set of 50, 40, 30, 20 and 10 words (with each case averaged over 20 different subsets). Each data point shows the average and standard error over the nine participants.

The consistency or reliability of the advantage of our input vectors over the Mitchell et al. input vectors appears to increase slightly as the training sets get smaller until a floor effect begins as the set size reaches 10 words. Using paired t-tests to gauge statistical significance of this advantage, it was significant for all training + test set sizes (apart from 10) and the level of significance increased as the training + set size decreased (apart from 10), and hence the difficulty of learning increased giving support to the suggestion that the advantage of our vectors increases as the task increases in difficulty until performance suffers for the regularised models when the set size reaches 10.

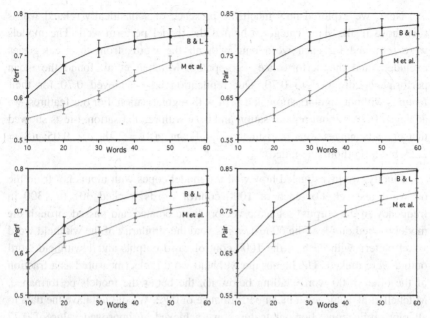

Fig. 4. Effect on performance of the number of words in the training data set: *Perf* (left) and *PairPerf* (right), non-regularised (upper) and regularised (lower). Individual lines correspond to using our corpus vectors (B & L) and the Mitchell et al. features (M et al.).

6. Further Comparisons

In addition to the main test of their model, described above, Mitchell et al. presented three further tests of its performance that we now apply for our richer representation of semantics.

First, since the 60 test words each fall into one of 12 semantic categories, it is instructive to compare the performance for the 120 word pairs that fall within a category, to the full set of word pairs. The within-category task is obviously harder than the full task, and Mitchell et al. did find a performance drop to 0.62. Our replication achieved 0.61 for their features without regularisation and 0.60 with regularisation. For our features, we achieved 0.58 without regularisation and 0.62 with regularisation. The differences between their results and ours was not significant ($t(8) = 0.89$, $p = 0.20$ and $t(8) = 0.69$, $p = 0.26$). This indicates that the improvements arising from our vectors come primarily from the remaining 1650 word pairs that fall across categories.

Next, we explored how much the presence of semantically related words (i.e. those in the same category) helped the model perform well. The models were retrained for each word pair with all the words from their categories excluded, and the performance recomputed. Mitchell et al. found the mean performance dropped to 0.70. Our replication also achieved 0.70 for their features without regularisation, and 0.74 with regularisation. For our features, we achieved 0.78 without regularisation and 0.79 with regularisation. t-tests showed that our advantages were statistically significant: $t(8) = 2.48$, $p < 0.05$; $t(8) = 2.23$, $p < 0.05$ (both one-tailed).

Finally, we investigated how well the model copes with inputs not from the 60 word test set. For each of 1000 control words (ranked 301 to 1300 in frequency in the corpus) semantic vectors were created and passed through the model trained on 59 of the 60 test words, and the similarity of the withheld word voxel pattern with each of the 1000 control word outputs and 1 withheld word output were ranked. The higher the withheld word ranks (measured as a fraction of the other 1000 words falling below it), the better the models performance. Mitchell et al. achieved a mean performance of 0.72. We did not have the data to attempt replication. For our features, we achieved an improved value of 0.77 without regularisation ($t(8) = 2.1$, $p < 0.05$, one-tailed).

The relatively marginal statistical significance for these last two tasks, despite approximately 5% increases in mean performance, is a reflection of the small number of subjects and the large variations between them. Some subjects consistently perform better with our corpus vectors than with the Mitchell et al. features, and others show the opposite pattern. This could be due to individual differences in the strategy chosen by the participants to perform Mitchell et al.'s relatively unconstrained task being captured better by one set of vectors than another. This is something that is worthy of future investigation, and may well hold the key to refining the whole approach.

7. Conclusions and Discussion

We have been able to closely replicate Mitchell et al.'s results and have shown that regularisation improves them slightly for the original task and more so when the task increases in difficulty. We have also provided results for the single word measure (*Perf*) that we believe is a more generally reliable indicator of performance than Mitchell et al.'s word pair measure (*PairPerf*).

Our richer semantic representations perform better across most of the tasks we have tried. Although the improvements are modest, they are consistent and statistically significant. It appears that the advantage of the much larger and semantically richer feature vectors increases as training set sizes decrease, which may be because the much larger vectors contain enough distributional information to make up for the smaller number of items. It was unsurprising that regularisation was required for our much larger input vectors, but perhaps unexpected that it made so little difference even after the regularisation parameter was optimised. Our average performance peaked when we used 10,000 frequency-ordered components demonstrating that even with a training set of 60 items, the computation of co-occurrence with large numbers of other words was advantageous.

Like Mitchell et al., we found that for this training set, optimal performance overall was achieved by using the 500 most stable voxels. For those individual participants with relatively high average stability values, however, a larger number of voxels was optimal. As with optimising our corpus vectors, there appears to be a trade-off between increased information and increased noise as more components are added.

While we were writing this paper, we discovered other recent work that had also used the Mitchell et al. data set and tested performance for a variety of alternative sets of input features[3,6,13]. It is interesting to note that all of these papers report useful results using different input features, but none of them convincingly exceed the performance levels achieved using the Mitchell et al. or our input vectors.

Perhaps the most puzzling aspect of this research is the apparently rather poor results achieved by all of the methods we have described. It is maybe worth speculating on what might be causing such a ceiling effect. It is certainly true that the BOLD signal is always small and subject to large amounts of noise, and that any head movement (which should be reflected in the "stability" measure) will cause problems for a voxel-pattern based approach. However, to train on 58 items and test on the remaining 2 is not an intrinsically difficult task. Mitchell et al.'s input feature set of 25 items performs well above chance and one might expect that our 10,000 element vectors would boost performance more than they did.

It would be instructive to further analyse the degree to which noise in the measurement of voxel BOLD response may be leading to an upper bound in the performance of the learning models reported here. The voxel patterns themselves do not cluster well using the CLUTO algorithm and this may indicate measurement noise. We are currently exploring the degree to which this kind of noise affects the performance of the models by constructing idealised voxel patterns that cluster perfectly and testing how learning performance drops off as noise is added.

It may also be instructive to repeat these modelling methods on a different stimulus set. The particular words chosen by Mitchell et al. are sometimes ambiguous and are always paired with line drawings. It is likely that lexical semantic processes are being confounded with visual ones in ways that differ between the different words. We hope to further investigate these issues using data derived from stimuli that are purely word-based.

Acknowledgments

We are very grateful to Tom Mitchell and Kai-min Kevin Chang for making their data available and for help in replicating their original results. We also thank Eddy Davelaar and an anonymous reviewer for helpful comments on the draft of this paper.

References

1. Bullinaria, J. A. & Levy, J. P. 2007. Extracting semantic representations from word co-occurrence statistics: A computational study. *Behavior Research Methods*, **39**, 510–26.

2. Bullinaria, J. A. 2008. Semantic categorization using simple word co-occurrence statistics. In: M. Baroni, S. Evert & A. Lenci (Eds), *Proceedings of the ESSLLI Workshop on Distributional Lexical Semantics*, 1–8. Hamburg, Germany: ESSLLI.

3. Devereux, B., Kelly, C. & Korhonen, A. 2010. Using fMRI activation to conceptual stimuli to evaluate methods for extracting conceptual representations from corpora. In Proceedings of the First Workshop on Computational Neurolinguistics, Los Angeles, California, USA. Association for Computational Linguistics.

4. Ferraresi, A. 2007. Building a very large corpus of English obtained by web crawling: ukWaC. Masters Thesis, University of Bologna, Italy. Corpus web-site: http://wacky.sslmit.unibo.it/

5. French, R. M. & Labiouse, C. 2002. Four problems with extracting human semantics from large text corpora. *Proceedings of the Twenty-fourth Annual Conference of the Cognitive Science Society*, 316–322. Mahwah, NJ: Lawrence Erlbaum Associates.

6. Jelodar, A. B., Alizaseh, M. & Khadevi, S. 2010. WordNet based features for predicting brain activity associated with meanings of nouns. In Proceedings of the First Workshop on Computational Neurolinguistics, Los Angeles, California, USA. Association for Computational Linguistics.

7. Karypis, G. 2003. CLUTO: A Clustering Toolkit (Release 2.1.1). Technical Report: #02-017, Department of Computer Science, University of Minnesota. Web-site: http://glaros.dtc.umn.edu/gkhome/views/cluto.

8. Landauer, T. K. & Dumais, S. T. 1997. A Solution to Plato's problem: The Latent Semantic Analysis Theory of Acquisition, Induction and representation of knowledge. *Psychological Review*, **104**, 211–240.

9. Lund, K. & Burgess, C. 1999. Producing high-dimensional semantic spaces from lexical co-occurrence. *Behavior Research Methods, Instruments & Computers*, **28**, 203–208.

10. Manning, C. D. & Schütze, H. 1996. *Foundations of Statistical Natural Language Processing*. Cambridge, MA: MIT Press.

11. Mitchell, T. M., Shinkareva, S. V., Carlson, A., Chang, K-M., Malave, V.L., Mason, R.A. & Just, M.A. 2008. Predicting human brain activity associated with the meanings of nouns. *Science*, **320**, 1191–1195.

12. Naselaris, T., Kay, K. N., Nishimoto, S., & Gallant, J. L. in press. Encoding and decoding in fMRI, *Neuroimage*.

13. Pereira, F., Botvinick, M., & Detre, G. 2010. Learning semantic features for fMRI data from definitional text. In Proceedings of the First Workshop on Computational Neurolinguistics, Los Angeles, California, USA. Association for Computational Linguistics.

14. Tyler, L. K., Moss, H. E., Durrant-Peatfield, M. R. & Levy, J. P. 2000. Conceptual structure and the structure of concepts: A distributed account of category-specific deficits. *Brain and Language*, 75(2), 195–231.

308

15. Zhao, Y. & Karypis, G. 2001. Criterion functions for document clustering: Experiments and Analysis. Technical Report TR #01–40, Department of Computer Science, University of Minnesota. Available from: http://cs.umn.edu/karypis/publications.

VARIABILITY IN THE SEVERITY OF DEVELOPMENTAL DISORDERS: A NEUROCOMPUTATIONAL ACCOUNT OF DEVELOPMENTAL REGRESSION IN AUTISM

MICHAEL SC THOMAS
VICTORIA CP KNOWLAND
ANNETTE KARMILOFF-SMITH

Developmental Neurocognition Lab, Centre for Brain and Cognitive Development, Department of Psychological Sciences, Birkbeck, University of London, Malet Street, London WC1E 7HX, UK

Developmental disorders show wide variations in severity even when, on genetic grounds, it is known that there is a common underlying cause. We use connectionist models of development combined with population modelling techniques to explore possible mechanistic causes of variations in disorder severity. Specifically, we investigate the plausibility of the hypothesis that disorder variability stems from the interaction of the common cause of the disorder with variations in neurocomputational parameters also present in the typically developing population. We base our simulations on a model of developmental regression in autism, which proposes that this phenomenon arises from over-aggressive synaptic pruning[1]. We simulated a population of 1000 networks in which 641 exhibited the behavioural marker of regression in their developmental trajectories in learning a notional cognitive domain. Aside from the known single cause of the disorder (an atypical connectivity pruning parameter), we then analysed which neurocomputational parameters contributed to variation in a number of characteristics of developmental regression. These included the timing of regression onset, its severity, its behavioural specificity, and the speed and extent of subsequent recovery. Results are related to existing causal frameworks that explain the origins of developmental deficits.

1. Introduction

Developmental disorders are notable for the range of severity with which they affect children. In the case of acquired disorders in adults, variations in the severity of behavioural deficits can usually be assigned to the degree of brain damage. For developmental disorders, the origins of variations in severity are less well understood. It is not clear, for example, whether variations in severity of deficits stem from the same causes which produce individual differences in cognitive ability in typically developing individuals. At present, many developmental disorders are defined on behavioural grounds, such as autism, dyslexia, and attention deficit hyperactivity disorder. On the face of it, the variation observed in behaviourally defined disorders could arise from at least two sources: these disorders could just represent the bottom tail of the normal distribution in population performance on social skills or reading or attention, in which case the underlying causes of variability in the tail would be no different from those producing variation in the normal range (see Kovacs et al.[2]); or the behaviourally defined disorders could in fact represent a heterogeneous mix of underlying causes, which would be unified by diagnosis but differ in their precise phenotype, thereby generating the observed variability in severity.

Somewhat more puzzling is the variability that is observed in developmental disorders with known genetic causes. Disorders such as Down syndrome (DS) and Williams syndrome (WS) are associated with well-characterised genetic mutations (an additional copy of chromosome 21 in the former case, a deletion of genes from one copy of chromosome 7 in the latter case). Yet, despite individuals in each disorder having a common genetic cause, they exhibit marked variation in the severity with which the genotype impacts on the cognitive profile and, more practically, on the ability of children and adults with these disorders to function in everyday life.

There are four likely sources of variation in the severity of developmental disorders of known genetic cause. (1) The environment: two individuals with the same disorder genotype might diverge through differential environmental influences. For example, phenylketonuria is a genetic disorder associated with a deficiency in an enzyme necessary to metabolize the amino acid phenylalanine to the amino acid tyrosine. This deficiency leads to a build up of phenylalanine, which causes developmental brain damage. An individual exposed to the environment of a low-phenylalanine diet will experience a much less severe version of the disorder. (2) Where genes are mutated, the genes may be polymorphic and vary in the normal population. For example, the additional chromosome 21 in DS contains many genes, some of which may differ between individuals and have different consequences. Additionally, such genetic differences may be exaggerated by gene-environment interactions. (3) The genetic mutation may occur to identical genes in two individuals, but epigenetic effects that alter gene expression might subsequently produce different effects. For example, in an extreme case, Angelman syndrome and Prader-Willi syndrome are two different disorders with the same genetic mutation (deletion of genes on chromosome 15). If the mutation is on the copy of chromosome originating from the mother, the result is Angelman syndrome; if the mutation originates from the father, the result is Prader-Willi syndrome. Parent-of-origin is an epigenetic effect that alters the gene expression from the same DNA code (in this case, the epigenetic effect is called 'imprinting'). (4) The mutated genes are the same in two individuals, but there are individual differences in the rest of the genotype, and the mutated genes interact with those other genes. For example, mouse models of DS have an additional copy of the equivalent of human chromosome 21 and such mice show a range of physical and cognitive abnormalities. When gene expression was examined in these mice, it was found to be altered in a large number of other genes on different chromosomes, suggesting interactions between normal and mutation genes (e.g., Saran, et al.[3]). Once more, interactions between mutated genes and other polymorphic genes may be exaggerated by gene-environment interactions. Together, these four causes contribute to what is called the *expressivity* of a given disorder genotype, that is, the extent of the phenotypic variation given the genotype.

It should become apparent that, for the goal of explaining differences in the severity of behaviourally defined developmental disorders, the fact that we know variability occurs even when there is a common known genetic cause makes the picture more complex. That is, even if a disorder such as autism were to have a common underlying genetic cause in all individuals with autism, one would still expect individual variation in the severity of the disorder. But, of course, autism may not be a single disorder but several disorders unified by behavioural diagnostic criteria. Alternatively, in terms of underlying mechanism, autism may not be a causally distinct disorder at all, rather one end of a spectrum of normal population variation for some set of behavioural traits.

1.1. *Computational models of variability in developmental disorders*

Relatively little attention has been paid to the possible mechanistic basis of variations in the severity of developmental disorders. Thomas[4] used a connectionist pattern associator to investigate whether it was possible on behavioural grounds to distinguish between a group of simulated individuals with a common underlying disorder (plus individual differences) from a group of simulated individuals diagnosed with a disorder on behavioural grounds but actually constituting heterogeneous underlying deficits (plus individual differences). Those simulations indicated that homogeneous and heterogeneous disorder groups were not necessarily distinguishable in their mean performance levels on a range of behavioural metrics. However, they were distinguishable on the basis of group variability: the heterogeneous, behaviourally defined group had the least variance on the measure that defined the disorder while the homogeneous, common cause group had comparable variance across measures. This prediction was confirmed empirically in a comparison of naming abilities in individuals with Williams syndrome and a group of children with behaviourally defined word finding difficulties.

In another model exploring variability, Kan et al.[5] examined developmental trajectories in a small, two-node dynamical system. They demonstrated that small stochastic differences in the start state in a self-organising learning system could become exaggerated across development. From the current perspective, such stochastic differences constitute effects of the environment. Since stochastic differences occur in the brain development even of identical twins, the model explains how identical genotypes could diverge across developmental time (see refs [6,7] for similar theoretical proposals).

In this paper, we investigate the hypothesis that a common underlying genetic cause of a developmental disorder can interact with individual differences elsewhere on the genome; that these interactions can occur at the neurocomputational level; and that such interactions contribute to the variability in severity of the disorder at the behavioural level (or, indeed, whether an individual exhibits a disorder at all). This was an exploratory model with two goals: (a) to evaluate emergent effects in complex learning systems that stem from the interaction of many simultaneously interacting components, in this case serving to modulate the severity of a simulated developmental disorder; (b) to propose candidate causal mechanisms that can explain empirical observations of variations in severity, and therefore widen the range of available inferences from behaviour to causal mechanism. We took a behavioural feature found in a subset of children with autism spectrum disorder, that of *developmental regression*, and built a set of models to test our hypothesis. There were three key features of the simulations. First, there were three sources of variability in behaviour: (i) intrinsic differences in neurocomputational properties, (ii) extrinsic variability in the composition of the learning environment, and (iii) the possible presence of a disorder affecting a single neurocomputational parameter. Second, behaviour was the outcome of an extended developmental process involving interaction of the individual with a structured environment. Third, simulated individuals were classified as having a disorder on behavioural grounds.

1.2. *Developmental regression*

In developmental regression, behaviours that emerge in early development subsequently disappear. There is then a later recovery and advance of these skills to a variable level. Regression is almost unique to autism but is not a universal feature of the disorder[8]. It occurs in 20-40% of cases, with skills typically disappearing between 15 and 24 months of age, and its cause is unknown[9,10]. Empirical data have hitherto mostly been based on retrospective parental reports, which indicate the loss of children's social and communication skills in the second year of life, including early productive vocabulary, eye contact, gestures, reciprocal games like peek-a-boo, and sometimes a loss of play and fine motor skills.

Our simulations extended a proposal by Thomas, Knowland and Karmiloff-Smith[1] that the cause of developmental regression in autism is over-aggressive synaptic pruning. Typical brain development involves initial over-production of neural resources, and in particular, the generation of synapses which allow for the plasticity of functional circuits; and then, later in development, the pruning of unused resources[11,12,13]. Using a connectionist population modelling technique[14], Thomas, Knowland and Karmiloff-Smith[1] investigated the hypothesis that regression may be caused by variations in synaptic pruning. A large number of simulated individuals were exposed to an abstract learning task. One neurocomputational parameter, which determined the severity of connectivity pruning following its onset, was set to be atypically extreme. This induced developmental regression because pruning ate into functionally established pathways instead of eliminating unused connections. The extreme pruning parameter was the *sole cause of the disorder*. However, the population also incorporated background variability in a range of other neurocomputational parameters, corresponding to normal individual differences; and variability in the composition of the learning environment to which individual networks were exposed. This provided the potential for interactions between different constraints within the simulated learning systems, which might in turn modulate (negatively or positively) the severity of the regression observed in behaviour.

In the following simulations, we explored the extent to which such interactions could lead to emergent variations in (a) the timing of regression during development, (b) the severity of regression, (c) the rate at which behaviour declined, (d) its specificity to particular types of behaviours, (e) the rate at which behaviour then recovered, and (f) the final level of performance. Lastly, although our simulations assumed a genetic disorder with a single underlying cause, disorder status was behaviourally defined on the basis of observed developmental regression. We were interested in whether such sampling created a disorder population with a different correlational structure among its neurocomputational parameters compared to the full population. That is, we considered the possibility that the *sampling* inherent in behaviourally defined disorders produces 'ghost' correlations between attributes that have no direct bearing on underlying cause of the disorder (which is this case was fully known).

2. Method

2.1. *Target learning problem*

For the purposes of these simulations, the training set was considered only as an abstract mapping problem, corresponding to a notional cognitive domain. The mapping problem was quasi-regular, in that it included a predominant regularity, which could be generalised to novel input patterns, and also a set of exception patterns. The learning environment was designed to assess role of similarity, type frequency and token frequency in development, together determining the difficulty of target behaviours. The mapping problem was defined over 90 input and 100 output units, using binary coded representations. The training set comprised 508 patterns. This was complemented with a generalisation set of 410 patterns.

The predominant regularity required the network to reproduce the input pattern on the first 90 units of the output layer, and then add a binary code on the last 10 units of the output layer. There were 410 regular patterns in the training set. The regular pattern had a high type frequency and formed a consistent set of mappings, and so will be referred to as *Easy*. The generalisation ability of each network was tested on 410 novel patterns that were similar to the *Easy* patterns, in that they shared 60 of the 90 input elements. This set will be referred to as *Generalisation*. There were three different classes of exception pattern in the training set, which fell on a continuum of (dis)similarity from the predominant regularity: (1) Reproduce the input but do not add the final code [N=20]. (2) Reproduce only a portion of the input and again do not add the final code [N=68]. (3) Associate an arbitrary binary pattern with the input and again do not add the final code [N=10]. The first exception type was most similar to predominant regularity, and third type the least similar. All three possessed a lower type frequency than the predominant regularity. The combination of dissimilarity and low type frequency created a continuum of difficulty. We refer to the first exception type as *Hard*, the second as *Harder*, and the last as *Hardest*. Finally, the arbitrary mappings were sufficiently difficult that they needed to be repeated in the training set to be learned at all. They therefore provide an opportunity to assess whether greater practice provided immunity to regression or perhaps allowed better recovery from regression. The third pattern type is therefore referred to as *Hardest-practised*.

2.2. *Basic architecture*

The simulations employed a connectionist pattern associator network trained using the supervised backpropagation learning algorithm. This type of architecture has been used in a number of cognitive-level models of development, for example, applied to infant categorisation, child vocabulary, semantic memory, morphosyntax, and reading development (see ref [15] for review). The model simulates a child's developmental profile in the notional cognitive domain.

2.3. *Variations in the learning environment*

The full training set was considered the ideal learning environment. For each individual, a subset of this training set was stochastically selected to represent the family conditions in which each simulated child was being raised. Each individual was assigned a *family quotient*, which was a number between 0 and 1. The value was used as a probability to sample from the full training set. Thus for an individual with a family quotient value of 0.75, each of the 508 training patterns had a 75% chance of being included in that individual's training set. Family quotients were sampled randomly depending on the range selected for the population. For the population we considered, the quality of the environment was reasonably good. Family quotients were sampled in the range of 0.6 to 1.0.

2.4. *Variations in the basic architecture*

Fourteen neurocomputational parameters in the basic architecture were allowed to vary between individuals, together serving to alter the learning capacity of each network. The parameter settings allowed for over 2000 billion unique individuals. Parameter values were randomly selected for each simulated individual and independently for each parameter; therefore any correlations between parameters occurred by chance. The parameters, split by their role, were as follows: *Network construction*: Architecture (two-layer network, three-layer network, or a fully connected network incorporating a layer of hidden units plus direct input-output connections); number of hidden units (10 to 500); range for initial connection weight randomisation (±0.01 to ±3.00); sparseness of initial connectivity between layers (50% to 100% of potential connectivity). *Network activation*: unit threshold function (logistic function, sigmoid temperatures between 0.0625 and 4); processing noise (0 to 6); response accuracy threshold (0.0025 to 0.5). *Network adaptation*: backpropagation error metric (Euclidean distance or cross-entropy); learning rate (0.005 to 0.5); momentum (0 to 0.75). *Network maintenance*: weight decay (0 to 2×10^{-5} per pattern presentation); pruning onset (0 to 1000 epochs); pruning probability (0 to 1); pruning threshold (0.1 to 4.0). Detailed explanations of the role of each parameter can be found in Thomas et al.[14].

The pruning process was central to simulating developmental regression. Networks were created with initial connectivity, determined by the sparseness parameter and the weight variance parameter. After a number of epochs of training determined by the pruning onset parameter, pruning commenced. After each epoch of training following onset, all the connection weights were assessed. Any connection whose magnitude was less than the pruning threshold was deemed an unused resource and could be permanently pruned. If a connection was less than threshold, pruning was then stochastic, occurring with a probability determined by the pruning probability parameter. Benchmarking suggested that of the 14 parameters varying in the simulations, the pruning threshold was the sole parameter that produced developmental regression. At levels up to 1.0, little regression was found (for comparison, initial weights were most often randomised in the range ±0.5). Levels above 1.0 were associated with regression. In the following population, pruning thresholds varied up to 4.0. This range implemented the hypothesis that the cause of the disorder is an accumulation of risk gene variants that allows a neurocomputational parameter to take on more extreme values than found in unaffected individuals. Under the hypothesis, both genetic risk and the neurocomputational causal factor are continuously valued.

2.5. *Creation of a population*

Parameter sets for 1000 individuals were generated at random. A family quotient value was generated in the appropriate range and the quotient used to create each individual's bespoke family training set. Each network was initiated with random weight values (in the range determined by the individual's weight range parameter), and then trained for 1000 epochs, where one epoch was an exposure to all the patterns in the individual's training set, presented in random order. Performance was measured on the five pattern types (*Easy, Generalisation, Hard, Harder, Hardest-practised*) according to the full training set and the full generalisation set.

3. Results

Developmental regression was defined on behavioural grounds as a noticeable drop in performance over development in one or more of the five behavioural measures (*Easy, Generalisation, Hard, Harder*, and *Hardest-practised*) against the level of variability exhibited by a given simulated individual. Developmental trajectories were plotted for all 1000 individuals and coded by hand for whether or not they exhibited developmental regression. Hand coding was used because trajectories were often non-monotonic and noisy, rendering automated classification problematic. Double coding was carried out on a sub-sample to ensure consistency. Figure 1 depicts sample trajectories for four typically developing networks (defined here as those not exhibiting regression) and four networks that showed regression. When regression was observed for a given pattern type, six measurements were made: peak performance prior to regression; the epoch at which regression occurred; the size of the drop in accuracy; the number of epochs over which that drop occurred; the rate of recovery (five qualitative categories were used: no recovery, slow recovery, medium recovery, fast recovery, almost instant recovery); and the final level of performance at the end of training (1000 epochs). We defined *four levels of severity* of the disorder, based on the size of the decline in accuracy: level 1, corresponding to a drop in accuracy of between 0 and 20%; level 2, corresponding to a drop in accuracy of 20 to 40%; level 3, corresponding to a drop between 40 and 60%; and level 4, corresponding to a drop of 60 to 100% in accuracy. Of the 1000 simulated individuals, 641 cases of regression were recorded in one or more behaviour.

3.1. *Variations in severity*

The single cause of regression was increasing the size of the pruning threshold parameter. However, there was no direct relationship between increasing this parameter and the subsequent severity of the observed regression. Table 1 lists the probability of observing regression at each severity level, for the five separate mapping types. It is evident that increases in the value of the pruning threshold produce an increased liability to exhibit regression, and regression of a more severe level, but the outcome was not deterministic (e.g., not 100% likely even with the highest threshold). Comparison of the behavioural categories indicated that *Easy* and *Generalisation* were more robust to regression, with all hard patterns more vulnerable. Notably, the *Hardest-practised* mapping exhibited a bimodal distribution for most extreme pruning levels: regression was either absent (23%) or at the severest level (61%). This is because the combination of exception mappings and extra practice caused networks to learn such mappings using a small number of weights (more localist representations). These weights were then stochastically preserved or lost during the atypical pruning process. More distributed representations demonstrated a dose-response relationship.

318

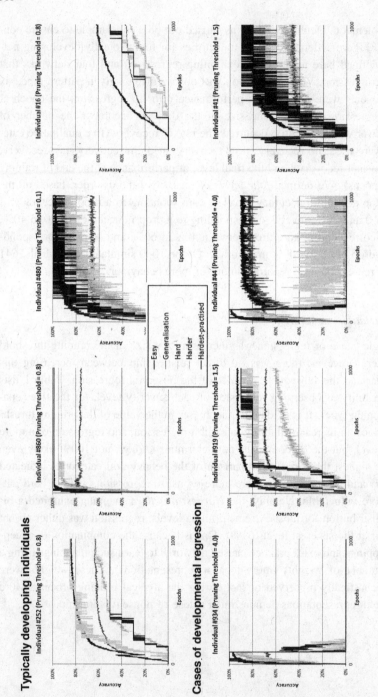

Fig. 1. Illustrative developmental trajectories for four typically developing networks and four networks exhibiting regression.

A statistical stepwise logistic regression analysis was used to identify the relationship between variation in neurocomputational parameters and the *presence of* regression. As expected, the atypical setting of the pruning threshold parameter accounted for most of the variance (Nagelkerke R^2 = 59.7% of the variance explained).

Table 1. The probability of a network exhibiting developmental regression, split by the level of severity (None, least severe I, II, III, or most severe IV). Probabilities are shown separately for each pattern type.

Severity	Pattern	Pruning Threshold								
		.1	.75	1.0	1.5	2.0	2.5	3.0	3.5	4.0
None	Easy	.98	.90	.72	.35	.24	.16	.14	.14	.04
	Generalisation	.98	.90	.72	.40	.33	.22	.17	.17	.10
	Hard	.98	.95	.75	.37	.29	.23	.16	.22	.11
	Harder	.98	.90	.71	.34	.23	.19	.13	.17	.11
	Hardest-Practised	.98	.95	.80	.42	.31	.19	.27	.23	.23
Severity I	Easy	.00	.07	.22	.24	.20	.17	.09	.09	.08
	Generalisation	.01	.03	.03	.24	.27	.20	.18	.22	.11
	Hard	.01	.00	.02	.11	.16	.20	.20	.15	.25
	Harder	.00	.00	.02	.06	.12	.28	.39	.40	.52
	Hardest-Practised	.01	.09	.24	.30	.20	.22	.13	.13	.04
Severity II	Easy	.01	.01	.02	.20	.30	.25	.28	.26	.24
	Generalisation	.00	.00	.01	.08	.12	.18	.20	.22	.25
	Hard	.00	.00	.02	.02	.05	.13	.23	.22	.36
	Harder	.00	.00	.02	.02	.01	.01	.03	.03	.05
	Hardest-Practised	.00	.04	.11	.10	.09	.07	.12	.05	.05
Severity III	Easy	.02	.01	.10	.24	.27	.28	.21	.17	.18
	Generalisation	.00	.00	.02	.28	.34	.41	.49	.54	.61
	Hard	.00	.00	.04	.06	.08	.08	.17	.16	.18
	Harder	.01	.08	.16	.19	.13	.24	.14	.15	.10
	Hardest-Practised	.00	.00	.06	.24	.30	.23	.17	.13	.13
Severity IV	Easy	.01	.02	.03	.16	.26	.26	.38	.40	.48
	Generalisation	.00	.01	.05	.05	.02	.04	.06	.05	.08
	Hard	.00	.01	.09	.06	.08	.07	.05	.07	.04
	Harder	.02	.02	.02	.18	.13	.18	.10	.12	.04
	Hardest-Practised	.00	.02	.05	.28	.46	.52	.51	.53	.61

However, individual differences in other neurocomputational parameters also modulated the risk. The following parameters showed a significant relationship: unit threshold function (Nagelkerke R^2 = 6.8%), architecture (1.2%), pruning probability (1.0%), hidden unit number (0.5%), sparseness (0.3%) and momentum (0.3%). Variations in the family quotient did not reliably modulate regression risk. In the case of pruning probability, this parameter directly affected the pruning process. All the other parameters acted indirectly by increasing or decreasing the size of the connection weights produced by learning prior to the onset of pruning. A statistical stepwise linear regression analysis was used to identify which parameters predicted the *severity of regression*, that is, the size of the drop in accuracy during regression. Twelve computational parameters were significant contributors at the .05 level; only 6 individually accounted for more than 1% of the variance: pruning threshold (10.0%), unit threshold (5.8%), processing noise (2.5%), architecture (2.3%), pruning probability (1.9%) and learning algorithm (1.4%). Pattern type explained 3.9% of the variance and family quotient 0.8%. Once again, the value of the atypical pruning parameter explained much of the variance in severity of regression, but many other parameters varying in the population as a whole also contributed to predicting severity.

3.2. *Variability in onset*

The onset of regression approximated a normal distribution with a mean of 101 epochs and a standard deviation of 69.[a] A statistical linear regression analysis indicated that the pruning onset parameter explained 51.1% of the variance. Only unit threshold and learning rate (0.3% each) also reached significance. Regression, then, was triggered by the normal onset of the pruning process.

3.3. *Variability in the rate of decline*

The rate of decline was assessed for each pattern type, separately across severity levels. More severe regression showed slower declines, and the *Hardest-practised* showed fastest decline amongst the pattern types. The statistical stepwise linear regression analysis implicated 8 computational parameters in explaining the variability in how quickly performance declined, with only 3 explaining more than 1% of the variance: pruning probability (5.3%), pruning threshold (1.5%) and unit threshold (1.5%). The amount of unexplained variance in this case reflected the stochastic nature of the pruning process.

---

[a] Plots illustrating population variation for data reported in Sections 3.2 to 3.6 can be found at http://www.psyc.bbk.ac.uk/research/DNL/techreport/NCPW12plots.pdf

3.4. *Variability in the rate of recovery*

Recovery rates were faster for milder regression and for *Easy* and *Generalisation* patterns. High type frequency and consistent mappings were thus recovered more easily. The statistical stepwise linear regression analysis implicated 8 computational parameters in explaining the variability in recovery rates, with 4 accounting for more than 1% of the variance: pruning threshold (9.9%), unit threshold (2.2%), processing noise (1.7%) and response accuracy threshold (1.4%). Pattern type explained 8.8% of the variance and family quotient 0.2%. Recovery, then, depended on how severe the loss of resources had been, and the difficulty of the behaviour being recovered. It was little affected by differences in the quality of the environment, indexed by the family quotient parameter.

3.5. *Variability in recovery levels*

The level of recovery can be considered in two ways: either the final outcome level or how far the network has recovered behaviours compared to their pre-regression peak. The former includes the differential difficulty of learning each pattern type while the latter corrects for this difference. The statistical stepwise linear regression analysis indicated that up to 13 of the 14 computational parameters were implicated in explaining the variability in recovery levels. The parameters split into three groups: those relating to the *level of damage*, those relating to the *level of background plasticity*, and those relating to *quality of processing*. Focusing on the relative measure, the main contributors were pruning threshold (21.6%) and pruning probability (0.9%), both indexing damage; unit threshold (10.7%) indexing plasticity; and processing noise (3.7%) indexing quality of processing, respectively. Pattern type explained 6.2% of the variance, with *Easy* and *Generalisation* showing higher recovered levels. Notably, practise for the *Hardest* patterns did not benefit recovery. Family quotient explained only 0.2% of the variance in recovery.

3.6. *Sampling and correlational structure*

In the full population, the 14 parameters that defined each individual network were sampled independently and at random (see Methods). We did not, therefore, expect any systematic relationship between parameters in the full population, other than those spuriously generated by multiple comparisons. Table 2 shows that three correlations were significant at the .01 level in the full population. We then repeated the correlations on just those 641 individuals who exhibited the behavioural marker of regression. The former three correlations were no longer reliable at the .01 level, but five new reliable correlations appeared. Two of these involved the pruning threshold parameter, which was the cause of regression. Three correlations were between parameters involved in background variation, which when interacting with each other could together elevate risk for regression. For example, sparse connectivity was a protective factor because it encouraged larger connection sizes more resistant to pruning, but not if the learning rate was low. Notably, then, the simulations suggest that the *selective sampling* involved in a behaviourally defined disorder can create correlations between processing parameters that are related, but sometimes only indirectly, to the underlying cause of the disorder.

Table 2. Correlations between neurocomputational parameters either in the full population of 1000 networks, just those exhibiting developmental regression (N=641), or those not exhibiting regression (N=359). Given the large number of potential correlations, only those with p<.01 (2-tailed) in either the full or sub-populations are included. Manipulation to the pruning threshold parameter was the sole cause of regression. Values show Pearson Correlation and significance in brackets.

Parameter 1	Parameter 2	Whole population (N=1000)	Those exhibiting Regression (N=641)	Those not exhibiting Regression (N=359)
Pruning threshold	Unit threshold	.046 (.143)	-.166 (<.001)*	-.142 (.007)*
Pruning threshold	Momentum	.031 (.325)	.118 (.003)*	.046 (.389)
Response accuracy	Weight variance	.091 (.004)*	.090 (.023)	.092 (.083)
Pruning onset	Learning rate	-.021 (.515.)	-.105 (.008)*	.095 (.073)
Pruning onset	Weight variance	.087 (.006)*	.086 (.030)	.088 (.097)
Pruning onset	Learning algorithm	-.043 (.171)	-.120 (.002)	.052 (.329)
Pruning onset	Sparseness	.084 (.008)*	.100 (.011)	.064 (.229)
Learning rate	Sparseness	-.063 (.046)	-.104 (.008)	.009 (.872)

* significant at .01 level (2-tailed)

4. Discussion

In the model, the disorder of developmental regression was caused by a single underlying computational cause, over-aggressive pruning of connectivity[1]. Nevertheless, background variability in other neurocomputational parameters present in the whole population led to marked variation in the severity and characteristics of the disorder, such that there was no deterministic relationship between the primary underlying cause and its surface manifestation in behaviour (see Thomas[16] for related work in the field of resilience to cognitive decline in ageing). Statistical analyses revealed that the relevant properties of background neurocomputational variation depended on the behavioural characteristic under consideration. Variance in some behavioural characteristics was predicted by only a few parameters: the onset of pruning and the speed of the decline involved only the details of the pruning mechanism. Variance in other behavioural characteristics, such as the severity of regression and the speed and final level of recovery, involved contributions from a wide range of parameters, including those involved in network plasticity and the quality of processing. Moreover, the type of behaviour also influenced the characteristics of regression. Mappings with higher type frequency and consistency were more robust and, if lost, faster to recovery. Idiosyncratic mappings were hard to recover even with practice. Differences in the composition of the learning environment, at least for the range considered, explained little of the variance in regression or recovery. Lastly, we noted that even when there was a single underlying mechanistic cause, diagnosis of a disorder on behavioural grounds created a ghost correlational structure between the neurocomputational properties of affected individuals that were an artefact of sampling, and only indirectly related to the underlying cause.

In the Introduction, we identified four possible sources of variability in the severity of disorders with a single underlying cause. The current simulations showed some evidence for environmental effects (source #1), albeit not from variations in the learning environment but from stochastic events (e.g., *Hardest-practised* patterns showed either no or very severe regression depending on whether by chance certain key connections were pruned). We presented extensive evidence that interactions with background population-wide variability could confer a probabilistic relationship between underlying cause and behavioural manifestation (source #4). However, in the simulations, interactions occurred at a neurocomputational rather than genetic level. Gene-environment interactions emerged in training pattern effects, which modulated both regression and recovery. However, statistical analyses revealed little evidence that variations in the composition of the learning environment (implemented here by family quotient) contributed to the severity of the disorder (at least, when the learning environment was on the whole of good quality; see ref [1] for a consideration of the effects of very impoverished learning environments). Since the underlying cause of regression was taken to be an accumulation of risk genes present in the normal population rather than a genetic mutation, we did not model the possibility of disorder variability arising from variations in mutated genes (source #2). Epigenetic effects were also beyond the scope of the simulations (source #3).

324

More widely, the causal account of disorders we have offered is consistent with recent proposals by Bishop[17] that the medical model is more appropriate than adult neuropsychological dissociation methodology for understanding the origin of developmental deficits. In the medical model, disease status is conveyed probabilistically based on risk and protective factors, rather than necessary and sufficient causes.

The value of the current model is threefold. First, it demonstrates a mechanistic rather than statistical basis for why the relationship between disorder cause and behavioural outcome should be non-deterministic. Second, through implementation, it provides a framework to investigate this mechanistic basis in quantitative rather than qualitative terms. The investigation revealed, for example, that separate individual difference factors might contribute to variations in regression onset and speed, compared to severity and recovery. Third, the simulations showed the benefit of considering disorders within a population setting, where variability is a dependent variable rather than a source of noise to be overcome by averaging, and where individual differences in symptom severity are a target phenomenon to be explained. This approach sets the stage for using computational models of development to predict interventions that are tailored to individual manifestations of a disorder rather than to an idealised average disorder that may not be observed in any individual child.

Acknowledgments

This research was supported by ESRC grant RES-062-23-2721 and MRC grant G0300188 to the first author and an ESRC studentship to the second author.

References

1. M. S. C. Thomas, V. Knowland & A. Karmiloff-Smith, *Manuscript submitted for publication* (2010).

2. Y. Kovas, C. Haworth, P. Dale & R. Plomin, *Monographs of the SRCD*, **72(3)**, serial. No. 188, 1-144 (2007).

3. N. Saran, M. Pletcher, J. Natale, Y. Cheng & R. Reeves, *Human Molecular Genetics*, **12(16)**, 2013-2019 (2003).

4. M. S. C. Thomas, *Dev. Sci.*, **6(5)**, 537-556 (2003).

5. K. Kan, A. Ploeger, M. Raijmakers, C. Dolan & H. van der Maas, *Dev. Sci.*, **13**, 11-27 (2010).

6. A. Karmiloff-Smith, *Trends in Cog. Sci.*, **2**, 389-398 (1998).

7. A. Oliver, M. Johnson, A. Karmiloff-Smith & B. Pennington. *Dev. Sci.*, **3**, 1–23 (2000).

8. A. Pickles, E. Simonoff, G. Conti-Ramsden, M. Falcaro, Z. Simkin, T. Charman, et al., *JCPP*, **50**, 843-852 (2009).

9. G. Baird, T. Charman, A. Pickles, S. Chandler, T. Loucas, et al., *J. Autism Dev. Disorder*, **38**, 1827-1836 (2008).

10. J. Richler, R. Luyster, S. Risi, W. Hsu, G. Dawson, et al. (2006). *J. Autism and Dev. Disorders*, **36(3)**, 299-316. (2006).

11. M. Johnson, *Developmental cognitive neuroscience (2nd Ed.)*. Oxford: Wiley-Blackwell (2005).

12. P. Huttenlocher, *Neural plasticity*, Cam. Mass.: Harvard Uni. Press (2002).

13. P. Huttenlocher & A. Dabholkar, *J. Comp. Neurol.*, **387**, 167–178 (1997).

14. M. S. C. Thomas, A. Ronald & N. Forrester, *Manuscript submitted for publication* (2011).

15. D. Mareschal & M. S. C. Thomas, *IEEE Transactions on Evolutionary Computation*, **11(2)**, 137-150 (2007).

16. M. S. C. Thomas, *Proc. 30th Annual Conference of the Cog. Sci. Soc.*, 2089-2094 (2008).

17. D. Bishop, *Qu. J. Exp. Psych.*, **59**, 1153-1168 (2006)

HOW DO WE USE COMPUTATIONAL MODELS OF COGNITIVE PROCESSES?

T. Stafford

Department of Psychology, University of Sheffield,
Sheffield, S10 2TP, UK
* E-mail: t.stafford@shef.ac.uk
http://tomstafford.staff.shef.ac.uk/

Previously I outlined a scheme for understanding the usefulness of computational models .[1] This scheme was accompanied by two specific proposals. Firstly, that although models have diverse purposes, the purposes of individual modelling efforts should be made explicit. Secondly, that the best use of modelling is in establishing the correspondence between model elements and empirical objects in the form of certain 'explanatory' relationships: prediction, testing, existence proofs and proofs of sufficiency and insufficiency. The current work concerns itself with empirical tests of these two claims. I survey highly cited modelling papers and from an analysis of this corpus conclude that although a diverse range of purposes are represented, neither being accompanied by an explicit statement of purpose nor being a model of my 'explanatory' type are necessary for a modelling paper to become highly cited. Neither are these factors associated with higher rates of citation. The results are situated within a philosophy of science and it is concluded that computational modelling in the cognitive sciences does not consist of a simple Popperian prediction-and-falsification dynamic. Although there may be common principles underlying model construction, they are not captured by this scheme and it is difficult to imagine how they could be captured by any simple formula.

1. Introduction

We might expect computational modellers to be very concerned with theory and meta-theory. For one reason, computational modelling is a relatively young branch of psychology and neuroscience. Not only this, but it is a field in which innovation abounds, as the rise and rise of computational power opens up new possibilities. Historically, this kind of tumult has been associated with discussion of the scope and purpose of a discipline, and with discussion of the standards of comparison that should be applied to different investigations. A second reason we might expect computational modellers to concern themselves with theory and meta-theory, is that modelling generates no data in itself. Modellers are forced to exist in the world of theory; to simulate the underlying structures responsible for the patterns in the data, to propose different explanations for the data and to test relationships between proposed theoretical entities in our computational mini-worlds.

For these reasons we might expect computational modellers to resist the urge to view their work as a mere technical challenge, but remain alive to the theoretical claims that modelling work must be situated among for it to be scientifically meaningful. For the same reasons, we might expect computational modellers to be alive to the ongoing metatheoretical questions that concern computational modelling: what scientific role can modelling play, how should computational models be evaluated and what are legitimate motivations for instigating a computational modelling project? These kinds of questions are the domain of the philosophy of science.

Philosophy of science has a mixed reputation among scientists. It has been said that there is a remarkable disparity between the actual conduct of science and the picture presented by mainstream philosophy of science. One reason is the greater attention paid in philosophy of science to how science ought to be conducted — that is, to the logical requirements and structure of scientific claims — rather than how it is — in fact — conducted. The physicist Richard Feynmann is reported to have said "Philosophy of Science is as useful to scientists as ornithology is to birds". The implication being that philosophy of science is an artificial and wholly conceptual domain of knowledge which is irrelevant to the way scientists conduct themselves. It would be surprising, however, if scientists were able to "do" science with quite the same instinct, grace and spontaneity that birds fly (even Feynmann).

There are at least three good reasons that philosophy of science is not just of interest, but a necessity for scientists. What is more, these three reasons are especially pertinent to the field of computational modelling. Firstly, an articulation of principles is required to support the acceptance of a new field. In the case of computational modelling it is not the case that everyone accepts its value as a scientific activity. For example, neuroscientist and Nobel Laureate Francis Crick accused neural network modelling of being 'a rather low-brow enterprise' [2] and a vent for frustrated mathematicians. Segalowitz and Bernstein [3] were clearer but equally condemnatory in their criticism, dismissing modelling and explaining that 'models cannot tell us anything about the world...nor can they provide new information about brain organisation or function'. Although these criticisms concern the historical period when computational modelling was still struggling for acceptance in psychology and neuroscience, it is still possible to find similar sentiments, along the lines that modelling is an indulgence or irrelevance, expressed informally today. Indeed, the division of psychologists or neuroscientists into 'modellers' and 'non-modellers' suggests that modelling has not been fully integrated into the wider discipline.

Secondly, philosophy of science informs debates that we have within a field. Among modellers substantial disagreements exist concerning the correct approach to modelling. As evidence of this assertion, let me pick two discussants from a debate that occurred on the comp-neuro mailing list in 2008. James Bower expressed the opinion that modellers should perhaps "give up on cerebral cortex for several hundred years and all study tritonia instead" .[4] Although he was making this suggestion to illustrate a point, it does resonate with his apparent preference for low-level 'computational neuroscience' modelling. In contrast, in the same debate, Randall O'Reilly wrote that "the hippocampus is essentially a "solved problem" in terms of the general framework for how its biological properties enable its well-established role in memory" .[5] Not only should we, *contra* Bower, continue to study cerebral cortex, but we have in fact essentially solved a major part of it! Bower initiated the discussion on the email list to illustrate to a group of graduate students that many fundamental issues within computational neuroscience are not agreed upon. This it illustrated admirably and the reader is encouraged to review the discussion to enjoy wide-ranging consideration of levels of modelling, ways of assessing the value of a model, the value of modelling in general. All of these issues are the business of philosophy of science and a modeller-scientist cannot avoid having a position of them, albeit if only implicitly.

Thirdly, and finally, a philosophy of science is necessary to educate the next generation of scientists. Even if we could do science as instinctively as birds fly, we would still wish to articulate the philosophy underlying our practice of science so that we could best convey it to future scientists. It is perhaps surprising, then, that of four major textbooks in computational neuroscience and psychology [6-9] very little space is devoted to the topic of what role computational models play in science. Perhaps the silence of the textbook authors is in recognition of the seemingly-intractable nature of many debates in philosophy of science, and a consequent desire to avoid unfruitful discussion. I recognise the risk that claims concerning the philosophy of science may evoke counter-claims and so on *ad infinitum*. In the current paper, my discussion of the purposes of computational modelling is grounded by a survey of how computational models are presented in the literature. In this way I hope to combine consideration of how computational modelling *should* proceed with consideration of how it *does*, in fact, proceed.

2. Three claims about computational models

Previously, I have proposed a scheme for categorising the purposes of computational models .[1] The details of this scheme are less important, for the purposes of this paper, than three claims which I will use here to motivate the current work. The first claim is that there are many purposes for which you might build a computational model. This is a reflection of the fact that it is difficult to elaborate a single formula which captures what all modellers are trying to achieve with every model. Therefore, it is likely the case that different modellers are trying to achieve different things, and so there must be many purposes for which computational models are built. The second claim, which recognises the first, is that models ought to be accompanied by some statement of what the modeller hopes to achieve by that model. If models can have many different purposes, then appropriate assessment of a model will take account of those purposes for which a model is designed. And this is made easier if the model-builder reveals their purposes rather than leaving them to be inferred. The third claim of Stafford (2009) is that, although there are many purposes for model building, the best purposes are those which relate to providing explanations. This is the claim that models that use correspondences between model parts and real-world entities to make, refine or test predictions. In this claim I am influenced by Popperian philosophy of science [10–12] and the auxilliary assumption that modelling is a kind of theory construction. This assumption makes natural the application of the centrality of prediction and falsification from Popperian philosophy of science to computational modelling.

The scheme for categorising model purposes developed by myself ,[1] and extended here, is shown in Table 1. There are four major categories of model purposes according to this scheme. Exploratory model building includes the sub-categories *capacity*, which is the demonstration that a model has the capacity to perform a certain kind of function, without reference to how that model might relate to psychological or neuroscientific theory. For example, the demonstration that a Hopfield network can store patterns would be such a demonstration of capacity. *Data fitting* is the demonstration that a model can generate data which resembles the data generated in psychology or neuroscience investigation. *Biological plausibility* is the adjustment of an existing model to increase the extent of its correspondence to the biological structure it purports to model. *Reinterpretation* is the use of suggestive results from a model to widen the scope of plausible explanations. *Problem definition* is the use of modelling to explore and more fully definite the domain in which a psychological or neuroscientific function is performed.

Table 1. Model paper categorisation scheme.

Major category	Sub-categories
Exploratory	Capacity
	Data fitting
	Biological plausibility
	Reinterpretation
	Problem-definition
Analysis	—
Integrative	—
Explanatory	Prediction
	Testing
	Sufficiency
	Existence proof
	Insufficiency

The second and third major categories are models used for *analysis* (e.g. a statistical model such as a linear regression) and modelling for *integration*, which is the construction of a model which combines models from two separate domains or levels of description.

The fourth and final category, which I claim is the one that the most scientifically useful models belong to, is of models with *explanatory* purposes. To understand my breakdown of this category I will need to rehearse an argument made previously,[1] which attempts to understand explanation in terms of the "modelling is just tautology" accusation quoted earlier.[3] My argument, briefly, was that models must, in some sense, be only tautology but they derive their power from the correspondence between the parts of the model and real-world entities. All mathematical equations are tautological, but this does not mean that computation cannot be used to reveal new facts about the world. If you take the length of the shadow of a tower at noon in one place, and the length of the shadow of a tower at another place at noon you can compute the circumference of the earth. The result is an inherent and necessary result of the information you put into the computation. In this sense it is tautological, but it would be obtuse to argue that the computation has not revealed new information about the world.

We can take the simple example of $1 + 2 = 3$ — another tautology — and use it to illustrate the value of modelling-as-tautology. If the model elements on the left-hand side of the equation ('$1 + 2$') correspond to known real-world entities then the model predicts the presence of the entities that correspond to the right-hand side elements ('3'). If entities corresponding to both left- and right-hand side elements are known that the model demonstrates that the left-hand side elements are *sufficient* to produce those entities corresponding to elements on the right-hand side. If, alternatively, the entities known to exist are more than represented by elements on the right-hand side (for example, not '3' but '4' maybe) then the model constitutes a demonstration of *insufficiency* (particularly, of those entities represented by the left-hand side of the equation to produce those entities on the right). If the existence of the entities corresponding to elements of the model is in doubt, or the particular interrelation represented by the model is in doubt, then the model can constitute a form of *existence proof* that these entities can exist in the particular inter-relation captured by the model. These four types of explanation, which correspond — I suggest — to the canonical Popperian category of prediction and three examples of what Kukla [13,14] calls *theory amplification* make up the four subcategories of my fourth class of model purpose. Note that the categorisation of a model depends on its relationship to wider theory, not on its internal structure.

3. The current work

3.1. *Aims*

The current work is concerned with an empirical investigation of how computational modelling work is presented to the scientific community. My hope was that a set of highly-cited modelling papers would act as a proxy for successful or admirable modelling work. By systematic investigation of the properties common to this set we might get some insight into the characteristics of modelling papers that are associated with success (as defined in terms of high rates of citation). The scheme outlined above is used to categorise the modelling papers investigated, so this investigation also acts as a test of the adequacy of this scheme for categorising modelling paper type.

3.2. *Corpus*

Table 2.   Search terms used to identify modelling papers from each source

Source	Search criteria	
Nature	Topic=(computational)	AND
	Topic=(neuroscience OR psychology)	
Nature Neuroscience	Topic=(computational)	
Neural Computation	ALL	
Cognitive Science	Topic=(model)	
Connection Science	ALL	
NCPW11	ALL	

The papers selected for this survey were the fifty most highly cited modelling papers from five journals, plus the papers from the 11th *Neural Computation and Psychology Workshop* (NCPW) held in 2008 .[15] The journals were selected to contain a range of papers for a specialist and generalist audience, and to capture some difference in impact factor. The search terms used to identify modelling papers are shown in Table 2. Non-modelling papers identified by these searches were discarded without replacement. Papers with less than 10 citations were also discarded, resulting in a total number of papers included in the survey of 173.

Figure 1 shows the log of the number of citations of the papers initially selected for inclusion in the survey, from the five journal sources, using the search times given in Figure 2. As expected, journals with higher impact factors have more highly cited papers.

4. Results

4.1. *Is making explicit your purpose for building a model associated with publication in quality journals and/or higher citation counts?*

To address this question each paper in the corpus was coded as to whether it made explicit in the abstract what the purpose of the modelling work presented was. The assumption here is that, because models have diverse purposes, if it is not said why a model is built then that model cannot easily be assessed or used by the non-modelling community.

For the NCPW11 conference, the proportion of papers which, in their abstracts, were explicit about the purpose for which their model was constructed was 66%. In other words, most, but far from all, models were

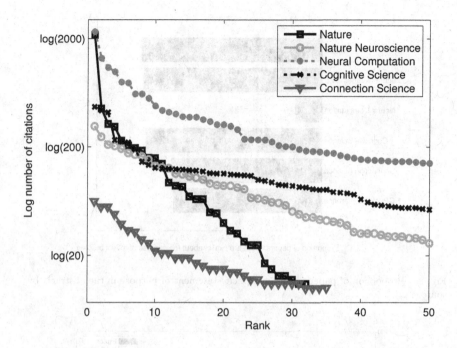

Fig. 1. Log citations for the fifty highly cited papers included in the survey

explicit about their purpose. This finding confirms an informal observation that I made while at NCPW11. One researcher I spoke to during NCPW11 acknowledged that this state of affairs was sub-optimal, but expressed the opinion that it was due to the nature of the papers at a conference. In other words, this was provisional work. Papers accepted for publication in a journal would have a far higher proportion of those which were explicit about their purposes. The results of my survey, shown for all the sources in the corpus, are shown in figure 2.

The details of these results are discussed below. Because it seemed that in general that most, but by no means all, papers were explicit about their modelling purpose, an additional analysis was carried out. The mean of the citation counts was calculated for each source, divided according to those papers which were explicit about their purpose and those that were not. If, on average, papers which were explicit were more highly cited (even among this corpus of highly cited papers) then this analysis should reveal it. The results are shown in figure 3. There is no clear superiority, in terms of citations counts, of the 'explicit' papers compared with the 'non-explicit'.

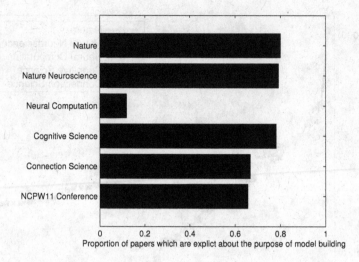

Fig. 2. Proportion of papers with an explicit statement of purpose in the abstract, by source.

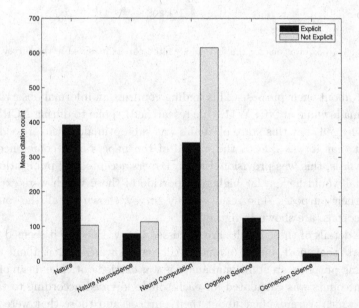

Fig. 3. Mean citation count for papers with and without an explicit statement of purpose in the abstract, by source.

4.2. *What purposes are associated with highly cited papers?*

The full results of the survey with respect to the primary purpose of the modelling paper analysed, are shown in table 3. Each paper can contribute to only one cell.

Note that there are over twice as many 'exploratory' than 'explanatory' papers. Of the exploratory papers the majority are of the 'capacity' kind. The second largest subcategory of the exploratory type is 'data fitting'. These two categories are very similar in nature, but distinguished in that 'capacity' papers demonstrate that a model can do some abstract or general task, whereas 'data-fitting' papers demonstrate that a model produces data of the same form as some experimental procedure.

Note also that the full range of proposed modelling purposes is found by the survey. In other words, there are no empty cells in the categorisation table (although there are some empty cells with respect to individual sources in the corpus).

In order to further address the question of the superiority of explanatory modelling, compared with models built for other purposes, the proportion of models with explanatory purposes for each source in the corpus was calculated. The results are shown in figure 4. It is clear that a majority of papers, in nearly all sources, are **not** presented as fulfilling explanatory purposes. Even for the single source for which more than half of papers in the corpus were explanatory, the proportion was not very much greater than half.

An analysis of mean citation counts for explanatory compared with non-explanatory papers from each source is shown in figure 5.

5. Discussion

The results covered in the previous section put us in a position to address the claims asserted previously and discussed at the beginning of this current paper (section 2). The first claim is that there are many purposes for which computational models are built. The results confirm this. Across the entire corpus examples of each purpose in the categorisation scheme were found. Two categories were well-populated, against previous expectations. The importance of modelling for providing theory integration and novel frameworks (as reflected in the 'integration' category), and the importance of modelling for providing new methods/techniques (as reflected in the 'capacity' category) was unanticipated from the perspective of my previous analysis .[1]

Table 3. Survey results, model paper types by source.

Major category	Minor category	Nature	Nature Neuroscience	Cognitive Science	Connection Science	Neural Computation	NCPW11	TOTAL
Exploratory	Capacity	2	5	4	18	22	17	68
	Data fitting	0	1	6	0	0	6	13
	Biological plausibility	0	0	1	2	0	5	8
	Reinterpretation	1	0	1	0	0	2	4
	Problem-definition	0	0	1	1	0	0	2
Analysis	—	2	1	2	0	0	2	7
Integrative	—	1	5	5	7	3	6	27
Explanatory	Prediction	1	4	3	1	1	3	13
	Testing	0	0	6	2	0	1	9
	Sufficiency	2	7	3	3	0	2	17
	Existence proof	0	2	0	0	0	0	2
	Insufficiency	1	0	0	2	0	0	3

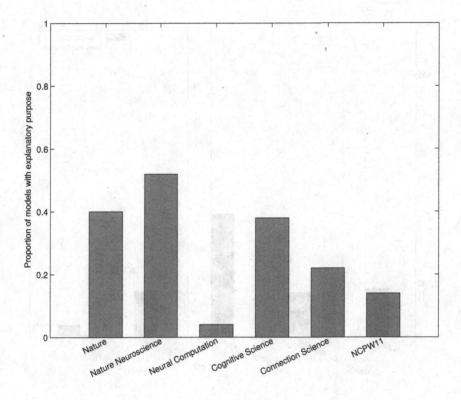

Fig. 4. Proportion of models with an 'explanatory' purpose, by source.

The second claim is that models ought to be accompanied by an explicit statement of what the modeller hopes to achieve by that model. These data cannot address this claim, since it is normative by nature, but they can inform us as to what occurs 'in the wild' with respect to model publishing. Evidently, many highly cited papers are not accompanied, in their abstracts, by an explicit statement of the purpose for which they are built. Further, it does not seem as if models accompanied by an explicit statement of purpose have a higher citation count among the corpus, on average (Figure 5. Although the mean citation count is higher for 'explicit' models for those published in *Nature* (see figure 3), the opposite patten was true for models published in *Neural Computation*. Furthermore, the highly skewed distribution of citation counts (see figure 1) means that a small number of highly cited papers have a disproportionate impact on these mean figures, and so although the difference between the 'explicit' and 'non-explicit' means

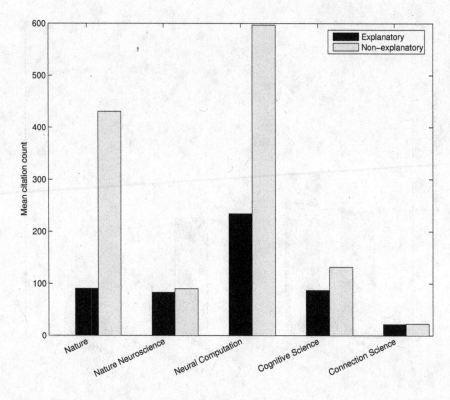

Fig. 5. Mean citation count for 'explanatory' and 'non-explanatory' modelling papers, by source.

seems large, it is probably not reliable. This inference is supported by the fact that although the differences are large for both *Nature* and *Neural Computation* journals, they are in opposite directions. Although I would still support the normative claim that models *should* be accompanied by an explicit statement of their purpose, this support is not reinforced by the data presented here. Many successful modelling papers do not contain such a statement.

The third claim is that the best model purposes are those which relate to providing explanations. Considering the proportion of explanatory papers from each source, it does not seem as if there is a strong association between better quality journals and a higher proportion of explanatory papers. Three higher impact journals, *Nature*, *Nature Neuroscience* and *Cognitive Science* do seem to have elevated levels of explanatory papers, compared with the NCPW11 conference and *Connection Science*. An exception to this pattern is the *Neural Computation* journal, which has a very high impact factor, but a very low proportion of papers with explanatory purpose. The reason for this can be deduced from table 3. Nearly all the papers in *Neural Computation* are demonstrations of capacity.

Note, however, that for all sources the proportion of explanatory papers is low. The mean citation counts for explanatory compared with non-explanatory papers shows there is no evidence that explanatory papers have higher rates of citation. If anything, there is some evidence that non-explanatory papers have higher rates of citation, although the distribution of citations (as discussed above) could make the means unrepresentative, and the results for the *Neural Computation* journal should probably be excepted. (The differences between the type of papers published in *Neural Computation* and the other sources in the corpus are probably due to the fact that it is a specialist journal with an engineering slant, rather than a general scientific or cognitive science journal like the others in the corpus).

A large minority of papers fell into the 'integrative' category, something which was unanticipated from my initial theorising, although it is in line with Kukla's analysis of the scope of theoretical psychology (alongside which I would include modelling) .[14]

It is surprising, perhaps, that so many of this corpus of highly cited modelling papers are of the 'data-fitting' category. An influential review by Roberts and Pashler [16] condemns data-fitting as a criterion for model assessment.

5.1. *Final words*

A limitation of the current design is that the categorisation of papers was done by one person (myself). The use of a single reviewer means it is impossible to assess the reliability of the categorisation. A possible extension of this work would be to fully formalise the criteria for the categories used and to have papers categorised and rated with respect to whether they include an explicit statement of purpose by independent reviewers who were blind to the source and authors of the paper.

Nonetheless, even allowing for some minor to moderate level of intra- and inter-reviewer variability, the major conclusions of this review would hold true: highly cited modelling papers appear to be constructed for a wide variety of theoretical purposes, they are often not explicit about what their purposes are, and often these purposes are not 'explanatory' according to this scheme. Neither being explicit nor having an explanatory purpose appear associated with higher rates of citation. This suggests that although previously I have suggested that these are desirable properties of a modelling paper, their absence does not conspicuously hinder the reception of a modelling paper.

The results presented here could be further investigated by looking at modelling papers cited outside of modelling journals — in other words, by experimentalists. This would give a valuable insight into how modelling work affects mainstream cognitive science. Another productive avenue would be to look how modelling papers build on and test existing models. The cumulative nature of research programmes, and how theories succeed or are replaced, is another area where analysis of the nature of computational modelling could be informed by philosophy of science .[17–19]

The current review is an investigation of how science, at least in this corner of the domain, *is* carried out, rather than how it *should be* carried out. In this sense the review is in the spirit of Feyerabend [20] and seems to echo his conclusion that "anything goes". He used this phrase to summarise his conclusion that there are no principles which hold universally in the conduct of scientific investigations. Here we might take it in a weaker sense to reflect the conclusion that successful modelling papers are not of one type and their nature is not captured by my initial hypothesis about what makes a good modelling paper (i.e. explicit statement of purpose, explanatory purpose).

A reasonable extension of this conclusion would be that 'naïve Popperianism' [11] is demonstrably wrong, at least in this domain of science. There is far more to computational modelling in the cognitive sciences than prediction and falsification. Although we may still hope that there are general principles governing the desirable features of modelling papers, this review suggests that they are not captured by this level of analysis. General principles, if it is possible to find and articulate them, are likely to be complex. Like all modellers, I continue in the belief that modelling is a powerful scientific tool. But if modelling is a tool it is clear that it is a multipurpose tool, used by different scientists in different ways.

6. Acknowledgments

Thanks The Redwood Center for Theoretical Neuroscience at UC Berkeley for hosting me while I did this work, and Bruno Olshausen and Nicol Harper for facilitating my visit there, to Eddy Davelaar for advice before and during preparation of this paper, and to an anonymous reviewer for a thorough reading of a draft of this paper.

References

1. T. Stafford, What use are computational models of cognitive processes?, in *Connectionist Models of Behavior and Cognition II: Proceedings of the 11th Neural Computation and Psychology Workshop*, ed. N. R. . K. P. J. Mayor (World Scientific, 2009) pp. 265–274.
2. F. Crick, *Nature* **337**, 129 (1989).
3. S. Segalowitz and D. Bernstein, Neural networks and neuroscience: What are connectionist simulations good for, in *The future of the cognitive revolution.*, (Oxford University Press, 1997)
4. J. M. Bower. Email to comp-neuro@neuroinf.org, 12/08/2008, 16:47 GMT available from `http://www.neuroinf.org/pipermail/comp-neuro/2008-August/thread.html`.
5. R. C. O'Reilly. Email to comp-neuro@neuroinf.org, 12/08/2008, 18:19 GMT available from `http://www.neuroinf.org/pipermail/comp-neuro/2008-August/thread.html`.
6. R. C. O'Reilly and Y. Munakata, *Computational Explorations in Cognitive Neuroscience: Understanding the Mind by Simulating the Brain* (MIT Press, Cambridge, MA., 2000).
7. P. Dayan and L. Abbott, *Theoretical neuroscience: Computational and mathematical modeling of neural systems* (MIT press Cambridge, MA:, 2001).
8. R. Ellis and G. Humphreys, *Connectionist Psychology : a text with readings* (Psychology Press Ltd, Hove, UK, 1999).
9. J. L. Elman, *Rethinking Innateness: A Connectionist Perspective on Development* (MIT Press, 1996).
10. K. Popper, *The Logic of Scientific Discovery* (Hutchinson, London, 1968).
11. B. Magee, *Popper* (RoutledgeFalmer, 1974).
12. A. Chalmers, *What is this thing called science?* (Univ. of Queensland Press, 2006).
13. A. Kukla, *New Ideas in Psychology* **13**, 201 (1995).
14. A. Kukla, *Methods of Theoretical Psychology* (MIT Press, Cambridge, MA., 2001).
15. J. Mayor, N. Ruh and K. Plunkett (eds.), *Connectionist Models of Behavior and Cognition II: Proceedings of the 11th Neural Computation and Psychology Workshop* (World Scientific, 2009).
16. S. Roberts and H. Pashler, *Psychological Review* **107**, 358 (2000).
17. A. Roelofs, From Popper to Lakatos: A case for cumulative computational modeling, in *Twenty-first century psycholinguistics: Four cornerstones*, ed. A.Cutler (Lawrence Erlbaum, Mahwah, NJ, 2005)
18. I. Lakatos, Falsification and the methodology of scientific research programmes, in *Criticism and the Growth of Knowledge*, eds. I. Lakatos and A. Musgrave (Cambridge University Press, Cambridge, 1970) pp. 91–195.

342

19. T. Kuhn, *The structure of scientific revolutions* (University of Chicago Press, Chicago, 1996).
20. P. Feyerabend, *Against Method (revised edition)* (Verso, New York, 1988).

SOME ISSUES IN COMPUTATIONAL MODELLING; OCCAM'S RAZOR AND HEGEL'S HAIR GEL[*]

RICHARD SHILLCOCK[†]

School of Informatics and School of Philosophy, Psychology and Language Sciences, University of Edinburgh, UK

MATTHEW ROBERTS

School of Philosophy, Psychology and Language Sciences, University of Edinburgh, UK

HAMUTAL KREINER

Department of Behavioural Science, Ruppin Academic Center, Israel

MATEO OBREGON

School of Philosophy, Psychology and Language Sciences, University of Edinburgh, UK

We look at some of the assumptions made in the computational modelling of cognition. In particular, we look at some of the problems raised by the conventional modelling goal of *simplicity*. We review why cognitive modellers make certain choices and we emphasise the central role of *abstraction*. We conclude that Occam's Razor is only half the story in using implemented computational models to explain cognitive processing, and we raise a number of questions that point the way to a materialist position in computational cognitive modelling.

1. Introduction

In this paper we present some critical questions for computational cognitive modellers, which we attempt to address comprehensively from a materialist standpoint elsewhere[1]. We will begin by looking at some normal practice in the computational modelling of cognition, and then we will look at some of the philosophical assumptions that underlie this current practice. We will then present some problems that seem to us to represent a crisis requiring a principled response, and we will conclude with some questions, and brief illustrations of answers, that indicate the general direction along which we believe that response

[*] This work was partially supported by project grants R39195 and R39942 from the ESRC (UK).

lies. Overall this discussion will lead us to look closely at the role of *simplicity* in cognitive modelling.

2. Standard practice in cognitive modelling

Computational cognitive modelling is recognized as a central paradigm, perhaps *the* central paradigm, in cognitive science. At its best, it is seen as proceeding hand in hand with experimental work – a virtuous spiral in which each informs the other, and in which the modelling makes predictions that can be tested in the laboratory.

Since cognitive science became an identifiable enterprise several decades ago, implemented computational models have been based on a range of computational substrates and on a number of different formal approaches, including production rules[2], interaction-activation models[3], distributed connectionist architectures[4], and Bayesian probabilities[5]. Biological and ecological criteria have variously been employed to argue for the plausibility, or lack of plausibility, of particular approaches.

In the history of cognitive science, the TRACE model of spoken word recognition[3] is a good example of how the main features of an ordinary-language theory – the Cohort Model[6] – can be computationally implemented so as to (a) reproduce the basic data on which the ordinary-language theory was founded, (b) force cognitive scientists to make concrete decisions about aspects of representation and process that might not be salient to informal theorising, (c) generate a useful and productive conceptual vocabulary, and (d) make behavioural predictions that are experimentally testable.

Thus, TRACE was shown to reproduce behaviours in which candidate words in the lexicon compete to represent specific stretches of the continuous speech input. Its authors took the categories of formal phonology (words, phonemes, phonetic features) and instantiated them in the model. They made specific proposals about the direction of interaction between such levels of processing (proposals which fuelled a decades-long psycholinguistic controversy [see, *e.g.*, refs 7, 8]). They raised the issue of speech segmentation "emerging" from word recognition without a specific segmentation stage; segmentation was seen simply as the other side of the coin of recognizing potential words and their beginnings and endings. They also characterised different types of temporary conspiracy – "gang effects" – in which small groups of similar words in the model's lexicon could become partially activated in the course of perceiving any one stretch of speech input and produce complex effects of competition. The model has motivated a substantial volume of experimental work on speech processing, and has constituted a particular position within theorising about speech perception.

TRACE is an example of a successful cognitive model that has advanced our understanding of speech processing. But this is not to say that everything in the wider cognitive modelling enterprise is rosy, or even to absolve TRACE of its own specific limitations.

3. Two challenges

A number of issues demand the attention of the present cognitive modelling community. The first – not specific to the domain of cognitive science – is the sheer volume of data. *Google Scholar* provides a striking demonstration: taking examples from the study of eye-movements in reading, a search for "saccade" yields "about 47,500 results", "eye movements" "about 567,000 results", and "word recognition" "about 209,000 results"[†,‡]. Anyone sceptical of the necessity of researchers addressing the philosophical aspects of their cognitive modelling, and who says "never mind about philosophy, just give me the facts!", faces no shortage of facts. The response to this scepticism is "state the reasons for choosing to include or exclude this fact or that fact in your model". *Abstraction* is central to the whole enterprise of cognitive modelling; how does the researcher work with something other than the full, real-world complexity of the brain, the stimulus environment, and human behaviour?

The second issue becomes apparent when we use another current electronic search tool, *Citeseer*, as a crude way of gauging the influence of a particular cognitive model by plotting its citations by year. In comparison with most cognitive models, TRACE fares well. All too often, a model attracts a little, temporary interest in the literature, like the Venerable Bede's description of life as the "short, swift flight of the sparrow through the brightly-lit banqueting hall". How is it that a typical implemented cognitive model does not become more securely incorporated into the scientific enterprise of understanding cognition? How should the model relate to the rest of cognition, to very closely associated behaviours and models?

---

† These results are a snapshot from the time of writing. In fact, hits may accrue to some searches at rates that make it unlikely that a single researcher can read each new article.

‡ On the one hand, electronic search now means that observations with a low electronic profile risk being lost to researchers, but on the other hand, "library-type research" can reveal new real connections between data. Electronic search is itself conditioning the abstractions we make; as one reviewer points out, apparently similar searches can even give different numbers to different researchers.

These questions have long been recognised as central to modelling. The responses to these questions all revolve around the issue of *simplicity*, as we will see below when we look at some of the philosophical assumptions that have been carried into the computational modelling of cognition.

4. Some underlying philosophical assumptions

In reality, most actual modelling research follows an existing modelling paradigm, introducing variations in form and content, and researchers do not typically feel the need to articulate the philosophical assumptions underlying the research. This may even be so when a new modelling paradigm is introduced. Such philosophical assumptions are nonetheless present.

We can identify a number of beliefs and assumptions in current cognitive modelling, all concerned one way or another with simplicity and with varying practical, scientific and epistemic significance. Cognitive modellers dramatically simplify real cognitive processing, and, indeed, simplicity is typically seen as a goal in itself – the simpler the model, the better the explanation. Occam's Razor is readily cited: do not multiply entities in explanations. Behind this is the longstanding positivist desire to emulate physics by supplying what Godfrey-Smith[9], in the context of modelling evolution, calls a "master equation", such as $F=ma$; see also Chater and Brown's[10] discussion of simplicity in the sense of a "law". At the level of particular algorithms and representations, there are formal approaches that seek to show that simpler processing accounts are more likely to be true, and thus should be preferred[11]. In related fields, parsimony features centrally in discussions of method[21]. Finally, there are ill-defined aesthetic preferences for simplicity in modelling.

Drawing on a recent review of idealization in science by Weisberg[12], we can catalogue a number of ways in which researchers simplify the world in order to model it, or make other modelling choices that have implications for the simplicity of the model.

First, a simple model can be used as a means of investigating the dynamics of a particular cognitive process, with the implicit aim of eventually trying to test whether the behaviour survives when the model is made more complex, or the range of the data is extended to make it more realistic. See, for example, Frank's use of a microworld to model sentence comprehension[18]. This is the classic "Galilean idealization", in which a temporary, unreal simplification is introduced to make modelling or theorizing tractable[§]. As an example of Galilean

---

[§] Indeed, the scientific program of Artificial Intelligence as a discipline was initially based on this principle: "block worlds" typically replaced real world complexity, and the goal was to discover

idealization, eye-movement modellers have typically ignored the hemispheric division of the brain and other anatomical information in modelling the interaction of different types of information in reading and scene viewing; such a move simplifies the situation, removing highly complex and usually unknown details from consideration, and leaves only what is seen as the functional interaction of different types of information. Thus such a model might contain a cyclopean visual input mechanism that does not exist in the real world.

Second, Weisberg defines "Minimalist Idealization" in which the modeller strips away irrelevant aspects of the situation in order to reveal that which is causally important. The creation of such minimal models is closely tied up with the goal of explanation. The researcher may specify a level of fidelity that the behaviour of the model is expected to attain, so that the enterprise avoids the risk of trivializing any explanation by extreme minimalization. In cognitive science, such models are rarely expanded to take in real-world levels of complexity; rather they are seen as having done their job in their simple form. The implicit assumption is that if they were fleshed out, and scaled up (and still worked), then the simple model would be related to the complex model by "structural realist" considerations[16] – that is, by an isomorphism between the relations between the entities of the simple and the complex model.

There has been a longstanding distinction between Galilean idealization and Aristotelian idealization. In the latter, objective aspects of the world are removed, to reveal something that is still itself an objective aspect of the world. Thus, in eye-movement models of reading, a model might contain only the optically relevant aspects of the two eyes (or one eye specifically intended to be, for instance, the right eye). Jones[13] suggests it may be useful to distinguish between omitting details (abstraction) and adding simplification (idealization), but elsewhere in the literature on abstraction, the distinction between adding simplicity and subtracting complexity is queried[17]. Below, we will argue that a better question to ask concerns the *reality* of entities in the model.

Third, Weisberg identifies "Completeness" as one possible representational ideal "associated with classic accounts of scientific method". The aspiration here is the inclusion of as much as possible of the real world detail pertinent to the

---

the principles that would solve these toy problems. Latterly, the complexity of the real world has been restored to its rightful place to some extent in some branches of cognitive science, but typically not because the toy approaches succeeded and required to be fleshed out; rather, real-world complexity has been seen to offer richer prospects for understanding complex behaviours, and, indeed, sometimes real-world commercial applications in certain domains have achieved results far ahead of "pure science" results in that domain. In other modelling cases, the model can be a "probing model" [20], in which the interest lies primarily in exploring just what a particular architecture is able to do.

phenomenon under study, while still retaining the clarity of the causal explanation produced by the prior simplification. With a radically simple model, there is always the question "Would the explanation still go through in the same way in all the complexity of the real world?"

Fourth, Weisberg discusses an approach that concentrates on the primary causal factors in a process, the factors that *make a difference* to whether or not the phenomenon actually presents itself, as opposed to factors that simply fine-tune the phenomenon. Again, the issue arises that we can't know exactly what does and does not make a difference until we have related the simple model to the full complexity of the real world.

Fifth, Weisberg discusses cases in which the theorist aims to maximize the precision and accuracy of the model's output in some way that does not prioritize the transparency of the causal mechanism that produces the output. In some connectionist modelling of cognition, the "microstructure of cognition" may be opaque but the desired outputs may nevertheless accurately emerge.

5. Some problems to be addressed

The picture of simplification that emerges from this one recent review of approaches to abstraction and idealization is a complex one across all the sciences. The range of approaches in the computational modelling of cognition is narrower, with TRACE being a good example. The concentration is on minimalization. Often the categories used in the modelling are adopted from existing theory or ordinary language; for instance, the authors of TRACE incorporated the categories of "phoneme" and "feature" from phonology.

As we saw, it is relevant to ask how often the goal of "scaling up" is ever carried through in cognitive modelling, where "scaling up" can also mean incorporating real entities into the model. How often do researchers increase the contents of one dimension of the model so that it resembles real-world complexity? How often do researchers incorporate in their model a component that can be said to be "real"? In cognitive science research, the quickest rewards frequently come from "picking the low-hanging fruit". There are often diminishing returns from augmenting the precision and extent of the modelling: such work necessarily takes longer for reasons of scale; sometimes the algorithms themselves are unforgiving of such scaling up; confirming the simple model may be unremarkable, and disconfirming the simple model by scaling up the demands on the model may be unconvincing if, for instance, the simple model had no claim on biological realism or if other unspecified additional processing might be expected to intervene in some way – for instance, unspecified effects of semantic processing might intervene to simplify a very large competition between partially activated lexical candidates in speech recognition. Overall, though, when scaling up is not attempted it is typically for the reason that the researcher judges, implicitly or explicitly, that the minimal model is a satisfactory explanation of the cognitive process under study. In these cases there is no detailed consideration of the question "would this model work with a realistic range of x", where x might be the number of words in a model of reading, number of eyes (i.e. two) in a model of eye-movements, degree of phonological reduction in a speech processing model, range of lighting conditions in a model of visual processing, and so on. Overall, the very word "model" is taken to convey simplicity as a goal.

The outcome of this general approach to simplicity in cognitive modelling is that the models are typically limited in their scope for development. Adding new components runs the risk of obscuring the researcher's initial insight by complicating the architecture. The operation of the model may make it unattractive or inappropriate to attach it to other models of related processes, in anything other than an *ad hoc* way. This is the general situation in which cognitive modellers find themselves, producing models that are inherently limited in the extent to which they can be developed, and in the implications they have for the rest of the field. The attitude towards simplicity in modelling is at the heart of this impasse.[**] This is not to downplay the successes that have been achieved in cognitive modelling, in providing new conceptual vocabularies for cognition and in enriching experimental investigation. Rather, it is to ask whether we can identify some principles underlying our best practice, so as to consciously develop that best practice.

Concern about the philosophical assumptions in contemporary cognitive modelling is not new. Churchland, Ramachandran and Sejnowski[14] present a critique of what they call the Theory of Pure Vision. They characterise this latter "commonsense" underpinning of vision science as consisting of three assumptions: (a) that the goal of vision is to reproduce the 3D visual scene in all its richness in the brain, (b) that visual processing is hierarchical, and (c) that there are dependency relations between higher and lower order processing. (See, also, Marr[15]). While acknowledging the success that this conventional approach

---

[**] This issue of simplicity does not necessarily result from the fact that we are dealing with "higher-order" entities in cognitive modelling. If we were modelling neural behaviour we would still need to make motivated abstractions from the totality in which the neurons are embedded. Modellers at the neural level may still need to address whether the model would still work if it were embedded in a population of astrocytes, if the full range of synapse types was used, if the population of neurons was a realistic size, and so on.

has had in the past, they question the adequacy of such assumptions for future progress. Their scepticism is based on the case that they make for what they call Interactive Vision, in which they question the artificial consideration of vision isolated from issues of motor control, and consider examples of processing that subvert conventional notions of hierarchy and dependency relations. They acknowledge that their Interactive Vision is sketchy, and they call for a new set of concepts adequate to describing interactive systems. It will be clear from our discussion here that what is at the core of Churchland et al.'s disquiet over the direction of vision science is how vision scientists have applied *abstraction* to their subject matter; indeed, this interpretation is clear from Churchland et al.'s own very brief consideration of the issue of idealization (p. 23). Issues of causality and explanation follow in the wake of any discussion of abstraction and idealization.

Overall, we have directly and indirectly identified a number of questions in this brief excursion into the role of simplicity in cognitive modelling. In the following list we indicate what we see as a productive direction of travel. We will give examples from the domain of eye-movement (EM) models of reading, for which we are currently developing a more philosophically grounded approach[1]. We suggest that the best way of proceeding is to consider particular domains and problems, rather than trying to suggest general principles for theorizing and modelling. There are no "philosophical" shortcuts to selecting the answer to specific scientific problems; what we hope is that suggesting a philosophical grounding may clarify and advance existing best practice as represented in the literature.

1. What is the best way to simplify the complexity of real world cognition? Are there criteria for taking away something that appears not to be contributing to the behaviour of interest, to leave that which we judge to be crucial?

We suggest that, in the range of entities created by modellers in a particular domain, priority should be given to real entities (i.e. the result of Aristotelian rather than Galilean abstraction). We do not seek to say how modellers should explore whether to abstract this or that aspect of the domain; modellers take into account the whole previous experience of the field. Models typically contain mixtures of entities, some necessarily "fictional" (in the non-pejorative sense employed in the abstraction literature to refer to non-observables), some "real" in a materialist sense that does not trade on any of the fine distinctions made in the realism debate[16,19]. The position of a fixation point in a word is an example from EM models of reading, contrasting with the necessarily fictional mechanisms of competition between entries in the lexicon. Anatomical distinctions available in the visual pathways are also candidates for such real components. Even though our models may be ontologically heterogeneous, we can still prioritise real entities in the model, as we will argue below.

2. Should we ever (re-)introduce real-world details into a typical, relatively simple model with a heterogeneous ontology? Just what is our goal for the "final" model?

We want to say that the aspiration of the modeller should be to reproduce the full, real-world complexity of the domain under study. Of course, this can never be achieved in the implemented model, but it can be aspired to in the theory. This does not mean that all we have ended up with is nothing but the same inscrutable complexity as the original subject of the study. As we will see below, we will also know every step away from and back to that real-world complexity.

3. How far should abstraction go? How do we know if we have taken away enough irrelevant, or less relevant, material in modelling a domain?

Abstraction should go as far as possible, in the attempt to reveal just what is left to mediate the domain under study. In our theorizing about EM models for reading, the farthest abstraction we have made is to the spatial relationship between the principal visual axes of the two eyes and their fixation points on the page. We are then interested in the role played by this farthest abstraction in the domain.

4. What is the point of knowing about this farthest abstraction? What is the connection between populating our model with simple entities (and with this farthest abstraction) and understanding how the model captures the domain under study?

We want to suggest that the goal of the modelling is to identify a particular far abstraction (which, remember, is still itself an objective aspect of the world) that has the role of mediating everything else in the domain under study. We want to be able to say that we have identified some objective aspect of the domain that has *necessary implications* for all of the rest of the domain. This means that we can take our very abstract view of the domain and then progressively repopulate it with real-world detail, as in (2) above. We will thus know the route *down* to the furthest abstraction and back *up* to the full complexity of the real world. A worked example will clarify this very abstract characterization of the process[1]. In our modelling of eye-movements in reading, the farthest abstraction we have identified is, as described above, the spatial relationship between the principal visual axes of the two eyes and their fixation points on the page. This very sparse feature of the reading domain is all that is left when everything else has been taken away in our theorizing. Yet it plays the crucial role. When it is cashed out in terms of interactions with real-world details, such as the anatomy of the visual pathways to the cortex, it speaks critically to every aspect of the reading domain, principally by means of the hemispheric division of the brain. Thus, our farthest abstraction has very important implications for lexical access, attention, saccade control, and other components of reading. Even though we can only characterise lexical access in "fictional" terms (we cannot observe how it actually works), it is still necessarily conditioned by our "core" abstraction described above. Because this core of the system is a material aspect of the domain, it cannot be defeated by, for instance, the sudden discovery of the comprehensive microscopic details of lexical access. Rather, it can only constrain those details in real ways.

5. How long does the model last? Do we expect a particular model to be only temporary and to be quickly updated as laboratory experimentation reveals more of the true picture? How can a model be updated and how can it retain its original integrity and the insights of its authors?

We want to say that having an objective aspect of the world as the "core" of the model (in that it mediates the operation of everything else in the domain) guarantees the model against being defeated by new data and means that it can always be updated in ways that maintain the transparency of its operation. That this is so, is the confirmation that we have identified the relevant farthest abstraction in the domain. We have seen that the model will necessarily still contain some fictional elements. The goal is to replace these, when possible, by real constituents. Even before then, though, such elements interact with the farthest abstraction we have identified, as it contacts and influences everything else in the domain.

6. How are we to understand causality in all of this? Should we start speaking about causation at the most abstract level that we have characterised, perhaps identifying the primary causal factors cited by Weisberg?

In the materialist tradition causality is ultimately in the totality of the interactions in the complete model. Of course, we also have a clear picture of causality in that we have seen how the real-world domain has been stripped down to the farthest abstraction, and then built up again in the implemented model, as all of the necessary interactions with the rest of the domain are added in again.

7. How are we to understand explanation in all of this? At what point do we have an adequate explanation, at what point a full explanation?

Explanation is constituted by the process, described in (6) above, by which we move down from the real world domain to the farthest abstraction, and back up again to the real world in all its complexity. Indeed, the philosophical picture we draw (which we take from the Vygotskyean tradition in Psychology) has strong resonances with compression-type procedures in mathematical descriptions of particular domains.

8. What about simplicity and Occam's Razor? Is this an argument against Occam's Razor if we are aiming for a maximally complex model that will resemble the real world?

We have obeyed Occam's Razor in stripping down the real-world domain to find that farthest part of the system that mediates everything else. In proposing to return to the full complexity of the real world, we are complementing Occam's Razor with Hegel's classic dictum "the truth is in the whole". Occam's Razor only gives half of the story. It is a half that is still visible even when we have returned to the full complexity of the real world.

In conclusion, we have returned to this issue of completeness, cited by Weisberg; the Hegelian aspiration that the model should reflect real-world complexity as fully as possible, while still retaining the contours of an explanatory, causal structure. It brings us to our provisional conclusion concerning simplicity, explored and illustrated more fully elsewhere[1], that the seeming impasse in much cognitive science modelling may be resolved by adopting this modelling goal – the fullest possible representation of the real-world complexity of the modelling domain (and with additional criteria for identifying a real part of the domain that pervades every other aspect of the domain). We adopt this position in opposition to the exclusive concern with simplicity in contemporary cognitive science modelling. This is not to say that demonstrations of the role of simplicity in relation to probability and cognitive processing are wrong – rather, it is the epistemic sense of simplicity that concerns us. Nor is it to say that Occam's Razor is wrong – just that it only tells us half the story. To have the fullest explanation and understanding of a cognitive process we need to be able to see it both in its simplest manifestation and in its fullest manifestation. Indeed, the more real-world details are added around the critical component we have identified, the more parsimonious the model becomes! We need to be able to answer the question, Does it scale up? Our goal in this paper has been to make this single point, against solely relying on simplicity, and for taking the fullest

354

complexity into consideration in our theorising about cognition and in our computational modelling of cognition. This point about completeness, about the fullest complexity and the whole, has been made before in other domains of study, and we repeat it here in the case of computational cognitive modelling. Our whimsical title comes from a desire to produce a name as memorable as "Occam's Razor", and staying within the tonsorial metaphor, for the method of revealing and accentuating the most elaborate structure possible ... hence "Hegel's hair gel"[††].

References

1. Shillcock, R., Roberts, M.A.J., Kreiner, H., Obregón, M., and Monaghan, P. (*in prep.*) Principles in the modelling of eye-movements in reading; two types of abstraction, two types of universal.

2. Anderson, J. R. ACT: A simple theory of complex cognition. *Amer. Psych.*, **51**, 355-365 (1996).

3. McClelland, J.L., and Elman, J.L. The TRACE model of speech perception. *Cog. Psych.*, **18**, 1-86 (1986).

4. Seidenberg, M. S. and McClelland, J. L. A distributed, developmental model of word recognition and naming. *Psych. Rev.*, **96**, 523-568 (1989).

5. Norris, D. The Bayesian reader: Explaining word recognition as an optimal Bayesian decision process. *Psych. Rev.*, **113**, 327-357 (2006).

6. Marslen-Wilson, W.D., and Welsh, A. Processing interactions and lexical access during word recognition in continuous speech. *Cog. Psych.*, **10**, 29-63 (1978).

7. Norris, D., McQueen, J.M., and Cutler, A. Merging information in speech recognition: Feedback is never necessary. *Behav. & Brain Sci.*, **23**, 299-370. (2000).

8. McClelland, J.L., Mirman, D., and Holt, L.L. Are there interactive processes in speech perception? *TICS*, **10**, 363-369 (2006).

9. Godfrey-Smith, P. *Darwinian populations and natural selection* (2009).

10. Chater, N., and Brown, G.D.A. From universal laws of cognition to specific cognitive models. *Cog. Sci.*, **32**, 36-67 (2008).

11. Chater, N., and Vitanyi, P.M.B. Simplicity: A unifying principle in cognitive science? TICS, **7**, 19-22 (2003).

[††] Thanks to Jon Oberlander for this joke, and for innumerable insightful discussions.

12. Weisberg, M. Three kinds of idealization. *The Journal of Philosophy*, **104**, 639-59 (2007).

13. Jones, M. Idealization and abstraction: A framework. In M. Jones and N. Cartwright (eds.), *Idealization XII: Correcting the Model: Idealization and Abstraction in the Sciences* (New York: Rodopi), 173-217 (2005).

14. Churchland, P., Ramachandran, V., and Sejnowski, T. A critique of pure vision. In C. Koch, & J. Davis (Eds.), *Large-scale neuronal theories of the brain* (pp. 22-60). Cambridge, MA: MIT Press (1994).

15. Marr, D. *Vision*. New York: W. H. Freeman (1982).

16. Ladyman, J. (2009). Structural Realism. *The Stanford Encyclopedia of Philosophy* (Summer 2009 Edition), Edward N. Zalta (ed.), URL = <http://plato.stanford.edu/archives/sum2009/entries/structural-realism/>.

17. Humphreys, P. (1995). Abstract and concrete. *Philosophy and Phenomenological Research*, Vol. LV, No. 1, 157-161.

18. Frank, S.L. (2005). Sentence comprehension as the construction of a situational representation: A connectionist model. In: *Proceedings of AMKLC 2005, International Symposium on Adaptive Models of Knowledge, Language and Cognition*, pp. 27–33. Helsinki University of Technology, Espoo.

19. Boyd, Richard, "Scientific Realism", The Stanford Encyclopedia of Philosophy (Summer 2010 Edition), Edward N. Zalta (ed.), URL = <http://plato.stanford.edu/archives/sum2010/entries/scientific-realism/>.

20. Frigg, R., & Hartmann, S. (2006). "Models in Science", The Stanford Encyclopedia of Philosophy, (Edward N. Zalta, ed.), http://plato.stanford.edu/entries/models-science/

21. Fitzpatrick, S. (2008). Doing Away with Morgan's Canon. *Mind & Language*, *23*, 224-246. doi:10.1111/j.1468-0017.2007.00338.x

HOW IS HAIR GEL QUANTIFIED?

MARK A. PITT

Department of Psychology, Ohio State University, 1835 Neil Avenue, Columbus, Ohio, 43210, USA

JAY I. MYUNG

Department of Psychology, Ohio State University, 1835 Neil Avenue, Columbus, Ohio, 43210, USA

Shillcock et al suggest that the preoccupation with simplicity in cognitive modeling has been detrimental to the discipline. They propose instead an approach in which the complexity of the real world should be the objective of modelers. We discuss some of the difficulties in achieving this goal from the standpoint of quantitative methods of model selection.

1. Introduction

In the target article[1], Shillcock, Roberts, Kreiner and Obregon (SRKO), review some of the philosophical assumptions in the contemporary computational modeling of cognition, and are troubled by what they perceive as an over-emphasis on simplicity in modeling, which they believe has been detrimental to the advancement of cognitive science.

According to SRKO, the notion of simplification has become too much of a guiding principle in current cognitive modeling, to the point that simplification (obeying Occam's Razor) is routinely taken as a goal of modeling in itself. They opine that this approach is myopic, incomplete, and potentially misleading. Instead, SRKO contend that simplification should be done with much greater care to ensure that the model, even after simplifying abstractions and idealizations, still contains the most basic yet essential kernel of truth. In the end, SRKO adopt the position that an alternative, more productive path would be to model "the fullest possible representation of the real-world complexity of the modeling domain..." (p. xx). SRKO clarify their approach and provide guidance for potential adopters in the form of eight questions for modelers to consider.

Although it is difficult to disagree with the gist of their argument, we believe that the proposal to "reproduce the full, real-world complexity of the domain under study" (Shillcock, et al., p. xx) may be unrealistic and unrealizable in practice because of the many conceptual and implementational challenges it poses.

2. Models Are Just Tools

We preface our main point with one that sometimes gets forgotten in discussions of cognitive modeling. Models are quantitative stand-ins of psychological theories that are developed from data acquired through experimentation. The idealized, naive goal of modeling is to identify the underlying regularities (truth) from which the data are actually generated. This goal, however, is not achievable, for at least two reasons. First, there are never enough observations (i.e., data) to pin down the truth exactly. Second, the truth may be quite complex, beyond the modeler's imagination, and thus is likely to be different from any one of the candidate models the modeler may contemplate, as captured by the famous quote "All models are wrong but some are useful" credited to George E. P. Box (1975).

A utilitarian paradigm of cognitive modeling that echoes George Box is to view models as no more than tools with which to study the brain and behavior. Viewed from this perspective, models are used primarily to increase the precision of theoretical predictions, generate novel and experimentally testable hypotheses, provide insights into complex behavior, etc. Samuel Karlin nicely sums up this aspect of modeling when he said, "The purpose of modeling is not to fit the data but to sharpen the questions"[2].

From this perspective, a realistic goal of cognitive modeling is to identify the one model, among a set of candidate models, that represents the closest possible approximation to the cognitive process of interest so that the identified model would capture the real-world complexity of the process under study, not necessarily fully but in some meaningful ways. Although we suspect SRKO would not disagree with this rather uncontroversial statement, the devil is in the implementational details. For example, a key issue is that of how one should select one model, from a set of competing models, that best approximates the cognitive process. This is the topic of model evaluation and comparison. In the remainder of this commentary, we discuss a few of the challenges that will arise when Occam's Razor must be balanced with other criteria, such as considering real-world complexity.

3. Model Evaluation and Comparison: Where Hair Gel Becomes Sticky

The ever-increasing popularity of modeling in cognitive science has resulted in the introduction of a great number of computational models within and across content areas. Although their purposes vary, from being proof-of-concept demonstrations to modeling a complex cognitive process such as reading, what has lagged considerably are methods for evaluating the quality of the models and comparing between competing models. The nuts and bolts of model evaluation are a critical component in model development, as they assist in justifying a range of choices, whether it be in the design of a model or the selection of one model over another.

Although standard practice is to compare empirical data with model output, this sufficiency test is minimally informative and it would be prudent to develop model analysis tools as well in tandem. With a set of tools that provide keener insight into model performance (answering *how* and *why* a model performs the way it does), the current modeling practice would likely be more productive and suffer less from some of the problems that SRKO rightly highlight, such as a short lifespan.

Cognitive science is a particularly challenging discipline in which to develop formal model comparison methods because of the diversity of the types of models – How does one compare a simulation-based neural network model[3] with an algebraically formulated model? The task is not impossible, and we have suggested methods for doing so[4]. The challenge is to envision its implementation in SRKO's paradigm, where model breadth must also be considered.

In the context of model comparison, to abide by Occam's Razor is not the same as adhering to simplicity. Rather, it is intended as a check on excess, unnecessary model complexity (flexibility in performance). The principle is instantiated in quantitative model selection methods as a means of justifying the additional complexity held by one model over its competitors. A complex model (e.g., one with more parameters, more hidden units, or a more complex functional form) will be preferred, but only as long as it is justified by the complexity of the cognitive process under study. Specifically, one uses Occam's Razor to identify the model that is sufficiently complex to capture the regularities underlying the data but not too complex to enable it to capitalize on ever-present random noise in the data[5]. By relaxing this criterion, an overly complex model could be favored, one that might fit virtually any data pattern (both regularity and noise), but reveals little of psychological relevance. This would surely drive cognitive science to an impasse.

Looked at in another way, Occam's Razor emphasizes a very strong bottom-up (i.e., data-driven) orientation. This ensures the model maintains maximum contact with what is known about the cognitive process under study. Although SRKO acknowledge a need for parsimony, it would have to be loosened in an effort to accommodate a wider range of phenomena.

Such a rebalancing of parsimony with a model's explanatory breadth would result in a few problems. One problem is that the source of superior model performance, whether measured as a more exact simulation or a better fit to the data, is difficult to isolate in the model. With a highly complex model, good performance could be attributable to the accuracy of the model (i.e., it is a good approximation of the underlying cognitive process) or to its excess complexity (i.e., its ability to reproduce a wide range of data patterns). Only by some means of simplification, such as turning off unnecessary parts of the model, could this question begin to be answered.

Another problem that emerges when models become highly detailed is behavioral tractability. What parts of the model are responsible for its many behaviors? SRKO touch on this point briefly when criticizing the current practice of cognitive modeling, but do not explain how it can be overcome in their approach. Without intimate knowledge of model behavior, it can be very difficult to improve model performance, largely because the sources of performance gains are not transparent or non-unique, with one part of the model able to compensate for deficiencies in other parts. As one can imagine, this type of flexibility stymies modeling.

SRKO cite the abundance of data in the literature as evidence that the current modeling paradigm is not working, and what is needed is a more comprehensive, integrated approach. From the vantage point of model evaluation, the problem is just the opposite: Data that can convincingly discriminate models are in short supply. Models under consideration can often mimic each other so closely that they differ in primarily subtle quantitative predictions. What is more, it can be very difficult to determine how two models actually differ, even when comparing models that generate simple data patterns. It is not surprising, then, that it can be exceedingly difficult to design experiments that stand a good chance of discriminating between models. It is unlikely that this situation will change by trying to model the "whole." The increased complexity that accompanies more detailed models may well result in greater mimicry, not less.

4. Conclusion

The desire to model real-world complexity is probably held by most modelers. This commentary is intended to point out what we believe is a formidable challenge in practicing this type of modeling, how to balance model parsimony with model breadth in model selection. If Occam's Razor "only tells us half the story," how is the other half quantified in a mathematically rigorous way so as to facilitate model selection? It is hard to imagine hair gel ever going out of fashion, but style-conscious modelers have a formidable task ahead of them.

References

1. Shillcock, R., Roberts, M., Kreiner, H., and Obregon, M. Some issues in computational modeling; Occam's Razor and Hegel's hair gel. In E. J. Davelaar (Ed.), *Proceedings of the Twelfth Neural Computation and Psychology Workshop* (London, UK: World Scientific), xxx-xxx (2011).
2. Karlin, S. The 11th R. A. Fisher Memorial Lecture. *The Royal Society 20 Meeting* (1983).
3. McClelland, J. L., and Elman, J. L. The TRACE model of speech perception. *Cog. Psych.*, **18**, 1-86 (1986).
4. Myung, J. I., Tang, Y., and Pitt, M. A. Evaluation and comparison of computational models. *Methods in Enzymology*, **454**, 287-304 (2009).
5. Pitt, M. A., Myung, I. J., and Zhang, S. Toward a method of selecting among computational models of cognition. *Psych. Rev.*, **109**, 472-491 (2002).

WHAT DO HUMANOID ROBOTS OFFER TO EXPERIMENTAL PSYCHOLOGY ?

Jochen J. Steil

Research Institute for Cognition and Robotics & Faculty of Technology
Bielefeld University, 33615 Bielefeld, Germany
E-mail: jsteil@cor-lab.uni-bielefeld.de
www.cor-lab.de

I discuss challenges and chances offered to cognitive psychology by the recent groundbreaking progress in humanoid robot technology. The focus is on three developments. First, the robots' humanoid appearance in combination with their cognitive capabilities facilitates intuitive interaction with users and causes strong anthropomorphism and encourages the systematic investigation of the human's

"theory of robotic mind". Second, experimental investigation of interaction by means of systematic variation of robot behavior provides new approaches to investigate human behavior, which yield methodical challenges. Third, humanoid robots increasingly face similar learning and behavioral problems as humans and their performance can give insights into the structure of such problems. Finally, it has often been argued that compared to computational models robots provide an alternative way of understanding human behavior by means of synthesis of intelligent behavior. I argue that humanoid robots can provide testbeds for hypothesized models, but – regarded as models for cognition – face similar fundamental considerations in their validity from a point of view of philosophy of science as computational models in cognitive psychology do.

1. Humanoid robots

At least since Leonardo da Vinci's fantastic drawings of complex machines it has been a dream to build human-like mechanical artifacts. With the advent of artificial intelligence, researchers have tried to display intelligent behavior on such platforms. Since the 1970s, the first prototypes of humanoid robots have been built at Waseda University, Japan.[1] However, until recently these have remained singular research platforms that were not ready for more widespread use. It lasted until 2001 with the introduction of Honda's ASIMO[2] that the first humanoid complied to industrial standards and was built in larger numbers [a]. Since then, the field of humanoid robot technology has seen a breathtaking development towards high-end research platforms (QRIO (SDR-4X II), HRP3, Sarcos DB, iCub, CB2, to name only a few). Also mid-size and mid-level systems like KHR-1 and Nao have appeared, the latter now being the standard platform for RobotCup. While about ten years ago the focus was still on implementing particular skills like movement control,[3] platforms with the explicit goal to serve as models for human behavior, cognition, and development have been introduced more recently.[4,5] Other platforms are becoming affordable products that are shipped together with an ever increasing amount of built-in cognitive capabilities for e.g. movement control, path planning, map building, person and simple object detection, audio-localization etc.[6]

These platforms have created a substantial new research field in robotics, as can also be seen e.g. from the strongly increasing number of participants at the IEEE Conference of Humanoid Robotics[b]. Engineering-wise this implies that research for the first time can go beyond demonstrating capabilities in exemplary singular research scenarios and results can be reproduced and compared across different laboratories. For non-engineering disciplines like cognitive psychology and neuroscience these developments imply that for the first time the technology allows the use of robots as research tools in interactive experiments. Arguing from the viewpoint of robotics, I will discuss in the following that a number of new chances and challenges arise for cognitive and experimental psychology from this development.

1.1. *Why Humanoid Robots?*

Robots are typically attributed "humanoid" if their morphology is human-like as a whole or at least in parts. In more traditional automation applications repeatability and accuracy are the main goals of robot use and humanoid appearance and morphology is typically regarded as unimportant. The robot's environment is fixed and tailored to the capabilities of the technical system. In the automation context, only human intelligence and flexibility allows the user to adapt to interaction formats that such robots can understand – mainly programming and engineering methods. Humanoid robotics takes off from a different viewpoint: it is assumed that the robot shall behave in a human's natural environment and in close interaction with the human, which implies that the machine needs to be

---

[a] About 60 ASIMO robots overall have been built up to today.
[b] More than 400 participants in 2009.

tailored towards the natural interaction and communication formats that humans are using. This facilitates communication and acceptance,[7,8] usage of the same tools (that has been a strong motive behind the development of the NASA robonaut project[9]) and mobility in our human-tailored environment. For interaction and communication in particular, common ground routing in similar experiences is important and the embodiment and humanoid shape allow for such "similar" experience e.g. for a concept like "sit" that can be connected with respective sensori-motor patterns only for humanoid robots with legs. While the validity of such far reaching analogies can certainly be debated, we accept for the time being that there are interesting problems that can be explored during the interaction with humanoid robots. We focus on interaction and learning and consider three aspects: how does anthropomorphism occur for humanoid robots, what do they offer for experimental investigation of interaction, and what do we learn about learning and development from humanoids?

2. Investigation of Interaction and Antropomorphism

Encountering humanoids often leads to strong anthropomorphism, i.e. users attribute many cognitive capabilities to such robots and often are strongly touched emotionally. This has been identified as very important for social interaction[10,11] and has been taken to the extreme by designing android robots after the image of real persons.[7] The possible enrichment of human-robot interaction by anthorpomorphism towards humanoid and emotional robots has frequently been emphasized,[12] but already since the 1970s it has also been theorized that an "uncanny valley" might exist – a robot that is too similar to a human may become scary to a user[13] and some experimental investigation has addressed this in the context of androids.[14] There are, however, very few methodologically sound and systematic studies on the perception of the robots by humans and the "theory of robotic mind" the users may have. A recent fMRI-study has demonstrated that there is an increasing tendency to build such a model of a "robots mind" with respect to increasing human-likeness.[15] Another very recent work applies psychological methods to develop a perceptual scale for humanoids.[16]

The development of the user's anthropomorphism with increasing exposure to robots and interaction experience is yet unexplored. The current research in cognitive robotics still concentrates on building better robots that also display emotions e.g. by face animation.[4,17] Furthermore, it is commonly known that humans are very sensitive to perceive movement as more or less "natural",[18] making movement also an important means of robot-human communication.[19] The interplay of movement capabilities, emotional display and task-related intelligence has not yet been investigated.

Humans also have dedicated strategies to adapt their "theory of mind" of the interaction partner. Characteristic behavior modifications towards cognitively less-developed interaction partners are known from comparing adult-adult interaction vs. adult-child[20,21] and can be used to scaffold robot learning.[21] Consequently the robot can be equipped with particular means to detect when a user engages in a teaching situation.[22]

I conclude that a major target of investigating anthropomorphism is to understand more of particular features of human-robot interaction with the goal to improve the robot behavior. The design of better feedback channels, the reasonable use of emotional displays, the coordination of movement, speech, and other feedback are only a few examples. The field here is still at the beginning, but we regard it a crucial factor to investigate the user's "theory of robotic mind", because it determines expectations to be confirmed or violated and defines the common ground assumed by the user as the basis for interaction and communication.

3. Experimental Science of Humans and Robots

Experimental cognitive psychology has developed a culture of very fine-grained investigation of small-scale phenomena with high sophistication and strict control of experimental setups and variables. While this is the silver bullet to explain basic mental processes such as attention, perception, or memory, the corresponding reliable measurement of variables requires to control as many variables as possible and leads to restrictive experimental displays. They are often limited to computer displays, the presentation of simplified stimuli, or action in simulated toy worlds. It is practically impossibe to live up to such standards in the investigation of interaction behavior in the real world. However, humanoid robots now start to offer opportunities to systematically and reproducibly manipulate behavior of the (robotic) interaction partner – behavior can be "presented" in a controlled way. This has been identified as important in animal cognition,[23] but now can be scaled up to human behavior. Consider for instance an attentive robotic gazing system, where certain cues are systematically ignored or exaggerated, or where the system systematically ignores the interacting human from time to time.[24] The goal is to overcome the currently prevailing strategy of "data-harvesting" in exploratory studies of human-robot interaction in favor of hypothesis-driven experiments matching methodological standards of psychological research. This refers for instance to theory-driven experimental design, randomization of subjects, statistical analysis, the role of the experimenter etc. We must, however, be aware that real-world interaction always introduces uncontrollable variability already by the mere complexity of the setup and the involvement of robots often adds distracting factors for the humans. The investigation of interaction is therefore demanding from a theoretical point of view: a methodology of "semi-controlled" experiments including quantitative and qualitative elements needs to be established to lift human-robot exploratory interaction studies toward meaningful experiments.

4. Humans and Robots Facing Real World Learning

With increasing complexity of the humanoid robots, these machines increasingly face learning problems that are similar to those that humans encounter in their daily life. It has frequently been emphasized that physical embodiment is a crucial factor for intelligent systems,[25] particularly with regard to motion,[26] but only recently robots have come close enough to humans and animals to allow some reasonable degree of comparison. In this discussion on embodiment, the physical models are seen complementary to computational models in the sense that they aid thinking about cognition and foster developing theories of intelligence. In the combination of robot technology and the recent maturing of machine learning there are new perspectives: insights about the structure of learning problems that robots and humans face in similar ways can be gained. Examples reach from acquiring basic skills for body coordination[27] to sensori-motor planning on high behavioral levels using e.g. probabilistic rules.[28] Learning is of course also at the heart of the field of developmental robotics.[29-31] The basic hypothesis is that only an incremental addition of increasingly complex skills can succeed in reaching a reasonably complex level of cognition in robots. On the other hand, it is hoped that this shall lead to a better understanding of human development.

We would like to stress a different aspect that roots in a more theoretical point of view: the comparison of humans and robots allows insight in the structure of learning problems, regardless of how they are solved in detail. We explain this approach with the example of computational and physical models of learning full body motor control, that is the bootstrapping of inverse kinematics. Inverse kinematics is the problem to choose joint angles to reach a given target posture, e.g. to choose arm joint angles to position the hand. The problem is difficult, because the inverse model has to learn and select one of typically infinitely many postures that are possible to attain with the rest of the body when the hand is fixed. It is known that inverse kinematics models are typically locally low-dimensional and therefore can be learned very efficiently by local models.[32] Computational models in this domain have hypothesized error quantities like motor error[33] or a distal teacher[34] that are physically not measurable. Others learn a forward model and invert it analytically.[35] Our recent model has concentrated on bootstrapping motor coordination from observable information only.[27] The respective learning algorithm can be set up such that it is not more difficult to learn in high-dimensional spaces than in lower dimensions, i.e. learning to reach with the full body is not more difficult than with the arm only. This somewhat counterintuitive result from robotics can now be tested in motor learning experiments with humans, which closes the cycle and shows that results from robotics can lead to new ideas about human behavior. Certainly many more such analogies wait to be explored jointly by roboticists and experimental psychologists.

5. Humanoids and Computational Modeling

A number of comprehensive treatments have recently discussed what robotics can contribute to cognitive psychology (see e.g.[23,29,36]). They emphasize in different ways that robots can impact our understanding of animal and human cognition. Many robots serve as physically embodied models that always have a computational background for their control. Whereas we agree with the general direction of arguments, we comment on some specifics related to humanoid robotics and what humanoid robotics possibly have to offer in particular. Not the least, leading researchers in humanoid robotics have emphasized that one main motivation of humanoid robotics is to model and thereby understand human intelligence, development and behavior.[7,30] In this respect humanoid robots and their software systems are understood as physically embedded models, in particular in the domain of developmental cognitive robotics.[29] They can therefore – with respect to this function – be analyzed in the very same way as other computational models in psychology, as for instance is done in this volume by Shillock et al. and Stafford.

Following Stafford (in this volume) models can be made for different purposes and modellers in cognitive psychology are often not explicit about the goals they pursue with their models. They share this with humanoid roboticists. Very often there is a mixture of goals that can be exploratory or explanatory (see Stafford). Many robotic applications are – at times very sophisticated – demonstrations of capacity of certain skills where biological plausibility with respect to the morhpology is an important constituting factor of humanoid robotics. This has been put to the extreme by defining soccer as the ultimate challenge for humanoid robots in the context of RoboCup.[37] Further, embodiment of controller models in a physical system has defining character: it brings about many problems that non-embodied models can ignore, e.g. all hardware and control-related neccessities. A particular issue often overlooked by both roboticists and psychologists is the systemic aspect of architectural integration. Whenever many capabilities and basic skill have to be integrated in a common cognitive control architecture, the realization of the architecture itselfs imposes constraints on how components can be implemented and which functions they can exhibit. Humanoid robots necessarily face this problem because they are by definition rather complete and complex systems. That distinguishes them from embodied robotic models of minimal cognition that mostly ignore the systemic level: they try to be exploratory and provide proof of concept implementations on both a skill and a systemic level. Whereas this is hopeless by way of top down programming, an incremental pathway of learning cognitive capabilities has been identified as the most promising route to achieve this goal.[7,30,31]

Computational models from cognitive sciences are used and implemented in the respective robot control systems and thereby subjected to two aspects that can be ignored in stand-alone computational models: systemic integration and a necessary link to physical entities. In both aspects, robots define an real-world embedding of minimal complexity that the computational model can not simplify further - a real-world test. Their control system representations always refer to some physical items or processes. Most cognitive roboticists aim to show sufficiency in the sense that a (mostly minimal) set of algorithms and data processing is sufficient for a humanoid robot to perform some skill in the real world. It turns out that many computational models do not pass this test in the sense that the prerequisites they need can not be implemented on in an actual robot. For instance, a model that is designed for perfect object recognition in general scenes – as many computational models of visual search are – is practically not feasible, because no visual recognition algorithm can provide this precondition.

Shillock (in this volume) now argues that researchers shall strive for adding as much detail to the computational models as possible because "To have the fullest explanation and understanding of a cognitive process we need to be able to see it both in its simplest manifestation and in its fullest manifestation". A similar claim is widely accepted in the robotics domain. The starting point is that roboticists, like cognitive modelers, often simplify their scenarios because of the limitations in perception and motor-capabilities, which all currently exisiting robots still have. For instance, objects are limited to blocks, colors are uniform and nicely segmentable, obstacles remain static, only one control process can be active at one time, and so on. Most work in cognitive robotics is devoted to gradually extending these limits starting from relatively simple worlds and often such work is judged by the degree of robustness a robot has with regard to variation in this world. Following Shillock (in this volume): " We need to be able to answer the question, Does it scale up ?" This indeed is also the major question in cognitive robotics.

On the flipside, how complex should the environment be? The human cognitive system does simplify the perceptions of the external world. For example, in vision, Byrne et al. (this volume) note that perceptual constancies are due to minimal cognitive inferential processes. Similarly, the aforementioned example of inverse kinematics highlights the computational benefits obtained in pursuing simplicity. Finally, the problem of perfect object recognition highlights the problem of pursuing full complexity. Cognitive roboticists may be seen to aim for striking the right balance between computational simplicity and necessary complexity to solve problems in a dynamic real world.

Revisiting the goals roboticists pursue with their models, particularly in humanoid developmental robotics, there is always the tacit assumption that the robots could also be explanatory, e.g. make predictions about human behavior based on the robotic models. This ambition, however, has hardly been put into practice and in fact only very few researchers have tried to directly model and implement experimental work e.g. from child development in robots and succeeded to reproduce experimental data. One prominent example is,[38] where an experiment in language learning was repeated and the authors explicitly state that the ultimate goal of this research is that "(...) robot models generate new predictions tested in children." I believe that with the degree such approaches are successful, the impact of humanoid robotics on cognitive psychology will drastically increase. There is a wide and under-explored field particularily in testing learning paradigms developed on humanoid robots in cognitive psychology.

6. Challenges and Chances

In summary, I argue that contemporary humanoid robotics matures to a degree where interdisciplinary cooperation between humanoid robotics and psychology is feasible and can advance our knowledge about cognition in several ways: by creating experiments on the humans' "theory of robotic mind", by using robots as research tools in "semi-controlled" interactive experimentation, and by exploring the structure of learning problems that humans and robots face in the real world in similar ways. However, this proposed cooperation yet has to meet severe challenges: experimental human-robot interaction has to elevate methodology beyond "data harvesting" and subsequent ad-hoc interpretation of these data, a methodology for systematic investigation of interaction with robots is needed, and finally of course our current robots and machine learning methods have to be improved to let comparisons to humans be more insightful. In performing such research, both roboticists and psychologists need to be aware of their goals and should make explicit in which respect they use computational and physical models. Whereas this remains a complex endeavour, I believe that the preliminary examples presented in this chapter show that all three discussed approaches are feasible and offer new and fascinating opportunities to advance our understanding of human and artificial cognition.

Acknowledgments

I would like to thank Werner X. Schneider for discussion on the ideas in section three and the terminus "Experimental Science of Humans and Robots", which we have developed jointly. I would also like to thank Eddy Davelaar for inviting me to NCPW and many remarks that helped to greatly improve the manuscript.

References

1. S. Hashimoto, S. Narita, H. Kasahara, K. Shirai, T. Kobayashi, A. Takanishi, S. Sugano, J. Yamaguchi, H. Sawada, H. Takanobu *et al.*, *Autonomous Robots* **12**, 25 (2002).
2. Y. Sakagami, R. Watanabe, C. Aoyama, S. Matsunaga, N. Higaki and K. Fujimura, The intelligent ASIMO: system overview and integration, in *Proc. IEEE Conf. on Intelligent Robots and Systems*, 2002.
3. S. Schaal, *Trends in Cognitive Sciences* **6**, 233 (1999).
4. N. Tsagarakis, G. Metta, G. Sandini, D. Vernon, R. Beira, F. Becchi, L. Righetti, J. Santos-Victor, A. Ijspeert, M. Carrozza and D. Caldwell, *Advanced Robotics* **21**, 1151 (2007).

5. T. Minato, Y. Yoshikawa, T. Noda, S. Ikemoto, H. Ishiguro and M. Asada, CB2: A child robot with biomimetic body for cognitive developmental robotics, in *Proc. IEEE Conf. Humanoid Robots*, 2009.

6. http://www. aldebaran-robotics. com.

7. T. Minato, M. Shimada, H. Ishiguro and S. Itakura, Development of an android robot for studying human-robot interaction, in *Innovations in Applied Artificial Intelligence*, eds. B. Orchard, C. Yang and M. Ali, LNCS, Vol. 3029 (Springer Berlin / Heidelberg, 2004) pp. 424–434.

8. J. Goetz, S. Kiesler and A. Powers, Matching robot appearance and behavior to tasks to improve human-robot cooperation, in *Proc. IEEE Conf. Robot and Human Interactive Communication*, 2003.

9. R. Ambrose, H. Aldridge, R. Askew, R. Burridge, W. Bluethmann, M. Diftler, C. Lovchik, D. Magruder and F. Rehnmark, *Intelligent Systems and their Applications, IEEE* **15**, 57 (2002).

10. C. Breazeal, *Robotics and Autonomous Systems* **42**, 167 (2003).

11. T. Fong, I. Nourbakhsh and K. Dautenhahn, *Robotics and autonomous systems* **42**, 143 (2003).

12. T. Shibata, *Proceedings of the IEEE* **92**, 1749 (2004).

13. M. Mori, *Energy* **7**, 33 (1970).

14. C. Bartneck, T. Kanda, H. Ishiguro and N. Hagita, Is the uncanny valley an uncanny cliff?, in *Proc. IEEE Conf. Robot and Human interactive Communication*, 2007.

15. S. Krach, F. Hegel, B. Wrede, G. Sagerer, F. Binkofski and T. Kircher, *PLoS one* **3**, p. 2597 (2008).

16. H. Kamide, Y. Mae, T. Takubo, K. Ohara and T. Arai, Development of a scale of perception to humanoid robots: PERNOD, in *Prod. IEEE Conf. Intelligent Robots and Systems*, 2010.

17. I. Luetkebohle, F. Hegel, S. Schulz, M. Hackel, B. Wrede, S. Wachsmuth and G. Sagerer, The bielefeld anthropomorphic robot head "Flobi", in *Proc. IEEE Conf. on Robotics and Automation*, 2010.

18. M. Giese and T. Poggio, *Nature Reviews Neuroscience* **4**, 179 (2003).

19. T. Kanda, H. Ishiguro, M. Imai and T. Ono, Body movement analysis of human-robot interaction, in *Int. Joint Conference on Artificial Intelligence*, 2003.

20. R. Brand, W. Shallcross, M. Sabatos and K. Massie, *Infancy* **11**, 203 (2007).

21. Y. Nagai and K. Rohlfing, *IEEE Trans. on Autonomous Mental Development* **1**, 44 (2009).

22. L. Schillingmann, B. Wrede and K. Rohlfing, Towards a computational model of Acoustic Packaging, in *Proc. IEEE International Conference on Development and Learning*, 2009.

23. P. Oudeyer, *IEEE Trans. on Autonomous Mental Development* **2**, 2 (2010).

24. C. Muhl and Y. Nagai, Does disturbance discourage people from communicating with a robot?, in *Proc. IEEE Conf. on Robot and Human Interactive Communication*, (Jeju, Korea, 2007).

25. R. Pfeifer, *International Journal of Cognition and Technology* **1**, 125 (2002).

26. C. Atkeson, J. Hale, F. Pollick, M. Riley, S. Kotosaka, S. Schaul, T. Shibata, G. Tevatia, A. Ude, S. Vijayakumar *et al.*, *Intelligent Systems and their Applications, IEEE* **15**, 46 (2002).

27. M. Rolf, J. J. Steil and M. Gienger, *IEEE Trans. Autonomous Mental Development* **2**, 216 (09/2010 2010).

28. T. Lang and M. Toussaint, *Journal of Artificial Intelligence Research* **39**, 1 (2010).

29. M. Asada, K. Hosoda, Y. Kuniyoshi, H. Ishiguro, T. Inui, Y. Yoshikawa, M. Ogino and C. Yoshida, *IEEE Trans. on Autonomous Mental Development* **1**, 12 (2009).

30. G. Metta, L. Natale, F. Nori, G. Sandini, D. Vernon, L. Fadiga, C. von Hofsten, K. Rosander, M. Lopes, J. Santos-Victor *et al.*, *Neural networks* (2010).

31. L. Berthouze and T. Ziemke, *Connection Science* **15**, 147 (2003).

32. S. V. Aaron D'Souza and S. Schaal, Learning inverse kinematics, in *Proc. IEEE Conf. on Intelligent Robots and Systems*, 2001.

33. D. Wolpert and M. Kawato, *Neural Networks* **11**, 1317 (1998).

34. M. Jordan and D. Rumelhart, *Cognitive Science* **16**, 307 (1992).

35. A. Baranes and P.-Y. Oudeyer, Intrinsically motivated goal exploration for active motor learning in robots: A case study, in *Proc. IROS*, 2010.

36. R. C. A. M. T. Z. A. Morse, C. Herrera, *New Ideas in Psychology* (2011), in press.

37. H. Kitano and M. Asada, *Advanced Robotics* **13**, 723 (2000).

38. A. Morse, T. Belpaeme, A. Cangelosi and L. Smith, Thinking with your body: Modelling spatial biases in categorization using a real humanoid robot, in *Proc. CogSci*, 2010.